Political Traditions in
Foreign Policy Series

KENNETH W. THOMPSON

Editor

The values, traditions, and assumptions undergirding approaches to foreign policy are often crucial in determining the course of a nation's history. Yet, the interconnections between ideas and policy for landmark periods in our foreign relations remain largely unexamined. The intent of this series is to encourage a marriage between political theory and foreign policy. A secondary objective is to identify theorists with a continuing interest in political thought and international relations, both younger scholars and the small group of established thinkers. Only occasionally have scholarly centers and university presses sought to nurture studies in this area. In the 1950s and 1960s the University of Chicago Center for the Study of American Foreign Policy gave emphasis to such inquiries. Since then the subject has not been the focus of any major intellectual center. The Louisiana State University Press and the series editor, from a base at the Miller Center of Public Affairs at the University of Virginia, have organized this series to meet a need that has remained largely unfulfilled since the mid-1960s.

American Diplomacy and the Pragmatic Tradition

American Diplomacy
and the
Pragmatic Tradition

Cecil V. Crabb, Jr.

Louisiana State University Press

Baton Rouge & London

Copyright © 1989 by Louisiana State University Press

All rights reserved

Manufactured in the United States of America

98 97 96 95 94 93 92 91 90 89   5 4 3 2 1

Designer: Barbara Werden

Typeface: Linotron Meridien

Typesetter: The Composing Room of Michigan, Inc.

Printer: Thomson-Shore, Inc.

Binder: John H. Dekker & Sons, Inc.

Library of Congress Cataloging-in-Publication Data

Crabb, Cecil Van Meter, 1924–

American diplomacy and the pragmatic tradition/Cecil V. Crabb,
Jr.

p.   cm.—(Political traditions in foreign policy series)

Includes index.

ISBN 0-8071-1460-X (alk. paper)

1. United States —Foreign relations—Philosophy. 2. United
States—Foreign relations—20th century. 3. Pragmatism. I. Title.
II. Series.

E183.7.C698 1989

327.73—dc19   88-15509

                                                                                    CIP

The paper in this book meets the guidelines for
permanence and durability of the Committee on Production
Guidelines for Book Longevity of the Council
on Library Resources. ∞

Contents

Acknowledgments

Any study of this scope is, of course, immensely indebted to the efforts of others for the information and ideas reflected in it. This analysis of pragmatic thought and of American foreign policy draws extensively upon the history of the modern philosophical tradition and upon studies of the nation's diplomatic record. Many of these sources are cited in the documentation accompanying each chapter.

Louisiana State University has generously supported my research activities for this and other projects. The Department of Political Science has also been extremely cooperative in providing research support services and in arranging a teaching schedule that is conducive to research.

The Earhart Foundation awarded me a substantial research grant for the completion of this study. The White Burkett Miller Center for Public Affairs at the University of Virginia also provided financial support for the project. The assistance and encouragement of its director, Kenneth W. Thompson, is acknowledged with gratitude.

Several graduate students assisted in the research stage. Special thanks are owed to Gregory Russell for research assistance and for his informed criticisms of portions of the manuscript. The professional staff of the Troy H. Middleton Library at LSU was invariably helpful and resourceful in meeting my research needs.

As in all of my research and writing activities, my capable wife, Harriet, made an indispensable contribution in proofreading and criticizing earlier drafts of the study.

The contribution of others, of course, does not relieve the author of ultimate responsibility for errors of fact or interpretation which may be found in the study. These are mine alone, for which I accept complete responsibility.

American Diplomacy and the Pragmatic Tradition

Introduction

By the late 1980s, the adjective most frequently employed to describe the diplomatic behavior of the Reagan administration was *pragmatic*. The concept of pragmatically based diplomacy was epitomized by Ronald Reagan's second secretary of state, George Shultz. Although he was inexperienced in the foreign policy field, in time Shultz acquired a reputation for valuing "quiet diplomacy," for concentrating his efforts upon immediate and concrete problems facing the United States abroad, and for avoiding an overtly ideological approach to such issues as Soviet-American relations.

Evidence that the Reagan-Shultz approach to international issues commanded the support of a majority of the American people was provided in the presidential election of 1984, when the voters returned Reagan to the White House with one of the largest electoral majorities in the nation's history. The election results left little doubt that the "Great Communicator" understood the deeply entrenched pragmatic inclinations of Americans and that, in both foreign and domestic affairs, his policies were generally in accord with them. Although Reagan's administration of foreign affairs was often characterized by a high level of right-wing ideological rhetoric, in the end his diplomatic actions reflected the American preference for pragmatic solutions to human problems. After Reagan's electoral landslide victory, several leaders of the Democratic party (Governor Mario Cuomo of New York, for example) called upon their political colleagues to return to the pragmatic "mainstream" of American life. Indeed, this step was widely viewed as imperative if Democrats hoped to defeat their Republican opponents in the next national election.

The common theme uniting the chapters of this study is that pragmatically derived attitudes and behavior patterns on the part of the American people and their leaders are no isolated or exceptional phenomena. To the contrary, throughout some two centuries of its existence as an independent republic, the American nation has acted pragmatically in responding to myriad internal and external challenges—to such an extent that pragmatism has become synonymous with the "American way of life." From the earliest days of colonization and settlement to the present era, time and again Americans have indicated their preference for the pragmatic mode of problem solving. (Chapter 2 provides a more detailed discussion of the principal elements in the pragmatic approach.)

The nature and implications of this reality have been widely recognized and examined in the sphere of domestic policy. The views of the philosophical pragmatists, for example, were a major force contributing to many of the reforms undertaken on the national and state levels in the early 1900s. Again, pragmatic ideas were prominent in many of the New Deal measures of the Roosevelt administration. On still another front, the ideas and theories of one of the leading pragmatists, John Dewey, profoundly affected the evolution of the American educational system.

Yet for the most part, the impact of the mode of thought known as pragmatism on the diplomatic behavior of the United States has largely been ignored by serious students of American foreign policy. Instead, alternative modes of analysis (such as idealism, *Realpolitik*, and certain more recent behavioral approaches—game theory, systems theory, and decision-making theory) have been used to explain American viewpoints and actions abroad.

Both implicitly and explicitly, the analysis in this book concedes that useful insights into the diplomatic behavior of the United States can often be gained by employing these alternative theories, particularly in selected cases. The diplomacy of Woodrow Wilson or of Franklin D. Roosevelt or of Jimmy Carter, for example, cannot be intelligently understood without some knowledge of American idealism. Similarly, an understanding of America's containment policy, or of the diplomatic efforts of the Nixon-Kissinger foreign policy team, is greatly enhanced by acquaintance with the precepts of *Realpolitik*. A fundamental tenet of pragmatism—and a central assumption of this study—is that *no unicausal or monistic theory is capable of explaining reality*, including the limited dimension of American diplomatic experience.

Yet, though they may sometimes be useful and defensible in accounting for American diplomatic behavior in selected instances, these theories invariably leave substantial gaps or areas in American diplomatic activity for which they are unable to account satisfactorily. To date, no single theory of the behavior of the United States in foreign affairs enables us to predict Washington's conduct abroad with a high degree of accuracy.

For example, the American national ethos undeniably contains a high idealistic content. During several periods, symbols of American idealism—such as Presidents Woodrow Wilson, Franklin D. Roosevelt, John F. Kennedy, and Jimmy Carter—have had a decisive influence on external events, and they are often remembered for their diplomatic accomplishments. Every informed student of American diplomacy is aware that such idealistic pronouncements and developments as the Monroe Doctrine (1823), the Atlantic Charter (1941), and the United Nations Charter (1945) have been landmarks in the nation's diplomatic record. Moreover, every incumbent president since World War II has from time to time expressed idealistic principles which have long been identified with American democratic experience.

Yet Americans are too practical—and they are too influenced by the lessons taught by experience—to accept idealism alone as an adequate basis for the nation's foreign policy. If they were not always aware of it, Americans learned during and after World War II that peaceful and stable relations with the Soviet Union required more than gestures of goodwill, friendship, and concessions by national leaders to the demands of the Soviet hierarchy. (Some Americans remember that FDR's idealistic efforts to win and retain Soviet cooperation during the war led to pervasive disillusionment with that diplomatic course in the early postwar period.) As is true of the philosophy of pragmatism itself, American foreign policy has always had—and it doubtless always will contain—an idealistic component. But in the era of internationalism, few Americans believe that idealism alone can serve as an adequate basis for the foreign policy of a superpower.

For different reasons, relatively few Americans are prepared to adopt *Realpolitik* as an acceptable set of diplomatic guidelines for the United States. Such Old World ideas as the acquisition and pursuit of national power, the concept of balance of power, and highly ethnocentric definitions of the national interest have historically held little appeal for the American mind. As the Vietnam War and the Reagan administration's subsequent diplomacy in Central America clearly demonstrated, Americans have traditionally been—and they remain—apprehensive about the projection of national power abroad in behalf of diplomatic ends. Sooner or later, as the Johnson administration discovered, the American people demand that their leaders demonstrate how the application of national power is related to the achievement of worthwhile human goals. In a word, Americans expect that power will be used legitimately, that it will promote (and be widely perceived as promoting) some purpose related to human welfare. Machiavelli, Hobbes, Richelieu, Bismarck, and other Old World practitioners of *Realpolitik* are not widely admired figures in the United States. It was not totally coincidence, for example, that a contemporary advocate of political realism, Henry Kissinger, experienced increasing criticism from Congress and some segments of the American public during his period of official service in the Nixon and Ford administrations.

As for more recent behavioral theories of international politics and American foreign policy, three brief points may be made. In the first place, relatively few Americans (including most public officials) understand these theories, in part because with the passage of time they have become increasingly intricate and have given rise to a growing number of variations and subtheories. Second, with rare exceptions, the proponents of behavioral explanations are usually severely challenged to show how they apply to *specific issues* confronting the United States abroad, such as arms-control negotiations between the superpowers, American efforts to prevent a new round of violence in the Arab-Israeli conflict, or ongoing political turbulence in Central America. By their own admission, devotees of most behavioral theories of international politics acknowledge that they are unable to provide policy makers with useful guidance on the microanalytical level—the realm with which national officials are most urgently concerned. And third, most behavioral theories presuppose a level of knowledge and interest in foreign affairs which greatly surpasses that possessed by the ordinary American citizen. The average American is neither familiar with such theories nor motivated to understand them intelligently. Modern behavioral theories, therefore, have thus far been unable to serve as the basis for broad public perception of, and support for, the nation's diplomatic activities.

For reasons that are not altogether clear even today, the tendency of Americans to approach foreign policy, no less than domestic policy, questions pragmatically has received very little systematic analysis. The omission is as mystifying as it is serious. It is puzzling because one of the fundamental attractions of what may be called a "pragmatic world view" is that it allows Americans to "be themselves" in dealing with external problems. In contrast to alternative approaches, pragmatically based diplomacy does not require that Americans exhibit one set of attitudinal and behavior traits at home and a different set abroad.

The pragmatic world view rests upon the reasonable assumption that Americans approach both foreign and domestic issues from a common and familiar set of underlying beliefs, values, goals, and behavior traits. Moreover, our analysis presupposes considerable transfer between these two realms. As a rule, on the basis of limited interest and knowledge, Americans assume that behavior patterns derived primarily from domestic experience are applicable to the foreign policy field. As the reader is made aware more fully in Chapter 8, this tendency has both positive and negative consequences for the United States in foreign relations.

In brief, the primary theme of this study is that, better than any competing theory of American diplomatic behavior, a pragmatic world view *accurately describes customary American viewpoints and conduct in foreign affairs.* From time to time, there will be departures from the pragmatic norms identified here. President Ronald Reagan's public views on diplomatic issues—particularly, on Soviet-American relations—were at times highly ideological, and the diplomatic actions of the Reagan White House were sometimes unquestionably influenced by his right-wing ideological propensities. Nevertheless, as a generalization for which a substantial body of supporting evidence is available, one may contend that American attitudes and actions abroad usually exhibit a high degree of conformity with the main principles and tenets of pragmatic thought.

The general answer to the frequently asked question, What *is* American foreign policy? is that the diplomatic behavior of the United States reflects the nation's pragmatic tradition. Insofar as Washington's diplomatic conduct can be accurately predicted (and this study acknowledges that sometimes it cannot be), the actions of the American nation abroad will be governed by the main precepts of pragmatic thought. (As the discussion that follows will indicate in greater detail, a distinguishing feature of pragmatic thought is that it freely acknowledges the existence of contradictions or paradoxes in our understanding of the universe and, consequently, in the human response to it.) It follows that better acquaintance with the pragmatic mode of thought is indispensable if American attitudes and conduct in dealing with international issues are to be intelligently understood.

This book begins with an examination of the impact of pragmatic patterns of thought and conduct upon American domestic experience. Chapter 1 focuses selectively on five significant dimensions of the subject: the process of colonization and settlement, the revolutionary war experience and constitutional development, American religious life and beliefs, the evolution of the capitalistic economic system, and finally, the nature and continuing development of the American political system.

The school of philosophy known as pragmatism was the American society's most original contribution to the philosophical heritage. Pragmatism's main tenets are identified and analyzed in Chapter 2, in which the discussion focuses on the contributions of three representative pragmatic thinkers: Charles Peirce, William James, and John Dewey.

In Chapter 3, the main tenets of pragmatic thought, as they are applicable to international political relationships, are examined in detail. Specific attention is devoted to how the pragmatically oriented mind perceives the nature of political relationships, the concept of democracy, the concept of national power, the existence of violence among nations, and the idea of global political community.

In the chapters that follow, the emphasis is directly on the diplomatic experience of the United States, with particular reference to the era of American internationalism since World War II. Chapter 4 provides detailed evidence supporting the contention that pragmatic principles have influenced the postwar diplomatic behavior of the United States at every turn. Specifically, it calls attention to the insights provided by two fundamental pragmatic tenets: experience as the standard for the determination of truth, and the concept of the pluralistic universe in understanding America's relations with other nations.

The same subject is continued in Chapter 5, where attention is directed to the crisis nature of American diplomacy and to the role of the pragmatic concept of habituation in the foreign policy of the United States.

In Chapter 7, the pragmatic concept of the pluralistic universe is applied directly to the foreign policy process *within* the United States. According to this pragmatic idea, the formulation and administration of American foreign policy must be understood as resulting from the interplay of a long list of major and minor forces, whose precise impact upon diplomatic decision making varies from one international issue to another (even sometimes within the same administration in Washington).

The list of fourteen pragmatic diplomatic guidelines offered in Chapter 7 represents a distillation of ideas and insights contained in the previous chapters. In effect, these guidelines provide a convenient summary (usually with brief explanation) of the customary, normal, and expectable behavior of the United States in foreign relations. For both citizens within the United States and governments and observers abroad, familiarity with these guidelines should contribute to making American diplomatic conduct more predictable and less mystifying.

Pragmatically grounded diplomacy, of course, is both an asset and a liability for the United States. Chapter 8 assesses the positive and negative implications of a pragmatic world view. Ultimately, of course, the reader must balance the diplomatic books and decide whether, all things considered, a pragmatic approach to foreign relations is a source of diplomatic strength or weakness for the American democracy.

Regardless of the verdict, it seems certain that America's pragmatic tradition will continue to exert a potent influence on the nation's perceptions and actions in the foreign policy field for many years to come. As this book will demonstrate, the pragmatic nature of American diplomacy under the Reagan administration provides merely an unusually graphic example of a well-established tendency under successive administrations. Reagan's diplomatic pragmatism is, so to speak, American diplomatic conduct writ large. More intelligent understanding of the diplomatic implications of the pragmatic tradition is, therefore, essential and long overdue if the international role of the most powerful nation in history is to be comprehended intelligently.

One

The Pragmatic Ethos and American Life

The underlying thesis of this chapter is that a pragmatic orientation to problem solving has been a recurrent characteristic of American society since the colonial era. The tenets of the pragmatic school of philosophy (to be analyzed more fully in Chapter 2) were therefore particularly congenial for Americans, and, at many points, formed a link with their traditions and customary behavior patterns. As one student of American intellectual history has concluded, the pragmatic school of philosophy was "but a pale reflection of an ingrained attitude [among Americans] affirming the supremacy of experience over thought." The most seminal idea expressed by such early American thinkers as John Winthrop and Jonathan Edwards, as well as later figures including Walt Whitman, William James, and John Dewey, was the notion that experience is to be preferred over reflection "as the primary resource in formulating beliefs."[1]

Pragmatic Impulses in American Culture

That this is an accurate depiction of the American mentality has been attested to by numerous observers from the colonial period to the contemporary era. In 1835, for example, the perceptive Frenchman Alexis de Tocqueville observed that "in no country in the civilized world is less attention paid to philosophy than in the United States." During Tocqueville's era, the political forces that were seeking to democratize the American society were "not

---

1. John J. McDermott, "Philosophical Prospects for a New World," in Peter Caws (ed.), *Two Centuries of Philosophy in America* (Totowa, N.J., 1980), 244.

guided by any profoundly articulated political philosophy." Instead, they consisted of a "shrewdly managed, large combination of democrats operating without benefit of a unifying metaphysics or theology."[2]

A contemporary student of American culture has referred to the "amiable vagueness" that has always characterized thought in the United States. Lacking an established religion and a political dogma, Americans have relied on their experience "as antidote to dogmatism and utopianism." In every segment of their national life, they have seldom hesitated to combine logically incompatible and inconsistent ideas—a task that was "messy, philosophically speaking," but that often worked remarkably well.[3]

Another analysis of intellectual currents and behavior patterns in the United States has concluded that among all the modes of thought, "pragmatism has seemed to many to be the most distinctively American in outlook." For a variety of reasons—the diverse motives that led the settlers to the New World; the widely varying geographical conditions existing on the American continent; the lack of rigid social and class distinctions between mental and physical labor; the democratic ideal and the extension of the franchise; and other factors—the American environment was uniquely favorable for the emergence of the pragmatic school of philosophy. To many Americans, its birth meant that "the spirit of democracy has at last reached the metaphysician" and "the democratic ideal is destined to transform our thinking as well as our conduct."[4]

The American setting, another commentator has observed, has always been "chary of ideology, particularly of an eschatological cast." Historically, Americans have been "more interested in *saving experiences* than in salvation outside of time." Americans "are people deeply skeptical of final solutions and philosophies of history that provide principles of total accountability." Instead, Americans have always valued "pluralism," which has meant setting one philosophical "nostrum against another, in effect trimming the claim of each by the indulgence of many." Embracing the goal of "healing and amelioration," instead of accepting the idea of an "ultimate resolution" of society's problems, Americans may well have "stumbled on the only viable philosophy of history for a pluralistic world culture."[5]

From a different perspective, Max Lerner, a student of modern philo-

2. See the analysis of intellectual currents in nineteenth-century America in Morton White, *Pragmatism and the American Mind: Essays and Reviews in Philosophy and Intellectual History* (New York, 1973), 5–6.

3. Daniel J. Boorstin, *Democracy and Its Discontents: Reflections on Everyday America* (New York, 1974), 49–50.

4. Joseph L. Blau, *Men and Movements in American Philosophy* (New York, 1955), 228–30.

5. McDermott, "Philosophical Prospects," 248.

sophical movements, has observed that during the nineteenth century, because of its uncontested naval power, Great Britain "ruled the waves"; on the basis of its preeminence in philosophy, Germany "ruled the clouds"; and on account of the "applied" and practical nature of their knowledge and their preoccupation with down-to-earth problems, Americans "ruled the ground." Convinced that a "strain of empiricism" has connected all stages of American history, Lerner believed that "Americans find their ideas in things: they understand generalizations in terms of the operations involved in using them." It was no accident, therefore, that the school of philosophy known as pragmatism achieved its highest expression and most enthusiastic support within the American society.[6]

A recent student of American political experience has called attention to the historical coincidence that the Declaration of Independence and the publication of Adam Smith's classic study *The Wealth of Nations* both occurred in the same year, 1776. For this commentator, this fact signified the close conjunction between the concepts of "empirical politics" and "empirical economics," which became evident in the subsequent experience of the American republic. The study points out that America's most revered political figures and ideological sources—George Washington, Thomas Jefferson, Adam Smith, David Hume, Edmund Burke, and others in the Western tradition—were not revolutionaries in the true sense. In the main, they approved of the society of which they were a part, though they often advocated gradual and piecemeal changes and reforms to improve selected aspects of it. These thinkers nearly always avoided "political messianism," but called for "rebuilding" human institutions to make them more responsive to society's needs. Their "calmer view of democracy" served in the United States as an influential antidote to totalitarianism and other forms of political extremism.[7]

Foreign observers have also frequently commented upon the pragmatic propensities of American society. In his classic study *The American Commonwealth* (1891), Lord James Bryce, for example, pointedly contrasted the attitudes, ideas, and behavior traits of the New and the Old Worlds. Americans, Lord Bryce found, lived a simpler and less intense life than their European counterparts. Americans lacked the "passion in the [ideological] struggles" normally encountered in Europe. In the United States society was largely devoid of the "ideas . . . shooting to and fro" among rival groups often wit-

6. Max Lerner, *America as a Civilization: Life and Thought in the United States Today* (New York, 1957), 212.
7. See the review by Paul Johnson of Irving Kristol's *Reflections of a Neoconservative Looking Back, Looking Ahead* (New York, 1983), in *New York Times Book Review*, October 2, 1983, pp. 7, 25.

10

nessed on the European continent, producing ideological contests which Europeans tended to view as "fateful." Americans, however, rarely regarded such ideological clashes in these terms; for the ordinary American, they had little relevance or meaning for the solution of concrete, day-to-day problems. Americans were not, as a rule, attracted to "serious and sustained thinking" about underlying philosophical, political, social, and other principles; they seldom engaged in "minute investigation and patient reflection on the underlying principle of things." Fundamentally, in Lord Bryce's judgment, Americans were conservative people who were unwilling to "pull up the plant to see whether it has begun to strike root." At the same time, Americans were willing to "listen to suggestions from any quarter" for the improvement of society, and they exhibited "practical shrewdness" in the solution of their problems. Accordingly, the American republic was like a great tree that had put down deep roots but continued to grow and to change its shape with each passing year.[8]

Another thread in American cultural experience has been an anti-intellectual strain, directed particularly at the idea that only a small intellectual elite is capable of formulating and answering questions related to ultimate meaning and that ordinary citizens are dependent upon this minority for its insights. Nearly all outstanding American thinkers—for example, Jonathan Edwards, Ralph Waldo Emerson, and William James—in some measure reflected this anti-intellectual bias. As a group, American theologians and philosophers believed that "ordinary men were empowered to see truths beyond those arrived at by trained intellectuals." Immersion in the thought of American thinkers, therefore, inevitably leads to the conclusion that "vital truth" can be comprehended by processes and methods available to the average citizen. For want of a better term, that process of ascertaining truth and acting upon it could be called *common sense*—a concept that later figured prominently in the thought of leading exponents of pragmatism such as William James and John Dewey.[9]

The pragmatic outlook has also been prominent in the numerous reform movements that have been an integral part of American history for over two centuries. Rarely advocating revolutionary slogans or goals—and, in fact, usually viewing their causes as alternatives to more radical change—American reformers have usually concentrated selectively upon critical problems and abuses existing within the socioeconomic system. Devoting their atten-

8. See James Bryce, *The American Commonwealth*, ed. Andrew Hacker (2 vols.; New York, 1959), II, 310–13, 573.
9. White, *Pragmatism and the American Mind*, 88–91.

tion to a single problem (or at most a narrow range of related problems), the reformers usually called for gradual changes that would not produce social disruptions and political upheavals, and their efforts normally appealed "to the moderate goals of progress and the common welfare."[10]

Another student of American history has related the pragmatic mode of thought to one of the society's most distinctive qualities: its function as an ethnic and cultural "melting pot." The pragmatic school of thought was also a kind of philosophical melting pot of ideas and concepts. As it emerged on American soil, pragmatism proved to be "an inclusive, eclectic, philosophically omnivorous movement," drawing its basic tenets and methods from an almost infinite variety of domestic and foreign sources. As was true of the American society itself, pragmatic thinking did not comprise a neat system of philosophical principles; it was a dynamic and ever-changing body of philosophical axioms and scientific insights; it represented an "open" approach to truth, which continually benefited from the infusion of new ideas and criticism.[11]

As much as any other single individual, one of the American society's most revered folk heroes, Thomas Jefferson, exhibited the pragmatic and eminently practical orientation of the American mind. As the author of the Declaration of Independence and many political treatises and tracts, Jefferson has, of course, long served as the embodiment of the American democratic ideal. Jefferson's idealism is still known and admired throughout the world; the diplomatic behavior of the United States since World War II has often been criticized for its failure to reflect his idealistic principles.

Yet by his own admission, Jefferson had little interest in, or patience with, abstract philosophical principles such as those expressed in the works of a classical philosopher like Plato. Jefferson may well have been the American society's foremost interpreter of the principles of Enlightenment philosophy and of the French Revolution. His thought, however, was not outstanding primarily because of its originality; it was creative mainly in the sense that Jefferson applied preexisting political ideas to the American context in an effort to solve a series of specific problems and challenges confronting the American people before and after independence. Anticipating the approach

10. Lerner, *America as a Civilization*, 722–26; Richard Hofstadter, *The Age of Reform: From Bryan to F.D.R.* (New York, 1981); Lewis L. Gould (ed.), *The Progressive Era* (Syracuse, N.Y., 1974); Arthur M. Schlesinger, *The American as Reformer* (Cambridge, Mass., 1951).

11. See the Preface to Robert J. Mulvaney and Philip M. Zeltner (eds.), *Pragmatism: Its Sources and Prospects* (Columbia, S.C., 1981), vii–x.

of pragmatic thinkers a century or so after his era, Jefferson's ideas were ambivalent, fragmentary, unsystematic, and incomplete.

It has been pointed out, for example, that there is a tension between idealistic and realistic impulses in Jefferson's ideas. Jefferson continues to be widely cited as a prototype of American idealism, yet his life and thought could equally well be regarded as a noteworthy example of political adaptation and expediential policy making. When he was confronted with what one student of Jeffersonian ideas has called "the demands of reality," practical and hardheaded calculations of American national interest often outweighed Jefferson's professed ideological principles.[12]

This tendency was clearly exemplified by what must be viewed as one of the master strokes of American diplomacy: Jefferson's purchase of the Louisiana Territory from France in 1803 for the sum of $15 million. In agreeing to this transaction with Napoleon, Jefferson temporarily abandoned his cherished strict constructionist view of the Constitution. Jefferson feared that as president he was liable to impeachment for exercising constitutional powers he did not possess. Yet he was also mindful of certain overriding realities: the opportunity to acquire the Louisiana Territory might never arise again under such favorable terms (Napoleon's government was experiencing severe financial stringency), and the acquisition of this vast region would immeasurably strengthen the security of the vulnerable American republic from foreign powers having designs upon the New World. Accordingly, Jefferson instructed his agents to accept Napoleon's offer. Subsequently, he requested Congress to appropriate the necessary funds to complete the transaction, and in doing so he urged the House and Senate not to let "metaphysical subtleties" about the exact provisions of the Constitution or the scope of the president's authority interfere with this crucial transaction. Following Jefferson's recommendation, Congress overlooked philosophical and constitutional niceties and provided the $15 million required to acquire the title to the Louisiana Territory. The result was, in the words of one diplomatic historian, "the greatest real-estate bargain in history."[13]

The foregoing discussion illustrates the existence of pragmatic tendencies in nearly every significant sphere of American national life. It is neither

12. See Richard Hofstadter, *The American Political Tradition and the Men Who Made It* (New York, 1948), 18–44.
13. The negotiations leading to the Jefferson administration's purchase of the Louisiana Territory (1803) discussed more fully in Dumas Malone, *Jefferson and His Time* (6 vols.; Boston, 1970), IV, 284–311; and Alexander De Conde, *This Affair of Louisiana* (Baton Rouge, 1976).

possible nor necessary here to analyze the evidence illustrating pragmatic behavior in all aspects of the nation's experience; rather, this analysis will be concerned with five representative dimensions of American experience.

Colonization, Settlement, and the "Pioneer Spirit"

The colonization and settlement of the North American continent ex-emplified many ideas and behavior traits later reflected in the pragmatic philosophical tradition. The early explorers of the New World, followed by the Pilgrim fathers and thousands of other settlers who made the arduous voyage to American shores, were living embodiments of the idea that prevailing conceptions of the universe and of human society's relationship to it were in many respects faulty and incomplete. Almost daily, the early explorers operated on the premise (fundamental to the thought of the pragmatic school of philosophy) that the universe remained "open" and that nature's truths are accessible to adventurous and inquiring human minds. In the New World, early settlers received repeated object lessons in what might be called "the nature of nature." On one hand, they were reminded daily that nature was sometimes a formidable adversary and that environmental forces can pose extraordinarily difficult obstacles to human endeavor. On the other hand, they often discovered that natural forces could be overcome, controlled, or contained for mankind's benefit. They learned that human effort and ingenuity were capable of devising means for working with nature to achieve worthwhile purposes.

The frontier imparted another lesson to those living on it: in this strange and often hostile environment, there was no substitute for experience in coping with the conditions of frontier life. More often than not, the pioneers learned by trial and error, by experimentation, and by adaptation how to survive and, in time, how to improve the quality of life on the edge of civilization. Frontier existence became a distinctive blend of "rugged individualism" and of various cooperative and collectivist undertakings in the solution of common problems. (That classical political philosophers customarily re-garded individualism and collectivism as antithetical and mutually exclusive ideas was of little abstract concern to the early settlers of America. Experience taught that both concepts were essential for survival on the frontier, and both were relied upon as needed to promote the security and well-being of colonial communities.)

Other behavior traits and ideas were exhibited in the exploration and colonization of the New World that subsequently became prominent in the philosophy known as pragmatism. By emigrating to America, the settlers were cutting their ties with the Old World and creating a New World. To their minds, history was given a "new start" by this process, a fact most colonials believed in time would prove highly beneficial for the Old World as well. Yet even though they turned their backs on their country of origin, the American colonists brought with them foreign political principles and concepts, particularly those that had long formed part of the Anglo-Saxon tradition. In almost all cases, these ideas were adapted to the American setting and in the process often modified substantially—to the point ultimately of producing a distinctively American version of democracy, of Protestantism, of capitalism, and of other concepts which Americans believed had been greatly improved by the modifications made in the New World.

To cite merely one example of this phenomenon, the English common law became a foundation of American jurisprudence, but in time, there were significant differences between the English and American versions. So far was this overall process of adaptation carried throughout the thirteen colonies that many historians concluded that by the late eighteenth century America in fact had thirteen distinct "identities." The national motto—*E Pluribus Unum* ("one out of many")—testified to this reality. As the motto suggests, politically and in other respects a pluralistic universe was a fact for Americans. No theory or explanation of American life would be complete without taking account of this pivotal reality.

Frontier life encouraged another behavior trait noteworthy in the American ethos. The explorers and early settlers had been motivated to embark upon their quest by a variety of disparate reasons, ranging from highly idealistic to intensely self-serving and ignoble impulses. Some came to America solely to promote their own financial gain and to enhance their personal influence and prestige. Others were no doubt impelled by the spirit of adventure to seek a new life on the frontier. As every student of American history is aware, many early settlers left the Old World to escape religious and political persecution. Still other groups looked upon the New World as an opportunity to carry out some utopian scheme for the improvement and salvation of society (most of which ultimately failed). As Thomas Jefferson complained in the Declaration of Independence, among the early settlers were convicts and others who had come to the New World "involuntarily" and whose backgrounds did not bear overly close scrutiny! These various motivations for settlement of the American continent in turn engendered an attitude of judging individuals by what they were and by their evident accomplishments rather than by their past or previous social status. Irrespective of the reasons why a particular individual emigrated to America, the main question became how he was using the opportunities available to improve his own and society's condition.

The distinguished historian of the frontier Frederick Jackson Turner felt that the members of frontier communities needed no reminder that the "stubborn American environment is there with its imperious summons to accept its conditions." Yet few early Americans were content to "accept" conditions as they found them on the frontier. They viewed the environment as "a new field of opportunity, a gate of escape from the bondage of the past." The frontier instilled attitudes of "freshness, and confidence, and scorn of older society." Americans became convinced that through "struggle and conquest" they could achieve mastery of nature and harness environmental forces for useful human ends.[14]

For these reasons, many commentators believe that the pragmatic frame of mind in America derives in no small measure from the frontier experience. Frontier attitudes and behavior patterns, one study concludes, are clearly discernible in William James's philosophy of pragmatism. John Dewey later acknowledged the indebtedness of pragmatic thought to the nation's pioneer experience.[15]

William James, another commentator has concluded, "was as distinctly American as was Daniel Boone." Like James, Daniel Boone "was a civilized man who preferred to be the maker of civilization rather than to be its victim. He preferred to blaze his own way through the forest." For James philosophically, and for Boone literally, truth "was a continent awaiting settlement. First, the bold pathfinders must adventure into it. Its vast spaces were infinitely alluring." Both became convinced that the "universe must not be finished or inclosed." Once the universe was viewed by others as finished or fenced in, both men sought new insights and discoveries in unexplored vistas of life or thought.[16]

14. Frederick Jackson Turner, as quoted by Boyd H. Bode, "William James in the American Tradition," in Max C. Otto *et al.*, *William James: The Man and the Thinker* (Madison, 1942), 112–15; Turner, *The Frontier in American History* (New York, 1920).
15. See Otto, *William James*, 112–13; and John Dewey's observations concerning the impact of the frontier experience upon the American ethos in Stow Persons, *American Minds: A History* (New York, 1958), 401.
16. See the commentary in Charles H. Compton (comp.), *William James: Philosopher and Man* (New York, 1957), 73–75.

The American Revolution and Constitutional Development

A second realm of American life which nourished the pragmatic philosophical tradition and made it highly congenial to Americans was the Revolutionary War experience, followed by the drafting, ratification, and evolution of the Constitution. The American Revolution was, of course, an epochal event for the United States, a turning point in modern history, and a source of inspiration for countless foreign societies since 1776. Yet both at home and abroad, the revolutionary struggle in America has often been more venerated than clearly understood.

Strictly speaking, in the modern understanding of the term, the American Revolution was not a "revolution" at all. It was essentially *an anticolonial contest* in which, after a heroic struggle against great odds, Americans won their freedom from British colonial rule. Upon the surrender of General Charles Cornwallis, the British military band played "The World Turned Upside Down"—and from the British perspective, that may have been a fitting commentary upon the event. For the ordinary American, however, the world was not "turned upside down" in the sense that life was radically transformed for the Frenchman after the French Revolution (1789–1793) or for the Soviet citizen after the Communist seizure of power in Russia in 1917.

Although American foreign policy toward the Third World is discussed more fully in later pages, here it is appropriate to observe that in the post–World War II era, many Third World societies have experienced revolutions combining two struggles that were waged more or less simultaneously. One of these was directed at liquidating the existing (nearly always European) colonial regime and, after independence was achieved, at avoiding new forms of colonial dependency (sometimes described as neocolonialism). The other struggle sought to transform newly independent societies, often radically, by eliminating the *ancien régime* and creating new social, economic, and political processes and institutions which will contribute to the pervasive Third World goal of modernization and national development.

After gaining their independence, however, the American people preserved their domestic society largely intact. With relatively few exceptions, the Revolutionary War produced no revolutionary transformation of the American way of life. After 1783, of course, the American society was no longer part of the British Empire. Despite the residual Anglophobia that was detectable among some segments of American opinion as late as the 1930s (and, among Irish-Americans, for example, is still present), admiration for British ideas, customs, manners, fashions, and the like remained strong in

17

America. Throughout the nineteenth century, whether they chose to acknowledge it or not, Americans remained heavily dependent upon British naval power for their security and for the enforcement of important diplomatic declarations such as the Monroe Doctrine (1823) and the Open Door policy (1898–1899). Washington's acquisition of the isthmus of Panama and the subsequent construction of the Panama Canal (completed in 1914) were made possible by close Anglo-American cooperation. Beginning with World War I—and eventually formalized by the North Atlantic Treaty (1949)—a *de facto* alliance or special relationship has existed between the United States and Great Britain.

If, as foreign observers (especially in the Third World) have been heard to complain in the recent period, America has "forgotten its own revolutionary heritage," the explanation seems simple. The American society has no "revolutionary" heritage or tradition in the customary sense. Before resorting to insurrection against British authority, the American colonies repeatedly invoked their "rights as Englishmen"; time and again, they urged London to correct the abuses and injustices that were corroding the colonial relationship—to no avail. Most Americans were extremely reluctant to revolt against British rule, and they finally did so after they decided that circumstances had left them no alternative. In brief, one study has found, the revolutionary experience was characterized by "fundamental contradictions," unanswered questions, anomalous actions and viewpoints, and the total absence of a coherent revolutionary ideology for the remaking of American society.[17]

Another interpretation of this epochal event concludes that, "although radical at the time, in perspective the revolution appears moderate or even conservative." Its goal was "neither the overthrow nor the radical alteration of the existing social structure but the preservation of the sacred political liberty of Englishmen." Most Americans believed that "revolution would change the spirit of man and the fabric of society, which was more essential then merely changing the political structure." In America, the revolutionary process had been "a product of compromise, modification and even improvisation"; from its combined English and colonial heritage "it chose and discarded until it produced something new and different."[18]

17. See Jonathan R. Dull, "American Foreign Relations Before the Constitution: A Historiographical Wasteland," in Gerald K. Haines and J. Samuel Walker (eds.), *American Foreign Relations: A Historiographical Review* (Westport, Conn., 1981), 9.

18. See Robert Blackey and Clifford Paynton, *Revolution and the Revolutionary Ideal* (Cambridge, Mass., 1976), 75–84.

As events after the peace treaty with Great Britain soon demonstrated, from the perspective of strict historical accuracy it would be appropriate to refer to the American *evolution*. From 1778 to 1789, the American society endeavored to govern its affairs under the Articles of Confederation. Almost miraculously, and despite the increasingly evident weaknesses of this system of government, the colonials won the Revolutionary War. The defects of the Articles were soon revealed, however, as economic hardships, trade wars among the colonies, and political unrest swept the newly independent nation. By 1787, demands for constitutional change had become pervasive; and on May 25, 1787, that distinguished group of Americans known as the Founding Fathers convened in Philadelphia for the express purpose of revising and improving the system of government established by the Articles of Confederation. That the Constitutional Convention subsequently met in secret, and that its members were at pains to reassure the country that radical departures from existing political principles were not planned, testify eloquently that most Americans did *not* favor radical change in the existing constitutional system.

The results of the prolonged deliberations in Philadelphia are, of course, well known and require no lengthy recapitulation here. After the ratification process was finally completed, on April 30, 1789, George Washington was inaugurated as the first president of the American republic under the new Constitution, which has now provided America's constitutional framework for some two hundred years. Five points about the American constitutional system deserve emphasizing.

First, the Constitution was drafted and ratified in response to a crisis that Americans increasingly perceived as urgent and affecting their everyday lives. In time, Americans demanded significant improvements in the existing system of government; but it was also clear that the Founding Fathers had no popular mandate for radical and far-reaching departures from familiar and acceptable principles of government.

Second, in the new scheme of government produced at Philadelphia, the founders were careful to preserve considerable continuity with the existing system under the Articles of Confederation. Experience gained and lessons learned under the Articles were invaluable to the Founding Fathers at Philadelphia.

Third, the drafting of the United States Constitution was a continuous exercise in compromise, accommodation, adaptation, flexibility, adjustment, and comparable traits—all concepts which, a century or so later, were central in the thoughts of pragmatic philosophers. At Philadelphia, innumerable major and minor compromises were required before a majority was willing to approve the new Constitution. Proponents of states' rights versus centralized government; slaveholding states versus nonslaveholding states; large versus small states; advocates of strong versus weak executive authority; and (in the ratification stage) disagreements between those who wanted a long list of enumerated citizens' rights versus those who believed the Constitution already protected such rights—these were among the principal conflicts that had to be satisfactorily resolved before the Constitution was drafted and adopted. From beginning to end, the process served as a case study in the reasonable, moderate, "common-sense" approach to the resolution of political issues that has historically appealed to Americans and was later extolled by William James, John Dewey, and other spokesmen for the pragmatic tradition.

Fourth, after it emerged from the process of drafting and ratification, the American Constitution was an extremely untidy, and in some ways illogical, document. From a strictly logical perspective, the Constitution was filled with incongruities and inconsistencies; it left innumerable loose ends and unanswered questions; and its drafters depended upon experience in the years ahead to give tangible meaning to many of its provisions. Reflecting a concept integral to Enlightenment political philosophy, for example, many of the delegates at Philadelphia were more interested in *limiting* the powers of the national government than in facilitating the emergence of unified national policies. Throughout American history, learned constitutional authorities have disagreed over key constitutional concepts—federalism, separation of powers, and due process of law. Even more crucial perhaps, these concepts have impeded national officials who were endeavoring to formulate and administer cohesive policies in response to urgent internal and external problems.

To cite merely a single example of the constitutional conundrum that continues to engender controversy among government officials and citizens alike, even by the 1980s, the exact scope of the president's constitutional power to use the armed forces to achieve diplomatic objectives continued to elicit sharp debate and highly divergent interpretations. In this sphere, as in countless others involving the meaning of constitutional provisions, ultimately experience was likely to prove crucial in resolving the question. It was evident, for example, that the meaning and value of the War Powers Resolution (1973)—a forceful effort by Congress to limit the president's reliance upon armed force to achieve diplomatic goals—were being determined primarily by the degree to which the resolution did (or did not) contribute to the achievement of American foreign policy objectives.[19]

Yet in spite of such gaps and unresolved questions, the American constitutional system has worked remarkably well. It has provided the American people with a highly adaptive instrument of government, making the United States a model of political stability in a world of often radical change.

The fifth—and for our inquiry, possibly the most significant—feature of the American constitutional system was highlighted by the opinion of Chief Justice John Marshall that the Constitution of the United States was intended to "endure for ages to come and consequently [to] be adapted to various crises in human affairs." Or, as one of the Constitution's most eminent interpreters, Edward S. Corwin, said, the Constitution as a formal document came from the Founding Fathers, "but as *law* the Constitution comes from and derives all its forces from the people of the United States of this day and hour." Consequently, to his mind the only correct perspective from which to interpret the Constitution was to regard it "as a living statute, palpitating with the purpose of the hour."[20]

The dynamic and evolving nature of the American constitutional system was underscored by Marshall's opinion in the landmark case of *McCulloch* v. *Maryland* (1819), in which he rejected the view that the powers of the national government must be construed narrowly and restrictively. Such a rigidly narrow interpretation of the Constitution, Marshall asserted, would be "an unwise attempt to provide, by immutable rules, for exigencies which, if foreseen at all, must have been seen dimly, and which can best be provided for as they occur." For the Supreme Court to interpret the Constitution according to any other principle would negate its underlying purpose and deprive Congress "of the capacity to avail itself of experience, to exercise its reason, and to accommodate its legislation to circumstances." Elsewhere in the case, Marshall emphasized that the powers of the Constitution emanated ultimately from the American people. "Its powers are granted by them, and are to be exercised directly on them, and for their benefit." The rationale relied upon by Marshall in enunciating the constitutional doctrine of "implied powers"

19. See, for example, the detailed analysis of the War Powers Resolution in Cecil V. Crabb, Jr., and Pat Holt, *Invitation to Struggle: Congress, the President and Foreign Policy* (2nd ed.; Washington, D.C., 1984), 139–52.

20. The views of Chief Justice John Marshall, Edward S. Corwin, and others are cited in the Preface by Senator B. Everett Jordan, in Library of Congress, *The Constitution of the United States of America: Analyses and Interpretation* (Washington, D.C., 1973), vii–ix. See also Sheldon Goldman, *Constitutional Law and Supreme Court Decision-Making: Cases and Essays* (New York, 1982), 1–2.

would have been thoroughly understood and approved by the philosophical pragmatists several decades later.[21]

In contrast to other nations with written constitutions (like France), Americans take pride that they have had the same constitutional system for some two hundred years and that it has proved sufficiently flexible to accommodate the momentous changes that have occurred within the United States since the late eighteenth century. Since World War II, for example, in several key respects the constitutional system has been forced to adapt to the United States' emergence as a global superpower with a wide range of major and minor international responsibilities.

The Articles of Confederation, it would be correct to say, "grew" into the Constitution of the United States. The original Constitution was adapted by the addition of the first ten amendments (the Bill of Rights) in the stage of ratification. Since 1789, the Constitution has grown by the addition of twenty-six formal amendments (the last in 1971), covering such diverse subjects as the emancipation and enfranchisement of blacks, the direct election of senators, presidential succession, and (most recently) the extension of the franchise to teenagers. Other proposed amendments (*e.g.*, calling for an equal rights amendment, advocated by certain women's organizations and other groups, or requiring Congress to maintain a balanced budget) are currently being publicly discussed.

Yet as every informed student of American government is aware, in many respects these formal changes may be less influential than a long list of informal amendments, modifications, and practices identified with the American constitutional system since the late eighteenth century. This list includes precedents, traditions, usages, conventions, procedures, and the like that have become an established part of the constitutional pattern of the United States. Collectively, these form part of what is often referred to as the "unwritten Constitution" (unwritten only in the sense that these provisions are not found in the original Constitution and its formal amendments). For example, by the late twentieth century several thousand judicial decisions interpreting the meaning of the Constitution have been delivered by the courts (the process of judicial review, whereby the Supreme Court ultimately decides upon the constitutionality of laws and government actions, is itself a firmly established principle forming part of America's unwritten Constitu-

21. *McCulloch* v. *Maryland* 4 Wheaton 316 (1819).

tion).[22] Other examples—the president's appointment of a cabinet, the emergence of political parties, the direct election of the president by popular vote, the inclusion of legislators in important diplomatic negotiations since World War II, the president's dominant role in the foreign policy process, Congress' deliberations upon a budget submitted by the White House—are merely leading examples of precedents and practices that have now become integral to the American constitutional system. In nearly all instances, these have arisen to fill gaps in the written Constitution and to make its general provisions applicable to a host of contemporary problems unforeseen by the Founding Fathers.

American constitutional experience, one commentator has concluded, involved the process of translating the idea of a social contract or a "theory considered semimythical even by its upholders" into "a concrete historical fact."[23] According to another study, as it emerged from the proceedings at Philadelphia, the Constitution was a highly "ambiguous" document. References to the "intentions" of the founders, or the literal meaning of constitutional provisions, often could not resolve future disputes over the Constitution's meaning or requirements. "The framers left a great deal of room for their successors to adopt methods and apply values of their own." In trying to determine what the Constitution means in any given era of American experience, "we have to think. And we have to respond to experience." These behavior guidelines were repeatedly advocated by William James, John Dewey, and other pragmatically oriented thinkers in more recent American history.[24]

The cultural historian Max Lerner has commended the Founding Fathers for devising "intricate but effective means" for solving the constitutional problems confronting them; in doing so, they exhibited "the same pragmatic spirit" that actuated later American political leaders such as Abraham Lincoln and Franklin D. Roosevelt. Americans, Daniel J. Boorstin has said, view the Founding Fathers as "still alive"; the Constitution they drafted is still "adored

22. See the landmark case of *Marbury v. Madison*, 1 Cranch 137 (1803); and the more extended analysis of the concept of judicial review in Goldman, *Constitutional Law*, 10–12.

23. See the commentary on the American constitutional process in William H. Coates *et al.*, *The Emergence of Liberal Humanism: An Intellectual History of Western Europe* (2 vols.; New York, 1966), I, 296.

24. Warren Christopher, "Ceasefire Between the Branches: A Compact in Foreign Affairs," *Foreign Affairs*, LX (Summer, 1982), 989–1006. In this article, a former State Department official calls for needed changes in American constitutional practice to produce greater unity between the president and Congress in the foreign policy field.

because it still works." To American minds, the changes made in their constitutional system constitute "a single broad stream" forming "the unbroken living current of an American Way of Life." The past—or America's perception and understanding of experience—continues to give "meaning to our present."[25]

A leading student of American constitutional history in the modern period concluded that "the Constitution reveals a panoramic mixture of continuity and change." Throughout successive eras of American history, leading constitutional principles have been reinterpreted and presented "in the dress of new circumstances." His prediction—and events have in no way altered its accuracy—was that in the future, as in the past, new and unpredictable developments would play a crucial role in determining the meaning and evolution of the Constitution of the United States.[26]

American Religious Life and Thought

A comparable process of pragmatic adaptation to novel and changing circumstances has also been evident in American religious thought and life since the colonial era. Religious ideas—as reflected in the Mayflower Compact (1620), the charters of several of the American colonies, the Declaration of Independence, and the Constitution—have profoundly influenced American constitutional and political development, as well as nearly every other major sector of national life. America was (and remains) predominantly a Protestant society, drawing its theological inspiration from such Reformation leaders as Martin Luther and John Calvin. Although the Protestant community in the United States came in time to be divided into an almost infinite variety of denominations, sects, and subsects, the most typical expression of American religious belief was embodied in what has been called "Puritan Protestantism" (embracing such denominations as the Congregationalists, Baptists, Presbyterians, Methodists, Unitarians, Quakers, Disciples of Christ, the Salvation Army, and some branches of the Anglican church).

This particular version of Protestantism was in turn influenced primarily by three separate and often dissimilar Old World religious movements: Calvinism, spiritualism, and the Baptist sect movements. From the inception, therefore, American Protestantism was syncretistic: its approach to religious

25. Lerner, *America as a Civilization*, 401; Daniel J. Boorstin, *America and the Image of Europe* (New York, 1960), 82–83.
26. Carl B. Swisher, *American Constitutional Development* (Boston, 1943), 1017–18.

truth included both an emphasis on an intellectual understanding of spiritual reality and a sometimes highly emotional and individualistic "experience" of religious truths, leading to personal salvation. To the American mind, both dimensions of religious life were essential, and few Americans were troubled by the paradox or incongruity implicit in that fact.[27]

As expressed in the sermons and essays of influential colonial ministers such as Jonathan Edwards (1703–1758), the Puritan faith alternately emphasized the omnipotence and omniscience of God and the possibility of human redemption through the exercise of free will. The Puritan belief in predestination was no barrier to the idea that, in the end, every believer determined his own spiritual destiny. To the Puritan mind, the realization of the Kingdom of God depended upon man's choices; spiritual regeneration is always possible, but it is contingent upon the individual's decision initially to seek it and then to exemplify his spiritual rebirth by living a Christian life. Puritan life was also characterized by intense theological disputation. Yet Puritan religious beliefs did not remain static; they were always receptive to new knowledge and insights, and believers sought relief from rigid theological dogmas and established religious hierarchies. Puritan thought did not comprise a systematic and coherent body of belief. Rather, it was always "a collection of basic attitudes rather than . . . a specific and static ideology." In America, Puritanism combined the contradictory ideas of deep assurance and certainty on fundamental theological questions with an openness and receptivity to new ideas and spiritual insights, requiring continuous modifications in accepted creeds and dogmas.[28]

With Martin Luther, Puritans accepted—and were not unduly troubled by—the fact that the human mind was perhaps incapable of comprehending "ultimate" spiritual reality. Man could, however, comprehend what Luther had called *deus revelatus*—God's nature as revealed in the person of Jesus Christ. The believer was capable of knowing and experiencing Christ and of accepting His life and teachings as the touchstone of the Christian life. In Luther's view, therefore, faith was not merely a matter of giving intellectual assent to theological propositions. Instead, it was a matter of what Luther termed *assensus*, or accepting a personal commitment to take a risk or "joyous leap . . . across the abyss of sin and guilt, despair and death." In opposition to an abstract philosophical search for truth, Puritanism insisted that God could

27. William L. Miller, "American Religion and American Political Attitudes," in James W. Smith and A. Leland Jamison (eds.), *The Shaping of American Religion* (Princeton, 1961), 88.
28. Paul K. Conkin, *Puritans and Pragmatism: Eight Eminent American Thinkers* (Bloomington, 1976); see also J. S. Whale, *The Protestant Tradition* (London, 1959), 13–20.

be known for "what he is, by what he has done . . . for his mighty *acts.*"[29]

The American version of Protestantism was a product of the interaction among a number of highly influential and diverse forces that shaped and sustained it. The deep religious convictions of the early settlers and their determination to practice their religion freely were potent influences upon virtually every aspect of American life, not least the evolution of the American educational system. From the beginning, the lack of an acknowledged religious establishment or authoritative source of biblical interpretation meant that individual ministers and laymen possessed wide latitude to study and interpret the essentials of the Christian faith for themselves.

Down to the end of the nineteenth century, the existence of the frontier was another reality momentously affecting the course of religious life and thought in the United States. Inevitably, religious beliefs and practices reflected the exigencies of frontier life. Congregations were widely scattered, and communication among them was difficult. Church members—and sometimes even the clergy—possessed little formal education and had even less interest in abstract theological discourses unrelated to the often harsh demands of frontier existence. In frontier society, the church or "camp meeting" played a key role not only in providing spiritual guidance and revitalization but as a social and recreational center. (The joy or "rapture" often accompanying religious services on the frontier was a welcome relief from the usual austerity and sometimes tragedy that were the norm for frontier families.) Frontier existence was an almost daily exercise in survival, adaptation, improvisation, learning by doing, and eclectic problem solving in an effort to overcome unfamiliar and often ominous environmental forces. Understandably under these conditions, American attitudes toward religious questions reflected these same down-to-earth, practical, and eclectic qualities.

After the adoption of the Constitution, the principle of religious toleration—and the related concept of the separation of church and state—became part of the organic law of the United States, embodied in the First Amendment. With rare exceptions (such as the persecutions endured by the Mormons and other minorities from time to time), public adherence to these principles has spared the United States the fanatical religious strife that has destroyed—and by the late 1980s in many parts of the Third World continues to imperil—the fabric of other societies. Yet if Americans have been extremely tolerant of religious differences, nonetheless they have continued to insist on the idea that moral-ethical precepts do govern human conduct, even the

29. Whale, *Protestant Tradition*, 13–20, 318.

behavior of the state. In 1974, as a result of the Watergate episode, they threatened to impeach—and did succeed in removing—an incumbent president for failing to observe this principle. Throughout American history— from the utopian societies of the eighteenth and nineteenth centuries to the religious communes and political organizations sponsored by fundamentalist religious groups in the contemporary era—a wide range of groups has championed diverse interaction between religious teachings and political authority. This tendency has given added momentum to the already pluralistic nature of religious life in American society.

A salient characteristic of religious life in America has been its remarkably adaptive and dynamic nature. In the words of one study, religious groups in America have nearly always rejected the idea of "passive piety" in favor of "the cooperation of man with God in making a better world as well as a better life." Mainline Protestantism in the United States, therefore, has exhibited a "great capacity" for adaptability and reform. As every student of American history is aware, not infrequently reform movements in the economic, social, and political spheres have been powerfully influenced by religious teachings, and their reforms have been championed by religious organizations.[30]

Another observer of American religious life is convinced that its distinctive orientation can largely be explained by reference to three outstanding qualities: its *empiricism*, its *pluralism*, and its *catholicity*. In the American religious tradition as it has evolved, there is now an "expectancy of revision" of theological principles to conform to realities. The devout American is profoundly interested in "the relation between dogma and concrete experience"; he expects to discover "the connection between Christian faith and an intelligible world view."[31]

Still another study has pointed out that in a spectrum between the polarities of order and movement, or structure and process, American Protestantism has been "nearly always drawn toward the dynamic side." The American Protestant envisioned life as a "story of past pilgrimages now continued, and of encounters between God and man to be reenacted in every generation." American Protestant thought thus always had a twofold theme: the founding of the church and its reform. A recurrent motif has been the belief that the church and human society were "forever being created, forever falling, forever being raised again." More than did their European counterparts, American Protestants conceived of the history of the church as the story of "shaken

30. Nelson R. Burr, *A Critical Bibliography of Religion in America* (Princeton, 1961), 551–53.

31. Daniel D. Williams, "Tradition and Experience in American Theology," in Smith and Jamison (eds.), *Shaping of American Religion*, 445–46.

27

foundations and new construction on the ruins." In effect, the evolution of American Protestantism was a record of continual "movement" and of "many reformations," giving rise to ongoing schisms, and a profusion of denominations, cults, and subcults within the American environment.[32]

Another conspicuous feature of religious life in the United States has been what is sometimes called the "chaos of cults" or the continuing proliferation of denominations, sects, and subsects. These cults and fringe movements have unquestionably testified to the American love of freedom and to acceptance of the principle of freedom of conscience, and they call attention to American distaste for the idea of an established church whose hierarchy prescribes religious doctrines and dogmas. According to one interpretation, cults are also expressions of a "creative religion in the hands of the people," symbolizing the "very substance of democracy." Yet despite the chaos of cults in American society, other commentators have emphasized that it would be a mistake to ignore the substantial degree of agreement among these denominations and sects on essential tenets of the Christian faith. As every viewer of television in the contemporary era is aware, often these separate religious denominations consist of the followers of a charismatic leader whose religious insights and teachings are far from original.[33]

Theological currents in America have also been distinctive, reflecting the unique milieu within which they flowed. Two qualities of American religious thought have been especially notable. One is the remarkably adaptive nature of theology. As religion in the American context was compelled to confront one new development and tendency after another—the break with Great Britain, the westward movement, the agricultural and industrial revolutions in the nineteenth century, the momentous impact of Charles Darwin's scientific findings, the advent of psychology (especially the Freudian school), the demands of an almost endless list of reformers and critics of existing society, the emergence of the United States as a superpower during World War II, and the ensuing cold war between the United States and the Soviet Union—Protestant theologians have seldom been at a loss to accommodate their teachings to the demands of the contemporary world. A leading student of American religious life has noted the extent to which theological ideas in America have been "subject to constant change"; in the United States, re-

32. H. Richard Niebuhr, "The Protestant Movement and Democracy in the United States," in *ibid.*, 22–24.

33. Leland Jamison, "Religions on the Christian Perimeter," in *ibid.*, 230–31; William Miller, "American Religion and American Political Attitudes," in James W. Smith and A. Leland Jamison (eds.), *Religious Perspectives in American Culture* (Princeton, 1961), 84.

ligious teachings have moved "toward rapproachment now with biology, now with psychology, now with the mind of the day as expressed in literature." In the American setting, theology has thus been "orthodox and liberal and fundamentalist and neo-orthodox in turn. There is no standard theologian . . . to whom all . . . religious interpreters refer." The Protestant community has been extraordinarily "pluralistic" regarding the fundamentals of the Christian faith. Protestant groups in America have evolved from a religious movement less interested in "structure" than "directed toward action."[34]

The other outstanding characteristic of Protestant theology in America has been its declining role in the nation's religious life approaching the point in some periods when, in the view of some commentators, theology in the United States has been in effect "bankrupt." According to one interpretation, from Jonathan Edwards to Josiah Royce "America did not produce a first rate religious philosopher." American religious thought has moved rather steadily away from the "mystical and contemplative" toward the "individualistic" and the "immediate." For American religious thinkers, "awareness of the ultimate" has tended to give way "to the concerns with the practical life." The thrust of religious thinking in the United States has progressively been toward an emphasis upon moral behavior and conduct or the application of religious ideas to everyday life.[35]

According to George Santayana, theological studies in the United States have clearly demonstrated the extent to which the American experience has profoundly affected both the methods and the conclusions of indigenous thinkers. Above all, theologians in the United States have been interested in "the relation of doctrine to the religious life [of society] and to the life of the church." In contrast to many European Protestant thinkers, the reference point of American theologians has been *experience*—particularly the ability of the church to adapt to the dynamic pattern of new experiences that have been characteristic of American society. For the most part, religious thinkers in America have been concerned with "perceiving the relation between dogma and concrete experience" and with demonstrating "the connection between Christian faith and an intelligible world view."[36]

The deemphasis upon abstract theological speculations within the American religious community was typified by the remark of the dean of

34. Miller, "American Religion," 24–31.
35. *Ibid.*, 93–94.
36. George Santayana's views on American theological ideas are quoted in Williams, "Tradition and Experience in American Theology," 445–48.

Harvard Divinity School in 1946 that "Christianity is a quality of life rather than a fixed system of doctrine." What has been called American religion's "retreat from metaphysics" is the culmination of a long historical process in which—not only in their religious life but in related spheres of activity including domestic politics, economics, and foreign policy—Americans have traditionally shunned rigid doctrinal positions in favor of flexible, eclectic, and common-sense solutions to immediate problems, nearly always by a process of accommodation, adaptation, and compromise. Meanwhile, widely expressed fears that in the process the central core of Christian teachings will have been compromised out of existence—or the conviction of a small minority that "God is dead!"—find very little acceptance among the majority of the American people.[37]

Our emphasis on the nature and evolution of Protestant thought in the United States should not be interpreted to mean that other religious faiths in the American society are uninfluential or that they have not also been affected by the New World environment. Roman Catholicism in the United States, for example, differs not only from its counterparts in Europe, Latin America, and other regions, but pronounced regional variations in it can be discerned within the United States as well. A number of commentators have called attention to the uniquely "Puritan" character of American Catholicism. Paradoxically, Catholics in the United States have often appeared "more Puritan than anybody else" and have emerged as the champions of Puritan values long after many Protestant denominations had evolved beyond them.

Roman Catholicism in the United States is, in the words of one scholar, a faith which "is always adapting and adjusting in nonessentials" so that it may better serve its members and fulfill its larger mission. In the main, American Catholics have supported efforts (like Vatican II, convened in the early 1960s) to update the teachings of the church and to apply its doctrines to concrete human problems. With other Americans, Catholics share the conviction that growth and change must occur within the religious sphere no less than in other realms of life.[38]

American Judaism has also been a dynamic and adaptive faith. More than its counterpart in other countries, in the United States Judaism has

37. James W. Smith, "Religion and Science in American Philosophy," in Smith and Jamison (eds.), *Shaping of American Religion*, 430–31; George Gallup, Jr., and David Poling, *The Search for America's Faith* (Nashville, 1980), 91–133.

38. See the discussion of Roman Catholicism in the United States in Conal Furay, *The Grass-Roots Mind in America: The American Sense of Absolutes* (New York, 1977), 114–17; and Henry J. Bourne, "Catholicism in the United States," in Smith and Jamison (eds.), *Shaping of American Religion*, 71–121.

deemphasized the role of formal theology, to the point of raising a recurrent question about whether it has any theological cohesion. In America, Judaism has been a "way of life" rather than a system of specified religious principles and dogmas. American Judaism has always exemplified "pragmatism and latitudiarianism." The very term *Judaeo-Christian tradition* underscores the extent to which Jews in America have endeavored, with a high degree of success, to demonstrate the compatibility of their beliefs with Western culture. The pragmatic character of American Judaism was demonstrated after the creation of Israel in 1948. The American Jewish community generously supported it financially, politically, and in other respects, yet relatively few Jews in the United States showed an inclination to emigrate to Israel, to advocate political principles derived from Talmudic doctrines, or even to approve all of Israel's internal and external policies.[39]

American Economic Development

The basic thesis of this discussion of the American economic system is well illustrated by a lecture given several years ago to an American audience by the Indian ambassador to the United States. Speaking on the subject of Indian socialism, the ambassador described India's intensive efforts to devise and administer its own distinctive economic system, which, he assured the audience, would be different from the American, the Soviet, or any other country's model. Sensing perhaps that socialism was not a topic that aroused great enthusiasm among Americans, he described in detail India's efforts to establish a government-sponsored retirement system for workers, to provide adequate medical care for its citizens, to eliminate poverty, and to undertake other long-needed reforms. The climax of his lecture came when he concluded by saying that over a period of years India's goal was to create a socioeconomic system that was as "socialistic" as the system currently existing in the United States!

By the late twentieth century, the American economic system would be unrecognizable to advocates of *laissez faire* such as Adam Smith, or even to a "captain of industry" around 1900. Indeed, by the 1980s some features of that system would be unfamiliar to the architects of the New Deal of the 1930s. For two centuries or more, Americans have described their system of economic enterprise by the term *capitalism*, a principle that, in the popular

39. See Oscar Handlin, "Judaism in the United States," in Smith and Jamison (eds.), *Shaping of American Religion*, 122–61.

mind, "made America great" and continues to be a superior economic system to its competitors abroad. Despite Soviet Premier Nikita Khrushchev's famous boast of the late 1950s—"We will bury you!"—in most key spheres of economic life the United States continues to outpace the Soviet Union. Meanwhile, increases in Soviet productivity have often been achieved only because the Kremlin has permitted certain overtly capitalist principles and practices (as in the agricultural sector) to become established within Soviet society.

One of the modern era's most eminent thinkers, Jacques Maritain, has commented at length on what he has called "a phenomenon of great historical importance—the striking success of the 'unsystematic American [economic] system.'" The industrial regime which Americans inherited from the Old World "has now become unrecognizable in this country." America has produced "new economic structures which are still in the making," which remain in "a state of fluidity," and which "render both capitalism and socialism things of the past." After being transplanted to American soil, traditional Western concepts like free enterprise and private ownership evolved into forms "entirely different from those of the nineteenth century." Moreover, the road is still open to new transformations in the future.[40]

Since World War II, a number of commentators have directed attention to the disparities evident in the theory and practice of American capitalism. A number have called for a "new name" for the American economic system since, among other reasons, in modern history capitalism had widely become a synonym for foreign intervention and internal economic oppression by the owners of production to the detriment of the masses. Highly diverse terms, ranging from *new capitalism* and *democratic capitalism* to the less familiar designations *managementism* and *economic humanism*, have been proposed, but thus far none of these modifications has gained wide currency.

However it is described, the crucial reality is that as the American economic system has evolved, it now embodies traditional capitalistic principles, numerous adaptations of these principles to the exigencies of American national life, and innovative concepts and practices designed to solve specific economic problems confronting the American society in any given era. In many respects, Americans long ago abandoned classical *laissez-faire* precepts, not (as Marxists had predicted) through "sudden, violent and destructive revolution, but through steady, constructive—and unsystematic—transmutation." A more recent analysis of American economic experience arrived

40. Jacques Maritain, *Reflections on America* (New York, 1958), 101–20.

32

at a similar conclusion. Its basic thesis is that for the most part, the course of American economic development has not been determined by societal upheavals or adherence to ideological blueprints but by small and incremental choices made by millions of people over time.[41]

Emotionally and psychologically, Americans remain strongly attached to the concept of capitalism. Since World War II, for example, millions of Americans have interpreted the cold war contest with the Soviet Union as primarily a struggle between two antithetical modes of organizing society: one based on the principle of free enterprise, freedom of choice, and democracy; the other, on the theory of collectivism, coercion, and the paramount rights of the state over those of the individual. From the evidence of their respective performance records, few Americans doubt which system is superior and will ultimately win this global contest.

Yet it may be questioned whether the American society ever had a "pure" capitalist system. Since colonial times, economic enterprise in the United States has been diluted by economic practices and behavior patterns which were often at variance with capitalistic principles. The slavery-based plantation system of the South, for example, contravened a number of capitalistic tenets. As early as President George Washington's administration, Alexander Hamilton and other Federalists called for active government support and encouragement of business enterprise. Although Hamilton's economic theories were actively opposed by the Jeffersonians, they did have a residual impact on the American mind, and as time passed, many of them were accepted by a majority of American citizens. From an early date, it was axiomatic that a primary goal of the State Department was to create new opportunities for American business and commerce abroad. (Down to World War II, many Americans perhaps viewed this as the *only* worthwhile purpose of that department.)[42] Other developments such as opening up of western lands for private settlement and ownership, government assistance in fostering inventions, massive assistance by the states and the national government in constructing the nation's railroad network, and the establishment of the system of land-grant colleges and universities for the specific purpose of

41. The views of William E. Nichols on American economic evolution are discussed in *ibid.*, 112–14; see also Victor R. Fuchs, *How We Live: An Economic Perspective on Americans from Birth to Death* (Cambridge, Mass., 1983).

42. Louis M. Hacker (ed.), *Alexander Hamilton in the American Tradition* (New York, 1957); Donald Swanson, *The Origins of Hamilton's Fiscal Policies* (Gainesville, Fla., 1963); Herman F. Eilts, "Diplomacy—Contemporary Practice," in Elmer Plischke (ed.), *Modern Diplomacy: The Art and the Artisans* (Washington, D.C., 1979), 7–8.

benefiting American agriculture contributed to the emergence of a distinctive species of capitalism in the New World. During some periods also, high tariff walls protected American industry and labor from foreign competition, and with Washington's encouragement, American business groups actively established new markets and commercial opportunities abroad (as in China).

The heyday of rugged individualism economically at the end of the nineteenth century was followed by a period of adaptation and new relationships between business and government. Initiated by President Theodore Roosevelt and continued by President Woodrow Wilson before and during World War I, this process entailed far-reaching changes in the nature of American capitalism—a list far too extensive to examine in detail here.[43] It must suffice to make two general observations about these innovations.

First, in several key sectors of economic enterprise—regulating the policies and activities of trusts and other business combinations; recognizing and protecting the rights of labor; improving working conditions for children, women, and labor generally; and enforcing standards for the production of food, drugs, and other consumer goods—the power of the national government was relied upon to bring business practices into conformity with the general welfare. In many cases (as in more stringent government regulation of monopolies), the impetus for these innovations often came from business organizations and spokesmen who urged political leaders to protect them from injurious or unfair business practices by more powerful competitors.

Second, these changes before and during World War I were increasingly accorded constitutional legitimacy by the decisions of Justices Oliver Wendell Holmes, Jr., Louis D. Brandeis, and other "judicial pragmatists." In resolving constitutional questions posed by growing government intervention in business activity, the judicial pragmatists were usually guided by Holmes's widely quoted dictum that the life of the law is not reason but experience. On that premise, pragmatically oriented jurists carefully examined the consequences of government action (or inaction) in determining the constitutionality of particular laws. (The implicit assumption of this approach, of course, was that general concepts like "freedom" or the "general welfare" must always be defined within a specific context; and this requirement necessarily implied that their precise meaning was likely to change from one historical period to another). More often than not, on the basis of this test, pragmatically inclined

43. John M. Blum, *The Republican Roosevelt* (Cambridge, Mass., 1954); Richard H. Collins (ed.), *Theodore Roosevelt and Reform Politics* (Lexington, Mass., 1972). Woodrow Wilson's approach to economic issues is analyzed in John M. Blum, *Woodrow Wilson and the Politics of Morality* (Boston, 1956); and William Diamond, *The Economic Thought of Woodrow Wilson* (Baltimore, 1943).

jurists found that more stringent regulation of business activities by government met the standard of constitutionality.[44]

More than any other era of American history, however, the New Deal of President Franklin D. Roosevelt witnessed the most numerous and far-reaching changes in the nature of the capitalistic system. Elected to the presidency in 1932 as a conservative, FDR was dedicated to "saving" American capitalism from the effects of the most ruinous depression in the nation's history. His prescriptions for doing so throughout his tenure in office consisted of a profusion of new programs and regulations that simultaneously sought to revive economic activity in the United States and to impose new restrictions on business practices, making them more responsive to the public interest. From an ideological perspective, the New Deal was a grab bag or bewildering *mélange* of concepts and programs which the Roosevelt administration offered piecemeal. If FDR's approach to domestic problems had any ideological consistency or cohesion, students of the New Deal at the time and afterward were unable to discern it. (More than once, Roosevelt expressed his disdain for "-isms"; on one occasion, he said that he left the philosophical rationalization of his program to his advisers!)

The nature of American capitalism was also crucially affected by the attitudes, tactics, and demands of the American labor movement. In the words of one commentator, its traditional approach has reflected the "hard-headed, pragmatic unionism" identified with Samuel Gompers, the first president of the American Federation of Labor (AFL). Gompers evinced little interest in causes like the "revolutionary overthrow of state power." Instead, he advocated "pure and simple unionism," devoted to achieving "here and now" goals. His cryptic threefold expression of labor union demands—"more, more, and more"—epitomized the eclectic and nonideological orientation of mainstream labor organizations in the United States. Bitter, prolonged, and violent as they sometimes were, labor-management conflicts in America were conducted "within a framework of ultimate consent"; after the settlement, production was resumed. In time, the labor union movement was sanctioned and protected by the national government. Conversely, radical and militant labor groups such as the International Workers of the World (IWW) or "Wobblies" during the early 1900s, or communists and communist-controlled unions after World War II, nearly always found themselves

44. Melvin I. Vrofsky, *Louis D. Brandeis and the Progressive Tradition* (Boston, 1980); David Burton, *Oliver Wendell Holmes, Jr.: What Manner of Liberal* (Melbourne, Fla., 1979); Samuel J. Konefsky, *The Legacy of Holmes and Brandeis: A Study of the Influence of Ideas* (New York, 1956).

opposed by the mainstream labor organizations and by majority sentiment among the American people. In the post–World War II era, American labor leaders and organizations played an active role in opposing Soviet expansionism abroad and communist influence within the United States and other countries.[45]

More than any political movement in American history, however, the New Deal was the prototype of a pragmatic approach to challenges at home and abroad. Confronted domestically with the most serious economic crisis in national experience, FDR responded, "The country needs and . . . the country demands bold, persistent experimentation. It is common sense to take a method and try it. If it fails, admit it frankly and try another. But above all, try something." In 1934 Roosevelt told a nationwide radio audience, "I believe in practical explanations and in practical policies." His New Deal has been called "not so much a consistent, carefully planned, comprehensive program as it was a series of practical responses to the various problems arising out of the Depression." An experienced political analyst called Roosevelt "a man of action," who "cared greatly about results but rather little about how the results were obtained."[46]

Future chapters will provide examples of New Deal diplomacy. Here it suffices to note that Roosevelt's pragmatic orientation was also evident in the realm of foreign policy. European observers, for example, were convinced that FDR was "above all an empiricist" whose approach to international issues was "without doctrine or consistent plans." Other students of New Deal diplomacy believed that FDR's ideas (the "Four Freedoms" and the "Atlantic Charter," for example) reflected a "Rooseveltian synthesis" of conservative and liberal concepts. Still others believed that New Deal diplomacy embodied both isolationist and internationalist ideas. As the end of World War II approached, another commentator concluded, President Roosevelt was "as always . . . acting pragmatically, opportunistically, tactically. As usual, he was almost wholly concerned about the immediate job ahead—winning the war." Overall, FDR's foreign policies were "more a simple response to events abroad than to a set plan or program of foreign policy making at home." He

45. Lerner, *America as a Civilization*, 321–22; Ronald Radosh, *American Labor and United States Foreign Policy* (New York, 1969); symposium, "Labor's International Role," *Foreign Policy*, XXVI (Spring, 1977), 204–46.

46. FDR's views are quoted in Hofstadter, *American Political Tradition*, 311; Samuel I. Rosenman (ed.), *The Public Papers and Addresses of Franklin D. Roosevelt, 1934* (New York, 1938), 312–18; and Gerald Nash, *The Great Depression and World War II: Organizing America, 1933–1945* (New York, 1979), 18; see also Joseph Alsop, *FDR, 1882–1945* (New York, 1982), 9.

lacked a "firm strategy" diplomatically, and he was nearly always at a loss to discern the "meaning of affairs" overseas.[47]

Franklin D. Roosevelt was perhaps the prototype of the pragmatic chief executive. His remedies for the ills besetting the American society were avowedly eclectic, experimental, and dictated by the nature of the problems at home and abroad. Roosevelt was determined to avoid the "collectivist" solutions currently fashionable in Nazi Germany and communist Russia. He no less rejected the idea (pervasive in America during the 1920s) that government should refrain from interfering in the economy and permit unrestrained market forces to determine the level and nature of business activities. Consequently, the New Deal was a veritable potpourri of new government programs, laws, executive orders, guidelines, and suggestions to American business enterprises. Collectively, these steps were designed to stimulate American industrial and agricultural production, to reduce unemployment, to protect workers and their families from the adverse consequences of the business cycle, to revive foreign trade, to create a retirement program (Social Security) for millions of Americans, and, perhaps above all, to overcome the pervasive psychological malaise that gripped American society during the 1930s.

The Roosevelt administration laid the basis for the emergence of the welfare state in the United States. Judging by the decisive popular mandates he received while in office, FDR's ideas enjoyed the support of the overwhelming majority of the American people. Despite the conservative reaction that brought Ronald Reagan to the White House in 1981, there has been no concerted attempt since World War II to dismantle this welfare state.

As the end of the twentieth century approached, questions were widely raised about the future of the American capitalist system. Other countries (like Kuwait) have achieved a higher per capita income than the United States; and the long-dominant economic position of the nation was being challenged by a dynamic Japan. In several domestic industries both corporate executives and workers demanded protectionist legislation against the hazards of "unfair" foreign competition. Admittedly (and the American automobile industry was a prominent example), since World War II American

47. European reactions to FDR's diplomacy are quoted in Howard C. Payne, Raymond Callahan, and Edward M. Bennett, *As the Storm Clouds Gathered: European Perceptions of American Foreign Policy in the 1930's* (Durham, N.C., 1979), 28; Paul Seabury, *The Rise and Decline of the Cold War* (New York, 1967), 44; James M. Burns, *Roosevelt: The Lion and the Fox* (New York, 1956), 383, 469; and several commentaries on Roosevelt's foreign policy in Warren F. Kimball (ed.), *Franklin D. Roosevelt and the World Crisis, 1937–1945* (Lexington, Mass., 1973).

business enterprises have sometimes been slow to recognize the gravity of new challenges, to adopt technological innovations, and to recognize changes in consumer trends. A number of serious and intractable problems— high unemployment (especially among ethnic minorities), the obsolescence of certain productive techniques and job skills, the poor competitive position of some segments of American industry, and the perennially depressed condition of certain sectors of agriculture—remained unsolved. The strength of America, a Chinese economist observed in the early 1980s, lay in its capacity for creative innovation and "in Yankee ingenuity."[48]

A comparable pragmatic orientation to economic problems has been identified in recent years with many other foreign countries, notably the Soviet Union and the People's Republic of China. Political authorities in both nations were introducing (or in some cases officially tolerating) pragmatic innovations that had long been a hallmark of the American economic system. Reluctantly, Soviet leaders had been compelled to loosen ideological rigidities and to make concessions to peasants, workers, and managers in an effort to stimulate productivity throughout the USSR. Even then (as in agriculture) Soviet productive levels lagged considerably behind their goals. After the death of Mao Tse-tung in 1976, Chinese authorities initiated a series of sweeping and pragmatic changes and reforms, producing what was in time called China's new "responsibility system" (an interesting mixture of Marxist, traditional Chinese and Confucianist, and capitalistic ideas and practices). By the mid-1980s, in some economic sectors Chinese productivity had improved significantly.[49]

Whatever specific forms the American response to emerging economic challenges might eventually take, on the basis of national experience one outcome can be predicted with confidence. The American society's response will be in the spirit of the New Deal. It will be less concerned with ideological principles than with the solution of urgent and immediate problems. It will consist of a mixture of long- and short-range solutions—such as scientific and technological research and development programs, which will often produce important innovations for American industry and agriculture; new produc-

48. The views of the Chinese economist Zhau Jinglun, are quoted in *Newsweek*, C (September 20, 1982), 33.

49. For more detailed evidence of pragmatic tendencies in recent Soviet policies, see Joseph L. Nogee and Robert H. Donaldson, *Soviet Foreign Policy Since World War II* (2nd ed.; New York, 1984), 37–39. Comparable tendencies in recent Chinese policy are discussed in the symposium "The People's Republic of China," *Current History*, LXXXI (September, 1983), 241–81; in the New York *Times*, October 25, 1983; and in *Newsweek*, CIII (January 9, 1984), 55.

tive processes and techniques (including adaptations of ideas drawn from Japan and other foreign countries); innovative patterns of labor-management relations; significant modifications in the American educational system and vocational training programs tailored to anticipated changes in the American society; and new government programs and regulations—all directed toward keeping the American economy prosperous, dynamic, and stable. As in earlier eras, relatively few Americans will really care how the continuing evolution of the nation's capitalistic system is rationalized ideologically or whether these changes comprise a philosophically consistent approach. Paramount considerations in the years ahead, as during some two hundred years of American history, will be how well do they work and what are their principal consequences in accomplishing the goals widely shared by the members of American society.[50]

The American Political Experience

By some criteria, the realm of national experience that most poignantly illustrates the pragmatic tendencies of the American people is their political life. To this day, the democratic political system of the United States evokes bewilderment, mystification, and astonishment from observers at home and abroad. The American political process is routinely characterized by the existence of ideological inconsistencies and paradoxes; by continuity and improvisation; by what sometimes seems an almost total irrelevance to the serious public issues of the day; by the impact of powerful personalities; by periodic calls for a fundamental partisan "realignment" to give voters a more meaningful choice among candidates and parties; and by a public atmosphere of disdain and distrust for the political process and those directly involved in it. Yet by some inexplicable process, the American political system has worked reasonably well for two centuries. Most political scientists are convinced that there is an organic connection between the existence of the nation's two-party system and the successful operation of democratic government in the United States.

To no inconsiderable degree, the ambivalent reactions to the American political system can be attributed to the circumstances of its emergence in the

50. Lester R. Brown, "The Nation-State, the Multinational Corporation and the Changing World Order," in Harvey S. Perloff (ed.), *The Future of the U.S. Government: Toward the Year 2000* (Englewood Cliffs, N.J., 1971), 172–86; John Stack, *Policy Choices: Critical Issues in American Foreign Policy* (Guilford, Conn., 1983), 162–86; Seymom Brown, *On the Front Burner: Issues in U.S. Foreign Policy* (Boston, 1984), 80–134.

eighteenth century. In the words of one study, the concept of self-government "was never completely planned nor projected" in American society; many of its chief elements, including the two-party system, "were neither designed nor authorized," but developed as "unspecified improvisations and adaptations" to American conditions. The American political system evolved primarily because people "have had to be ingenious and resourceful and to contrive much." American political experience has, therefore, witnessed the emergence of "ever more intricate devices" to meet the political needs of the people. Not until the mid-nineteenth century did the American political process assume the form that is familiar to present-day observers.[51]

The illogical, untidy, and anomalous nature of the American political process has possibly become more pronounced in the late twentieth century than in any previous era of the nation's history, in part perhaps because on domestic and international issues, American public opinion seems extraordinarily confused and disunified. Thus in 1982, one study of Congress' highly inconsistent behavior in dealing with a broad range of national issues used the term *the politics of contradiction* to describe contemporary legislative behavior. One harassed legislator observed, "Whatever the flaws of [Congress], it reflects the mood of the American people, and basically they are ambiguous." Faced with the incompatible and ambivalent demands of millions of voters, Congress was compelled "to make hard choices among them."[52]

Within the executive branch a comparable tendency was discernible. President Ronald Reagan was simultaneously attacking the threat posed by "big government" to the ordinary American and proposing the largest Defense Department budget in the nation's history! Almost daily, Reagan denounced the Soviet Union as the world's most dangerous "evil empire"; concurrently, he repeatedly expressed his desire to engage in peaceful negotiations with Moscow. Describing the attitudes of the two major political parties toward foreign affairs in the mid-1980s, one commentator concluded that under Reagan's leadership the Republican party had "become diplomatically isolationist and militarily internationalist." By contrast, the Democrats "are becoming the opposite." These are examples of what one study has described as the "mildly schizoid" quality of American political life.[53]

51. Roy F. Nichols, *The Invention of the American Political Parties: A Study of Political Improvisation* (New York, 1967), xi–xii, 86.
52. See the views of several commentators on the American political system in *U.S. News and World Report*, XCIII (September 6, 1982), 80.
53. Richard Reeves, "The Ideological Election," *New York Times Magazine*, February 19, 1984, p. 92; Lloyd A. Free and Hadley Cantril, *The Political Beliefs of Americans: A Study of Public Opinion* (New York, 1968), 180.

In somewhat more philosophical terms, another recent study of the American political system referred to the gap that "has always existed between the ideals in which Americans believed and the institutions that have embodied their practice." The result has been "continuing disharmony between the normative and existential dimensions of American politics." The disharmony has been evident in every period of American political experience—and according to some standards, it may be more evident today than earlier. Ideological anomalies and contradictions; wide differences between professed theory and practice; a high degree of irrationality, buffoonery, and comic relief; a discernible gulf between the behavior of political leaders and the concerns of ordinary citizens continue to be appropriate descriptions of the political process in the United States.[54]

Many of these same puzzling and intriguing aspects of the American political system are highlighted by the numerous and continuing efforts made to identify the "mainspring" or primary causal force motivating American political contests. In this quest, countless explanations and theories have been offered. The political process in the United States has alternately been depicted as a contest between ideological adversaries, such as the proponents of "loose" versus "strict" construction of the Constitution, or the advocates of sweeping socioeconomic change ("modernizers") versus groups attached to the *status quo*; between the workers and the owners of the means of production (the Marxist explanation), or between slaveholders and nonslaveholders, or between property owners and propertyless classes; between different geographical interests, such as the North versus the South or, more recently, the East versus the West; between WASPs and other politically "established" groups versus ethnic minorities, disadvantaged groups, and others who feel excluded from access to political power; and between citizens who are strongly attracted to and those who oppose an influential political leader who symbolizes their viewpoints and aspirations. Then, as will be explained more fully below, by the late twentieth century there was an expanding group of Americans who found the whole political process distasteful and repugnant. Among this group, citizens believed that political contests in the United States involve little more than efforts by rival self-seeking and ambitious groups to promote their own interests at society's expense. Within the American society, the political process has few overt admirers—fewer today perhaps than in the past.

The truth, of course, is that in any given historical period, several of these

54. See Samuel P. Huntington, "American Ideals Versus American Institutions," *Political Science Quarterly*, XCVI (Spring, 1982), 1–37.

conflicts have existed in, and been influential in shaping, American political experience *concurrently*. This is perhaps the main reason why it has proved so difficult to arrive at a consensus concerning a unicausal explanation of American political development. In a society as variegated as the United States—and within a geographical area of continental dimensions—the political universe has always been *pluralistic*: normally, a number of highly diverse political forces operate within it simultaneously. As often as not, these influences have arisen unpredictably and fortuitously. The accidental presence of two opposite and forceful personalities—Alexander Hamilton and Thomas Jefferson—in the early history of the republic, for example, was crucial in the emergence of the American two-party system. The assassination of Abraham Lincoln was a no less epochal event in determining American political life after the Civil War. The personality of Franklin D. Roosevelt was a momentous force in shaping the New Deal and in determining the party realignment that occurred in the United States during his administrations.

Despite President George Washington's well-known admonition in his "Farewell Address" (September 19, 1796), indigenous political parties arose during his first administration. Led by Alexander Hamilton, John Jay, and other conservatives, the Federalist party was a coalition of groups and interests favoring a "loose" or flexible interpretation of the Constitution to permit an active role by the national government in fostering business and commercial activity. Opposed to the Federalists were the Anti-Federalists or Jeffersonian Republicans. Jefferson's followers were an even more heterogeneous assortment of aristocrats, workers, farmers, admirers of the French Revolution, and others who advocated strict constitutional construction, limited government, and states' rights. The Jeffersonian Republicans were the progenitors of the modern-day Democratic party (although it is an interesting commentary on the nature of the American political system that spokesmen for *both* major parties from time to time claim Jefferson as one of their political ancestors). In less than a generation, the Federalist party had disappeared as an organized political force. For a few years, many of its followers and ideas were represented in the short-lived Whig party, which was in turn superseded by the Republican party on the eve of the Civil War.

The Democratic party evolved from the Jeffersonian Republicans and was extremely influential during the Jacksonian era. Because of its close identification with the South and the cause of slavery, the party's political credibility was severely impaired by the Civil War. The period 1876–1896 was one of the few eras of true two-party competition—when there were no landslide electoral victories and control of Congress changed hands frequently—in American political experience. Yet from the end of the Civil War until 1932, the Republican party remained largely dominant in the national government. Then for the next twenty years, until the election of Dwight D. Eisenhower in 1952, the Democratic party usually controlled the White House and Congress. Since the Eisenhower period, each major party has controlled the White House several times, although the Democratic party has normally held a majority in Congress and continues to have more nominal members among the electorate then the GOP.[55]

Without attempting a detailed recapitulation of American political history, we may briefly call attention to several aspects of the nation's political experience that are especially pertinent for our subject. Beginning with the party struggles between the Federalists and Anti-Federalists, each major political party has had a heterogeneous constituency—the Democratic party perhaps even more than the Republican. Since the New Deal, and particularly since World War II, the Democratic party has been identified with three concepts uniting its members: internationalism in foreign affairs, support for the welfare state, and the promotion of civil rights. The dynamic nature of the American political system, however, is highlighted by the fact that on each of these broad issues, the Democratic party has become increasingly factionalized and severely challenged to forge an enduring consensus. Although its leader in the 1930s, Franklin D. Roosevelt, embodied the idea of active involvement by the United States in global affairs, by the 1970s many prominent Democrats and groups traditionally supporting the party espoused a "neo-isolationist" position, calling for significant limitations upon America's overseas commitments. Comparable factionalism could be discerned toward other issues advocated in recent history by the Democratic party.

Although less divided internally, the modern-day Republican party has also been hard-pressed to preserve its cohesion. According to some interpretations, the party is divided between the Yankees (eastern wing) and the Cowboys (western wing). From another perspective, the Republican party has two primary sources of strength, represented by Main Street and Wall Street. The former (New Englanders, midwestern farmers, and small businessmen) have epitomized "homely American virtues of self-reliance and frugality," and they have been intensely moralistic and antigovernment in

55. In recent years, among new voters especially, the trend toward political independence appears to be rising. See the data presented in James Sundquist, "Whither the American Party System?—Revisited," in Carl Ladd, Jr., and Charles D. Hadley, *Transformations of the American Party System: Political Coalitions from the New Deal to the 1970's* (New York, 1975), 586–89.

their ideological orientation. By contrast, the Wall Street wing, whose influence has been largely responsible for Republican electoral victories on the national level in the postwar era, consists of "sophisticated international money handlers and entrepreneurs." This group has supplied the impetus for "modern Republicanism," and it has accepted—and in some respects, pledged to improve—most of the New Deal programs introduced by Franklin D. Roosevelt and his political heirs.[56]

The ideological and policy differences between the two major political parties have become increasingly indistinct, to the point often of being undetectable. More often than not, they differ in matters of emphasis, degree, outlook, and timing rather than in fundamental principles. Conversely, a broad area of agreement exists between the two major political parties on domestic and foreign policy issues. Since 1932, for example, both parties have largely accepted the concept of the welfare state at home; and by the 1980s, spokesmen for both were seriously questioning some of the abuses and extravagances associated with it. Similarly, in foreign relations, Democrats and Republicans alike accepted the proposition that since World War II the United States was a superpower; that the primary threat to its security arose from the behavior of the Soviet Union; that it needed allies among the nations of the free world; and that it had a responsibility to assist societies in the Third World to engage in modernization and national development.[57]

It must be emphasized that in American experience, political loyalties have been—and available evidence indicates that they remain—subject to ongoing, and sometimes dramatic, change. This tendency was poignantly illustrated by the fundamental political realignment that occurred during the New Deal. One prevalent theory of American political life contends that "critical" elections, in which such realignments have periodically occurred, provide the key to understanding American political experience.[58]

The election of Ronald Reagan to the presidency in 1980 created genuine uncertainty among well-qualified observers of the American political scene. For some, it represented the fulfillment of political prophecy: the "emerging Republican majority" had become a reality. In other words, a new political

56. See Nelson E. Polsby, "Coalition and Faction in American Politics: An Institutional View," in *ibid.*, 160–64.

57. See S. I. Hayakawa, "The Two-Party System: A Personal Reflection," in Seymour M. Lipset (ed.), *Party Coalitions in the 1980's* (San Francisco: 1981), 47–48.

58. See, for example, V. O. Key, "A Theory of Critical Elections," *Journal of Politics*, XVII (February, 1955), 3–18; see also Bruce A. Campbell and Richard J. Triling (eds.), *Realignment in American Politics: Toward a Theory* (Austin, Tex., 1980); and Walter Dean Burnham, *Critical Elections and the Mainsprings of American Politics* (New York, 1970).

realignment had unquestionably occurred. For others, it was merely a political aberration, signifying little else than that voters were dissatisfied with Democratic President Jimmy Carter; on that basis there was no reason to anticipate that the political coalitions existing since the New Deal would be fundamentally changed.[59] Our interest in the question is confined to emphasizing that (as the leader of a numerically smaller party) Reagan could win the election only by convincing the American electorate that he was less ideologically rigid than he sometimes seemed and that he was prepared to control right-wing extremism among his supporters. In 1984, in his successful campaign for reelection, Reagan was at pains to convey an image of "moderation" to the voters and convince them of his willingness to be flexible and adaptive in attempts to solve such problems as the global arms race and the budget deficit at home.

Generalizing the point, one study of American political dynamics finds that voters in the United States seldom approach political issues in ideological terms; those voters who do so are a small minority of the American electorate. In the United States "there is a general lack of commitments to some set of abstract principles about the role of government in society" on the basis of which voters evaluate the two major political parties. In their political attitudes, "Americans are consistently neither liberal nor conservative on a wide range of issues." An individual voter is likely to be liberal on some issues, conservative on others, and have no opinion on still others. The outstanding fact perhaps is that voters tend to approach each issue "on its merits," without resort to ideological guidelines. Or expressing the same idea differently, another study of American political attitudes found that "the majority of Americans remain conservative at the ideological level" in the sense that they favor curbing the power of the federal government. Yet on the practical level of government programs and activities designed to benefit various segments of American society, the people's attitudes have consistently been "in liberal directions . . . since the days of the New Deal." Such incongruous and contradictory aspects of American public opinion perhaps serve as the strongest deterrent to any fundamental realignment of the American political system.[60]

Increasingly in recent American political experience, the outcome of

59. The sometimes widely varying interpretations by several authorities on the American political system are presented in Ellis Sandoz and Cecil V. Crabb, Jr. (eds.), *A Tide of Discontent: The 1980 Elections and Their Meaning* (Washington, D.C., 1981); and several of the essays in the same editors' *Election '84: Landslide Without a Mandate?* (New York, 1985).

60. William H. Flanigan and Nancy H. Zingale, *Political Behavior of the American Electorate* (4th ed.; Boston, 1979), 118–22.; Free and Cantril, *Political Beliefs of Americans*, 5–6, and the data presented in the Baton Rouge *Morning Advocate*, November 30, 1982, dispatch by Richard Reeves.

national (especially presidential) elections has been determined by three variables or factors that are largely independent of nomimal party affiliations or ideological preferences: the personality or "image" projected by the candidates in any given election; the decisions made by a steadily expanding number of voters who regard themselves as politically independent; and the particular and immediate issues confronting the American society at home and abroad, particularly those viewed as urgent during the months immediately preceding national elections.

If it has always been true in American political life, the personal appeal of candidates for high political office has become a crucial element in determining electoral outcomes in the age of television and instantaneous communications. To achieve maximum political appeal, candidates for the White House and Congress should convey an image of personal integrity, sincerity, and competence; of optimism, youth, and vigor; of reasonableness and moderation in their policy positions; of a genuine interest in people and an ability to "relate" to their urgent concerns; and of self-confidence and assurance (without at the same time giving an impression of superiority and arrogance). By contrast, ideological dogmatism and philosophical rigidity are not qualities that endear candidates to the American people.

One experienced observer of the American political process has described it as involving the "energetic politics of suspicion." Throughout their political history, but especially with the Populist party of the late nineteenth century, Americans have opposed "big government," even while their representatives in Congress were expanding the powers of government by adding new federal programs to benefit particular segments of the population![61]

As President George Washington's widely quoted warning about the evils of political parties indicated, Americans have historically been especially skeptical about "politics" and "politicians." Throughout the nation's history —from nineteenth-century humorists Mark Twain and Artemis Ward, to twentieth-century satirists Will Rogers, Mark Russell, and Art Buchwald— American political life has provided the raw materials for countless humorous scenarios. Artemis Ward's boast, "I am not a politician, and all my other habits air [sic] good!" perhaps typifies long-standing American negativism about the political process and those involved in it. In recent years, numerous public opinion surveys have documented the extent to which Americans exhibit a low degree of confidence in politicians and have repeatedly shown

61. Richard Reeves, "The Ideological Election," *New York Times Magazine*, February 19, 1984, pp. 80–91.

that parents rank politics at or near the bottom as a desirable career for their children. (Paradoxically, such attitudes do not inhibit Americans from viewing their own political system as superior to any other existing in the contemporary world.)

More than in any previous era of their history, Americans pride themselves on their political "independence." For many citizens, it has become a matter of principle, if indeed perhaps even of conscience, that they "vote for the man (or candidate), not the party" on election day. In recent years, the proportion of the American electorate not identified permanently with either major political party has grown steadily. This tendency has led to pervasive apprehensions among some observers about the "decomposition" of the American two-party system. As never before, Democrats and Republicans (but particularly the numerically smaller GOP) must make a concerted effort to appeal to the widening circle of independent voters, in part by convincing them that their approach to important public policy issues is moderate, reasonable, and conformable with the middle-of-the-road impulses of the ordinary American citizen.[62]

For some two hundred years—but even more in the contemporary period than in earlier eras—the electorate in the United States has usually been preoccupied with issues possessing what political scientists call a high degree of "saliency," that is, questions of public policy which voters perceive as having a significant, direct, and immediate impact upon their everyday lives. Professional politicians are, of course, well acquainted with the tendency of Americans to "vote their pocketbooks"; as a rule, economic issues are uppermost in the minds of voters on election day, and they are motivated to elect candidates who will "do something" about unemployment, declining production, high inflation, or other adverse economic conditions.[63]

The normal political behavior of the American people is subject to one noteworthy exception: the public response to the existence of a crisis (or a series of crises) abroad. Throughout American diplomatic history, but particularly since the 1930s, when a foreign crisis exists the American people have tended to close ranks behind the incumbent president, according the chief executive wide latitude in responding to it. The watchword of the World War I era—"politics is adjourned"—succinctly describes this state of mind. Simi-

---

62. See the analysis by William Schneider, "Democrats and Republicans, Liberals and Republicans," in Lipset (ed.), *Party Coalitions in the 1980's*, 181–82. A more extended discussion is Everett C. Ladd, Jr., *Where Have All the Voters Gone? The Fracturing of America's Political Parties* (New York, 1978).
63. See remarks on the 1984 national election in Sandoz and Crabb (eds.), *Election 84.*

larly, during World War II Americans were reluctant to "change horses in midstream," and as a result the Roosevelt administration was reelected to unprecedented third and fourth terms in office.

The era of limited war, it is true, has presented the American people with a novel challenge, and their reaction has not followed customary patterns. For example, the Korean conflict was highly unpopular with some segments of the American society and was widely labeled "Mr. Truman's war." More than a decade later, President Lyndon B. Johnson complained during the Vietnam War that he was the only American chief executive in history who had not received overwhelming popular support while the United States was involved in a foreign conflict. The Vietnam War, of course, destroyed the Johnson administration's political credibility. Yet by the end of the 1970s, the American people had "reverted to type." President Jimmy Carter lost his political mandate because *he did not act decisively in foreign affairs* and because he was widely perceived as a chief executive who either could not or would not protect the diplomatic interests of the United States. Ronald Reagan's pledge to "make America great again" contributed to his election to the White House in 1980. Subsequently, the Reagan administration's overt diplomatic defeat in Lebanon—along with a continuing series of diplomatic crises in Central America—did not discernibly damage its political credibility, primarily perhaps for two reasons. Most Americans approved of President Reagan's attempt to do something about challenges to American diplomatic interests abroad. And much as they may have disliked his policies, Reagan's critics were hard-pressed to formulate alternatives that were acceptable to the American people.[64] Significantly, even in the post–Vietnam War era, there was no detectable public demand for Congress to take charge of the foreign policy process. As always, Americans continued to look to an individual in whom they had confidence to solve problems with which they had little familiarity and which often appeared to be only remotely related to their daily lives.

Two other essential features of the American political system remain to be mentioned. One is the role of minor or third parties in the political process.[65] American political life has been punctuated by the meteorlike rise and

64. Bernard C. Cohen, *The Public's Impact on Foreign Policy* (Boston, 1973); Ralph B. Levering, *The Public and American Foreign Policy, 1918–1978* (New York, 1978); and Crabb and Holt, *Invitation to Struggle*, esp. 1–37, 235–53.

65. The principal third parties in American political experience were the Anti-Masonic party in the 1830s, the Abolitionist party before the Civil War, the Populist party during the 1890s, the Progressive party during the early 1900s, the Farmer Labor party in the 1930s, the

decline of a multitude of third parties. On the national level thus far no third party has been successful in displacing the two major political parties, although they have sometimes become potent political forces on the state and local levels.

Nevertheless, minor parties make a valuable contribution to the American political process in several respects. In many cases, they have performed the role of political *agent provocateur*: their vocal demands and challenges have alerted the major parties to neglected areas of public policy. As was conspicuously true of the Populist and Progressive parties before and after 1900, in time many third-party demands were eventually supported by the Democratic and Republican parties and enacted into law. In 1968 the political challenge presented by Governor George Wallace's American Independent party unquestionably forced the Democratic and Republican parties to adopt a more "rightist" (or anticommunist) position in foreign affairs. Third parties also operate as legitimate channels of dissent for Americans who believe that the political "establishment" is indifferent to their interests and viewpoints.[66]

One category of third parties, however, has been exceptional: those advocating radical, and sometimes violent, changes in the American constitutional system. Anarchists before World War I; radical socialists; fascist and crypto-fascist organizations during the 1930s, along with neo-Nazi groups after World War II; the Communist party of America and crypto-Marxist organizations; antiwar critics who relied upon illegal and violent methods to express their views have seldom received more than limited support from the American people and, in many cases, have alienated ordinary citizens by their extremist positions and tactics.[67]

The other notable feature of the American political process that serves as an essential adjunct to the two-party system is the complex network of pressure groups that has emerged in the United States since the late eighteenth century. In the contemporary period, this nexus includes thousands

Dixiecrat party during the late 1940s, and the American Independent party around 1970. Other fringe parties such as the Temperance party, the Communist party, and the Libertarian party have also been active from time to time on the American political scene. In the main, these third parties have had life spans of a few brief years, nearly always less than a decade.

66. See Howard P. Nash, Jr., *Third Parties in American Politics* (Washington, D.C., 1958); Seymour Lipset and Earl Raab, *The Politics of Unreason* (New York, 1970); W. B. Hesseltine, *The Rise and Fall of Third Parties* (Washington, D.C., 1948); John D. Hicks, *The Populist Revolt* (Minneapolis, 1931); Amos Pinchot, *History of the Progressive Party, 1912–1916* (New York, 1958); and David A. Shannon, *The Socialist Party of America* (New York, 1955).

67. See Lipset (ed.), *Party Coalitions in the 1980's*, 409; Flanigan and Zingale, *Political Behavior of the American Electorate*, 193–94; and V. O. Key, *Politics, Parties, and Pressure Groups* (5th ed.; New York, 1964), 273.

of large and small organizations representing every segment of American life. Besides the "big three"—business, labor, and agriculture—there is an almost endless list of interest groups representing small businessmen, independent trade unions, cattlemen, fishermen, the real estate industry, fundamentalist religious organizations and cults, veterans, peace groups, minorities and other disadvantaged citizens, *ad infinitum*. In this sense, no society in history is as highly organized as the American; and in no other is the magnitude and importance of lobbying such a prominent characteristic of its political process.[68]

Several brief observations seem warranted about the evolution of pressure group activity in the American political setting. One is that, by nearly all accounts, its level has increased significantly in the post–World War II era, and it shows no sign of diminishing. Although the total annual expenditure by pressure groups is impossible to calculate accurately, little doubt exists that it has climbed sharply in recent years and continues to escalate.[69]

Another interesting development has been the extent to which pressure groups have increasingly directed their lobbying activities at the executive branch of the United States government (along with the state governments). Though not neglecting Congress (the traditional target of lobbying efforts), interest groups have broadened the scope of their efforts to include the White House and executive agencies—a tacit admission that important laws usually originate with executive officials.

Still another significant tendency has been the extent to which the United States government has itself emerged as one of the most active and influential "lobbies" in the American political arena. Nearly every executive department and agency today has one or more offices devoted to public relations, congressional relations, or some comparable function. (It is an ironic commentary that Congress routinely provides the funds requested by executive agencies to lobby for the president's policies and programs on Capitol Hill!) A related development has been the forging of coalitions between government and private organizations to conduct lobbying campaigns for (or against) specific policy proposals and programs.[70]

68. Comprehensive and current information on lobbying activities is available in *The Washington Lobby* (4th ed.; Washington, D.C., 1982) and in later editions of this publication. See also "Middle East Lobbying," *Congressional Quarterly Weekly Report*, XXXIX (August 22, 1981), 1523–83. The State Department's relations with pressure groups are examined in William O. Chittick, *State Department, Press, and Pressure Groups: A Role Analysis* (New York, 1970).

69. Jeffrey M. Berry, *The Interest Group Society* (Boston, 1984), 16–45.

70. Crabb and Holt, *Invitation to Struggle*, 75–96, 114–29.

The growing influence of lobbying activities in the American political process is highlighted by the recent emergence of what is sometimes called "single-issue politics" in the United States, in which political action committees (PACs) often play a decisive role. Although the phenomenon probably applies more to congressional than to presidential elections, PACs have become increasingly influential in American political life. More than at any time in the past, today a candidate's position on a single political issue—for example, gun control, abortion, environmental questions, the protection of American industry and workers from foreign competition, or a nuclear "freeze" between the superpowers—can determine the outcome of elections. Largely unrestrained by federal laws designed to prevent them, PACs expend untold millions of dollars to influence political contests. Their activities, in turn, have become a major contributing factor in the almost prohibitive costs of conducting political campaigns in the United States.[71]

Overall, the American people in the late twentieth century are subjected to an almost constant barrage of public relations and lobbying campaigns designed to influence their political behavior and choices. That such activity has an impact—sometimes crucial—in determining the attitudes and behavior of the electorate cannot be denied. Yet the American electorate is remarkable for its almost unshakable preference for moderate, ideologically middle-of-the-road solutions to important national problems. If political fringe movements sometimes appear and gain notoriety for a brief period of time—for example, the more extreme anti–Vietnam War critics and advocates of the "New Politics" during and after that conflict—their history is almost invariably short-lived. As often as not, spokesmen for extremist political movements and causes in the United States are more likely to repel and alienate than to convert the voters.[72]

According to one student of public attitudes, Ben J. Wattenberg, the American state of mind about problems facing the United States at home and abroad can best be described by the term *cope*. Reviewing the American society's response to a host of challenges and problems in recent years, Wattenberg concludes, "Ingeniously, constructively, flexibly—these folk have coped. They have accommodated and they have held firm; they have listened, they have learned and they have spoken and have taught. One step at a time, sensibly, they have made material and attitudinal progress." Americans,

71. Michael J. Malbin (ed.), *Money and Politics in the United States: Financing Elections in the 1980s* (Washington, D.C., 1984), 112–72.

72. Ben J. Wattenberg, *The Real America: A Surprising Examination of the State of the Union* (Garden City, N.Y., 1974), esp. 283–95.

he believes, "can cope" with a wide range of problems from rapid inflation, to an energy crisis, to wrongdoing in the White House, to misadventures abroad. Americans "can cope—and they will cope" in the future.[73]

One final observation by Wattenberg highlights the basic thesis of this chapter about the pragmatic impulse in American life. After examining the attitudes of Americans toward war and peace, along with other recent international issues, he is convinced that the most noteworthy trait has been "the pattern of accommodation, eclecticism and shameless synthesis that the American public has demonstrated" in dealing with diplomatic questions. Toward international affairs, as in all other spheres of their national experience, Americans have consistently exhibited the same behavior pattern: "Exposed to new doctrines, to old doctrines, reformulated, to changing circumstances . . . the public made careful choices. In making their choices they remembered their past, considered the present and looked to the future. They put their choice to one essential test: *Did it make common sense?* If it did—fine. If not—back on the shelf." In his view, this "process of common-sense shopping-cart eclecticism, of supermarket synthesis and of attitudinal accommodation" recurs again and again and is an ingrained characteristic of American character.[74] In the next chapter, the pragmatic cast of the American mind will be approached from a more scientific viewpoint.

73. *Ibid.*, 320.
74. *Ibid.*, 211–12.

Two

Pragmatic Philosophy

Proponents, Principles, and Tenets

By general consensus, pragmatism is America's most original and influential contribution to the philosophical tradition. It was a distinctively New World mode of thinking, which, despite the often adverse reaction of rival philosophers, had a potent effect upon the development of modern philosophy. Significantly, the discoveries of modern science have increasingly supported (or been parallel to) a number of the major tenets of pragmatism, and during the past half-century, scientists have become progressively prone to present their ideas, theories, and conclusions in terms that would be highly congenial to the pragmatic movement in philosophy. It is imperative, therefore, that we become familiar with the main principles of pragmatic thought at an early stage.

The American Pragmatists and Modern Philosophy

A student of modern philosophical movements has said of William James, one of the founders of the pragmatic school of thought: "Among the philosophers of America, William James has no peer in the eyes of the world, whether it be in China or Great Britain, in Italy or Russia, or all the nations of the earth between, men celebrate him not merely as the greatest American philosopher, but as the great philosopher of America."[1]

In 1930 the University of Paris awarded John Dewey an honorary degree.

1. The views of Horace Kallen are quoted in H. B. Van Wesep, *Seven Sages: The Story of American Philosophy* (New York, 1960), 127.

This distinguished French institution honored Dewey as "the most profound and complete expression of American genius."[2]

To the minds of Charles Peirce, William James, and John Dewey the New World needed its own philosophical mode of thought no less than it needed novel modes of religious, economic, or political behavior. That requirement was supplied by the emergence of pragmatism as an identifiable school of philosophy in the late nineteenth century. Pragmatism has been described as "America's first original contribution to the mainstream of Western philosophical thought." It has also been observed that in the modern world, three potent philosophical currents have been in competition: revolutionary ideologies (exemplified by the teachings of Karl Marx and his disciples and in more recent years by religious leaders such as the Ayatollah Khomeini in Iran); existentialist philosophy (grounded in the teachings of Nietzsche, Kierkegaard, Heidegger, and other recent thinkers); and the concept of liberal democracy (as most ably represented in the thought of John Dewey). Building upon the ideas of Charles Peirce and William James, Dewey offered "the only major social philosophy which the liberal tradition has produced in the twentieth century." Another commentary has concluded that pragmatism "is the only unique contribution American philosophy has made to the tradition known as Western philosophy."[3]

One index of the significance of pragmatism for the modern world is that no other American mode of thought—and very few outside the United States—has had such a marked and pervasive influence on other societies as has pragmatism. An English journal, for example, called William James's ideas "the greatest spiritual force in the English-speaking world."[4] The pragmatic ideas of Peirce, James, and Dewey influenced the thought and behavior of India's great nationalist leader Mohandas K. Gandhi. Globally, the pragmatic mode of thought epitomized the democratic ideal as identified with American society; it became "a symbol of what is most precious and enduring in our American way of life." By contrast, William James's philosophy was also admired by, and influenced the thought of, the leader of the Italian fascist

2. *Ibid.*, 195.

3. John Dewey, *Problems of Men* (New York, 1946), 158; Guy W. Stroh, *American Philosophy: From Edwards to Dewey* (Princeton, 1968), 120; Albert J. Levi, *Philosophy and the Modern World* (Bloomington, 1959), 120; Edward C. Moore, *American Pragmatism: Peirce, James, and Dewey* (New York, 1961), vii.

4. The unidentified English journal is cited in Boyd H. Bode, "William James in the American Tradition," in Max C. Otto *et al.*, *William James: The Man and the Thinker* (Madison, 1942), 102.

movement after World War I, Benito Mussolini.[5] In many other spheres, from modern literature, to existentialist philosophy, to natural and social science, the ideas of America's pragmatic thinkers have often made significant and lasting contributions.[6]

At the outset of our discussion of the primary tenets of pragmatism, certain caveats and limitations about this mode of thought need to be recognized.

Caveats and Limitations

From its inception pragmatism has always suffered from what has sometimes appeared to be an extraordinarily high level of semantical imprecision and confusion, from seeming contradictions among some of its primary tenets, and from other disabilities that have raised continuing questions about its philosophical respectability and whether it deserves to be viewed as a "philosophy" at all. (To the minds of many commentators, it is in reality an *approach* to, or a method for ascertaining, truth.) The nature and evolution of pragmatic thought have admittedly contributed to uncertainty and confusion concerning its core meaning. On several occasions, for example, William James denied that his ideas comprised a coherent and logically consistent system of thought; James was extremely dubious about the value of such systems in explaining reality, including even a pragmatic system. John Dewey was no less skeptical about the utility of "closed" philosophical systems; and on more than one occasion he emphasized the evolving nature of his own thought in response to new evidence and new circumstances.

Undeniably also, significant differences can be discerned in the thought of Peirce, James, and Dewey. In time, for example, Charles Peirce became primarily interested in the application of pragmatic principles to mathematics and logic. Believing that there were important divergences between his thought and the ideas of William James, Peirce coined the ungainly term *pragmaticism* to describe his approach. By contrast, at one stage William James expressed his preference for *humanism* to describe his thought; on

5. Ignas K. Skrupskelis, *William James: A Reference Guide* (Boston, 1977), 161; Rao K. Ramakrishna, *Gandhi and Pragmatism* (Calcutta, 1968); and Bode, "William James in the American Tradition," 116.

6. Bernard P. Brennan, *William James* (New York, 1968), 157–58; Ralph Barton Perry, *The Thought and Character of William James* (New York, 1954), 357–58; and Skrupskelis, *William James,* 169.

other occasions, he referred to it as *radical empiricism*, and he also frequently used the term *pragmatism*. In turn, John Dewey's ideas were variously described during his long career by such terms as *incrementalism, instrumentalism, experimentalism,* and many others.

Significant differences (often more in emphasis than in substantive content) can also be identified in the ideas of leading American pragmatists. William James's thoughts exemplified the venerated American concept of *individualism*: the emphasis in his approach is upon the behavior, adjustment, and well-being of individual members of society. By contrast, John Dewey (who was by no means indifferent to the rights and responsibilities of individuals) was more prone to emphasize the individual *in his relationship to society* or in his *collective* behavior. As we shall see, in his political philosophy, John Dewey called attention to the role of groups and associations in determining political outcomes, and he believed that collective citizen opinion and action would in time crucially affect the nature of international politics.

As pragmatism evolved, it proved to be a highly prolific approach to knowledge. It gave rise to numerous species and subspecies of pragmatic thought, and its tenets significantly affected other philosophical movements. The distinguished philosopher A. O. Lovejoy once identified thirteen separate species of pragmatic thought! In the twentieth century, terms like *biological pragmatism* and *logical pragmatism* were applied to certain philosophical movements; as the years passed, other varieties such as *humanistic pragmatism, empirico-spiritualistic pragmatism,* and *fictional pragmatism* evolved. In the contemporary period, even natural scientists (especially in fields like quantum mechanics) frequently describe their methodology as *pragmatic*. It would be no exaggeration to say that, by the era of John Dewey, nearly every dimension of modern thought had in some way been affected by the emergence of pragmatism.[7]

Confusion about the core meaning of pragmatism and its adjectival form, *pragmatic*, is also engendered by the etymology of the word and its development in usage. Fittingly perhaps for the philosophy of pragmatism, in popular usage the term has experienced a continuing evolution. Derived from the

7. The varieties of pragmatic thought are identified and explained more fully in David W. Marcell, *Progress and Pragmatism: James, Dewey, Beard, and the American Idea of Progress* (Westport, Conn., 1974), ix–xii; Bertrand Russell, *Sceptical Essays* (New York, 1928), 61; Ralph Barton Perry, *Present Philosophical Tendencies* (New York, 1912), 214; Frederick Mayer, *A History of American Thought: An Introduction* (Dubuque, Iowa, 1951), 304–305; and William L. Reese, "Pragmatism," in the *Dictionary of Philosophy and Religion: Eastern and Western Thought* (Atlantic Highlands, N.J., 1980), 453.

Greek word *pragmatikos,* it originally designated skill in business and law; it was also a synonym for civic affairs; and it could describe a deed or an act. As time passed, it described an imperial decree or order by a sovereign (a king or parliament), and it also denoted the behavior of a busy, intrusive, overly ambitious individual (a "busybody"). Pragmatism was also often employed as an epithet, describing the behavior of an overly opinionated, conceited, and dogmatic individual. (As an illustration in the evolution of language, this last connotation is the *opposite* of what pragmatism customarily implies in current usage.)[8]

In contemporary American usage, the term *pragmatism* has several often conflicting connotations. If a political leader is described as pragmatic, this might mean one or more of the following: (1) he lacks clear ideological goals; (2) his actions do not appear to be guided by adherence to clearly defined moral-ethical principles; (3) he is motivated by immediate, here-and-now considerations, as distinct from long-term goals and strategies; (4) he is "opportunistic" and seeks to achieve the maximum benefit or gain from opportunities available to him; (5) he is skilled in compromise and gaining agreement among divergent positions; (6) he is flexible, capable of learning from experience, and of adapting his position to changing realities; (7) he is prudent, judicious, tends to avoid extremist solutions, and understands that politics is "the art of the possible."

From a philosophical viewpoint, the term *pragmatism* has become almost hopelessly vulgarized, having certain connotations that are in some cases diametrically opposed to the tenets of pragmatic philosophy. Two conspicuous examples of such vulgarization come to mind. One is that pragmatism is merely a synonym for *success*: the pragmatic individual is the successful individual. Thus the thought of William James and John Dewey has been widely (and erroneously) held to provide a convenient rationalization for the successful American businessman—the "man in the gray flannel suit"—whose climb to the top was marked by a total disregard for moral-ethical principles and the rights of others. The other example is that pragmatism is synonymous with action, motion, energy—or merely doing something with little awareness of why the action was undertaken or of its principal consequences. This meaning of pragmatism was frequently ascribed to the diplomatic activities of Henry Kissinger during the early 1970s, when, the implication was, Kissinger was a diplomatic "whirling dervish," whose assumption appeared

8. See the *Oxford English Dictionary* (New York, 1971), II, 725–26.

to be that activism, energy, and motion *per se* were equivalent to policy accomplishments.

Peirce, James, and Dewey, needless to say, would reject both these viewpoints as caricatures of their philosophy. For them, as we shall see more fully in later chapters, the only success that mattered was progress in promoting the growth and evolution of human society. Alternatively, the notion that pragmatism was synonymous with the mere expenditure of energy or motion for no apparent purpose is no less a misreading of the pragmatic approach to truth. Pragmatism teaches that intelligence, for example, must be applied to human problems *creatively*, in the solution of what John Dewey called "the problems of men." Such solutions almost invariably require the expenditure of energy in some form, but the mere expenditure of energy *per se* does not solve urgent human problems.

Despite the admitted ambiguity in the popular connotations of pragmatism, it is equally true that as a rule Americans react most favorably to evidence of "pragmatic" behavior by other governments. For example, Americans are nearly always heartened to learn that the communist hierarchy in the Soviet Union is taking a more pragmatic approach to internal and external problems. As articulated by George F. Kennan, the containment strategy, to which the United States has been committed for over forty years, anticipates a pragmatic objective: what Kennan called the "mellowing" of, or a significant evolution in the nature of, the Soviet system. The basic premise of containment was that Soviet leaders would learn in the light of experience that they could not act aggressively without incurring grave risks; and as they learned this lesson, they would in time modify their behavior at home and abroad.[9] During the 1950s, even that staunch "cold warrior" Secretary of State John Foster Dulles detected evidence of a pragmatic transition in Soviet foreign policy, inducing the communist hierarchy to adopt less belligerent policies abroad. Naturally, Dulles thought the United States should encourage this transition.[10]

By the 1980s, Americans widely applauded a comparable tendency in the People's Republic of China. After a prolonged era of ideological rigidity

9. Kennan's views are set forth succinctly in his widely circulated and influential article "The Sources of Soviet Conduct," *Foreign Affairs*, XXV (July, 1947), 556–83; see also his *Memoirs (1925–1950)* (New York, 1969); and Charles E. Bohlen, *Witness to History, 1929–1969* (New York, 1973), 211, 447, 497, 522, 542.

10. This was the gist of the assessment by Secretary Dulles at a briefing for legislative leaders held at the White House on July 12, 1955. See "Bipartisan Legislative Meeting," July 12, 1955, Legislative Meetings File, Box 1, Dwight D. Eisenhower Library, Abilene, Kansas.

and internal oppression, China was devoting its attention primarily to solving a multitude of critical problems and to making the ideological adjustments which this step demanded.[11] During the early 1980s, Syria's President Hafez Assad was described as a "consummate pragmatist," who was not likely to pursue his goals to the point of precipitating a new regional conflict in the Middle East. Similarly, the government of Mrs. Indira Gandhi in India was demonstrating a new "pragmatic respect" for India's ties with the West, which was interpreted as a favorable development for the future of Indo-American relations. Evidence of change and moderation was also discerned, and applauded, in the internal policies of the government of South Africa.[12] Meanwhile, State Department officials were confident that intractable problems in regions such as the Middle East would be solved on the basis of lessons "learned from long experience"; in this view, "progress comes slowly and only through painstaking effort and patience." Secretary of State George Shultz asserted, "The world has work to do for the realists, the pragmatists, and the free."[13]

The normal tendency of Americans to react favorably to evidence of pragmatic behavior by their own and foreign governments provides confirmation of the affinity between the American ethos and pragmatism as a formal school of philosophy. Throughout this discussion, unless otherwise indicated, the terms *pragmatism* and *pragmatic* will be employed in their formal philosophical connotation to signify behavior that accords with the principal tenets of the philosophical school of thought known as pragmatism. Yet it must be borne in mind that, even in this limited sense, pragmatism has been an "open," unfinished, and evolving mode of thought. As we have observed, significant differences can sometimes be detected among the ideas of leading proponents of pragmatism, and for all of them, it can accurately be said that they did not construct a unified, comprehensive, and totally consistent system of thought. Indeed, for thinkers like William James and John Dewey, *a priori* philosophical systems were a serious impediment to objective and continuing scientific investigations into the nature of an infinitely complex,

11. See papers from the symposium on the People's Republic of China in *Current History,* LXXXI (September, 1982), 241–304; and LXXXII (September, 1983), 241–304; and Donald S. Zagoria, "China's Quiet Revolution," *Foreign Affairs,* LXII (Spring, 1984), 879–904.

12. See the commentary by Joseph Joffe in the New York *Times,* December 13, 1983; the discussion of India's foreign policy in *Newsweek,* CX (March 21, 1983); and the dispatch by Flora Lewis in the New York *Times,* March 22, 1984.

13. Deputy Secretary of State Kenneth W. Dam, "Policy Options in Lebanon," in the State Department's series *Current Policy,* No. 536 (January 11, 1984), 1–3; and Secretary George Shultz, "U.S. Foreign Policy: Realism and Progress," *Current Policy,* No. 420 (September 30, 1982), 1–5.

variegated, and pluralistic universe. For its principal expositors, pragmatism was as unsystematic, dichotomous, and marked by discontinuities as the universe itself! In that sense, perhaps pragmatism more faithfully depicted reality than have most of its philosophical competitors. After reading the ideas of Charles Peirce, William James, and John Dewey, one often gets the impression that, in their view, paradoxes and logical incongruities are a more accurate depiction of reality than if they were absent—a conclusion increasingly shared in recent years by natural scientists who are endeavoring to understand and explain the nature of the physical universe.

Origins and Antecedents

William James's candid admission that pragmatism was merely a new way of expressing old ideas explicitly acknowledged the indebtedness of the pragmatic mode of thought to the philosophical tradition and to other sources. It is appropriate at this stage to refer briefly to the thoughts of earlier philosophers and scientists who contributed significantly to pragmatism's major tenets.

Charles Peirce, William James, and John Dewey were well versed in the thought of their philosophical predecessors, from the ancient Greeks to thinkers of the late nineteenth century.[14] James and other pragmatists traced the origins of their mode of thought back to Socrates and Aristotle. They also drew heavily upon the teachings and insights of Locke, Newton, Descartes, Berkeley, Hume, Comte, Kant, John Stuart Mill, Hegel, Marx, and other Western thinkers. Sometimes (as in William James's *The Varieties of Religious Experience*) pragmatic thought incorporated ideas from non-Western sources as well.[15]

American thinkers also contributed significantly to the broad philosophical stream that came to be called pragmatism. The Puritan theologian Jonathan Edwards, for example, had emphasized the idea that the believer demonstrated the depth and sincerity of his Christian faith by his behavior and actions. Benjamin Franklin's life and thought epitomized the cherished American concept of "applied" knowledge. Thomas Jefferson is often viewed as symbolizing American idealism. Yet Jefferson's life and thought also testi-

14. The complete title of William James's widely circulated essay on pragmatism was *Pragmatism: A New Name for Some Old Ways of Thinking* (New York, 1907).
15. William James, *The Varieties of Religious Experience: A Study in Human Nature* (New York, 1902).

fied to his devotion to empirically based knowledge, to experimentation, and to the improvement of the human condition. Along with Franklin, Jefferson placed little value upon abstract intellectual speculation divorced from concrete human needs.[16]

Other American thinkers contributed to the mode of thought that came to be designated pragmatism. In *Common Sense* (1776), Thomas Paine had emphasized that citizens of the New World had the power to transform nature and to create a new political order based on the principles of democracy. The new Constitution, anticipating the emergence of "a more perfect union," was widely described as America's "great experiment" in democratic government. In the nineteenth century, historian George Bancroft extolled the American experience; his historical studies conveyed a deep sense of optimism and bouyancy about the possibilities latent in American society. The great Transcendentalist philosopher Ralph Waldo Emerson praised the virtues of "self-reliance," urged his countrymen to realize the potentialities for self-fulfillment and growth that were within their grasp, and insisted that values must demonstrate their worth by leading to beneficial human behavior.

Other nineteenth-century thinkers rejected the long-standing view that nature constituted an immutable "system" of laws and phenomena impervious to the human will; rather, nature must be envisioned dynamically, as consisting mainly of "creative energy" that could be harnessed and utilized for worthwhile human purposes. In the age-old philosophical conflict between science and religion, American thinkers usually resolved the problem by saying in effect that these were by no means antithetical concepts. Instead, they were merely separate paths to, or different perspectives upon, cosmic truth. The nineteenth-century American mind viewed the universe as "unfinished"; how it came out depended in no small degree upon man's own understanding of and response to it. Moreover, in the nineteenth century, the emphasis in American thought was almost invariably upon ameliorating, improving, and reforming human society. Revolutionary schemes advocated by anarchists, socialists, Marxists, and other radical groups demanding a total transformation of human nature held very little appeal for American minds.

16. Carl Van Doren, *Benjamin Franklin* (New York, 1938); Gerald Stourzh, *Benjamin Franklin and American Foreign Policy* (Chicago, 1954). Jefferson's political ideas are presented in C. P. Patterson, *The Constitutional Principles of Thomas Jefferson* (Austin, Tex., 1953); Adrienne Koch, *The Philosophy of Thomas Jefferson* (Gloucester, Mass., 1953); and Richard Hofstadter, *The American Political Tradition and the Men Who Made It* (New York, 1951), 18–44.

Only a small minority of Americans was ever attracted to the various utopian schemes and programs that appeared intermittently in the New World before the late nineteenth century.[17]

In light of such antecedents, Lewis Mumford has observed that "in Mr. Dewey the American mind completed, as it were, a circle, and returned to its origins, amplifying by the experience of a century, the essential interests" of such earlier thinkers as Jonathan Edwards, Benjamin Franklin, and many others. Still others have called attention to pragmatism's "omnivorous" quality: pragmatic thinkers freely drew upon insights and precepts from almost every preexisting philosophical tradition. Or, as another student of modern philosophy has expressed the idea, while relying heavily on the contributions of their philosophical predecessors, the leading spokesmen for American pragmatism sought to "purify," refine, and apply these preexisting ideas. The result of this effort was what came to be known as the philosophy of pragmatism.[18]

Two other major intellectual developments of the nineteenth century deserve special mention for their contribution to the formulation of pragmatic philosophy. One of these was the emergence of psychology as a field of study—a process to which William James contributed significantly. The theories and findings of the early psychologists gained insight into how the mind perceives reality, the cognitive process, and how human personality is affected by environmental forces and changes.[19]

The other momentous development—one of the most far-reaching events in the history of science—was the publication in 1859 of Charles Darwin's seminal work, *On the Origin of Species.* Darwin's theory of evolution had a profound impact on the field of natural science, and its implications for social science and philosophy was scarcely less momentous. For our subject, Darwin's findings had both a positive and negative effect.

Positively, Darwin's ideas provided convincing scientific evidence that nature was a highly dynamic—not a static—phenomenon. "The fundamental fact about our experience is that it is a process of change," asserted William James. To his mind, experience must be viewed *as a process*, meaning that no statement about it could ever be viewed as definitive or final. Throughout human experience, James discerned "something like a law of nature" which is "everywhere going on." He speculated that perhaps this was really what

17. Marcell, *Progress and Pragmatism*, 52–92.
18. See the views of Lewis Mumford as cited in Gail Kennedy (ed.), *Pragmatism and American Culture* (Boston, 1950), 46–47; Moore, *American Pragmatism*, 13–15.
19. Moore, *American Pragmatism*, 7–9.

was meant by the process of "creation." Building on the thought of Darwin, the pragmatists believed that the human species had to adapt to changing circumstances or it would perish. Human history provided convincing evidence that such adaptation was possible and that it had frequently occurred.[20]

Negatively, Darwin's teachings spawned the application of the theory of evolution to a wide range of human relationships. Pragmatism was to no inconsiderable degree a reaction against this tendency. For example, Social Darwinism, as it came to be called, received its most forceful expression in the writings of Herbert Spencer (1820–1903), whose work *Social Statics* was initially published in 1850. Spencer's depiction of the natural environment as a harsh, unforgiving, uncompromising milieu, in which only the "fittest" survive, appeared to receive authoritative reinforcement from Darwin's theory of evolution. The ideas of Spencer and his disciples were widely invoked to justify the inevitability of war and conflict, the dominance of one group over another, and the irrelevance of moral and ethical principles for the conduct of human affairs.

More than any of their philosophical adversaries, Herbert Spencer and his disciples were perhaps the favorite targets of attack by American pragmatic thinkers. Pragmatic thought rejected virtually every premise and proposition associated with Social Darwinism. For example, one of pragmatism's fundamental tenets—that the natural environment is "open," dynamic, and capable of being shaped by the human will—clashed directly with the fixed and deterministic natural order impervious to human will depicted by Spencer. Against the Social Darwinists, the pragmatists contended that by the application of creative human intelligence, man was capable of comprehending and using natural forces for the benefit of human society.[21]

After taking note of the formal philosophical and intellectual antecedents of pragmatism, it is necessary to reiterate the basic point emphasized earlier. Pragmatism was a philosophical movement that can be stamped "made in America"; it was unquestionably the American society's most original and influential contribution to the Western philosophical heritage. The principal expositors of pragmatism were steeped in the nation's culture, ethos, and history. Ideas that had long been familiar to, and taken for granted

20. William James, *The Meaning of Truth* (Ann Arbor, 1970), 89–90; and H. M. Kallen (ed.), *William James's Some Problems of Philosophy* (London, 1916), 142, 214–15.

21. Richard Hofstadter, *Social Darwinism in American Thought* (Philadelphia, 1944); and see the briefer discussion in Herbert W. Schneider, *A History of American Philosophy* (2nd ed.; New York, 1963), 275–373.

by, Americans such as freedom, democracy, individualism, self-reliance, progress, and a decided preference for applied over abstract knowledge were intrinsic parts of the intellectual climate of the late nineteenth century. These concepts were "in the air" when the giants of American pragmatism were formulating and refining their ideas, and nearly every major precept of pragmatic philosophy reflects the influence of the American environment in which it emerged.

The neo-Thomist philosopher Jacques Maritain, for example, called attention to the "latent rebellion of the spirit of the [American] people in the logic of structure." In his judgment, the "vital, *pragmatic*, completely unsystematic pressure" exercised by Americans was transforming economic and other structures throughout the world. Still another commentator believes that the American genius lay in the idea that by using intelligence to solve specific problems, humans could "create a future satisfying . . . developing moral requirements."[22]

Charles Peirce: Founder of American Pragmatism

By general consensus among informed students of philosophy, the founder of American pragmatism was a little-known and eccentric genius, Charles S. Peirce (1839–1914). The son of a Harvard mathematician, Peirce became a logician, mathematician, and philosopher while spending most of his life as an official of the United States Geodetic Survey. Peirce was in many respects a tragic figure: a failure in interpersonal relations, he died impoverished, embittered, and without the recognition he and his admirers believed was his due. Yet William James and other pragmatists repeatedly acknowledged their indebtedness to Peirce's pioneering work.[23]

Charles Peirce was well grounded in the principles of classical philosophy, and he was familiar with the history of science, including the recent findings of Charles Darwin. He sought to devise an epistemology that would in effect reconcile the principles of philosophy and modern science. (Peirce believed that the former included or embraced the latter.) In time, Peirce

22. See Jacques Maritain, *Reflections on America* (New York, 1958), 22–23; italics added. See also Marcell, *Progress and Pragmatism*, 323–24; and Morton White, *Pragmatism and the American Mind: Essays and Reviews in Philosophy and Intellectual History* (New York, 1973), 88–91.

23. Amelie Rorty (ed.), *Pragmatic Philosophy: An Anthology* (Garden City, N.Y., 1966), 3–25; H. S. Thayer, "Pragmatism: A Reinterpretation of the Origins and Consequences," in Robert J. Mulvaney and Philip M. Zeltner (eds.), *Pragmatism: Its Sources and Prospects* (Columbia, S.C., 1981), 3–19; and Morton White, *Science and Sentiment in America: Philosophical Thought from Jonathan Edwards to John Dewey* (London, 1972), 144–56.

concluded that the key to this endeavor involved the meaning of evidence, data, sensations, perceptions, and the like available to the investigator. Peirce rejected all preexisting "mechanistic" theories of reality. Drawing upon the ideas of such earlier thinkers as Alexander Bain and other Scottish philosophers, Immanuel Kant, Georg W. F. Hegel, and the American philosopher Chauncey Wright, Peirce contended that all existing methods of scientific investigation were subject to criticism. Anticipating one of the twentieth century's most momentous discoveries—the Heisenberg principle—Peirce asserted that all scientific findings are influenced by the interaction between the observer and the observed.[24] Moreover—and this was perhaps his most original and influential proposition for the emergence of pragmatism—in his essay "How to Make Our Ideas Clear" (1878), Peirce contended that ultimately the truth of any proposition is dependent upon its future consequences. In Peirce's conception, the only ideas that really matter are ideas in action; ideas are not important for what they assert but for what they *do*. Time and again, Charles Peirce challenged his philosophical adversaries to demonstrate empirically what difference it really made whether their ideas were believed or not. For Peirce and later pragmatists, ideas that could not pass this test possessed no real meaning or utility. In effect, Charles Peirce elevated the old biblical precept "By their fruits, you shall know them" into the capstone of his new epistemology.

24. In 1927 Werner Heisenberg revolutionized the study of quantum mechanics by stating his "uncertainty principle," which was applicable to the investigation of extremely small particles of matter (such as electrons). According to the Heisenberg principle, it is impossible to determine simultaneously both the momentum and the position of a microscopic particle under investigation because the very act of observation alters its behavior. This limitation is "inherent in the very nature of the measuring process." It is a constraint imposed upon scientific inquiry *by nature itself*. In effect, the principle means that in opposition to earlier scientific expectations, the exact "future arrangement of an atomic system cannot be predicted with certainty. . . . Instead, only the probability that an electron will be at a given point at a given time can be predicted." See Harry B. Gray and Gilbert P. Haight, Jr., *Basic Principles of Chemistry* (New York, 1967), 209–10; and Farrington Daniels and Robert A. Alberty, *Physical Chemistry* (2nd ed.; New York, 1955), 461–62. The philosophical implications of the Heisenberg principle and other recent discoveries in the investigation of the behavior of subatomic particles have been staggering. Einstein, for example, refused for many years to accept the Heisenberg principle, exclaiming that "God does not play dice" with the universe. His philosophical adversary Niels Bohr believed that the principle—along with later discoveries in subatomic physics—had resolved for all time the old philosophical controversy about the "dual nature" of matter. In Bohr's view, the findings of modern science left no doubt that such dualities as between mind and matter, or subjective and objective knowledge, were false and untenable. As one student of Bohr's ideas expressed it, there are "no atoms, only observations. The atom is a creation of the human mind" or merely an idea needed to explain reality intelligibly. See Robert H. March, *Physics for Poets* (Chicago, 1978), 226–35. Or as another recent study has explained, an "atom" is merely "an idea, a theory" formulated "to account for the facts of experience" (Alfred Romer, *The Restless Atom* [Garden City, N.Y., 1960], 175).

A number of corollary ideas and principles derive from Peirce's teachings. These include the principle that any experience (such as a scientific investigation) always occurs in association with other experiences; that clarification of the meaning of reality is a continuous process, decreeing that all knowledge is, therefore, tentative and conditional; that a general idea has meaning only when it is connected with, or placed in the context of, experience that inescapably conditions its meaning; and that epistemology, logic, and scientific inquiry are inherently normative undertakings whose findings are influenced by, and in turn influence, the environment within which they occur.

Characteristically for thinkers in the pragmatic tradition, Peirce's ideas were fragmentary and incomplete; he left no fully delineated and consistent system of thought. In time, the eccentric Peirce even differed with William James over the appropriate designation of his approach (Peirce preferred the ungainly term *pragmaticism* to describe his ideas). Yet eventually Peirce came to be recognized as possessing one of America's most brilliant and original minds, and his ideas had a powerful impact on the development of modern philosophy.[25]

William James and the Emergence of American Philosophy

More than any other figure in the history of modern philosophical thought, the name of William James (1842–1910) became synonymous with the concept of pragmatism. By many criteria, he was acclaimed at home and abroad as the embodiment of the American ethos.[26]

"The intellectual biography of William James," one student of his thought has said, is almost "an intellectual biography of America." The German essayist and poet F. C. S. Schiller said of William James, "He interpreted American life, but in its universal aspects. Actual life is everywhere pragmatic." Still another commentator has observed that William James was the "first American philosopher to be read seriously throughout the world."

25. See Charles Harshorne and Paul Weiss (eds.), *Collected Papers of Charles Sanders Peirce* (Cambridge, Mass., 1931–35), Vols. I–IV; and A. W. Burks (ed.), *The Collected Papers of Charles Sanders Peirce* (Cambridge, Mass., 1958), Vols. VII–VIII.

26. William James was the author of some ten major books, along with numerous essays, articles, and published lectures. His major works were *Principles of Psychology* (New York, 1890); *The Will to Believe* (New York, 1896); *Varieties of Religious Experience* (New York, 1902); *Pragmatism* (New York, 1907); *A Pluralistic Universe* (New York, 1909); and *Essays in Radical Empiricism* (New York, 1912). A highly acclaimed biography and guide to James's ideas is Perry, *Thought and Character of William James*. Excerpts from James's writings may be found in Bruce Wilshire, *William James: The Essential Writings* (New York, 1971).

James has been called "America's Aristotle" and the embodiment of American ideas and behavior.[27] Perhaps the most eloquent tribute to James's thought is that many of his ideas appear to be even more relevant to the problems of human society today than during his lifetime. The distinguished philosopher Alfred North Whitehead believed that modern philosophy was inaugurated by William James. He was the first philosopher whose thought was harmonious with two basic principles of modern science: Albert Einstein's theories of relativity and the Heisenberg "uncertainty principle," which governs the study of quantum mechanics.[28]

William James was born on January 11, 1842, in New York City. His father was a theologian, and his brother was the famous novelist Henry James. As a young man, William James suffered a nervous breakdown, and continuing health problems always affected his outlook on life and his conception of the universe. In time, James became a distinguished member of the Harvard University faculty and, by the end of his career, a world-renowned writer and lecturer.[29] Although James achieved eminence as a philosopher, he was also one of the founders of modern psychology (he coined the term *stream of consciousness*, for example, to denote the continuing interaction between mental activity and the environment). Among his other contributions, James gave a democratic orientation to philosophy: he believed that insight derived from experience, rather than from the abstract speculations of learned philosophers, provided the most reliable path to truth. With other pragmatists, William James distrusted all *a priori* and "closed" systems of knowledge. Supranaturalism, naturalism, deism, Transcendentalism, Hegelianism, Social Darwinism, Marxism—these and all other monistic philosophical systems were viewed by James as impeding the quest for understanding. Invariably, they failed to account for a universe that was pluralistic, dichotomous, discontinuous, and paradoxical. In one way or another, most of these deterministic philosophies reduced man to a helpless or passive actor who had no real control over his destiny and little or no ability to influence the outcome of human society. William James found this concep-

27. These and other tributes to the thought and influence of William James may be found in Skrupskelis, *William James*, 104; Edward C. Moore, *William James* (New York, 1966), 1; Van Wesep, *Seven Sages*, 124; Charles H. Compton (comp.), *William James: Philosopher and Man* (New York, 1957), 73–75; and Marcus P. Ford, *William James's Philosophy: A New Perspective* (Amherst, Mass., 1982), 27.

28. See the Introduction by H. L. Thayer to William James's *Pragmatism* (Cambridge, Mass., 1975), xxxv. Whitehead's views are cited in Van Wesep, *Seven Sages*, 172.

29. Bruce Kuklick, *The Rise of American Philosophy: Cambridge, Massachusetts, 1860–1930* (New Haven, 1979), 159–338.

tion of man and his place in nature intolerable, and he became convinced that it was also scientifically indefensible. James's philosophical revolt was thoroughly in keeping with the New World's rejection of other modes of thought and conduct associated with the Old World.

One of William James's more distinctive ideas also was the notion (rejected by rival philosophers before and after his time) that religion, faith, and other forms of emotional and nonrational experience were capable of yielding valuable insights into reality. Faith was an inseparable element in experience—nowhere, as James assessed it, more than in the scientific enterprise itself. The scientist, for example, takes what James called a "leap of faith" when he assumes that the human mind and nature are in sufficient accord to make knowledge possible; when he further assumes that nature in the future will be like nature in the past (thereby allowing experiments to be repeated); and—perhaps the most basic presupposition of scientific inquiry—when he assumes that knowledge is preferable to ignorance. James accepted Charles Peirce's principle that it was the *interaction* between the observer and the observed—or, more generally, between man and nature—that was the key element in cognition; and this interaction always took place in some environmental setting that affected, and was affected by, it.[30]

To William James's mind, all creative mental activity is ultimately *purposive* and directed toward an identifiable end. Mental activity consists essentially of two components: what James called *percepts* (or perceptions), existing in a random, discontinuous, and undifferentiated "stream of consciousness" of images, sensations, ideas, and the like continuously impinging upon the mind from nature; and *concepts* or what he called "objects" carved out of percepts, which are discrete, tangible, and specific—for example, a beach, a forest, a new building, a better economic system, a more benign political system, and comparable mental constructs. For James, the intellectual life of man consists of substituting "a conceptual order for the perceptual order." The transition from perceptions to conceptions (in accordance with Peirce's principle) always leads to *consequences or actions*. As James defined it, the meaning of any particular concept "may always be found . . . in some particular difference in the course of human experience which its being true will make." In human experience, the isolated and fragmentary parts of nature embodied in percepts are "built into wholes by our conceptual additions."

30. William James, *The Will to Believe and Other Essays in Popular Philosophy* (Cambridge, Mass., 1979), 76–89; *The Meaning of Truth* (Cambridge, Mass., 1975), 68–73, 105–109, 111–12, 150–52; and *Essays in Radical Empiricism*, 47–57.

Humans "harness perceptual reality in concepts in order to drive it better to our ends."[31] In brief, creative intellectual activity has as its ultimate purpose the improvement of the human condition. The mind thus serves as a "problem solver" or what James once called a "transformer of the world." It seeks to bring into existence the world of our conceptions; and this in turn inevitably involves actions and consequences for the relationship between man and the environment.[32]

It would not distort his ideas unduly to say that William James's conception of the universe and man's place in it was analogous to the nineteenth-century American understanding of the challenge posed by the western frontier. On one hand, the universe unquestionably contained forces and phenomena that could be—and sometimes were—dangerous and inimical for human well-being. The frontier was a hazardous environment for what James characterized as "tender-minded souls," who were unwilling to recognize its dangers, to become familiar with the requirements of frontier life, and to accept the challenge implied in "conquering the frontier."[33] On the other hand, the frontier offered new vistas for human advancement and betterment; it provided countless opportunities for the solution of age-old human problems by the "tough-minded" who were able to respond to the challenge. The latter group, however, had to exhibit courage and faith, a spirit of adventure, discipline, physical and mental exertion, and a continual receptivity to new ideas—most especially those derived from experience—if they were to create a new and more satisfying life on the frontier. James and his fellow pragmatists, therefore, called upon professional philosophers, scientists, and laymen alike to join in an ongoing quest to comprehend reality and to use the knowledge gained for human betterment. In later pages, we shall refer more specifically to many of William James's ideas on subjects directly related to this study.

John Dewey: Philosopher of Modern America

William James's co-laborer in the cause of pragmatism was John Dewey (1859–1952). Dewey has been called "the St. Paul of pragmatism"; he not

31. See Kallen (ed.), *William James's Some Problems of Philosophy*, 48–60, 97–100.

32. See James's discussion of the purpose of cognition in his *Pragmatism* (New York, 1959), 20–21, 45–58, 63–64, 73–80; *The Will to Believe* (New York, 1903), 22–27, 57–59; and *The Varieties of Religious Experience* (New York, 1961), 51, 506–509.

33. See William James's description of "tender-minded" and "tough-minded" individuals in *Pragmatism*, 7–14.

only reiterated accepted pragmatic principles, but he also enunciated certain ideas and concepts of his own which came to be included in pragmatic doctrine. Best known perhaps for his educational theories, John Dewey was no less eminent for his contributions to the philosophical tradition and for his capable defense of a pragmatic orientation toward the acquisition of knowledge and its application to human affairs.[34]

Born and educated in Vermont, John Dewey received his Ph.D. from Johns Hopkins University. In 1895 he joined the faculty of the University of Chicago, where he became a leader of the renowned "Chicago school" of intellectuals who had a profound influence on the development of such fields as philosophy, sociology, and political science. In 1904 Dewey accepted a faculty position at Columbia University, where he remained until his retirement in 1930. For the remaining two decades of his life he was an indefatigable champion of the pragmatic approach to the discovery of truth and the solution of human problems.[35]

A prolific author and widely traveled lecturer, during his lifetime Dewey emerged as America's most distinguished contemporary philosopher; after his death, it would be difficult to name a twentieth-century American thinker whose ideas were more influential. John Dewey's thought was noteworthy for another reason directly related to our inquiry: his career as a philosopher spanned both the period of America's diplomatic isolation and, after world War II, its emergence as a superpower. With millions of his fellow citizens, Dewey was compelled to adapt his thinking to this "revolution" in American foreign policy. His thought clearly shows the impact of this momentous change, and his ideas reflect many of the dilemmas, perplexities, and incongruities that still characterize American attitudes in the new era of diplomacy.

With Charles Peirce and William James, John Dewey was well grounded

34. Frederick Mayer, *A History of American Thought* (Dubuque, Iowa, 1951), 304. John Dewey was a prolific author, and several helpful commentaries on his thought are available. His principal works included, with James H. Tufts, *Ethics* (New York, 1908); *The Influence of Darwin on Philosophy* (New York, 1910); *Reconstruction in Philosophy* (Boston, 1920); *Human Nature and Conduct: An Introduction to Social Psychology* (New York, 1922); *The Quest for Certainty: A Study of the Relation of Knowledge and Action* (New York, 1929); *Individualism, Old and New* (New York, 1930); *Liberalism and Social Action* (New York, 1935); and *The Public and Its Problems* (New York, 1927). An extremely useful bibliographical aid is Jo Ann Boydston (ed.), *Guide to the Works of John Dewey* (Carbondale, Ill., 1970). See also Milton H. Thomas and Herbert Schneider, *A Bibliography of John Dewey, 1882–1939* (New York, 1939). Two informative commentaries are A. H. Somjee, *The Political Theory of John Dewey* (New York, 1968); and Charles F. Howlett, *Troubled Philosopher: John Dewey and the Struggle for World Peace* (Port Washington, N.Y., 1977).

35. Darnell Rucker, *The Chicago Pragmatists* (Minneapolis, 1960).

in classical political thought, from which he drew heavily in his approach to truth. Yet the philosophical systems offered by Plato, Locke, Kant, Hegel, Marx, and other predecessors were inadequate for modern man's needs and incompatible with the teachings of modern science. Dewey believed, for example, that Platonic thought contained the seeds of modern totalitarianism. He was especially critical of the Social Darwinists, whose rigidly deterministic and pessimistic view of man's place in nature missed the main point of Darwin's discoveries. To Dewey's mind, the central lesson to be learned from Darwin's teachings was the necessity for the human organism *to adapt and develop* toward its fullest potential. Dewey agreed with William James that such successful adaptation was possible, that human intelligence played a crucial role in it, and that the *interaction* between the human species and the environment held the key to its outcome.

More even than most pragmatists, Dewey was repelled by arid and abstract intellectual speculations having no apparent relationship to real-life problems. Their results were always inconclusive, and they failed to reflect the idea that creative intellectual activity is focused on the solution of problems directly related to the evolutionary process. To Dewey's mind, age-old philosophical dichotomies such as the assumed difference between mind and matter, or between subjective and objective knowledge, were artificial and untenable. In the pragmatic conception, truth is *always* a product of the observed and observer; all human knowledge is contingent and subject to revision in light of new evidence; and the evolutionary process governs not only the meaning of truth during a particular historical era but also methods for *ascertaining truth*.[36]

For John Dewey and other pragmatists, scientific inquiry is concerned with values, fully as much as other approaches to truth. The basic premise of scientific inquiry, for example—the assumption that expanding the frontiers of understanding is desirable or beneficial for man—asserts in effect that knowledge is better than ignorance. Yet the validity of this idea (which, of course, Dewey accepted) could be verified only by reference to the realm of human experience. In Dewey's view, scientists, philosophers, and others engaged in the search for truth should, therefore, recognize overtly and candidly that their goal was to change or improve the world. Scientific thought always had been, and remained, in Dewey's words, "an instrument for the realization

36. See Sidney Hook, Introduction, to Jo Ann Boydston (ed.), *John Dewey: The Later Works, 1925–1953* (12 vols.; Carbondale, Ill., 1981), xviii–xix.

of values."[37] Dewey's thought, therefore, was sometimes described as *instrumentalism*. As this pragmatic tenet was expressed by one of Dewey's literary contemporaries, "The answer to the enigma of life, so far as there is any, is not for the man who sets up some metaphysical theory, but for the man who . . . acts."[38]

Drawing upon the earlier thought of Hegel and William James, Dewey asserted that the results of creative mental activity tend in time to be embodied in society's traditions and institutions, or what James had called society's "habits." These habits are subject to change, but nearly always by a slow, trial-and-error process, whereby one set of established habits is gradually substituted for another set having greater utility.

This concept placed pragmatic thinkers in the middle of the philosophical spectrum. On one hand, pragmatists rejected the idea (identified with ultraconservatives and reactionary political groups) that change is neither necessary nor desirable. On the other hand, pragmatists no less disagreed with anarchists, radicals, and revolutionaries (Marxists or certain revolutionary movements active in the contemporary Third World) who called for a sudden and dramatic transformation in the nature of individuals and society. A favorite concept with pragmatic thinkers was amelioration or "meliorism." This idea implied that growth and progress were always possible and should be the constant goal of human society. At the same time, it suggested another pragmatic conviction: that progress was in no sense inevitable or automatic. The evolution of human society was not guaranteed or decreed by ideological laws; many species of animal life had in fact retrogressed, disappeared, or otherwise failed to adapt successfully to environmental challenges. Human society was capable of adaptation, but only as creative intelligence was employed to replace one set of society's "habits" by another, more beneficial, set as indicated by experience.[39]

Two other aspects of John Dewey's pragmatism deserve brief mention. One (and on this point differences, at least in emphasis, can be discerned in the thought of Dewey vis-à-vis William James) was Dewey's emphasis on *society and the community*. To Dewey's mind, all scientific inquiry was essentially a *community undertaking* (as suggested by the term *scientific community*.)

37. Dewey's views are quoted in the Introduction by Sidney Morgenbesser (ed.), *Dewey and His Critics: Essays from the Journal of Philosophy* (New York, 1977), xliii. See also John Dewey, *Reconstruction in Philosophy* (New York, 1920), 121–22, 212–13; and *Experience and Nature* (Chicago, 1926), 325.

38. See the views of Irving Babbitt cited in J. David Hoeveler, *The New Humanism: A Critique of Modern America* (Charlottesville, Va., 1977), 42.

39. See James, *Will to Believe*, 87–88.

This community sustained the scientific enterprise, created and maintained the conditions under which it flourished, publicized and applied its findings, and provided the laboratory within which its findings were tested. As Dewey viewed it, individuals always had rights and responsibilities deriving from their membership in society, and nearly all worthwhile human enterprises involved some direct or indirect cooperative relationship among the members of society. In his *Individualism, Old and New*, Dewey emphasized that the cherished American idea of "rugged individualism" was now obsolete and inadequate. He observed "combination in all phases of life"; individual life was increasingly characterized by "dominant corporateness." Throughout the world, new social movements were emerging to which individuals must relate if human society is to evolve successfully.[40] As we shall see, this motif in Dewey's thought must be distinguished from both the idea of the corporate state (prominent in modern fascism) or the concept of collectivism (as exemplified by communism and other varieties of Marxist thought).

A second conspicuous theme in Dewey's publications and lectures was his clear preference for, and belief in the superiority of, *democracy*. In this respect also, of course, pragmatism was a characteristically American mode of thought. Only in a democratic milieu was it possible for a society to "learn by doing" or conduct the ongoing investigation and reexamination of existing knowledge that were essential for human development. Dewey did not disguise his preference for a democratically organized society. Yet he was convinced that democracy has meaning only by reference to a particular society's values, traditions, customary behavior patterns, and needs. As was implicit in his visit to republican China in the 1920s, new and novel forms of democracy were emerging. Dewey's thought, as explained in Chapter 3, provides useful guidance for contemporary Americans, who are often mystified by strange and unfamiliar versions of democracy that have been witnessed in the Third World since World War II.

Nature, Cognition, and Intelligence

A perennial question that has preoccupied philosophers throughout history is the "ultimate" nature of reality vis-à-vis its apparent nature as revealed by the senses. On this point, a substantial consensus existed among pragmatic thinkers: since the validity of all truth must in the end be determined by reference to experience, the question was meaningless and irrelevant. Experi-

40. Mayer, *History of American Thought*, 255; Dewey, *Individualism, Old and New, passim.*

ence *was* truth. If truth existed "outside" the realm of human experience, it was inaccessible to the mind and could not govern human behavior. Meanwhile, the task of philosophy and all other quests for knowledge was to concentrate on what could be comprehended about reality and to apply it to the conduct of human affairs. For pragmatic thinkers, the old antimony between observable and ultimate truth was another of those irrelevant historic "dualisms" that was untenable and that actually *impeded* the quest for knowledge.[41]

For pragmatically oriented minds, a key fact about the universe was its essentially plastic, unfinished, and pluralistic nature. The universe, said William James, "stands really malleable, waiting to receive its final touches at our hands."[42] Two facts about the universe were central to the pragmatic conception of it. One was that the universe was "pluralistic" or characterized by discreteness, concreteness, uniqueness, and randomness. This idea differentiated pragmatism from other (what William James called "block" or closed) conceptions of the universe depicting it as intrinsically unified, coordinated, and totally rational and predictable in the relationship among its components. A phenomenon familiar to anyone with an elementary grasp of modern physics illustrates the pragmatic conception: the dichotomous nature of light. For certain purposes (as in the science of optics) light is treated as consisting of waves, and its behavior is explicable and predictable by reliance on wave theory. For other purposes (as in photography), light is conceived of as consisting of "packets of energy" (photons), and its behavior must be explained by a different set of principles and theories derived from quantum mechanics. Neither theory alone can account adequately for the behavior of light, and neither is able to explain the "real" nature of light. Modern science has found such paradoxes and incongruities to be commonplace in the natural environment. Their existence, of course, does not prevent man from learning a great deal about the nature and behavior of light or other physical phenomena and of applying this knowledge for the welfare of human society.

Pragmatic thinkers did not deny the possibility that ultimately the overall unity of nature might be demonstrated. To date, however, this had not occurred; and the evidence remained preponderantly on the side of those who believed that the universe was pluralistic and discontinuous. Integrated sys-

41. See John Dewey, *Problems of Men* (New York, 1946), 5–7, 19.
42. James is quoted in Patrick K. Dooley, *Pragmatism as Humanism: The Philosophy of William James* (Chicago, 1974), 178.

tems of relationships (as in the relationship among the planets in the solar system) exist in nature; so do individuality, uniqueness, change, and unpredictability. A major corollary of the idea of pluralism, therefore, William James asserted, was the idea of a "world imperfectly unified" or a "commonsense world, in which we find things partly joined and partly disjoined." It might turn out, James believed, that the world may be "eternally incomplete, and at all times subject to addition or liable to loss."[43] Or, as John Dewey expressed the same idea, the "entire human predicament" was merely a reflection of nature itself. Nature exhibited both "individualities and uniformities, finalities and efficacies, contingencies and necessities." In nature there could be found both "harmony" and "disharmony"; and it was this "peculiar intermixture" or *paradoxical* quality of nature "which constitutes experience."[44]

A second key characteristic of a pluralistic or open universe is conveyed by one of William James's most widely quoted statements about the nature of truth. In the Jamesian view, truth is not "discovered" or "found": "The truth of an idea is not a stagnant property inherent in it. Truth *happens* to an idea. It *becomes* true, is *made* true by events." An event or natural phenomenon only *exists*: it is neither *per se* true nor untrue: it only becomes true or false as the human mind connects it in some way with experience (as in a scientific experiment) and thereby demonstrates its truthfulness or falsity.

A phenomenon exists on the subatomic scale, for example, which scientists call an "electron" (it could be given any number of other designations). If the statement is made that the electron has a certain orbital velocity of X, the truth or falsity of that statement can be proved only by precise scientific observation, involving measurements comprehensible to the human mind—in a word, by *experience*. In the pragmatic view, it is impossible to determine whether this proposition is true or false, independent of human experience. In that sense, the statement is made or becomes true by the process used to verify it.

Truth, then, in the pragmatic conception, is a quality imparted to a phenomenon by the encounter between man and the environment.[45] Truth is *made* just as health, wealth, and strength (or their opposites) are made in

43. For William James's views on the nature of the universe, see Joseph L. Blau (ed.), *William James's Pragmatism and Other Essays* (New York, 1963), 57–74. James's ideas are developed more fully in his *Pluralistic Universe*; and see Kallen (ed.), *William James's Some Problems of Philosophy*, 101–108.
44. Dewey, *Experience and Nature*, 421.
45. James, *Meaning of Truth*, xxix–xxx.

the course of experience. As a student of William James's thought has expressed it: "From atom bombs to earth satellites, men literally construct a world. The world is made by our efforts. Its future is a function of the choices we make, and the things we do." Or as Horace M. Kallen has generalized the point: "The pragmatic mind is an open mind confronting an open world, where, so long as it lives, it has a chance to *make* destiny and not merely submit to destiny; where the inevitable is the contingent. For the pragmatic spirit, there is no conflict between Freedom and Reason." Reason, in brief, is "creative intelligence."[46]

The unfinished nature of the universe—and the opportunities this fact provides for human creativity—is one of the most important and, at the same time, one of the most *misunderstood* tenets of pragmatic thought. This aspect of nature, pragmatists are convinced, poses a challenge and an opportunity for man. Man might, or he might not, respond to it constructively. Those critics are incorrect, therefore, who regard pragmatism as merely a "fair weather" credo. Pragmatism never asserted that there was anything inevitable about human evolution; human society might—and on several occasions, James, Dewey, and other pragmatists expressed concern that in fact it would—*fail* to meet the challenge successfully.

In William James's view, humans could make four possible responses to the unfinished nature of the universe. (1) They could follow the advice of many philosophers (especially certain schools of empiricism) by withholding judgment and waiting until all the evidence was available about the nature of the universe; in other words, the individual would do nothing in the interim. (2) They could take the route of the philosophical cynics, who held (in accordance perhaps with the physical law of entropy) that the universe will ultimately fail, and human society will fail with it. (3) They could operate on the premise that human and nonhuman forces within the universe are capable of producing beneficial results for society, and they could exert themselves to the fullest to produce this result. Or (4) humans could flounder indefinitely in indecision, torn between conflicting evidence that the universe is inimical and that it is benign, in regard to the welfare of mankind. For William James and other pragmatists, the matter was not in doubt: humans should choose the third possibility and by doing so "create the conclusion of the universe."[47]

Implicit in the pragmatic conception of the universe was the belief that

46. Moore, *William James*, 158; and Horace M. Kallen, "John Dewey and the Spirit of Pragmatism," in Sidney Hook (ed.), *John Dewey: Philosopher of Science and Freedom* (New York, 1950), 40–41.
47. Kallen (ed.), *William James's Some Problems of Philosophy*, 230.

nature was neither essentially hostile nor benign. Nature *per se* was neither "for" nor "against" man's endeavors; nature was neutral in the sense that it contained some forces that were inimical to, and others that were beneficial for, human purposes. A river, for example, might be a source of devastating floods, diseases, and other harmful effects; it might also be a source of food, energy, transportation, recreation, and other constructive uses. X-rays and ultraviolet radiation cause skin cancer and other debilitating disorders, but they can also be used therapeutically to cure cancer and other diseases. In these and comparable cases, whether nature is hostile or benign—whether its impact on human society is deleterious or beneficial—will depend to no insignificant degree upon *decisions made by man*; and in making such decisions, human intelligence plays a decisive role.[48]

Pragmatism thus rejects two extreme positions widely encountered in the philosophical tradition. One is identified with certain mechanistic and "deterministic" conceptions of nature (expressed in many forms of supranaturalism and Social Darwinism), holding that man is merely a helpless creature whose fate will ultimately be determined by the inexorable operation of natural or supranatural forces over which he has no control. Besides being unsupported by the evidence from human experience, in the pragmatic view this conception of the natural order reduces the concepts of human freedom and will to a mockery. The other position is exemplified by the "nature lover" who believes that the natural environment in all its manifestations and expressions is an essentially benign force which everywhere promotes human well-being. (This idea was implicit in the image of Rousseau's "noble savage," who lived "close to nature" and whose well-being was jeopardized only by human civilization.) To this group, the pragmatist would point out that though certain primitive groups today (like the aboriginal tribes of New Guinea or the Amazon Valley) live "close to nature," most are rapidly becoming extinct! Even if this is not the case, they normally suffer from high incidences of disease, malnutrition, and other disabilities which debilitate them and make life little more than a precarious struggle for existence.

As a mode of thought potently affected by the teachings of Charles Darwin, pragmatism accepted the idea that change is a law of nature and that man is capable of evolution. Yet pragmatists underscored the notion—and this tenet placed their thought in opposition to other philosophical traditions deriving from Darwin's thought—that creative human intelligence plays the

48. Dewey, *Human Nature and Conduct*, 310–11; Dewey, *Quest for Certainty*, 210–11.

decisive role in determining whether human society will evolve or retrogress. Implicit in the pragmatic idea, of course, is recognition of a fundamental distinction between change and progress: progress demands change, but all change is not necessarily progress. (Certain species of animal life, pragmatists are aware, had changed in the sense that they had *lost* their ability to adapt to the environment, and some had disappeared entirely.)

A prevalent misconception about pragmatism, therefore, was the notion that it believed in, or rationalized the idea of, "inevitable progress" in America or other societies. Pragmatic thinkers were convinced that progress in human affairs *was* possible; but it was by no means a certainty. Humans may well fail in their efforts to achieve it (William James and John Dewey, as we shall see in future chapters, pointed to innumerable examples of such failure during their lifetimes). Consequently, pragmatism has been called the "philosophy of possibilities" that are open to human society. In James's words, life was for the "tough-minded," rather than the "tender-minded," for those who were prepared to take risks, to the point perhaps of staking their lives upon their expectation that man's own creative efforts could make a difference in determining his ultimate destiny.[49]

In an unfinished and pluralistic universe, pragmatists are skeptical about all *a priori*, deterministic, and "closed" belief systems purporting to depict reality fully and accurately. William James, for example, freely acknowledged his indebtedness to earlier philosophers, including the distinguished German Idealist Georg W. F. Hegel. Yet he totally rejected Hegel's determinism, which, in effect, nullified the idea of human will and choice. Similarly, James and other pragmatists repudiated Social Darwinism, which made human destiny merely the outcome of certain supposedly "inexorable" biological laws.[50]

John Dewey was no less critical of the determinism implicit in Marxism. One of his most telling criticisms of Marxism was the idea that, not only was the fund of human understanding of experience constantly expanding, but the *methods of acquiring knowledge* also evolved. Neither Marxism nor any other *a priori* belief system, therefore, was capable of explaining reality. (Marxist thought, for example, takes virtually no account of what modern, post-Newtonian science has learned about the nature of matter.)

It is worth noting in this context that even many of Marxism's propo-

49. Dewey, *Quest for Certainty*, 244; Marcell, *Progress and Pragmatism*, 246–47; White, *Pragmatism and the American Mind*, 198; Preface by James M. Edie, in Wilshire, *William James*, xiii–xiv; and Blau (ed.), *William James's Pragmatism and Other Essays*, 8–10.
50. James, *Will to Believe*, 114–40.

nents have implicitly conceded the validity of this pragmatic idea. The periodic "revisions" and modifications in Marxist ideology—as epitomized by the concept of "creative Marxism"—testify to the value of this pragmatic insight. To cite but one example, the dangers implicit in the nuclear age have compelled the Soviet Union and its followers to make key modifications in classical Marxist thought on the subject of relations with capitalist countries and reliance on violence to achieve Marxist goals.[51]

Validation of the pragmatic precept has also been provided by the unprecedented "knowledge explosion" in the post–World War II era. From astronomy and astrophysics to investigation of subatomic particle behavior and genetics and in countless other realms, preexisting theories of the universe have had to be drastically modified or altogether abandoned. As pragmatic thought anticipated, the more scientists have learned about natural phenomena, the more they have become impressed with how much more there is to learn and with the degree to which the universe is pluralistic, anomalous, mystifying, and paradoxical.

Recent experience—and no better example is available than America's space program—has time and again focused attention upon another tenet of pragmatic thought. This is what might be regarded as the essential dilemma at the heart of scientific investigation. Space probes have simultaneously added to man's understanding of the universe and posed a long list of new and intriguing problems for future scientific investigation. In the popular phrase, space probes "raise as many questions as they answer." As the frontiers of space are explored, they continually recede beyond man's ability to answer many fundamental questions about the nature of the universe. In human affairs, pragmatic thinkers have emphasized the reality that every answer or proposed solution for a human problem engenders a new problem, which in turn requires a solution, *ad infinitum.*

Creative human intelligence thus has nearly always had a twofold impact upon the interaction between man and nature. In David W. Marcell's words, it has offered "new possibilities for both resolution [of a particular problem confronting society] and for the further inquiry such resolution might occasion."[52] Paradoxically, in solving one human problem man has almost invariably created the conditions for the emergence of another.

51. See, for example, the discussion of the Soviet view of détente in Coral Bell, *The Diplomacy of Detente: The Kissinger Era* (New York, 1977), esp. 54–79, 201–50; and in Adam B. Ulam, *Dangerous Relations: The Soviet Union in World Politics, 1970–1982* (New York, 1983), 39–82.

52. Marcell, *Progress and Pragmatism*, 225–26.

Experience and the Validation of Truth

A cornerstone of the pragmatic philosophical structure—and one of prag-matism's most distinctive tenets—is the idea that the verification of all propo-sitions about reality must be found *in the realm of experience*. This contention, of course, destroys the old philosophical distinction between the spiritual and actual, or between the subjective and objective, qualities of reality. According to Charles Peirce's axiom, truth has no existence or meaning apart from experience; truth depends upon experience for its validation; truth is always a product of the interaction between the observer and the observed in a particular environmental milieu. As William James emphasized, truth is not discovered but *made*: it comes into being as the result of an experiential interaction between man and nature.

Experimentation, for example—the method utilized by natural science to test the validity of propositions and theories about the physical universe— consists of acts engaged in by individuals whose measurements and other activities always occur within a specific social context. For investigations on the microcosmic level at least, scientists themselves have questioned whether certain subatomic particles and other phenomena really exist apart from the act of investigating them. Similarly, the truth of propositions about man's social, economic, and political behavior must be tested by experience—in the laboratory of human behavior. In John Dewey's words, in all realms of human experience, the "hypothesis that works is the true one; and truth is an abstract noun applied to the collection of cases, actual, foreseen and desired, that receive confirmation in their works and consequences." A "truthful" propo-sition is one that, on the basis of experience, "works" best in enabling us to account for or explain reality.[53]

Now it is essential to guard against certain distorted and simplistic in-terpretations of Charles Peirce's maxim that the truth of an idea is revealed by its consequences for experience. Echoes may be found in this principle, it is true, of such popular American aphorisms as "experience is the best teacher" or the most useful education is the one acquired "in the university of hard knocks." Pragmatism also unquestionably exhibits the long-standing Ameri-can aversion to abstract philosophical speculation having little apparent rela-tion to everyday life. In the sense that William James, John Dewey, and other

53. Dewey, *Reconstruction in Philosophy*, 156–57; Kallen (ed.), *William James's Some Problems of Philosophy*, 10–28; and Alfred N. Whitehead, *Science and the Modern World* (New York, 1925), 46.

pragmatists shared this aversion, their thought no doubt mirrored the anti-intellectualism that has often been identified in the American ethos.

Yet Peirce's principle must not be construed to mean that "one experience is as good as another" for the purpose of validating truth. The effect of such crude relativism would be to cast human society adrift aimlessly upon a sea of subjectivism or unrestrained individualism unrelated to the ultimate goal of human society: its *evolution* or development to a higher state of accomplishment in all spheres of life. Nor does Peirce's criterion justify the idea that any conceivable experience is "as good" as another in its contribution to the individual's and society's well-being. (William James, John Dewey, and other pragmatists, for example, believed there was an enormous qualitative difference between the value of war and peace, or between good and poor health, as experiences affecting the life of man.) Nor does Peirce's guideline assert that "experiencing" truth (as, for example, occurs in a highly emotional and mystical state) can be substituted for logical analysis and experimental verification as methods for ascertaining truth.

It will be helpful perhaps in understanding this important pragmatic axiom if we contrast it with other standards sometimes employed in answering Pontius Pilate's celebrated question: "What is truth?" Proponents of several supranatural philosophies would answer that the truth of a proposition is determined by the degree to which it accords with divinely revealed verities (as contained, for example, in the Ten Commandments, the Beatitudes, and other portions of the Old and New Testaments). For Transcendentalists, like Ralph Waldo Emerson and his followers, truth was accessible primarily by intuition and the development of a sense of spiritual union with nature. For rationalists, like Aristotle, Cicero, Leibniz, and Descartes, a true proposition was one that can be proved by reliance upon a formal system of rigidly logical analysis. For empiricists, like Hobbes, Locke, and Hume, the "true" was that which can be proven by a careful and objective examination of evidence available to the senses (some empirical thinkers concluded that no proposition could really be certified as "true" according to this criterion). By contrast, the utilitarians, like John Stuart Mill and Jeremy Bentham, believed that a proposition was true to the degree that it was "useful" or that it promoted the "greatest happiness for the greatest number" of people. In the more recent period, existentialists would measure truth by the degree to which it accorded with their tragic sense of life and their perception of suffering and alienation, promoted their sense of individuality, and contributed to their ability to control their own destiny.

As in nearly all aspects of their thought, pragmatic thinkers drew freely upon the philosophical tradition. For example, pragmatism unquestionably reflected the ideas and principles expressed by the empiricists and the utilitarians; yet there were also fundamental differences between pragmatism and these schools of thought. In contrast to some empirical thinkers, for example, pragmatists asserted that man was capable of ascertaining truth (even if his conception of it was nearly always incomplete and marked by incongruities, subject to modification in the light of new evidence). Among pragmatic thinkers, William James was convinced that spiritual and religiously derived insights must be included as part of human "experience," which served to validate truth. Pragmatism also rejected the traditional dichotomies between ideas and matter, or between objective and subjective knowledge, that were accepted in many other philosophical schools.

To illustrate this dimension of pragmatic thought concretely, let us examine a proposition that has been central to American foreign policy since the end of World War II. This is the assertion that the policies of the Soviet Union pose a threat to the peace and well-being of the United States and other countries. How is the validity of this assertion to be most reliably tested?

The supranaturalist would examine the extent to which communist ideology and Soviet policies since 1917 accord with the precepts of the Judaeo-Christian tradition and perhaps other religious systems such as Islam or Buddhism. The philosophical rationalist would analyze the meaning and logical consistency of communist ideology and of Soviet policies deriving from it. The existentialist thinker would evaluate Soviet policies in the light of his own highly subjective belief system; and he would be interested in whether Soviet thought and conduct do, or do not, contribute to a pervasive sense of alienation, fear, and meaninglessness among individuals. The empiricist would base his evaluation upon a thorough examination of the evidence—limited to data available to the senses—relevant to the question. Since much of this evidence even now is unavailable (as, for example, in ascertaining Moscow's real aims in building up Soviet military power steadily since the late 1960s), many empiricists would conclude that the proposition cannot be adequately tested and verified one way or the other.

The pragmatic standard for verifying the proposition would be to examine Soviet behavior since 1917. Pragmatically oriented thinkers would contend that the most reliable and meaningful criterion for ascertaining the validity of the proposition is the testimony provided by experience with Soviet conduct at home and abroad. What have been the observable *conse-*

quences of communist ideology as they have been expressed in the record of the Soviet Union's behavior in its relations with other countries? This fundamental pragmatic tenet easily translates into guidelines that have been prominent in American diplomacy since World War I. We shall examine them more fully in Chapter 4. Meanwhile, it suffices to mention two leading examples briefly.

Beginning with the Truman administration in 1945, spokesmen for every incumbent administration for some forty years have said that Washington expected "deeds—not words" from Moscow as evidence of the Soviet Union's professed dedication to peace, brotherhood, security, and other goals widely shared by other nations. Then by 1970 and afterward, basically this same idea was implicit in the concept of "linkage," which, to the official American mind, was crucial in efforts to achieve détente between the superpowers. Again, Moscow's desire for "peaceful coexistence" with the United States would be tested by (or "linked" with) Soviet *behavior* in Poland, in Afghanistan, in East Africa, in Latin America, and in other settings. Washington consistently refused to accept a Soviet definition of détente that permitted Moscow to support peaceful coexistence verbally while undermining it in practice by contrary behavior in its relations with other countries. If they were compelled to choose between Soviet words and Soviet behavior, millions of Americans had no hesitation in accepting the latter as the most convincing evidence of the "meaning" of communism.

Pragmatism and Its Corollaries

In conclusion, let us briefly summarize the discussion thus far of the pragmatic mode of thought by attempting to define pragmatism and by taking note of its major corollaries. As a school of philosophy that emerged in American society in the late nineteenth century, pragmatism has been variously designated by such terms as *radical empiricism* (the phrase often used by William James), *instrumentalism* (the term frequently applied to John Dewey's thought), the *new humanism, voluntarism, functionalism, experimentalism, operationalism,* and several others. The core idea of pragmatism is the belief that the most reliable criterion for ascertaining and validating truth lies in the degree to which it accords with *human experience.* Pragmatists are convinced that the *interaction* between the human species and its environment is the key fact of experience; that the environment is dynamic and pluralistic; that human society must continually adapt and evolve or perish; and that the ultimate goal of all scientific, philosophical, and other forms of inquiry is the creation of an ever-widening *sense of community* which promotes the highest possible degree of human development and self-realization. Pragmatism thus attempts to serve as a "science of human affairs" by blending the principles of scientific inquiry with the practical knowledge and wisdom which humans derive from everyday life.

So defined, Pragmatism contains a number of significant corollary ideas:

· Pragmatism is a syncretistic mode of thought that draws heavily and freely from the philosophical tradition. It demands an "open" approach to truth, which is willing to derive insights from a wide variety of available sources.

· The pragmatic mentality, therefore, rejects all "closed" or *a priori* belief systems, viewing them as oversimplifying a highly complex reality and as impeding the ongoing search for new truths; pragmatists believe not only that our understanding of reality evolves, but that the scientific method and other approaches to ascertaining truth also undergo continuing modifications.

· In contrast with other philosophies, pragmatism holds that truth is not discovered by the process of abstract philosophical speculation; a proposition is *made* or *becomes* "true" to the degree that it is found to conform to experience and is, for that reason, accepted as being true; the search for truth, therefore, is an ongoing and never-ending process of examining, reexamining, accepting, modifying, and rejecting ideas in the light of experience.

· The pragmatic mind believes in the pluralistic nature of the universe; the universe is conceived of as being dynamic, unfinished, and "plastic"; it contains recurrent and unique, symmetrical and asymmetrical, predictable and unpredictable forces; human understanding of the universe, therefore, is always limited and contingent; and accepted truth must constantly be re-tested and modified in the light of new evidence.

· Sometimes called a "philosophy of change," pragmatism views a dynamic universe as being in the process of *becoming*; human destiny, therefore, is *undetermined*; it will be significantly affected, however, by the human *response* to challenges arising from the environment; therefore, it lies within the power of human beings, by relying on what John Dewey called "the method of intelligence," to influence the outcome of the universe.

· The pragmatist believes that cognition is essentially a process which William James called "living reason"; the mind responds to and interacts with the environment; an almost infinite number of stimuli, images, sensations, and the like impinge upon the human mind; in this "stream of consciousness," the old classical distinction between mind and matter, or between objective and subjective knowledge, becomes meaningless and untenable; it is always this *relationship* between the investigator and what is being investigated that leads to the discovery of truth.

· In the pragmatic conception, in the process of cognition the mind focuses attention upon challenges and problems directly affecting human well-being that require a response; as William James expressed it, the mind is "a fighter for freedom"; creative human intelligence guides individuals and groups to seek solutions for the problems confronting them within a particular context of time and circumstances; among the feasible alternatives available, intelligence guides humans to select the course of action which, on balance, best promotes human welfare.

· Since the cognitive process is viewed by pragmatists as primarily an exercise in *problem solving*, pragmatism believes that humans are normally concerned with immediate, here-and-now issues directly affecting their well-being; these issues always arise in a particular context of time, events, and circumstances and, therefore, invariably contain *unique* elements; the human response to them must, as a result, take full account of the context within which the problem exists and must be solved.

· Pragmatism holds a "fallibilistic" view of knowledge: human understanding of a pluralistic universe is always partial and incomplete; individuals must continually make decisions on the basis of fragmentary and incomplete evidence; such decision making more often than not involves calculated risks, entailing, of course, the risk of failure as well as success; yet the *failure to act* will, in all likelihood, entail an even greater degree of risk that the outcome will be inimical to human well-being.

· Pragmatic thought rejects the notion of "value-free" scientific or philosophical inquiry; those who seek to understand the universe always operate upon some set of values or exhibit faith in something (such as the idea that knowledge is preferable to ignorance, or confidence in the reliability of the results provided by using the scientific method); pragmatism calls for frank recognition that scientists and other investigators *always interact* with their environment; the explicit purpose of this interaction should be to *improve* the environment for human society's benefit.

· Pragmatists are genuinely and continuously concerned with what John Dewey called "the problems of men"; they are involved in attempts to solve human problems in a manner best conducive to human well-being; yet they are aware that the solution of one problem contains the seeds for a new one that must be solved, *ad infinitum*.

· The pragmatic mode of thought extols experimentation, trial-and-error methods, adjustment, and adaptation in all fields of human endeavor; key concepts in pragmatic thought are growth and development; though accepting the inevitability of change, pragmatism believes that, by relying on creative intelligence, man can guide and direct change to produce *evolution*; evolutionary change is preferable either to attempts to preserve the *status quo* or efforts to transform human society by means of revolutionary methods and programs, both of which will likely fail.

· According to pragmatic thought, progress in human affairs is *possible*, although it is by no means inevitable or automatic; progress is nearly always contingent upon the application of creative human intelligence to the solution of problems confronting human society; in the absence of continuing and intelligent human efforts, retrogression, rather than progress, will likely characterize human affairs; the leading pragmatic thinkers were what can be called moderately hopeful about the future of human civilization.

· The pragmatist believes that an "open" or democratic community is indispensable for the operation of the scientific method, for the pursuit of knowledge generally, and for the maximum degree of human development; for this reason primarily, pragmatism advocates democracy as the most desirable pattern for the organization of society; yet pragmatists also believe that democracy must be defined and created *within specific contexts*, which take full account of a particular society's values, traditions, and needs; the exact principles, institutions, and practices associated with it, therefore, are likely to vary from one society to another.

Three

Pragmatism and International Politics

This chapter focuses on pragmatic concepts and principles that are directly relevant for understanding human political behavior, with particular emphasis on international political relationships. The impact of pragmatic thought on American domestic political life has been identified and analyzed by numerous scholars.[1] The ideas of leading pragmatic thinkers sometimes momentously influenced internal political movements such as the Populist and Progressive parties during the late nineteenth and early twentieth centuries. They had an impact on certain citizens' organizations such as those opposing imperialism and war and (by the 1930s) those calling for adherence to America's traditional isolationist foreign policy. Pragmatism has also been closely associated with internal reform movements in recent American history, including those advocating the merit system and other civil service reforms, the democratization of the political process, more stringent government regulation of business, and the rise and strengthening of the American labor movement.

By the 1930s, the ideas of leading pragmatists were sometimes cited by

1. David W. Marcell, *Progress and Pragmatism: James, Dewey, Beard, and the American Idea of Progress* (Westport, Conn., 1974); Gail Kennedy (ed.), *Pragmatism and American Culture* (Boston, 1950); Bernard P. Brennan, *The Ethics of William James* (New York, 1961); Stow Persons, *American Minds: A History of Ideas* (New York, 1958); Alfonso J. Damico, *Individuality and Community: The Social and Political Thought of John Dewey* (Gainesville, Fla., 1978); Daniel J. Boorstin, *Democracy and Its Discontents: Reflections on Everyday America* (New York, 1974); Roger Burlingame, *The American Conscience* (New York, 1957); Henry S. Commager, *The American Mind: An Interpretation of American Thought and Character Since the 1880s* (New Haven, 1950); Richard Hofstadter, *The Age of Reform: From Bryan to F.D.R.* (New York, 1981); and Lewis L. Gould (ed.), *The Progressive Era* (Syracuse, N.Y., 1974).

both supporters and critics of the New Deal. Those who were apprehensive about the emergence of "big government" and the New Deal's collectivist orientation found ample support in the writings of William James, who championed the cause of individualism and was suspicious of "bigness" in industry, labor, government, and other settings. By contrast, those who welcomed the New Deal's emphasis on collective efforts to solve urgent national problems, and who favored its efforts to redefine democracy in social and economic terms, were often sustained by the writings and lectures of John Dewey. Yet it was a commentary on the ambivalent nature of pragmatic thought that Dewey's own assessment of the New Deal was decidedly mixed.[2] President Roosevelt's own distinctive ideology—or conspicuous lack of it— inevitably added fuel to the continuing controversy over the principles that motivated his administration's approach to domestic and foreign problems. On one occasion, FDR said, "I believe in practical explanations and in practical policies." A leading commentator on his policies said that the president liked to "keep his options open" in dealing with urgent problems confronting his administration at home and abroad. Another study has found that in foreign affairs, Roosevelt's decisions consisted mainly of "improvisations," resulting in a "wobbly if not downright erratic" diplomatic course. FDR has also been quoted as saying that he believed in *acting* and then leaving it to his advisers to explain and theorize about the meaning of his actions.[3]

Although John Dewey and many of his followers were often critical of the New Deal, it is significant that they refrained from endorsing the two principal alternatives to Roosevelt's highly pragmatic approach to national problems. One of these was a return to nineteenth-century *laissez-faire* capitalism. The other was a collectivist solution to national problems as was being attempted in the Soviet Union, Germany, Italy, and other nondemocratic states.[4]

The Nature of Political Relationships

To the pragmatic mind, the state—the political arm or organization of society—is an established and necessary instrument of society to facilitate what

2. See Sidney Hook, *John Dewey: An Intellectual Portrait* (New York, 1939), 226–39; A. H. Somjee, *The Political Theory of John Dewey* (New York, 1968), 156; and Charles F. Howlett, *Troubled Philosopher: John Dewey and the Struggle for World Peace* (Port Washington, N.Y., 1977), 125–26.

3. Samuel I. Rosenman (comp.), *The Public Papers and Addresses of Franklin D. Roosevelt* (13 vols.; New York, 1938–50), II, 312–18; Frank Friedel, *Franklin D. Roosevelt: Launching the New Deal* (Boston, 1973), 465–66; Lloyd C. Gardner, *Imperial America: American Foreign Policy Since 1898* (New York, 1976), 124–35.

4. George Dykhuizen, *The Life and Mind of John Dewey* (Carbondale, Ill., 1973), 253–54.

John Dewey called the "coming together" of its members. As an instrument of society, the state's purpose is to protect and promote the security of its members, to establish and dispense justice, and to promote what the American Constitution called the "general welfare" of the people. Accordingly, the behavior of the state must be judged by the same criteria which pragmatists applied to all other human institutions and activities, that is, the degree to which it enhances human well-being and provides opportunities for human development.[5]

As his thought evolved, however, Dewey came to believe that universal concepts like "the state" and "sovereignty" were largely meaningless: they tended to impede insight into real-life political behavior and relationships. Nevertheless, in the end Dewey and other pragmatists frequently resorted to the commonly used and familiar terms of political discourse. Consistent with the pragmatic tenets discussed in Chapter 2, pragmatically oriented thinkers nearly always concentrated on discrete, immediate, and urgent problems confronting Americans and citizens of other countries in the modern world. Dewey, for example, did not like the term *the state;* even less did he accept the age-old principle of *raison d'état* ("reason of state") as a legitimate explanation of state behavior. To his mind, only *states* existed. Each was different, and yet each was (or should be) an instrument for the solution of a particular society's problems. The common denominator of all states was that their performance had to be judged ultimately by the same standard.[6]

To pragmatic minds, the particular organization of a state—its constitution, form of government, political processes, and the like—was the product of many and diverse factors. These included the society's underlying moral-ethical values, its history and traditions, its experiences, its unique needs, and, not least, certain accidental and fortuitous forces that contributed to the emergence of liberal democracy in the United States, autocracy in czarist Russia, totalitarianism in Nazi Germany and the Soviet Union, monarchy in Ethiopia, military rule in Japan, and alternative forms.[7]

In the pragmatic conception, the policies and actions of governments derive from a highly pluralistic social environment, in which individuals and groups continually interact to produce consequences deemed useful or beneficial for themselves. In John Dewey's version of pragmatism especially, groups serve as the mainspring of government activity; as in all spheres of life, collaborative human effort is required to achieve worthwhile results. Al-

5. Somjee, *Political Theory of John Dewey,* 82.
6. *Ibid.,* 5–6.
7. Dewey, *The Public and Its Problems,* in Jo Ann Boydston (ed.), *John Dewey: The Later Works, 1925–1953* (12 vols.; Carbondale, Ill., 1901), II, 238–303.

though William James is often regarded as a tireless champion of American individualism vis-à-vis his younger pragmatic colleague, John Dewey, the line between James's "individualism" and Dewey's "collectivism" should not be drawn too sharply. As an educator, Dewey was keenly interested in the development of individuals; repeatedly throughout his career, he expressed concern about threats to individual rights posed by the actions of government at home and abroad. Nevertheless, as Albert W. Levi has expressed it, there was unquestionably a difference in emphasis between these two expositors of pragmatism. For Dewey, "the idea of democracy is defined less by political machinery than by the right of the individual to have a responsible share in forming and directing the activities of the groups to which he belongs, and in participating genuinely in the values which the groups promote." The individual realizes his fullest potential in "associated life," and "the achievement of democracy is nothing but the achievement of community."[8]

To say that twentieth-century pragmatists emphasized the group basis of political and other forms of social action is not, however, to assert (as some behaviorally oriented political scientists in the modern period have said or suggested) that all group activity is permissible and equally valuable for society, that *only* groups influence public policy, or that government itself is only one among many competing groups seeking to gain and hold the allegiance of members of society. Pragmatist thinkers recognized that, in several fundamental respects, government is *sui generis* (as, for example, in its monopoly in the use of force and its reliance on the legal concept of sovereignty). As a later section of this chapter will demonstrate, one unique activity of the state—its proclivity for war and other forms of violent behavior—was a problem to which William James, John Dewey, and other pragmatists devoted considerable attention.

Dewey was a leading member of the "Chicago school" of intellectuals, several of whose members were pioneers in the emergence of behaviorally oriented social science with its emphasis on precise measurement, quantification, and methodology.[9] For this group, as for John Dewey and other prag-

8. See John Dewey, *Reconstruction in Philosophy* (Boston, 1920), 209–10; *Freedom and Culture* (New York, 1939), 93–94; Albert W. Levi, *Philosophy and the Modern World* (Bloomington, 1959), 326; and Wayne A. R. Leys, "Dewey's Social, Political, and Legal Philosophy," in Jo Ann Boydston (ed.), *Guide to the Works of John Dewey* (Carbondale, Ill., 1970), 143.
9. The behavioral approach to political science is usually dated from the publication of Arthur Bentley's *The Process of Government* (1908). Concepts central to the behavioral orientation are an emphasis on the regularity of political behavior, the verification of data, the refinement of new techniques of observation (such as statistics), the quantification of data, the attempt to exclude values from scientific inquiry, and the integration of knowledge. See David Easton, "The

matists, natural science provided the model for efforts directed at acquiring accurate and comprehensive understanding of social, economic, and political relationships.

Yet though pragmatism in some measure unquestionably influenced behavioral inquiry in the social sciences, there were also some fundamental differences between them. Behavioral inquiry, its devotees have repeatedly claimed, is "value-free" and uninterested in philosophical questions. By contrast, as we have seen, a central tenet of pragmatism is that all scientific inquiry is inherently concerned with questions of value. For pragmatism, the only relevant question is *whose* values, or *what* values, will guide the quest for scientific understanding and the application of its findings to society's problems. If the scientific quest is "good," the pragmatist would insist, it must be *good for something* related to human experience and meaningful to human beings. In the pragmatic conception, the purpose of creative intellectual activity is to promote human development or evolution by enabling the members of society to respond successfully to challenges confronting them from the interaction between the human species and its environment. The mind is thus viewed as a problem-solving mechanism, and this conception inescapably implies that among all possible human responses to a particular challenge, some are preferable to others.

Relying upon his intelligence, in other words, man makes choices among alternative courses of action. He chooses the response that, under prevailing circumstances, is judged superior to other possible responses on the basis of its contribution to human well-being and development. For example, William James, John Dewey, and their followers clearly recognized the difference between various kinds of growth in human affairs. They did not equate the growth of disease, slums, poverty, and violence among groups and nations with the growth of knowledge, better sanitary and living standards, peace, and a heightened sense of community among peoples in terms of their value for human society. The natural scientist, and his imitator in the social sciences, routinely operates on the premise that a flourishing and expanding scientific enterprise (such as the space program) is better than its absence. On this crucial point, therefore, pragmatism and behaviorally oriented social science are philosophically antithetical.

In its approach to political relationships—international no less than do-

Current Meaning of Behavioralism in Political Science," in *The Limits of Behavioralism in Political Science* (Philadelphia, 1962), 1–25. A critical assessment of the behavioral approach is Bernard Crick, *The American Science of Politics: Its Origins and Conditions* (London, 1959).

mestic—the pragmatic viewpoint thus provides an approach that is reasonably distinct from both traditional political science (with its emphasis on political philosophy, laws, and institutions) and behavioral political science (with its emphasis on political processes, quantification and measurement, and prediction). For the pragmatic mind, the most fundamental questions relate to how the state *actually functions in terms of the consequences of its actions for individuals, groups, and society as a whole.* Whether the state's behavior promotes or impedes human growth and development is the primary concern of the pragmatist and the salient criterion by which all states' laws, institutions, political processes, and the like ought to be judged. (Pragmatic thought thus anticipated the emergence of a relatively recent emphasis in the study of political phenomena known as policy evaluation, in which the observer is less interested in the process by which a policy is formulated and adopted than in its actual effects, intended and unintended.) John Dewey believed that governments in the United States, the Soviet Union, and all other nations in the contemporary world would ultimately be evaluated according to this standard rather than by *a priori* ideological principles or other criteria. The demand since the Vietnam War that American foreign policy possess "legitimacy"—that, on the basis of the evidence, it produces results deemed beneficial by the American society—is a tangible expression of this pragmatic criterion.

From the fundamental pragmatic tenet that the universe is pluralistic and unfinished, it follows that the political environment exhibits a comparable diversity and incompleteness. Particularly in the United States, the milieu within which political decision making occurs is characterized by an almost infinite variety of individuals, groups, and institutions and by continuous interactions among them that ultimately produce government policies, programs, and behavior. As emphasized in Chapter 2, pragmatists reject all unicausal and *a priori* explanations of political phenomena as inadequately reflecting the enormous complexity and dichotomous nature of the political universe. In understanding this political universe, as in comprehending nature itself, pragmatism implicitly (and sometimes explicitly) acknowledges the limits of human comprehension and concedes the essential mystery of some dimensions of human experience.

To cite merely one example of this principle, the pragmatic mind is not surprised or especially disturbed by the numerous and highly diverse explanations of precisely when and how the Truman administration decided to make "patience and firmness" (later reformulated as "containment") the centerpiece of American foreign policy toward the Soviet Union in the early postwar period. Even President Harry S. Truman himself would most likely have been hard-pressed to have identified precisely the moment or process by which he ultimately decided to oppose expansionist Soviet behavior. It seems less controversial that the decision resulted from the interplay of many divergent factors and forces—from Truman's own personality traits and ideological inclinations, to the advice offered him by his principal diplomatic aides, to the influence of Congress on American foreign policy, to changes in American public attitudes toward the Soviet Union after World War II, to Moscow's actions and statements during and after the war. Collectively, these forces combined to produce a fundamental change in the diplomatic approach of the United States toward the Soviet Union.

The pluralistic nature of the political environment is especially pronounced in the case of the American society, so much so as to convince many political scientists in the United States that pluralism and democracy are synonymous.[10] The unique American system of government, based on such distinctive concepts as separation of powers, checks and balances, and federalism, makes the American political milieu unusually variegated and dichotomous. In foreign affairs, two additional factors since World War II have added to the complexity of the decision-making environment. One of these is the necessity for the United States to maintain relations with approximately 160 independent nations. The other is the progressive erosion in the traditional distinction between what once was regarded as foreign and domestic affairs. Today, that line has all but disappeared. President Lyndon B. Johnson's projected Great Society within the United States, for example, was largely undermined by the nation's prolonged and costly involvement in the Vietnam War; by the early 1970s, the energy crisis—precipitated by the embargo placed on foreign oil shipment by the Persion Gulf states in 1973— again had profound and lasting domestic consequences for Americans.

The pragmatist has no difficulty, therefore, accounting for the enormous diversity found in the ongoing interpretations of American diplomatic behavior since World War II. Thus some studies of American foreign relations in recent years have emphasized the economic forces and compulsions motivating the United States in international affairs. In turn, these may be divided into three subgroups: (1) the familiar Soviet and other Marxist interpreta-

10. See Robert A. Dahl, *Who Governs: Democracy and Power in an American City* (New Haven, 1972); and Theodore J. Lowi, "The Public Philosophy: Interest-Group Liberalism," *American Political Science Review,* LXI (1967), 5–24.

tions, in which American diplomatic moves are explicable by reference to the ongoing class struggle and the principles supposedly governing the behavior of capitalists; (2) various quasi-Marxist interpretations (such as those written from a socialist orientation); and (3) non-Marxist explanations in which economic compulsions and forces provide the key to understanding American diplomatic behavior.[11]

From a different perspective, other studies of recent American diplomacy have identified a deeply ingrained anticommunist impulse as the key factor accounting for the emergence of the cold war, the containment policy, and other major developments (including involvement in the Vietnam conflict) in postwar American foreign relations. Yet this interpretation is far from being unified in its basic conclusions. Some commentators attribute the anticommunist impulse to the class composition and right-wing ideological propensities of what are sometimes called the foreign policy establishment or "national security managers" who have largely controlled the diplomatic decision-making process in the United States since World War II. Drawn in the main from established, prosperous, and conservative families, these officials presumably have exhibited an intense dislike—amounting sometimes to an almost uncontrollable phobia—for communism as a force engendering revolutionary change, to which this elite is nearly always opposed.[12]

A still different approach to post–World War II American diplomacy emphasizes the importance of psychological factors in accounting for such developments as Soviet-American tensions and superpower competition in the Third World. Again, this perspective on American foreign policy is not monolithic. Such studies differ in *which* psychological forces they consider decisive in shaping American diplomatic moves and the relative influence of these moves. One point of view, for example, attributes the cold war—and, indeed, most great power conflicts in recent history—to "misperceptions" by key policy makers concerning the intentions and strength of their adversaries; diplomatic responses stemming from such misperceptions have usually resulted in an escalation of international tension and conflict. An alter-

11. William A. Williams, *The Tragedy of American Diplomacy* (2nd ed.; New York, 1972), 295–96. Economic determinism is also a major theme of the interpretation by Joyce Kolko and Gabriel Kolko, *The Limits of Power: The World and United States Foreign Policy, 1945–1954* (New York, 1972).

12. Interpretations of American diplomacy in this vein are David Horowitz, *The Free World Colossus: A Critique of American Foreign Policy in the Cold War* (New York, 1971); Richard J. Barnet, *Intervention and Revolution: America's Confrontation with Insurgent Movements Around the World* (New York, 1968); Richard J. Walton, *Cold War and Counter-Revolution: The Foreign Policy of John F. Kennedy* (Baltimore, 1973); and John C. Donovan, *The Cold Warriors: A Policy-Making Elite* (Lexington, Mass., 1974).

native explanation is that major postwar diplomatic undertakings (such as the containment policy) derived ultimately from a deep and recurrent sense of self-deception which Americans have consistently relied upon to conceal their nation's true aims in dealing with other countries. According to one interpretation, the nation's leaders are "unaware of what they are really doing," which in reality has been to engage in "aggression—American-style." A different psychologically oriented interpretation attributes American diplomatic moves during the 1960s in Southeast Asia and other settings to what is called "groupthink" or a decision-making process that places a premium on conformity, which stifles creativity, originality, and dissent and in turn, led to the Vietnam War and other diplomatic failures.[13]

A fundamentally different viewpoint on American diplomatic behavior since World War II has been offered by devotees of one of the oldest approaches to the study of political phenomena: *Realpolitik*. During and after World War II, Nicholas J. Spykman, DeWitt Poole, Walter Lippmann, Robert Strausz-Hupé, Hans J. Morgenthau, Henry Kissinger, and (for some aspects of his thought at least) George F. Kennan advocated an avowedly power-oriented approach to international politics by the United States. In this view, power is the pivotal concept in all political relationships; international politics involves a continuing "power struggle" among nations; nations are devoted primarily to the pursuit of their "national interests"; and maintaining a stable "balance of power" is the most reliable method for preserving global peace and stability. In the *Realpolitik* conception, ideologies and values are important in international political relationships only insofar as they rationalize and facilitate diplomatic moves stemming ultimately from power calculations.[14]

By contrast, innumerable studies of American diplomacy have emphasized the extent to which it has endeavored—and in many cases has been able—to achieve goals and purposes consonant with the American society's

13. John G. Stoessinger, *Nations in Darkness: China, Russia, and America* (3rd ed.; New York, 1981), and *Why Nations Go to War* (2nd ed.; New York, 1978); William H. Blanchard, *Aggression American Style* (Santa Monica, Calif., 1978); Irving L. Janis, *Victims of Groupthink* (Boston, 1972).
14. International relations literature written from a *Realpolitik* perspective is almost endless. A sampling of worthwhile studies includes Edward V. Gulick, *Europe's Classical Balance of Power* (New York, 1955); Nicholas J. Spykman, *America's Strategy in World Politics* (New York, 1942); Walter Lippmann, *U.S. Foreign Policy: Shield of the Republic* (Boston, 1943), and *Isolation and Alliances: An American Speaks to the British* (Boston, 1952); Hans J. Morgenthau, "The Mainspring of American Foreign Policy," *American Political Science Review,* XLIV (1950), 833–54, and *In Defense of the National Interest* (New York, 1951); George F. Kennan, *American Diplomacy, 1900–1950* (New York, 1952), and *Memoirs (1925–1950)* (New York, 1969); and Henry A. Kissinger, *American Foreign Policy* (2nd ed.; New York, 1974).

own traditions, values, and ideological objectives.[15] If *Realpolitik* tends to explain American diplomatic behavior by reference to common factors and influences affecting the diplomatic conduct of all nations, this approach highlights the uniqueness of the American experience and its significance in understanding the role of the United States in foreign affairs. It calls attention, for example, to the distinctive and original contributions often made by the United States to the practice of recent diplomacy. In conformity with the New World mentality, it asserts not only that Americans conceive of their international political behavior differently from other societies, but that in a number of crucial respects—the nation's historic policy of isolationism, its opposition to colonialism, its interest in the global extension of democracy, its attachment to peace and (as events during and after the Vietnam War indicated) its opposition to military interventionism abroad, its leadership role in creating new international and regional institutions—the diplomatic role of the United States is unique. To this list should be added another noteworthy feature of American diplomatic activity: the degree to which its behavior in foreign affairs has been influenced by pragmatic principles.

Since World War II, several behaviorally oriented approaches to the study of international political relationships shed light on the behavior of the United States in foreign affairs. Only two of these, game theory and systems theory, will be considered here. Game theory has been especially useful in understanding such international problems as the challenge of nuclear deterrence between the superpowers and arms-control negotiations. Game theory is a highly rational approach to international political relationships, in which presumably the participants (or "players") endeavor to make moves designed to enhance their own positions vis-à-vis those of their opponents and ultimately to win the contest.[16]

Systems theory takes a different approach. Drawing upon certain principles of natural science governing the operation of systems (as in the planetary

15. Frank Tannenbaum, *The American Tradition in Foreign Policy* (Norman, Okla., 1955); Dexter Perkins, *The American Approach to Foreign Policy* (New York, 1968), and *Foreign Policy and the American Spirit* (Ithaca, N.Y., 1957); Ernst B. Haas, *Tangle of Hopes: American Commitments and World Order* (Englewood Cliffs, N.J., 1969); and Philip W. Quigg, *America the Dutiful: An Assessment of U.S. Foreign Policy* (New York, 1971).

16. The principal behavioral approaches, with excerpts from representative studies, are identified in James N. Rosenau (ed.), *International Politics and Foreign Policy* (2nd ed.; New York, 1969). Useful summaries are contained in James E. Dougherty and Robert L. Pfaltzgraff, Jr., *Contending Theories of International Relations: A Comprehensive Survey* (New York, 1981). For game theory see Thomas C. Schelling, *Strategy and Arms Control* (New York, 1961), and *Arms and Influence* (New Haven, 1966); also R. Duncan Luce and Howard Raiffia, *Games and Decisions* (New York, 1957).

system or the human body's nervous system) and upon the economic theories of Kenneth Boulding and the sociological theories of Talcott Parsons, systems theory attempts to identify and analyze the behavior of the members of the "international system." Proponents of this approach assume that an international system exists; some are convinced that regional subsystems (such as the Middle East and East Asia) exist within it.[17]

As with most other behavioral interpretations of American diplomacy, systems theory confronts serious obstacles as a useful guide to foreign policy. Many informed observers believe that international politics is characterized more by anarchy and disorder than by the ordered relationships which the term *system* implies; and even if it is conceded that an international system actually exists, political scientists are in fundamental disagreement about how it ought to be defined and described. Systems theory is even less useful in describing the political relationships among states and political movements in regions like the highly volatile and turbulent contemporary Middle East.[18]

This list of diverse approaches to the study of international political relationships and American foreign policy is not, of course, meant to be exhaustive, merely illustrative. Other useful perspectives are available and shed light on selected aspects of international relations—so many in fact as to convince some students of the subject that a "theory of theories" is now needed to unify and correlate this growing profusion of individual hypotheses and theories purporting to account for the international behavior of the United States and other nations.

Attention to the problem here is dictated by the relevance of a pragmatic orientation to international political relationships for it. The extraordinarily wide diversity encountered among the interpretations of American diplomacy, for example, is a noteworthy feature of them. In no other country has there been such a remarkable range of interpretations or such disunity among well-qualified observers in accounting for the nation's diplomatic behavior. Relatively few of these studies could be called totally "wrong"; most are based

17. See David Easton, *The Political System* (New York, 1953); Charles C. McClelland, *Theory and the International System* (New York, 1966); Morton A. Kaplan, *Systems and Process in International Politics* (New York, 1957); Sidney Verba (ed.), "The International System," special issue of *World Politics*, XIII (October, 1961); and Romano Romani, *The International Political System: Introduction and Readings* (New York: 1972).

18. See, for example, Hedley Bull, *The Anarchial Society: A Study of Order in World Politics* (New York, 1977); and George W. Ball, *The Discipline of Power: Essentials of a Modern World Structure* (Boston, 1968). Several theories regarding the nature of the international system are identified and evaluated in Joseph L. Nogee, "Polarity—An Ambiguous Concept," *Orbis*, XVIII (Winter, 1975), 1193–1224.

on extensive research and reflect careful thought by their authors. What can be said about them collectively perhaps is that, at best, they contribute to better understanding of a *limited dimension* of American diplomatic experience. Almost never, however, do they account adequately for the totality of that experience; nor do they provide a comprehensive set of diplomatic guidelines for American foreign policy under a wide variety of novel and future circumstances.

The existence of this diversified body of scholarly literature on postwar international politics, in other words, provides convincing evidence of the central importance of one of pragmatism's basic tenets: the concept of a pluralistic universe. The American political universe is highly pluralistic, consisting of an almost infinite number of major and minor, rational and irrational, calculated and random, forces that combine in particular cases to produce a given foreign policy decision. It is possible to identify in very general terms (or in the "average case") what these forces will likely be, irrespective of whether one is interested in the diplomatic decisions of Franklin D. Roosevelt's administration, Reagan's administration, or those in between. It is infinitely more difficult—and, based on the evidence to date, virtually impossible—to predict how these forces will combine in reaching a particular diplomatic decision, or to anticipate what the relative influence of any one of them is likely to be in determining diplomatic outcomes.

To illustrate the point as concretely as possible, let us briefly apply these ideas to the diplomacy of merely one period in recent American foreign relations—the diplomacy of President Franklin D. Roosevelt. (With suitable variations, the same approach could be equally well applied to the diplomatic records of any other administration since World War II.) New Deal diplomacy resulted from the interaction of at least eight reasonably distinct and influential factors determining America's response to external problems. One of these was *personal and idiosyncratic factors,* such as FDR's unique administrative style, his strong ego, and his declining health, all of which influenced his approach to foreign policy issues. Another category of factors was the president's—and, more broadly, the American people's—*fundamental ignorance of international affairs* and traditional lack of interest in them. On some foreign policy issues (Russia's foreign policy goals before and after 1917 and China's internal political conflicts), FDR was poorly informed, and many of his advisers were only slightly better informed; and this fact was sometimes crucial in accounting for the results of New Deal diplomacy.

The foreign relations of the Roosevelt administration were also strongly colored by *ideological factors*. FDR was a tireless champion of democracy, anticolonialism, self-determination, and other principles fundamental to democratic ideology. His insistence that democratic regimes be established in Eastern Europe after World War II was one example of this ideological inclination; another was his vocal opposition to British, French, and other forms of colonialism.

Conversely, New Deal diplomacy was sometimes also influenced by *Realpolitik* calculations. As a master political manipulator, Roosevelt understood the concept of power and on occasion relied on his position as leader of the most powerful member of the allied coalition to gain his objectives. For example, FDR's "Grand Design" for the postwar world contemplated that the "Big Five" (in reality, often the "Big Two"—the Soviet Union and the United States) would effectively make the major international decisions.

Other diplomatic decisions by the Roosevelt administration reflected the influence of certain *historical and traditional factors* conditioning the American approach to foreign relations. A prominent example was FDR's inability to understand the intimate relationship between political and military decisions and his tendency to compartmentalize these two realms of national policy. As a result, in Eastern Europe, Korea, Indochina, and other locales military developments and decisions became decisive factors in determining the course of future political events. In the American tradition, General Carl von Clausewitz's principle that "war is the continuation of politics by other means" has never become widely accepted.[19]

Still another factor influencing FDR's diplomacy was the *lessons of experience*. In planning for the post–World War II order, for example, Roosevelt and his advisers were determined to avoid the mistakes of the Wilson administration, which failed to include legislators in planning and negotiating the League of Nations. Even before World War II ended, by contrast, the Roosevelt administration invited legislators to participate extensively in postwar planning. As a result, in 1945 the United Nations Charter was approved by the Senate by an overwhelming bipartisan vote (89 to 2).

Franklin D. Roosevelt's diplomacy was also *opportunistic* in the literal sense of the word: he took full advantage of opportunities that arose to pursue his goals abroad, and sometimes he deferred those goals when circumstances

19. Carl Maria von Clausewitz (1780–1831) was a Prussian officer who fought against Napoleon and was in time promoted to the rank of general. He is remembered for his celebrated posthumous treatise *On War*, in which he examined the relationship between the application of military force and the achievement of political objectives. A useful summary of his thought is Roger A. Leonard, *Clausewitz on War* (New York, 1967).

were unfavorable for their realization. Toward the end of the war, for example, he unquestionably relied on Moscow's interest in such questions as the future of Germany and Poland and the possibility of postwar American assistance to gain Soviet agreement for his new experiment in international organization, the United Nations. Roosevelt also took advantage of opportunities available during the war to exact concessions from the Soviet leader, Joseph Stalin, regarding the treatment of Soviet citizens by the communist regime.

Finally, the Roosevelt administration's foreign policy decisions not infrequently were influenced by *domestic political considerations.* In its endorsement of Zionist goals in Palestine, its strong advocacy of freedom for Poland and other Eastern European nations, its policies toward Nationalist China, and in other realms of external policy, New Deal diplomacy was responsive to internal political forces and calculations.

The Roosevelt administration's behavior in foreign affairs was thus pragmatic in the philosophical sense that it clearly reflected the pluralistic nature of the political universe within which diplomatic decisions are made and carried out. In contrast to most other interpretations of postwar American diplomacy, the pragmatic viewpoint also calls attention to the often crucial role of random and fortuitous factors, such as FDR's declining health and his charismatic personality, in shaping the course of post–World War II international relations. For at least some of the foreign policy decisions of the Roosevelt administration, these may well have been the most crucial factors influencing the American diplomatic record.[20]

Pragmatism and Democracy

As critics from time to time have assessed it, pragmatism fails to qualify as a true "philosophy" for several reasons, in part because it is not so much a coherent body of substantive ideas and concepts as it is an approach to truth. Many commentators are convinced that pragmatism offers merely a standard for validating truth but is devoid of substantive ideological content. This

20. Among the many informative studies of New Deal diplomacy are the following: Cordell Hull, *The Memoirs of Cordell Hull* (2 vols.; New York, 1948); William L. Langer and S. Everett Gleason, *The Challenge to Isolation, 1937–1940* (New York, 1952); James M. Burns, *Roosevelt: The Lion and the Fox* (New York, 1956); Robert E. Sherwood, *Roosevelt and Hopkins: An Intimate History* (New York, 1950); Warren F. Kimball (ed.), *Franklin D. Roosevelt and the World Crisis, 1937–1945* (Lexington, Mass., 1973); Gaddis Smith, *American Diplomacy During the Second World War, 1941–1945* (New York, 1966); Willard Range, *Franklin D. Roosevelt's World Order* (Athens, Ga., 1959); and Sumner Welles, *The Time for Decision* (New York, 1944).

interpretation, however, fails to recognize that pragmatic thinkers in the United States have been identified wth a reasonably distinct set of political principles and ideals. John Dewey, for example, is widely referred to as a tireless spokesman for liberal democracy in the United States and throughout the world. From the era of William James to the contemporary period, the thought of American's pragmatists leaves little doubt that they preferred certain political outcomes over others; they were convinced that, after applying the pragmatic standard for the validation of truth, some political results would ultimately be found to be more useful or beneficial for society than others.

Second, no serious doubt can exist that the pragmatists *presupposed the existence of certain political conditions* that were requisite for the pragmatic search for truth to occur. Some political environments are more conducive to the application of the pragmatic standard of truth than others; and, as we shall see, certain environments are highly inimical to—if not fatal for—the application of the pragmatic test of truth.

Third, this criticism of the pragmatic approach ignores one of the most fundamental tenets of pragmatism: the belief that "fact" and "value" are inseparable. In the pragmatic view, efforts by philosophers throughout history to separate fact from value not only have failed; they often have led to serious distortions in our understanding of the universe. As emphasized earlier, pragmatic thinkers rejected the idea of a sharp dichotomy between fact and value. To their minds, there is no such thing as value-free facts or fact-free values; both are found inextricably connected in experience, which serves as a laboratory for determining truth.

Among the political ideas most conspicuously associated with pragmatism is the concept of democracy. As in other aspects of their thought, pragmatists exhibited a deep and fervent commitment to the democratic ideal, which imparted to pragmatic thought much of its uniquely American quality. By democracy, the leading spokesmen for pragmatism meant *Western liberal democracy.* When they discussed the basic concepts, principles, and practices of democracy, James and Dewey nearly always took their examples from the experiences of the United States, Great Britain, France, Canada, and other Western democratic societies. The leading expositors of pragmatism did not conceal their bias toward, nor did they apologize for their undisguised preference for, democratic government.

William James's emphasis on the pluralistic nature of the universe led him naturally to value the same diversity in the political environment.

James's commitment to "meliorism" and gradual reform, to liberty, individualism, and the toleration of widely differing political viewpoints, along with his abhorrence of colonialism and war, reflected ideas already deeply embedded in the national ethos and identified with the American democratic system. Reflecting the nineteenth-century context of his thought, James tended in the main to equate democracy with the preservation and extension of individual rights, whereas Dewey's thought clearly reflected the twentieth-century emphasis on social, economic, cultural, and other connotations of democracy in their group or collective impact.[21]

Pragmatic philosophers found justification for democracy in the variations among the members of the species that Charles Darwin had observed in nature and that played a crucial role in the evolutionary process. The existence of such variations was essential for successful adaptation and evolution by the human species. Both James and Dewey deplored the tendency of democracy toward conformity, the degradation of standards and values, the vulgarization of language, literature, the arts, and other pursuits. A democratic society, however—especially one in which education was valued and supported—permitted the emergence of scientists, philosophers, scholars, and other "individuals of genius" who served as the inventors of society and who made indispensable contributions to its improvement and evolution.[22]

Pragmatists preferred democracy for another reason. The pragmatic method for validating truth—subjecting hypotheses and propositions to careful, objective, and ongoing examination in the laboratory of human experience—presupposed the existence of a democratic political order. (In both the contemporary period and earlier eras, valid scientific discoveries have occurred in nondemocratic political contexts, as in the Soviet Union or Nazi Germany. Despite such examples, pragmatic thinkers were convinced that the scientific method could be most consistently and optimally applied within a democratic setting.) The pursuit of knowledge and its application to human affairs requires certain conditions—the right to pursue truth objectively without fear of suppression for holding unpopular views, the right to criticize, freedom of speech, and the unhindered exchange of information across national frontiers—normally associated with democratic government. The ap-

21. John Dewey's views are quoted in Ignas K. Skrupskelis, *William James: A Reference Guide* (Boston, 1977), 117. See also Ralph Barton Perry, *The Thought and Character of William James* (New York, 1954), 295.

22. See William James's 1907 address "The Social Value of the College-Bred," in John K. Roth (ed.), *The Moral Equivalent of War and Other Essays* (New York, 1971), 17–25; and the excerpt from the analysis by Jack Lindeman, "William James and the Octopus of Higher Education," in Skrupskelis, *William James*, 168.

plication of new knowledge and insights also demands a willingness by society to change its institutions, behavior patterns, and public policies and political leaders in ongoing efforts to make them more responsive to human needs. Democracy, John Dewey contended, was "the best means so far found, for realizing ends that lie in the wide domain of human relationships and the development of human personality." In Dewey's view, democracy's essence is "the necessity for the participation of every mature human being in formation of the values that regulate the living of men together."[23]

As America's most distinctive contribution to the philosophical tradition, pragmatism has a natural and perhaps inevitable affinity for democracy. Both value open inquiry, experimentation, and a receptivity to change in all spheres of human activity. Particularly since the New Deal, American democracy has emphasized equality of opportunity, a concept fully consonant with Dewey's ideal of the highest development of human personality. To pragmatic minds, therefore, a democratic political system must be viewed as *sui generis*. It cannot be regarded merely as one among several possible systems of government. In Dewey's view, it was equivalent to "the ideas of community life itself" and the realization of the "experimental" social order he envisioned.[24]

Yet the pragmatic view of democracy is also characterized by the presence of several qualifications and caveats that go far toward counteracting its evident bias in favor of Western (specifically, American) political experience. Pragmatism, for example, does not equate democracy solely with America's or any other particular nation's institutions and political process. John Dewey's conception of democracy, for example, was closely akin to what is sometimes referred to as the "unwritten" British Constitution or the spirit of "fair play" in political life. As Dewey viewed it, democracy involved essentially a recognition of "the necessity for the participation of every mature human being in the formation of the values that regulate the living of men together." The common denominator was that a democratic system treats people humanely and provides ever-widening opportunities for their self-realization. There is, Dewey insisted, "no *a priori* rule" whereby "a good state will be brought into existence"; and "there is no form of state which can be said to be the best." As in all spheres of human life, the most desirable political institutions and processes must be created experimentally, by trial-and-error

23. Quoted in Joseph Ratner (ed.), *Intelligence in the Modern World: John Dewey's Philosophy* (New York, 1939), 100; and George R. Geiger, "Dewey's Social and Political Philosophy," in Paul A. Schilpp (ed.), *The Philosophy of John Dewey* (Evanston, 1939), 355.
24. See John Dewey, *Problems of Men* (New York, 1946), 157–58; and *Freedom and Culture*, 124–25, 148.

methods, and they must take full account of a particular society's values, traditions, and needs. Dewey cautioned that "democratic institutions are no guarantee for the existence of democratic individuals." Like truth itself, democracy is not a predetermined, unalterable, and static condition of the political order; societies (including the American) *become* democratic as they respond to concrete human problems and needs.[25]

In his approach to societies outside the United States, John Dewey's views reflected many of these ideas. During his travels to the Far East, for example, Dewey believed that, under Sun Yat-sen's leadership, a favorable prospect existed for the emergence of a distinctive version of democracy in republican China. Predictably, Dewey was convinced that the expansion of education would play a pivotal role in that process. Dewey was fully cognizant, however, that Chinese democracy would be unique, reflecting that country's own culture, values, and needs. Dewey also endeavored (with no conspicuous success) to persuade Japan's leaders to include democratic reforms as part of that country's modernization program.[26]

The pragmatic conception of democracy, however, must be carefully distinguished from what came to be called "participatory democracy" by certain political fringe groups during the 1960s and early 1970s, which often did not hesitate to employ violence and obstructionism to gain their ends. In Sidney Hook's view, the pragmatic understanding of democracy differed from participatory democracy because of the former's emphasis on the concept of majority rule; because of its belief that political elites and leaders are necessary for the successful operation of democratic governments; and above all, perhaps, because of its conviction that scientific inquiry and rational methods (rather than ideologically and emotionally based reactions) are indispensable for the functioning and extension of democracy.[27]

The pragmatic understanding of democracy provides valuable insight into one of the most important and, for Americans especially, mystifying global political phenomena since World War II: the emergence of novel and often highly disparate forms of democracy, particularly among newly inde-

25. Quoted in Ratner (ed.), *Intelligence in the Modern World*, 100; Dewey, *Freedom and Culture*, 124; see in Levi, *Philosophy and the Modern World*, 326; John Dewey, *The Public and Its Problems* (New York, 1927), 33; Wayne A. R. Leys, "Dewey's Social, Political, and Legal Philosophy," in Boydston (ed.), *Guide to the Works of John Dewey*, 143; George R. Geiger, "Dewey's Social and Political Philosophy," 353–54.

26. The impact of Dewey's thought on modern China is discussed in Ou Tsuin-Chen, "Dewey's Lectures and Influence in China," in Boydston (ed.), *Guide to the Works of John Dewey*, 361–63; Howlett, *Troubled Philosopher*, 46.

27. Sidney Hook, *Philosophy and Public Policy* (Carbondale, Ill., 1980), 172–73.

pendent Third World nations. This phenomenon has often bewildered and frustrated Americans. Paradoxically, sometimes the American society's understanding of it has been less perceptive than the Soviet or Chinese understanding. Admittedly, the invocation of democratic terminology, the use of democracy symbols, and the resort to ostensibly democratic political processes throughout the modern world have sometimes amounted to little more than ill-concealed efforts to disguise the reality of authoritarian or totalitarian rule. For a century and a half, for example, Latin America's verbal commitment to the democratic ideal has been legendary. In Eastern Europe, "peoples' democracy" today is often merely a synonym for communist hegemony. In most cases, even dictatorships find it necessary or useful to pay their respects to democracy by publicly using its concepts and rituals. (Even this hypocrisy, pragmatists would say, testifies to the existence of some deep impulse within the human species toward political growth and development in the direction of human freedom.)[28]

Allowing for such abuse, however, it remains true that since World War II throughout the Third World two apparently contradictory and antithetical political forces have been at work simultaneously. One is a strong commitment to the ideal or goal of democracy, derived in large part from exposure to Western experience and thought during the colonial period (but also derived in some instances from certain precolonial customs and traditional practices serving as democratic antecedents). The other force is the quest—it would not be an exaggeration in some cases to call it the compulsion—for national "identity" and self-realization among Third World societies. Politically, this quest has expressed itself in the belief that democracy is not a concept on which the United States or any other Western nation holds an exclusive patent. Just as democracy was a product of Western experience, new versions of it can and must reflect the experiences and needs of non-Western societies; and the precise meaning of democracy for a particular society must be defined by reference to its unique history, traditions, values, and goals. As pragmatic thinkers insisted, political leaders throughout the Third World have asserted in effect that democracy is an *evolving* concept, and the process of political evolution did not come to an end with the experience of the United States and other Western societies. Better acquaintance with the ideas of the philosophi-

28. See, for example, John Dewey's analysis of the prospects of democratic government in Turkey during the 1920s, in Jo Ann Boydston (ed.), *John Dewey: The Later Works, 1925–1953* (12 vols.; Carbondale, Ill., 1981), II, 181–210. See also Ratner (ed.), *Intelligence in the Modern World,* 100–101; and John Dewey, *Human Nature and Conduct: An Introduction to Social Psychology* (New York, 1930), 308.

cal pragmatists would equip Americans more adequately to comprehend this reality of the modern political universe and its implications. Expressed differently, it would prepare them to understand more intelligently, and to respond more constructively to, the "love-hate dichotomy" that has often been evident in America's relations with Third World nations in the postwar period.[29]

Pragmatic thinkers also discovered (it would be more accurate perhaps to say rediscovered) an idea that has preoccupied political scientists in recent years. This is the contribution made by elites to the democratic process. The strong pragmatic emphasis on democracy is also coupled with a twofold realization that elites exist, even within a democracy, and that they play an essential role in the operation of democratic government. The Western conception of democracy has always been intimately associated with the companion principle of egalitarianism. As Thomas Jefferson expressed it in the Declaration of Independence, "all men are created equal"; and the rallying cry of the French Revolution was "Liberty, Equality, and Fraternity." A basic requirement of American democracy is equality before the law. Since the New Deal at least, equality of opportunity has been added to the list of fundamental principles that are intrinsic to the existence of democracy.

Yet the leading pragmatic thinkers believed in egalitarianism and elitism concurrently! This was another paradox, however, that did not trouble William James and John Dewey. If it had to be attributed to some source, the blame lay with the nature of the political universe itself. Drawing upon Charles Darwin's findings, pragmatist thinkers believed that if evolutionary change were to occur, variations had to exist among the members of the human species; these variations were provided by an elite, or what William James described as a "natural aristocracy" distinguished by its insights into, and contributions in resolving, society's problems. The evolutionary process, James once asserted, depends upon the "educated intellect," whose only audience sometimes "is posterity." The existence of this elite serves as a corrective for a democratic society's tendency toward conformity, dullness, mediocrity, and apathy.[30]

From a different perspective, William James also recognized the decisive influence which gifted and forceful personalities have often exercised upon history. An Alexander the Great, a Napoleon, a Bismarck, a Wilson—in the more recent period, a Franklin D. Roosevelt, a Joseph Stalin, or a Winston

29. Democracy's meaning "is fixed in different ways in various cultural contexts." See Joseph L. Blau, *Men and Movements in American Philosophy* (Englewood Cliffs, N.J., 1955), 352–53.

30. See Skrupskelis, *William James*, 168; Perry, *Thought and Character of William James*, 240; and James's address "The Social Value of the College-Bred," 17–25.

Churchill—can have a momentous impact not only upon their own societies but upon the world. (As we shall see, James and other pragmatists were aware that this impact might be detrimental to, no less than beneficial for, human well-being.) As an ardent advocate of individualism, James was persuaded that "the true meaning of a moral idea is most obvious when a single man rises to challenge the status quo."[31]

Power, Violence, and Revolution

The Great Seal of the United States (printed on the back of every one-dollar bill) provides a graphic illustration of the ambivalence in the American mind toward the exercise of power in international political relationships. In one claw, the American eagle clutches a quiver of arrows; in the other, it holds the olive branch of peace. The eagle itself is both a symbol of great beauty and majesty, but it is no less a predator and a symbol of power and ferocity.

As America's most distinctive philosophy, pragmatism thus reflects the long-standing dualism in the American mentality about the concept of power. Americans routinely acknowledge the central importance of power in countless dimensions of human life; they rely upon power in many forms to achieve the "American way of life," particularly in its more innovative aspects; they extol the "power of positive thinking," the power of advertising, the principle that "knowledge is power," and—a concept that was invoked repeatedly to justify the nation's long attachment to an isolationist foreign policy—the power of example.

At the same time, Americans have traditionally been uncomfortable with, and suspicious of, the concept of power, especially in the political realm. They made the doctrine of separation of powers the foundation stone of their constitutional system, and they divided the power to rule between the national government and the states. Many of the constitutional amendments adopted after 1787 imposed restraints upon the powers of the national government and the states. The long-standing aversion to a standing army in the United States—expressed tangibly in popular opposition to conscription for raising military manpower except during periods of national crisis—is another manifestation of this popular aversion to power. Concepts like "power politics," "balance of power," and "power struggles" have never been popu-

31. See William James's view as cited in Paul K. Conkin, *Puritans and Pragmatists: Eight Eminent American Thinkers* (Bloomington, 1976), 333–37; and Patrick J. Dooley, *Pragmatism as Humanism: The Philosophy of William James* (Chicago, 1974), 77–78.

lar in the United States. Leaders who employed such terms (and a prominent example from recent diplomatic experience was Henry Kissinger during his career as the president's national security adviser and as secretary of state) have encountered considerable resistance and unpopularity from Congress and the American people.

Pragmatism faces this dualism about power in the American mind squarely and in several respects mirrors it. According to some critics, whose approach to political relationships is explicitly power-oriented, pragmatism lacks a "tragic sense of history." The thought of the genteel William James especially is sometimes viewed as much too "civilized," Victorian, and humane to provide guidance for a world that has witnessed two global wars and innumerable local and regional conflicts, has lived with the ever-present threat of nuclear annihilation, and in recent years has confronted a significant increase in international terrorism. It is a serious misconstruction of the thought of William James, John Dewey, and their followers, however, to believe that they were oblivious to the role of power and force, or what the theologian often calls the problem of evil, in human political behavior.[32]

The leading pragmatic thinkers have always acknowledged the power-seeking propensities of individuals, groups, and nations. Moreover, they understood the key role of power in determining political outcomes. Pragmatists have been fully aware that throughout history, human controversies have often been resolved by recourse to violence. They were cognizant not only that this tendency existed, but that if unchecked it jeopardized the future of human civilization. John Dewey, of course, lived long enough to witness the rise of modern totalitarianism, World War II, and the dawn of the nuclear age, and he became aware of at least some of the fateful implications of this new era for international politics.

More than once, James referred to the "ultimate cruelty of the universe" and of the "appetite for destruction that was discernible within it." Man, James believed, perpetually confronted "real evil, real crises," and "catastrophes." In James's pluralistic universe, "beauty and hideousness . . . life and death keep house together in this indissoluble partnership." Citing the views of the German philosopher Arthur Schopenhauer, James cautioned against "the illusoriness of the notion of uninterrupted moral progress by mankind," since the "more brutal forms of evil that go are replaced by others more subtle and more poisonous." To James's mind the universe is "enigmatical" and

32. Max Lerner, *America as a Civilization: Life and Thought in the United States Today* (New York, 1957), 397–98.

vulnerable; it is "liable to be injured by certain of its parts if they act wrong."[33]

According to one of his leading biographers, James condemned these and all other forms of moral or philosophical "escapism" that pretended that the problem of evil did not exist, that it would soon disappear, or that worthwhile and constructive human efforts would always triumph over violent, egocentric, aberrant, and other forms of antisocial behavior. Mankind, in James's view, was engaged in a "heroic struggle" against what he identified variously as "sick souls," "predatory lusts," the "animal instinct," the "powers of darkness," and comparable forces inimical to human well-being. Yet in James's concept of human nature and the "heroic life," the notion is implicit that power is a legitimate and necessary instrument for the achievement of worthwhile human purposes. As James made clear in "The Moral Equivalent of War," how a society uses its power is the central problem: the consequences of its use ultimately determine power's legitimacy.[34]

Similarly, John Dewey acknowledged that "chaos and anarchy are with us" in the environment; they are normal and seemingly are also ineradicable components of the political milieu; and by some criteria these conditions appeared to be even more prevalent in the modern era than in earlier stages of history. Throughout his life, Dewey so strongly advocated the principle of the peaceful resolution of political disputes and issues as to convince some people that he was a pacifist. Yet this characterization seems hard to defend, when it is noted that Dewey favored America's entry into World War I. Although he was much less enthusiastic about the nation's participation in World War II and was convinced that certain real dangers would accompany that act, Dewey nevertheless also opposed Axis expansionism. Time and again, he denounced the barbarities committed by totalitarian governments, and he pointed out that sometimes a surgeon must excise diseased tissue to promote the good health and recovery of the patient. In brief, in his attitude toward war Dewey might be called a typical American: he abhorred it, tried to avoid participation in it, was convinced that mankind must develop less violent methods of resolving political disputes, but (as in World War II) could think of no alternative under certain circumstances but to use armed force to promote society's well-being and security. Dewey's analysis of what he believed was

33. William James, *A Pluralistic Universe* (Cambridge, Mass., 1977), 41–45; *The Will to Believe and Other Essays in Popular Philosophy* (Cambridge, Mass., 1979), 6; *The Will to Believe* (New York, 1903), 131, 136; and "Is Life Worth Living?" in Roth (ed.), *Moral Equivalent of War and Other Essays*, 66–89.

34. See Ralph Barton Perry, "If William James Were Alive Today," in *In Commemoration of William James* (New York, 1942), 78–80; James's essay "The Moral Equivalent of War," in Joseph L. Blau (ed.), *William James's Pragmatism and Other Essays* (New York, 1963), 289–303.

America's principal mistake after World War I testifies to the paradoxical nature of his thought: it lay in the nation's failure to use its armed forces decisively to achieve the lasting peace that was consonant with America's announced war aims and with Dewey's conception of a just postwar order![35]

As storm clouds gathered in Europe and Asia during the 1930s, John Dewey was at the forefront of those Americans who urged the United States to preserve its traditional isolationist stance and to adhere to a policy of non-intervention in any new global conflict. Dewey believed that participation in another war would be a disaster for America and would release anti-democratic forces at home and abroad. Dewey supported efforts (culminating in the Kellog-Briand Pact in 1928) to outlaw war as an instrument of national policy; he remained unenthusiastic about the League of Nations as a peace-keeping mechanism, believing it to be unrepresentative of the views of the people and dominated by the power-seeking, revenge-minded nations of the Old World.[36]

For John Dewey, the gathering political storm precipitated by Axis expansionism involved agonizing decisions and diverse judgments that could not be embraced within a single, consistent viewpoint. With the vast majority of Americans, Dewey remained devoted to the isolationist credo and urged policy makers in Washington to avoid involvement in a new world conflict. Dewey also abhorred totalitarianism, recognized the danger it posed to global peace and well-being, and believed that Axis demands must be resisted. In the words of Charles F. Howlett, Dewey "abhorred the Nazi mentality and wished to see it crushed." In 1939 he joined a new organization opposed to totalitarianism; thereafter, his attacks on fascism and communism were unrelenting.[37]

After Pearl Harbor, Dewey supported the war effort halfheartedly and with little evident enthusiasm about the results to be expected from it. Dewey had little confidence in the new United Nations to maintain global peace, and he was deeply concerned that the emerging cold war between the United States and the Soviet Union would plunge the world into a new international conflict, in the process impairing democracy at home and abroad. In the last years of his life, Dewey called attention to the rapid advance of science (es-

35. Dewey, *Problems of Men*, 175–76; Merle Curti, *Peace or War: The American Struggle, 1636–1936* (New York, 1936), 258; and for a commentary emphasizing Dewey's pacificistic inclinations, see Howlett, *Troubled Philosopher*, 20–42.

36. Howlett, *Troubled Philosopher*, 40–42; and Dewey's views on the reasons for America's attachment to its historic policy of isolationism in Boydston (ed.), *John Dewey*, II, 167–72.

37. See Howlett, *Troubled Philosopher*, 146–47; and Dykhuizen, *Life and Mind of John Dewey*, 291.

pecially in its military applications) vis-à-vis the slower progress of mankind in applying scientific truths to social, economic, and political affairs. Ultimately, Dewey believed, only an enlightened, educated, and concerned public opinion could prevent international conflicts and apply his "method of intelligence" to the resolution of political controversies.[38]

John Dewey's pacifistic inclinations are undeniable, but his opinions on the subjects of war and violence exhibited the same ambivalence discernible in the thought of William James and countless American citizens in the twentieth century. Dewey neither venerated nor denigrated the crucial role of power in human relationships. He viewed power in ethically neutral terms; it meant essentially the "effective means of operation," and it denoted man's "ability or capacity to execute, to realize ends." Power was thus "the sum of conditions available for bringing the desirable end into existence." On one hand, Dewey rejected what he called the "sentimental" or romantic conception of power, the idea (common to many idealists throughout history) that power could be ignored or wished out of existence. Power was essential for building bridges and roads, for manufacturing, for progress in agriculture, for law enforcement, for scientific investigations, and for countless other worthwhile human pursuits.

On the other hand, wars among nations and conflicts among groups and between individuals were also examples of power, as were natural disasters like floods, hurricanes, and volcanic eruptions. The justification for the use of power (and on this question, pragmatic thought drew heavily from the earlier teachings of the nineteenth-century utilitarians) lay in the concept of what Dewey called "effectiveness." The relevant question always was the relationship between the use of power and the promotion of human well-being. If a close relationship existed, then reliance on power was justified; if not, the use of power was morally, ethically, and practically questionable. "The serious charge against the State," Dewey once wrote, "is not that it used force—nothing was ever accomplished without using force—but that it does not use it wisely or effectively." The standard for determining effectiveness was the familiar pragmatic test: What are the observable consequences for human society of relying upon power to accomplish a given end?[39]

Philosophically, therefore, pragmatism once again assumed a midway position between ideological antinomies. William James and John Dewey were overtly contemptuous of the "romantic" view of power (as expressed,

38. Howlett, *Troubled Philosopher*, 144–53.
39. Boydston (ed.), *John Dewey*, I, 320.

for example, in many of the statements of President Woodrow Wilson), believing this approach to be naive, utopian, and dangerous. (In actuality, of course, even Wilson relied on his own vast power over public opinion at home and abroad, and on his position as leader of the most powerful nation in World War I, to gain support for his political objectives.)

Yet pragmatism no less rejected the Old World or *Realpolitik* conception of power, which seeks to divorce its possession and use from the promotion of legitimate human ends. With millions of other Americans, the proponents of pragmatism were unwilling to accept the notion that the pursuit of power *per se* is a legitimate rationale for domestic and international political behavior; that the creation and preservation of a "balance of power" is the highest goal of statecraft; or that international politics involves an endless cycle of power conflicts whose outcome is determined by the respective power of the participants.

The pragmatic assessment of power becomes more meaningful when it is applied specifically to three problems that have been at the forefront of modern international relations: imperialism, war, and revolution. William James was one of the earliest and most vocal opponents of imperialism, and by the end of the nineteenth century, in the wake of the Spanish-American War, he was outspoken in warning American society against engaging in it. Nor did James favor the strong foreign policy championed by Captain Alfred T. Mahan, Theodore Roosevelt, and other influential Americans at the turn of the century. James denounced the war fever that had led to the conflict with Spain; he deplored demagogic and superpatriotic appeals to chauvinism that erupted from time to time within the American society; and he rejected the notion that America had a "great destiny" to play abroad, requiring it to become increasingly powerful and interventionist in dealing with other countries. James cautioned Americans about the dangers of trying to serve as what he called "missionaries of civilization" throughout the world. James's ideas today seem remarkably akin to those of certain anti–Vietnam War critics and others who have warned Americans about the deleterious consequences of endeavoring to serve as "the policeman of the world." John Dewey was similarly critical of America's Open Door policy toward China, viewing it as merely an ill-disguised form of imperialism. Dewey was also skeptical about the League of Nations (and later about the United Nations) in part because strong imperial interests would most likely control its deliberations and actions.[40]

40. See, for example, Perry, *Thought and Character of William James*, 245–46; Gay W. Allen (ed.), *A William James Reader* (Boston, 1971), 222–24; J. William Fulbright, *The Arrogance of Power* (New York, 1966); and Howlett, *Troubled Philosopher*, 24, 56–57.

One of William James's most widely circulated essays was "The Moral Equivalent of War" (1910), in which he dealt with one of human society's most durable and influential behavior patterns: the tendency of nations and smaller social units to resolve their differences by recourse to war. "Military feelings," James declared, are "deeply grounded" in human nature, and, as experience had demonstrated, they will be extremely difficult to eradicate. Modern man, said James, "inherits all the innate pugnacity and all the love of glory of his ancestors"; the record of human history has been "a bath of blood." The evidence convinced James that mankind liked violent behavior. War and other forms of violence entailed certain economic, political, psychological, and other rewards and gratifications that made human society loath to give up violent behavior, despite all the rational, moral-ethical, emotional, and other appeals that it do so. War and violence engender such virtues as faith, tenacity, heroism, conscience, inventiveness, vigor, a closer sense of community, sacrifice, and other noble human qualities. To James's mind, there was only one feasible answer to the problem: a "moral equivalent of war" or a new set of habits that retained many of the same features associated with war but without its bloodshed and destruction. Yet in calling for a moral equivalent to war, James knew that it would be extremely difficult to achieve, and the prospects for successfully doing so were not overly bright.[41]

William James's compatriot in the cause of pragmatism, John Dewey, was no less dedicated to the goal of world peace. As he witnessed the gathering of the war clouds during the 1930s, Dewey time and again urged the nations of the world to resolve their differences by peaceful means, and he advocated American nonintervention in any new global conflict. Yet devoted as he was to the cause of peace, Dewey was no less outspoken in denouncing other evils that also threatened the future of civilization—specifically, the threat of totalitarianism in the form of Nazism, communism, Japanese militarism, and other systems that oppressed their own citizens and endangered the security and well-being of other societies. On one occasion, Dewey labeled Nazism "by all odds the greatest threat to world peace today." Dewey was also one of the earliest influential Americans to call attention to the oppressive and dangerous features of the Soviet regime. Following the Japanese attack on Pearl Harbor, Dewey reluctantly reached the same conclusion shared by millions of other Americans: the United States now had no alternative except to defend itself and to use its vast power to assure an Allied victory in the war.[42] Dewey's subsequent endorsement of the war effort clearly lacked enthusiasm; and it

41. See James, "Moral Equivalent of War," 289–303.
42. Dewey's views on the Nazi menace are quoted in Howlett, *Troubled Philosopher*, 133.

was matched by his conviction that internal dangers (such as reliance on the emergency powers of the national government and an increasingly strong presidency to curtail the rights of citizens) also posed new dangers to American freedom. Nor could Dewey muster much enthusiasm for the nascent United Nations organization, created in 1945. He was skeptical that the United Nations would fundamentally alter the nature of international political relationships (and events after 1945 indicated that his forebodings were amply justified).

Dewey's views on the ensuing Soviet-American cold war tended to be in the same vein. He was highly critical of it and believed both superpowers shared the responsibility for postwar conditions of international tension and instability; and he was extremely apprehensive about its long term implications. Yet Dewey was never able to formulate a feasible alternative to America's containment policy, which did avoid the twin dangers of a new international conflagration and acquiescence in ongoing Soviet expansionism. Characteristically for pragmatic thinkers, Sidney Hook asked critics what their alternative was to America's cold war strategy of containment. He responded that there were only two. One was American acceptance of piecemeal Soviet expansionism and intervention in the internal affairs of other nations. Hook reminded his fellow citizens that during the 1930s, the policy of "appeasement" had not produced peace; it had led ultimately to the most destructive war known to history. The other alternative was all-out or "preventive war" against the Soviet Union. Whatever its defects, Hook was convinced that the containment strategy was an infinite improvement over either of these alternative policies. A fourth possibility—the creation of a sense of international community—is a long-term goal of pragmatic thinkers, but it is likely to be achieved very slowly, on the basis of incremental decision making advocated by John Dewey and other pragmatists. Hook pointed out that the term *cold war* also implies what we might call "cold peace," or limited collaboration with the Soviet Union implicit in the term *détente*. In fact, since the Vietnam War Soviet-American relations have been characterized by suspicion and limited cooperation.[43]

The pragmatic analysis of the problem of war reflected the same assessment that has for the most part guided American foreign policy in the new era of internationalism since World War II. This approach has usually steered a middle course between two philosophical extremes. On one hand, it has rejected the Old World or *Realpolitik* position or the notion that power politics is

43. See Hook, *Philosophy and Public Policy,* 105–107; Dewey, *Problems of Men,* 185–89; and *The Public and Its Problems,* 128–31.

a legitimate synonym for international relations; that the United States may permissibly employ its vast power anywhere in the world to achieve its goals, as calculations based on national interest dictate; and that moral-ethical and ideological principles are irrelevant to the conduct of international affairs. Acceptance by the United States of a military stalemate in the Korean War, and the eventual liquidation of the American military commitment in the Vietnam War in response to adverse public opinion at home and abroad, provide persuasive evidence that Americans are unwilling to be guided in foreign relations by an explicitly power-oriented doctrine of political behavior.

On the other hand, the pragmatic mode of thought no less rejects the idea—expressed most graphically in the pacifistic or "better red than dead" position—that a nation's reliance on military and lesser forms of power is inherently evil and impermissible. Pragmatic thought acknowledges that power is a crucially important element in political relationships. The United States cannot be oblivious to its own power or that of other countries, particularly its diplomatic adversaries. By acquiescence at least, even John Dewey conceded the principle that has in the main guided American foreign policy since World War II: in a pluralistic, vulnerable, and unpredictable political universe, some dangers or evils are worse than war and lesser forms of violence in human affairs.

William James died in 1910 and did not witness the two great global wars of modern history or the rise of totalitarian governments. Any attempt to apply his ideas to such phenomena must necessarily be speculative and contingent. Yet James once said that "evils must be checked in time, before they grow so great" as to make it impossible to eliminate them. James was also an outspoken opponent of bigness in all its forms, especially in government; and he was a tireless champion of individual freedom. He believed that what he called the "powers of darkness" frequently took advantage of expressions of sympathy and friendship toward them. For these reasons, some students of James's thought believe, he would have advocated resistance to tyranny and the goal of human freedom. John Dewey believed that any decision to employ military force had always to be made in a specific context of time, circumstances, and events. Sometimes reliance on force might be the least unpalatable alternative available to policy makers. In any decision to use force, Dewey was convinced, policy makers must understand that inevitably the political environment will be altered, and a host of new problems will result from their actions.[44]

44. Elizabeth P. Aldrich (ed.), *As William James Said: Extracts from the Published Writings of William James* (New York, 1942), 150; and Perry, "If William James Were Alive Today," 75–77.

A third concrete problem illustrating the pragmatic viewpoint toward violent political behavior is revolution. The concept of revolution gained currency from the French Revolution at the end of the eighteenth century, and in more recent history, it was given new impetus (and for some groups, respectability) by the Communist Revolution in Russia in 1917. The post–World War II external political environment has often been described as revolutionary. The challenge of American diplomacy, according to some commentators, is to respond constructively to the demands of a revolutionary age, particularly throughout the Third World. Conversely, recent American foreign policy has been condemned by some critics because of its antirevolutionary orientation and its refusal to come to terms with radical change throughout the world.[45]

The pragmatic view of revolutionary political change should be predictable. Reflecting the teachings of Charles Darwin, pragmatism advocated *evolutionary* change in all spheres of human experience. This idea also, of course, echoed the traditional American preference for gradual, trial-and-error methods of change, as well as the historical American aversion to political extremism.

Pragmatism's position on revolution was well illustrated by John Dewey's analysis of Marxism. Dewey became a highly controversial figure in some quarters because from time to time he overtly commended some of the goals and accomplishments of the Soviet regime after 1917. Dewey also cautioned Americans against engaging in emotional and dangerous anticommunist crusades (such as swept the United States after World War I and during the McCarthy era in the early post–World War II era). Nor did Dewey believe that all the blame for the emergence of the cold war could be attributed solely to the Soviet Union.[46]

Yet after 1917, John Dewey and most of his fellow pragmatists became increasingly disenchanted with Soviet communism and vocally critical of the Kremlin's behavior at home and abroad. For their part, defenders of the Soviet system came to view pragmatism—particularly Dewey's version of it—as little more than a rationalization of the bourgeois American mentality and as a philosophical apology for anticommunist behavior at home and abroad.[47]

45. Richard J. Barnet, *Intervention and Revolution: America's Confrontation with Insurgent Movements Around the World* (New York, 1968), 8–10.
46. Howlett, *Troubled Philosopher*, 140–41.
47. George Novack, *Pragmatism Versus Marxism: An Appraisal of John Dewey's Philosophy* (New York, 1975).

Dewey opposed Marxist ideology for several reasons, not least because of the conflict between its scientific pretensions and its patently unscientific methodology and *a priori* conclusions. It was ironic, Dewey observed, that Marxism, "the theory which has made the most display and the greatest pretense of having a scientific foundation should be the one which has violated most systematically every principle of the scientific method." The fundamental error of Marxism, Dewey believed, lay in its assumption that "a generalization that was made at a particular date and place" in history can "obviate the need for continued resort to observation, and to continual revision of generalizations in their office of working hypotheses."[48]

To Dewey's mind, Marxism was a prime example of a monolithic or "block" system of thought that was incapable of accounting for the existence of a pluralistic universe. Marxism was also a deterministic philosophy in that it made man a prisoner of economic forces over which he had little control and which he was powerless to change. Moreover, Marxism's so-called laws of history were in reality little more than crude adaptations of ideas already expressed by Hegel. Dewey was also extremely critical of Marx's dismissal of moral and ethical values as having no intrinsic importance for, or influence upon, society's behavior.

Even more fundamentally, Dewey indicted Marxism because it failed the pragmatic test: on the basis of experience since 1917, communism had not fulfilled the idealistic promises made by the instigators of the Bolshevik Revolution but had degenerated into what Dewey called a dictatorship and a "terrifying menace," which sought to crush freedom within Soviet society and to endanger its future in other countries. Soviet behavior, as Dewey assessed it, was "Byzantine" and inimical to human well-being. In the USSR, the "dictatorship of the proletariat" had in fact become the dictatorship "of the party over the proletariat," which, in turn, was replaced by the "dictatorship of a small band of bureaucrats over the party." To maintain itself in power, the Communist party was compelled to adopt "with greatly improved technical skills in execution, all the repressive measures of the overthrown Czarist despotism."[49]

Launched as a movement that professed to believe in equality, the Communist party of the Soviet Union had in reality achieved "great inequality of income" among the Soviet people, had imposed "one-party control" over nearly all aspects of Soviet society, and had engaged in "ruthless persecution"

48. Dewey, *Freedom and Culture,* 101, 87.
49. *Ibid.,* 168–70.

and suppression of dissent in an effort to perpetuate its own power. Instead of the "withering away of the state," as anticipated by Marxism, the opposite had occurred: the Soviet state had steadily become more powerful, more all-pervasive, and more detrimental to the interests of the workers and others in whose name the revolution had been undertaken. As Dewey analyzed it, Soviet experience provided an especially poignant example of a tendency that existed in, and was perhaps intrinsic to, all human endeavors: the displacement of the ends of policy by the means employed to achieve them, with the result that in time *the means become the ends.* In effect, this is what occurred in the USSR after 1917, and it was a likely outcome whenever insufficient attention was devoted to the crucial interrelationship between policy ends and means.[50]

As an American credo, pragmatism reflected a long-standing ambivalence in the American mind about the most effective method of achieving social, economic, and political change. All Americans, of course, are conscious of their own nation's successful revolution against British rule; and most are aware that to the minds of Old World political leaders, the concept of democracy was viewed as a revolutionary ideology having profound and disturbing implications for established governments and political movements throughout the world.

At the same time, Americans tended to view their own political revolution not as a discrete event in history but as an ongoing process of change, carried out daily, weekly, and monthly by millions of citizens and their leaders in all dimensions of national life. Ralph Waldo Emerson, for example, once called the legislative branch a "standing insurrection" against problems and conditions that impaired the good life for Americans.[51] America's "great experiment" in democratic government was a continuing phenomenon, as the meaning of democracy was continually redefined in light of new challenges and conditions.

The unique and paradoxical conception of revolution in the American ethos entailed the application of intelligence, flexibility, and foresight in the solution of national problems, expressing itself in an "ability to maintain the institutions of the past while remaking them to suit new conditions." Or as

50. Dewey, *Freedom and Culture,* 84–92; and see Boydston (ed.), *John Dewey,* II, 178; Dewey, *Human Nature and Conduct,* 273; and Dewey's conclusions about Soviet communism as a result of the trial and assassination of Leon Trotsky in the late 1930s, in James T. Farrell, "Dewey in Mexico," in Sidney Hook (ed.), *John Dewey: Philosopher of Science and Freedom* (New York, 1950), 351–77.

51. Arthur M. Schlesinger, *The American as Reformer* (Cambridge, Mass., 1951), 8.

Charles L. Sanford concluded, Americans were "inveterate reformers." In reality, since the earliest days of colonization and settlement, Americans have been engaged in "permanent revolution" devoted to achieving progress in social, economic, political, and other realms of national life. Or, as the eminent anthropologist Margaret Mead expressed it, Americans have traditionally believed that human problems could be solved "by purposeful thought and experimentation," a predisposition she related to the old Puritan idea that man was saved "by *intelligent* works." Earlier, John Dewey described most social, economic, and political problems confronting mankind as "engineering problems" that could and should be solved by the application of scientific and creative thought. For pragmatic philosophers, as for millions of Americans for two centuries or more, the effect of accumulated changes over time might be revolutionary; but the preferred method of achieving this result was *evolutionary,* usually consisting of piecemeal, gradual, and trial-and-error innovations and adjustments, introduced after experience indicated they were necessary and desirable.[52]

Pragmatism's attitude toward Marxism and other revolutionary political movements was also derived from the Jamesian concept of "habituation." Drawing on Hegel's thought, the pragmatists believed that the lessons a society learned from experience led to habitual conduct, which was in turn expressed in its traditions, institutions, laws, and customary behavior patterns. These habits evolved and were gradually modified, as new evidence and new experiences in time convinced society that changes were desirable.

By contrast, in their desire to achieve a sudden and radical alteration of society, revolutionaries customarily ignored habituation as a force that would almost certainly frustrate their efforts. "Habituations to the old persist long after the old has changed its form," John Dewey once wrote. The deeply ingrained habits of society are seldom changed "by what are deemed revolutions by those who record the course of history." Instead, the actual effect of revolutionary efforts is to create new and disruptive tensions produced by the conflict between the persisting habits of a society and required changes in its overt behavior, which will likely engender "confusion and conflict" within it for a prolonged period in the future. To Dewey's mind, the tendency of societies toward habituation was comparable to the concept of the momentum possessed by a physical body that has been set in motion along a certain path.

52. Richard Hofstadter, *Social Darwinism in American Thought, 1860–1915* (Philadelphia, 1945), 118; Charles L. Sanford, *The Quest for Paradise* (Urbana, Ill., 1961), 176–78; Margaret Mead, *And Keep Your Powder Dry: An Anthropologist Looks at America* (New York, 1965), 207; Dewey's views are quoted in Damico, *Individuality and Community,* 61.

(According to Newton's laws of motion, the body's tendency is to remain in motion along this course.) "Habit," said Dewey, "not original human nature keeps things moving most of the time, about as they have moved in the past." Neglect of this fact was a primary reason why revolutionary political movements rarely achieved their proclaimed goals. As in the Soviet case, "instead of the sweeping revolution which was expected," what actually occurred was "a transfer of vested power from one class to another." In more general terms, the projected "new order" for society that serves as the revolutionary vision is almost never accomplished because society continues to base its attitudes and behavior on habituation.[53]

One final pragmatic objection to revolutionary methods of political change remains to be mentioned. In the pragmatic analysis, all aspects of human society are subject to evolutionary change, *including methods of investigating human problems and effecting change in human relationships*. In Dewey's view, failure to understand this reality was one of the cardinal defects of Marxism. Basing their revolutionary program on evidence derived from the nineteenth century and earlier eras, Marx and his followers failed to realize two key facts: new evidence in the years that followed (as in the fundamental changes that occurred in the nature of American capitalism) in time made many of Marxism's conclusions obsolete; and advances in the scientific method and other modes of investigation increasingly made Marxism's claims to "scientific" validity highly questionable. For these reasons, in Dewey's words, "The radical who insists that the future method of change must be like that of the past has much in common with the hide-bound reactionary who holds to the past as an ultimate fact. Both overlook the *fact that history in being a process of changes generates change not only in details but also in the method of directing social change.*" Dewey believed that "mankind now has in its possession a new method, that of cooperative and experimental science which expressed the method of intelligence"—pragmatism.[54]

Any reasonably well-informed citizen who is familiar with the course of international politics since World War II can think of innumerable examples illustrating the relevance of the pragmatic critique of Marxism and other revolutionary movements, particularly in the Third World. From Latin America to East Asia, revolutionary groups have encountered deep-seated "traditionalism" (or habituation), which has in many cases frustrated their political

53. Dewey, *Problems of Men,* 190; *The Public and Its Problems,* 159–60; and Boydston (ed.), *John Dewey,* III, 205–206, 336.
54. See John J. McDermott (ed.), *The Philosophy of John Dewey* (2 vols.; New York, 1973), II, 659.

aspirations or, at a minimum (as in the recent experience of China), ultimately required ongoing and wholesale modifications in the regime's once ideologically rigid program.

As is true of certain other important aspects of their thought, in their approach to the problem of political change, the pragmatists occupied a midway position on the ideological spectrum. Against the views of ultraconservatives and reactionaries, for example, James, Dewey, and other pragmatists emphasized that preserving the political *status quo* is impossible, not to speak of the reactionary's hope of retreating into some imagined idyllic past. Reflecting the American preference for gradualism and reform, pragmatic thought advocated innovations in human affairs by methods variously described as melioristic, reformist, gradualist, incremental, and experimental. Thus in one of his speeches, President John F. Kennedy cited an observation by Thomas Jefferson that Americans had created a nation that would always be "in the full tide of successful experiment." Kennedy added that historically Americans had always believed "in progress by evolution, not revolution." For this reason, it could accurately be said that the United States "is the most dynamic nation in history.[55]

The United States has nearly always approached the issue of political change abroad on the basis of several fairly consistent presuppositions: (1) that socioeconomic and political change in other societies is desirable and should be encouraged; (2) that such change is inevitable, and attempts to prevent it are unrealistic and futile; (3) that change should be gradual and directed so as to involve minimum disruption to society, preserving its distinctive and valuable features; (4) that political stability and the prospects for democracy are enhanced to the extent that incumbent governments provide evidence of progress in instituting change and directing it constructively; (5) that experience should serve as the guide for determining the usefulness of particular innovations; and (6) that revolutionary political upheavals—especially those instigated and massively aided by the Soviet Union and its proxies (such as Cuba and North Vietnam)—will in the end produce more losses than gains for the society in question and will often jeopardize international peace and security.[56]

55. Kennedy's views are cited in Oscar Handlin (ed.), *American Principles and Issues: The National Purpose* (New York, 1961), 4–5; Schlesinger, *The American as Reformer*, 7–9; and Hofstadter, *Social Darwinism in American Thought*, 118.

56. As a recent example, see the change that has occurred in congressional attitudes toward the government of El Salvador, based primarily upon the latter's performance in carrying out democratic reforms, as reported in the New York *Times*, August 10, 1984, dispatch by Philip Taubman.

The keynote of this approach to the challenge of political change abroad was sounded early in 1947, when President Harry S. Truman enunciated the containment policy in connection with communist threats to Greece and Turkey. Neither country, Truman was fully aware, had political systems that met the American standard of democracy. Yet Truman was convinced that both countries required American assistance. Without it, the people and leaders of Greece "cannot make progress in solving their problems of reconstruction" and in restoring "internal order and security so essential for economic and political recovery." American aid would be used by Greece "in creating a stable and self-sustaining economy and in improving its public administration." The goal was to enable Greece to become "a self-supporting and self-respecting democracy." Truman acknowledged that the government of Greece was not perfect; it had well-publicized "defects," but it was capable of evolving in a democratic direction, and this process could occur only within a political atmosphere of stability and security. Toward Greece and Turkey, as toward other nations, the United States sought to "ensure the peaceful development of nations," free from coercion by antidemocratic movements at home and abroad. The purpose of American aid was to enable other societies "to work out their own destiny in their own way." Congress agreed with Truman's assessment and adopted the Greek-Turkish Aid Program by substantial majorities in the House and Senate.[57]

Goals, Planning, and the Concept of Community

A fundamental principle of pragmatic thought is that the cognitive process is directed toward the perception, analysis, and solution of immediate and concrete problems confronting the human species. In the pragmatic view, creative mental activity is essentially an exercise in problem solving.

Applied to the realm of foreign affairs, this tenet of pragmatism has several important corollaries. A nation's goals, for example, tend to be defined in no small measure by the problems and conditions it confronts abroad; and a society becomes aware of these conditions as it responds to challenges in the external environment, which often arise randomly, unexpectedly, and in no predictable sequence.

57. See the text of Truman's message to Congress on March 12, 1947, in *Public Papers of the Presidents of the United States: Harry S. Truman, 1947* (Washington, D.C., 1963), 176–80; and the discussion of the Greek-Turkish Aid Program in Truman's memoirs, *Years of Trial and Hope, 1946–1952* (Garden City, N.Y., 1956), 93–109.

From the pragmatic conception of the cognitive process also it follows that a nation's goals must be ranked in at least a crudely hierarchical order of priority. Some goals are more important and urgent than others. All states have what are sometimes called vital interests, and they have numerous second- and third-rank goals—merging into what become little more than visions and dreams—having little or no claim against their national resources.

Although these facts about a nation's foreign policy might appear to be axiomatic, the pragmatic approach emphasizes that the priority assigned to foreign policy goals will be determined in large part by the specific context within which diplomatic decision making occurs at any given time. As America has discovered on innumerable occasions since World War II, in most instances choices must be made between or among goals that are, in the abstract and in isolation, equally legitimate as objectives of national policy.[58] Thus, during World War II the United States had to choose between defeating the Axis threat and allying itself with nondemocratic governments abroad. As the war developed, the Roosevelt administration had to make a choice between close cooperation with the Soviet Union, in the interests of assuring an Allied victory, and refusal to do so, to avoid ideological contamination and identification with a totalitarian regime. It chose the former course.

After the war, at some point every administration in Washington has confronted comparable dilemmas—usually more than once. The Truman administration, for example, decided to confront the Soviet Union directly by relying on the containment policy. In the process, it perhaps accepted the reality that its move would all but eliminate any prospect of harmonious and cooperative relations with Moscow. Shortly after he entered office, Dwight D. Eisenhower threatened to use nuclear weapons if the Korean War were renewed. Inevitably, this decision gave impetus to the Soviet Union's determination to acquire a nuclear arsenal, and it may have encouraged other nations to do so as well. Time and again in the foreign aid program (as in the Alliance for Progress, initiated by the Kennedy administration for the modernization of Latin America), successive administrations have confronted a painful choice: to intervene in the affairs of Third World countries by attaching conditions to the foreign aid program, or to refrain from doing so in full knowledge that the goals of the program would probably not be achieved without such American-imposed conditions. President Richard M. Nixon repeatedly refused to permit his national security adviser, Henry Kissinger, to testify

58. Hook, *Philosophy and Public Policy,* 14.

before Congress concerning certain diplomatic decisions in Southeast Asia and elsewhere, thereby asserting the doctrine of executive privilege, which chief executives before and after have relied upon in their conduct of foreign relations. The result, however, was to provide new evidence that the policies of "tricky Dick Nixon" lacked credibility and could not stand public scrutiny. The Reagan administration made a decision to rely on armed force in dealing with Libya, thereby creating new sources of disunity within the Western alliance and engendering new waves of anti-Americanism in the Middle East.

The diplomatic goals of a nation are, like pragmatism itself, derived from a great diversity of sources, which means that they are not always logically consistent and compatible. Thus (as was evident in John Dewey's opposition to Nazism and communism), pragmatism accepts a cardinal principle of *Realpolitik:* nations have always been—and remain—deeply concerned about their security.[59] As philosophical Darwinists, pragmatic thinkers recognized that self-preservation is a primordial natural instinct; an organism cannot evolve unless it first survives. The evolutionary precept of the survival of the fittest underscores this fundamental reality. Almost never, therefore, do we find in pragmatic thought an impulse to political martyrdom. More than once, William James was derisive of those who operated under a romantic or "sentimental" view of the political process, which pretended that somehow political leaders and citizens could be indifferent to threats to society's well-being and existence. As John Dewey recognized during World War I, sometimes the preservation of security requires massive reliance on military power for its achievement. Pragmatic thinkers from time to time deplored this reality, but they did not deny it. Nor did they accept the pacifistic position that reliance on military force under all conceivable circumstances is ethically indefensible or unacceptable public policy.

By contrast, a term employed frequently by John Dewey to describe the American approach to foreign affairs was *practical idealism.*[60] Objectives that have long been identified with American diplomacy such as peace, the principle of nonintervention, the concept of self-determination, the strengthening and extension of international law, and the encouragement of democracy outside the United States were also leading goals in pragmatic thought. For idealists, as for pragmatists, the ultimate goal—creating a more durable and meaningful sense of international community—has been a conspicuous ob-

59. Hook, *Philosophy and Public Policy,* 171.
60. See, for example, Dewey's analysis of American isolationist attitudes after World War I in Boydston (ed.), *John Dewey,* I, 167–72.

jective from the Judaeo-Christian era to the administrations of Presidents Woodrow Wilson, Franklin D. Roosevelt, John F. Kennedy, and Jimmy Carter.

As Louis J. Halle and other experienced diplomatic officials have reminded us, the abstract formulation of diplomatic goals is perhaps the easiest and least demanding phase in the foreign policy process. For some citizens and groups, American foreign policy is (or should be) explicable by reference to a single unambiguous objective such as expanding American economic opportunities overseas, or enhancing the prospects for democracy abroad, or eliminating poverty in Third World nations. Pragmatic thought would categorize this approach as "diplomatic monism" that endeavors to "fit" a highly variegated political universe into a preexisting conception of what it ought to be. In the process, the approach distorts political reality seriously and may create insoluble problems for American diplomacy. As John Dewey's own responses to the fundamental changes in the external environment of American policy during the 1930s and 1940s illustrated, the pragmatic mind rejects the idea that political reality is explicable by reference to a single, rigidly held concept or principle.[61]

Another, and perhaps more pervasive, problem related to the foreign policy goals of the American society is a different tendency: the endless proliferation of diplomatic objectives by the United States, with little or no attention devoted to the means necessary for their successful implementation. As early as William James's era (in connection with America's acquisition of the Philippines and the enunciation of the Open Door policy toward China around 1900), Walter Lippmann believed, Americans began to exhibit this unfortunate tendency. Again during the 1930s, America wanted to preserve its cherished isolationism and to protect its territorial possessions (Hawaii and the Philippines) without allocating the military, financial, and other resources which achievement of this goal demanded. After World War II, millions of Americans desired international equilibrium and peace, placing the responsibility for attaining it upon the nascent, and largely impotent, United Nations.[62]

These are merely a few examples illustrating a more general problem to which pragmatic thinkers devoted considerable attention. This was the crucial interrelationship between the goals and means of public policy. In their

61. The problem of the formulation, adoption, and implementation of foreign policy goals by the United States is examined in detail in Louis J. Halle, *Civilization and Foreign Policy: An Inquiry for Americans* (New York, 1955).

62. Walter Lippmann, *U.S. Foreign Policy: Shield of the Republic;* the same idea is a basic theme of George Kennan's indictment of American diplomacy in his *American Diplomacy.*

view, the key to successful foreign or domestic policy was to be found in the *interaction between them*. To pragmatic minds, the goals of foreign policy are merely abstractions or mental constructs that can be and are endlessly conceived by the mind. They are little more than harmless mental exercises unless and until these goals are placed in some specific *environmental context* and *means* are devised for their realization that are appropriate to that particular environment.

Americans, for example, may believe—and traditionally have believed—that promotion of international peace is a high-ranking goal of the nation's diplomacy. Pragmatists would insist, however, that if the goal of peace is to have any practical significance, it must be related directly to a variety of specific problems confronting the United States abroad such as peace between the United States and the Soviet Union, peace in the Middle East, peace in southern Africa, or other concrete diplomatic challenges. After that, means for implementing the goal in these diverse contexts must be devised and used. In each instance, a different combination of means—diplomacy and negotiating skill, military power, financial resources, propaganda, moral principles and suasions, the influence of America's own example, and other methods—will be needed to make the goal of peace a meaningful objective of foreign policy.

This aspect of pragmatic thought emphasizes what can be called the "ends-means continuum" in national policy. Although few Americans perhaps are acquainted with the term, by the mid-1980s most had become familiar—in some instances, painfully familiar—with its implications for the diplomacy of the United States. Pragmatic thinking about this concept is analogous to its conception of truth, as explained in Chapter 2. A goal of foreign policy only really becomes such when it is actualized or, in Dewey's words, when "it is worked out in terms of concrete conditions available for its realization, that is in terms of 'means.'" In the diplomatic realm, the goals conceptualized by intellectual endeavor—or what Dewey sometimes called the "ends-in-view"—are given tangible expression and meaning only *in action;* and that occurs when ends are associated with the means required for their realization.

In one of pragmatism's most distinctive (and for some minds, most difficult) tenets, Dewey cautioned that a central problem of philosophical inquiry "concerns the *interaction* of our judgments about ends to be sought with the knowledge of the means for achieving them." Dewey cautioned against a human tendency to adopt "endless ends" or goals formulated apart from the

126

means needed for their implementation. It is always a mistake, he insisted, to differentiate sharply between the goals and means of public policy because "means and ends are two ways of regarding the same actuality." The value of goals resides, therefore, "not in themselves but in their capacity to work [as] shown in the consequences of their use."[63]

At first glance, such pragmatic insights may appear to be esoteric and to involve the same philosophical and verbal "hairsplitting" to which the pragmatists objected vehemently in the thought of classical philosophers. Yet upon reflection, it seems clear that Dewey and other pragmatic thinkers identified a problem that, in several instances since World War II, has impeded the realization of American diplomatic objectives. Throughout the postwar period the American people and their leaders have been prone to ignore or neglect the ends-means continuum in their relations with other nations. Certainly from the perspective of the nation or group overseas which the United States is endeavoring to influence, *how* American goals are given tangible expression in the methods adapted to implement them will often be decisive in testifying to what these goals are and what they mean. A foreign policy of good intentions divorced from concrete and adequate means for its realization, Dewey once warned, is a certain formula for diplomatic failure. America's devotion to peace, for example, is likely to be judged by what it does in resolving specific disputes such as military competition, controversies in the Middle East, and human rights disputes. The importance of America's belief in the abstract goal of equality in relations among nations will be determined in no small measure by how it *acts* toward its partners within the North Atlantic Treaty Organization (NATO) alliance and toward its less powerful friends in other regions. Its professions of concern about the future of the Third World will be assessed on the basis of how it responds to the financial needs, trade problems, and other paramount issues for leaders and masses throughout this zone.

A major corollary of the pragmatic emphasis upon the ends-means continuum is another idea applicable to the diplomatic activities of the United States and other nations in the contemporary world. There is nearly always a tendency for the means of national policy to displace the announced goals and in effect to become the goals the nation is pursuing abroad. This is not an unfamiliar phenomenon for Americans since World War II. Time and again, goal displacement has occurred in the diplomacy of the United States; in

63. John Dewey, *The Quest for Certainty: A Study of the Relations of Knowledge and Action* (New York, 1929), 37, 233–34; and his *Reconstruction in Philosophy* (New York, 1920), 145–46.

effect, action in time became the goal, and the original purpose (or purposes) of the action tended to be forgotten or ignored.

American diplomatic experience in the Korean and Vietnam wars, for example, provides ample evidence of the relevance of this pragmatic principle. In both cases, the reasons why American military power was committed to the region became increasingly obscured, yet the application of that power increased in scale and intensity in behalf of goals that were increasingly confused or uncertain for the American people. In the Vietnam conflict, the escalation of military power *per se* in time appeared to be the goal. How it was related to, or promoted the achievement of, diplomatic objectives in Southeast Asia was a question the Johnson and Nixon administrations had considerable difficulty answering to the satisfaction of the American people. Under the Johnson administration winning the war appeared to many observers at home and abroad to *be* the goal of Washington's policy—and yet even officials of the administration itself were unclear about just what was meant by "winning" the contest in Southeast Asia.

Many of these same questions arose concerning the Reagan administration's diplomacy in Lebanon in the mid-1980s. Ultimately, the administration's commitment of armed forces to preserve the stability of Lebanon was a conspicuous diplomatic failure, in large part because the means employed rendered the achievement of the original objectives of the Lebanese intervention unobtainable.[64]

Thinkers immersed in the pragmatic tradition do not find such results surprising or unusual. Reflecting upon the consequences of World War I, for example, John Dewey observed that this destructive encounter—in the American view, waged to "make the world safe for democracy"—in reality had the opposite results from those intended by the Allies. The demise of democratic governments in several Western nations; the precipitation of severe financial crises contributing to the Great Depression and the ensuing global economic chaos; the withdrawal of the United States into its isolationist shell; and the rise of totalitarian and expansionist regimes in Germany, Japan, and Italy were some of the direct or indirect results of World War I, which were totally contrary to the announced war aims of the Allies. To Dewey's mind, World War I was a classic example of nations' meaning well but being oblivious to the consequences of their actions. As a result, their

---

64. See the discussion of the Reagan administration's diplomacy in Lebanon in the New York *Times*, February 27, 1984, dispatch by Thomas L. Friedman; and *ibid.*, September 17, 1984, dispatch by John Kifner.

diplomatic goals were in time subverted or undermined by the means used to achieve them.[65]

Now it must be admitted that even today, the reasons why there is nearly always a tendency for the means of foreign policy to displace and eclipse the goals is a process that is imperfectly understood. From experience with American diplomacy since World War II (and the Korean and Vietnam conflicts offer especially pertinent examples) several possible explanations may be given. (1) The goals of American diplomacy were not clearly thought through, or were inappropriate, from the beginning. (2) The nation's objectives abroad were not adequately explained by officials in Washington and understood correctly by the American people. (3) Inappropriate means were chosen to achieve the goals. (4) The goals were subsequently changed in the light of developments abroad. (5) Pressure groups within the United States developed a strong vested interest in the continuation of a particular policy even after it became evident that the policy's goals were not being achieved. (6) Government agencies (and bureaus within agencies) developed bureaucratic interests in an existing policy. (7) High-ranking policy makers in time acquired strong ego commitments to a particular course of action and demanded its continuation. (8) In many cases, foreign governments applied pressure on Washington for the continuation of policies and programs. (9) In other cases, it was difficult for the American people and their leaders to agree upon a course of action they liked better than existing policies.

Another significant dimension of pragmatic thought related to the goals of diplomacy is the concept of planning. Even during their lifetimes, William James, John Dewey, and their followers confronted the criticism repeatedly that pragmatism was not a coherent philosophy but merely a disjointed collection of fragmentary, and sometimes contradictory, maxims for guiding human behavior. According to this indictment, pragmatism's preoccupation with immediate, real-life problems, its insistence that every problem must be analyzed and solved within an existing environmental context, and its overt disdain for abstract intellectual speculation have convinced many critics that pragmatism is little more than a rationalization for merely improvised behavior that is both devoid of principle and lacking in consistency and predictability.

One answer made by leading pragmatic thinkers to this charge was the concept of planning, especially conspicuous in the viewpoints of John Dewey. Dewey, of course, denied that a pragmatic approach to public policy was

65. Dewey, *Human Nature and Conduct*, 231–32.

synonymous with *ad hoc*ism or that it was merely a reflexive or reactive response to problems confronting human society. Dewey and other pragmatists believed that intelligence was capable of anticipating the emergence of serious problems and challenges to human society without waiting for them to reach crisis proportions, when effective solutions become very difficult, if not impossible. Fire prevention, after all, is the paramount goal of every fire department, no matter how skillful it may be in extinguishing fires. Physicians had rather prevent diseases than cure them. In the postwar era, the prevention of nuclear war (or deterrence) is infinitely preferable to dealing with its catastrophic consequences.

Because of his emphasis on planning in human affairs, John Dewey has sometimes been described as a "collectivist" in his political ideas. Yet Dewey's collectivism had little or nothing in common with the collectivist thought that was the foundation of totalitarian regimes in Nazi Germany and Soviet Russia. Consistent with his own pragmatic philosophy, Dewey was mindful that the concept of planning could also become an *a priori* idea or philosophical dogma, which, if applied rigidly and inflexibly, could serve as an impediment to imaginative and creative thought. Dewey was extremely critical of totalitarian regimes abroad, and he was unenthusiastic about certain features of the New Deal at home. He once called attention, for example, to the "immense difference" between the concept of a *"planned* society" and of a "continuously *planning* society." The former could lead—and in recent history, it has led—to the emergence of the all-pervasive state, which jeopardized human freedoms.

Planning could and should be conducted within a democratic context, as individuals and groups apply their creative intelligence to the identification and solution of emerging problems. As in other aspects of pragmatic thought, Dewey's concept of planning emphasized the identification and solution of discrete and concrete problems, on the basis of an objective analysis of the evidence, which were likely to confront society in the years ahead. An example from recent American experience is the energy crisis, a challenge that was anticipated and publicized for many years before it reached an acute state following the fourth round in the Arab-Israeli conflict in 1973.[66]

This analysis of the principal tenets of Pragmatism concludes by focusing on the concept that, for pragmatists as well as devotees of other philosophical

66. Dewey's views on planning are quoted in Geiger, "Dewey's Social and Political Philosophy," 357–58; in Ratner (ed.), *Intelligence in the Modern World,* 426–32; and Hook, *John Dewey,* 235.

schools, is often viewed as crucial in determining the nature of future political relationships. This is the idea of *community.* What man must seek "incessantly, with fear and trembling," William James once asserted, was "to act [so] as to bring about the very largest total universe of good which we can see." A "small community of true friends" was James's model for society as a whole. James was naturally aware that such a community rarely existed in human affairs, but it was the goal toward which mankind ought to strive.[67]

John Dewey carried James's idea one step further. To his mind, "some pre-existent association of human being is prior to every particular human being who is born into the world." The individual, in other words, has no meaningful existence, and cannot realize his full potential, apart from the community. The interaction among peoples will determine the outcome of human destiny.[68]

The ultimate goal of human interaction, therefore, was to bring into existence what Dewey called the "great community." To his mind, this quest is more important than political disputes over rival ideologies, types of government, differing political processes, and the like because, when conditions are favorable for creating the great community, they will engender their own specific and appropriate political forms. Yet until this community is brought into being, debates over ideology, systems of government, and other subordinate questions dissipate man's energies and divert him from the paramount objective.[69]

It was in the context of discussing the urgency of creating a new sense of community that Dewey enunciated his widely quoted dictum that "the cure for the ailments of democracy is more democracy." Dewey was not talking merely about changes in the institutions, forms, and processes of the American or any other government. He was concerned about the liberation of the mind and spirit of man, about human growth and development, about the application of scientific truth to human relationships. These were prerequisites of the emergence of the community Dewey envisioned. The great community was analogous to nature: it was continually in the process of becoming and of evolving. Achieving, sustaining, and improving the great community was man's supreme political challenge.

67. James, quoted in Aldrich (ed.), *As William James Said,* 48.
68. Dewey, *Human Nature and Conduct,* 59.
69. Dewey, *The Public and Its Problems,* 146–48.

Four

Pragmatic American Diplomacy

Recent Patterns, the Role of Experience, and Global Pluralism

─────────────

The basic thesis of the following chapters is that in its approach to foreign relations since World War II, American society has exhibited a pragmatic world view. This means that American attitudes and behavior patterns are, to a remarkable degree, in conformity with the tenets of pragmatism, which often expressed long-standing habits of mind and action identified with the American ethos.

Pragmatic Behavior: Some Postwar Examples

We may gain preliminary understanding of the nature and importance of a pragmatic world view by examining briefly three leading examples of incumbent presidents whose diplomatic activities exemplified this idea. One of these examples, Woodrow Wilson, is taken from the period of American isolationism. The other two, John F. Kennedy and Ronald Reagan, were Democratic and Republican leaders, respectively. Ideologically they differed widely in their viewpoints. Yet in both cases, the impact of certain pragmatic concepts and principles upon their diplomatic conduct is evident.

For many students of American foreign relations, Woodrow Wilson stands out as the personification of an idealistic approach to diplomatic issues. Internally, of course, Wilson's program of domestic reforms made significant changes in American national life and anticipated the even more sweeping innovations introduced later by the New Deal. In foreign affairs, Wilson was widely regarded as a forceful and tireless champion of American ideals; time and again, he denounced the tendency of powerful nations to pursue their goals by use of armed force, and he endeavored to prevent America's involvement in World War I. After failing in that goal, Wilson defined the global conflict as a "war to end wars" and "to make the world safe for democracy." His widely publicized Fourteen Points were hailed as an outstanding example of statesmanship and high principles and as laying the foundation for a just and lasting peace. His concept of self-determination was crucial in achieving the independence of several nations in central and eastern Europe. Wilson was also the main architect and proponent of the first modern experiment in international organization, the League of Nations.

Yet continuing research into Wilson's diplomacy reveals its extraordinarily complex, ambivalent, and often contradictory nature. Thus a recent survey of scholarly analyses of Wilsonian diplomacy emphasizes the consensus that it is explicable only by recourse to "multinational perspectives, multicausal analysis, and multidimensional explanations." America's entry into World War I, for example, can be accurately explained by a "complex combination of factors," ranging from calculations of national security, to moral and legal considerations, to diplomatic and economic influences. In his diplomacy, Wilson clearly exhibited idealistic, realistic, and other qualities. Under his idealistic diplomatic leadership, for example, Washington actually carried out more interventions in Latin America than under any other administration! Wilson—the tireless champion of idealism and "democratic diplomacy"—ordered the American navy to shell the Mexican city of Vera Cruz in his determination to "teach the Latin Americans to elect good men." Wilson and the other Allied leaders also negotiated the Treaty of Versailles in secret. During and after these negotiations, Wilson largely ignored Congress, and he showed little inclination to apply his principle of self-determination to the peoples living in the British, French, and other empires outside of Europe.[1]

Almost a half-century later, another Democratic chief executive also became a symbol of American idealism, youth, vigor, progress, innovation, and other qualities frequently associated with the American ethos. This was President John F. Kennedy, whose tragic assassination on November 22, 1963, ended his administration of "a thousand days." As a senator, Kennedy had

1. Edith James, "Wilsonian Wartime Diplomacy: The Sense of the Seventies," in Gerald K. Haines and J. Samuel Walker (eds.), *American Foreign Relations: A Historiographical Review* (Westport, Conn., 1981), 115–33; Arthur S. Link, *Wilson the Diplomatist: A Look at His Major Foreign Policies* (Baltimore, 1957), and *The Struggle for Neutrality, 1914–1915* (Princeton, 1960); Merle E. Curti, *Bryan and World Peace* (Northampton, Mass., 1931); Harley Notter, *The Origins of the Foreign Policy of Woodrow Wilson* (Baltimore, 1937); Charles C. Tansill, *America Goes to War* (Boston, 1938); and Daniel M. Smith, *The Great Departure: The United States and World War I, 1914–1920* (New York, 1965). *Realpolitik* influences upon Wilson's diplomacy are emphasized in Edward H. Buehrig, *Woodrow Wilson and the Balance of Power* (Bloomington, 1955).

demonstrated a genuine interest in and concern about the problems of the Third World, especially black Africa. Under his administration, American foreign policy clearly reflected this interest. The Kennedy White House also took the lead in formulating and promulgating the multi-billion-dollar aid program for Latin America, known as the Alliance for Progress. As president, Kennedy several times reminded Americans and foreigners of the potentially disastrous consequences of nuclear war between the superpowers; he urged his fellow citizens never "to fear to negotiate" with the Soviet adversary; and he cautioned Americans against a tendency to think that there was an "American solution" for every international or global problem. During the Cuban missile crisis of 1962, Kennedy was at pains not to provoke or humiliate Moscow, even while insisting that Soviet missiles be withdrawn from Cuba.

Yet Kennedy was also motivated in his approach to foreign relations by nonideological factors. In his campaign for the presidency in 1960, he emphasized the existence of a "missile gap" that presumably left the United States militarily inferior to the Soviet Union. (In time, this gap was found to be largely illusory.) Kennedy forcefully reiterated America's determination to defend Berlin from communist encroachments; and he both maintained and expanded America's commitment to the defense of Southeast Asia from communist hegemony. JFK authorized the ill-fated Bay of Pigs invasion of Cuba—an undisguised attempt to overthrow Fidel Castro's Marxist regime. On several occasions, he warned governments throughout the Third World about overly close associations with Moscow. And under Kennedy, the most serious Soviet-American confrontation since World War II—the Cuban missile crisis of 1962—brought the world to the brink of nuclear war. More than any in recent memory perhaps, the Kennedy administration's diplomacy typified the dualism implicit in the Great Seal of the United States: it *concurrently* emphasized such ideological values as peace and international understanding, along with *Realpolitik* calculations and careful attention to the nation's diplomatic and strategic interests.[2]

2. Arthur M. Schlesinger, Jr., *A Thousand Days: John F. Kennedy in the White House* (Boston, 1965); Roger Hilsman, *To Move a Nation: The Politics of Foreign Policy in the Administration of John F. Kennedy* (Garden City, N.Y., 1967); Robert F. Kennedy, *Thirteen Days: A Memoir of the Cuban Missile Crisis* (New York, 1968); emphasis on Kennedy's anticommunism and opposition to revolution abroad is found in Richard J. Walton, *Cold War and Counter-Revolution: The Foreign Policy of John F. Kennedy* (Baltimore, 1972). Some twenty years after Kennedy's death, one of his closest advisers, Theodore C. Sorensen, observed that although JFK's foreign policies had been diversely interpreted, to his mind they could most accurately be described by the term "pragmatic" (New York *Times*, November 22, 1983).

Lest it be imagined that such anomalous behavior patterns have been characteristic of Democratic presidents alone, the diplomatic record of the Reagan administration exhibited comparable paradoxes and incongruities. By many criteria, Ronald Reagan was perhaps the most overtly ideological chief executive to occupy the Oval Office since World War II. His strong antipathy toward communism infused nearly all his diplomatic statements and actions, amounting almost to an *idée fixe*. More than once, Reagan identified the Kremlin as the "locus of evil" in the contemporary world, and he tended to blame Moscow for a long list of international problems, from the necessity for an escalating American defense budget, to the continuation of instability in the Middle East, to ongoing political upheaval in Central America. Campaigning on a pledge to "make America great again," Reagan was determined to create an American military establishment "second to none"; to frustrate communist designs in the Caribbean, the Persian Gulf areas, and Western Europe; and to restore American diplomatic credibility as the undisputed leader of the noncommunist world.

At the same time, despite his undisguised right-wing ideology, Reagan engaged in diplomatic actions that were widely described as pragmatic, moderate, flexible, and realistic. Early in his administration, for example, he accepted a decision by the European allies to purchase natural gas from the Soviet Union and thereby averted a serious schism within NATO. Responding to the demands of American farmers, Reagan lifted the economic boycott (imposed by the Carter administration) on grain sales to the Soviet Union. The Reagan White House authorized a substantial emergency loan to Poland, saving that communist-ruled nation from bankruptcy and preventing a new crisis in Soviet-American relations. Reagan and his advisers also gave high priority to improving relations with the People's Republic of China, even while America simultaneously maintained close relations with the Republic of China (Taiwan). In the Middle East, down to 1987 at least, the Reagan administration managed to avoid direct involvement in the Iraqi-Iranian war. (In mid-1987, the USS *Stark* was fired upon by an Iraqi missile.) After his military intervention in Lebanon failed to bring peace and stability to that strife-torn country, Reagan "cut his losses" and ordered the Marines to evacuate Lebanon.

In Latin America, the Reagan administration was determined to counter communist expansion, as symbolized by its successful intervention in Grenada and its ongoing hostility toward Nicaragua's Marxist regime. Yet in its diplomacy toward Central America, the administration was also sensitive to congressional and public apprehension about another Vietnam. The scale of American involvement in the region was kept limited; and in time officials of the Reagan administration acknowledged that the security of El Salvador depended ultimately upon the honesty, efficiency, and commitment to progress toward democracy exhibited by its own government. Toward Moscow generally, in response to continuous congressional and public interest in the issue, spokesmen for the Reagan administration reiterated White House readiness to engage in arms-control negotiations with Soviet officials.[3]

On the basis of this survey—and comparable reviews might be undertaken for other administrations in the postwar era—certain preliminary conclusions about the conduct of American foreign relations seem justified. It may be said, for example, that every incumbent president since World War II has exhibited diplomatic behavior that correlates closely with the leading tenets of the pragmatic mode of thought. In their different ways, all have displayed attitudes and actions in the foreign policy field that were a mixture of highly diverse policy influences and motivations, that were responsive to crises and urgent problems abroad, that took account of the unique circumstances confronting the United States overseas, and that reflected awareness of the consequences of alternative courses of diplomatic action. Stated negatively, the diplomatic behavior of particular presidents has almost never been ideologically consistent or predictable according to their known ideological preferences; in most instances, little pattern or overall strategy could be discerned in their diplomatic activities; and their diplomatic moves (often in marked contrast to their rhetoric) were not characterized by a high degree of rigidity and adherence to *a priori* ideas. A prominent example of this frame of mind is provided by former senator and Vice-President Hubert Humphrey (D., Minn.). As one study of Humphrey's approach to foreign policy issues concluded, his position "flitted back and forth among the concepts of containment, competition, and cooperation" with the Soviet Union. Humphrey saw no contradiction between endeavoring to preserve peace and negotiating Soviet-American differences, on one hand, and preserving a strong national defense program capable of containing communism, on the other. In his words, in an "imperfect world," both approaches were needed.[4]

3. See the summary of the recommendations made by the National Bipartisan Commission on Central America, headed by Henry Kissinger, as presented in the State Department publication *Gist*, March, 1984, pp. 1–3.
4. See Barbara Stuhler, *Ten Men of Minnesota and American Foreign Policy (1898–1968)* (St. Paul, 1973), 199–201.

Paradoxical as it may appear, the consistency of American foreign policy in the era of postwar internationalism consists primarily in its correspondence with *the main tenets of pragmatic thought,* which is characterized by its philosophical untidiness, by the existence of logical loose ends, and by its unfinished nature. This is another way of saying that as a rule American foreign policy possesses a high degree of predictability: it may be confidently anticipated that, under any incumbent administration, the foreign policy of the United States will reflect the American society's belief in the leading tenets of pragmatism. To the perennial question, "But what *is* American foreign policy?" the best general answer is that the attitudes and actions of the American society abroad are best understood by reference to the nation's pragmatic tradition.

Pragmatic thinkers distrust all monistic explanations of reality, and that principle applies no less to the political universe. A pragmatic world view is not, therefore, the only useful perspective within which to understand American diplomacy. All informed students of American foreign relations are mindful, for example, that ideological factors sometimes crucially affected the activities of the United States abroad—as in Wilson's commitment to the concept of self-determination, Franklin D. Roosevelt's opposition to colonialism, and the American society's long-standing antipathy toward communism. Similarly, power calculations no less at times influence American diplomacy. For twenty years or more, a nuclear balance of terror has existed between the superpowers, and every incumbent administration has recognized the key role of nuclear and other forms of military strength in deterring aggression by the Soviet Union and other countries. Accordingly, familiarity with the *Realpolitik* approach to international politics is unquestionably essential for understanding the foreign policy of the United States.

Other approaches to the study of international politics can also be useful in illuminating various aspects of American foreign relations. Game theory, for example, sheds light upon such problems as Soviet-American disarmament negotiations and upon the strategy of deterrence in the nuclear age.[5] Decision-making theory calls attention to the complexity of formulating, administering, evaluating, and revising foreign policy by the United States and

5. A helpful introduction to game theory as it applies to international politics may be found in James E. Dougherty and Robert L. Pfaltzgraff, Jr., *Contending Theories of International Relations: A Comprehensive Survey* (2nd ed.; New York, 1981), 511–43. More detailed treatments are Thomas C. Schelling, *The Strategy of Conflict* (New York, 1963); and Martin Shubik (ed.), *Game Theory and Related Approaches to Social Behavior* (New York, 1964).

other nations. It affords some basis for comparability in the process employed by different nations in formulating their responses to external challenges.[6]

A number of psychological theories of American diplomatic behavior are also helpful. These focus on such influences affecting the policy process as the class background of decision makers, their mind-set and personal qualities affecting their actions, the degree to which a desire for consensus (or "groupthink") governs the decision-making process, and other variables. Still other studies have analyzed the degree to which economic incentives, pressures, and forces influence the behavior of the United States abroad.[7] A recent emphasis in such studies has been the activities of multinational corporations in foreign countries.[8]

A pragmatic frame of reference for understanding American foreign policy is not offered, therefore, upon the assumption that it can replace all existing interpretations of the diplomacy of the United States. A pragmatic world view, however, does have certain advantages over alternative explanations in making American diplomatic activity understandable and in unifying its disparate and separate features. A pragmatic perspective accords with many long-standing and deeply ingrained attitudes and behavior patterns of the American people. As explained in detail in Chapter 1, in their approach to domestic affairs Americans have traditionally engaged in pragmatic problem solving, and it is reasonable to expect that they bring that same mentality to the solution of external problems. In contrast to several other approaches, a pragmatic world view does not require us to assume that Americans behave

6. See Dougherty and Pfaltzgraff, *Contending Theories*, 468–511; Richard C. Snyder, H. W. Bruck, and Burton Sapin (eds.), *Foreign Policy Decision-Making* (New York, 1963); Joseph Frankel, *The Making of Foreign Policy: An Analysis of Decision-Making* (New York, 1963); John P. Lovell, *Foreign Policy in Perspective: Strategy, Adaptation, Decision-Making* (New York, 1970); and James M. Rosenau (ed.), *International Politics and Foreign Policy* (rev. ed., New York, 1969), 199–255.

7. See Hadley Cantril (ed.), *Tensions That Cause War* (Urbana, Ill., 1951); "International Relations: Psychological Aspects," in *International Encyclopedia of the Social Sciences* (12 vols.; New York, 1968), *VIII*, 76–79; Robert Berkowitz, *Aggression: A Social-Psychological Analysis* (New York, 1962); Leon Bramson and George W. Goethals (eds.), *War: Studies from Physiology, Psychology, Anthropology* (New York, 1968); Konrad Lorenz, *On Aggression* (New York, 1967); Anthony Storr, *Human Aggression* (New York, 1968); Jerome D. Frank, *Sanity and Survival: Psychological Aspects of War and Peace* (New York, 1968); Elton B. McNeil (ed.), *The Nature of Human Conflict* (Englewood Cliffs, N.J., 1965); and Irving L. Janis, *Victims of Groupthink* (Boston, 1972).

8. See Richard J. Barnet and Ronald E. Muller, *Global Reach* (New York, 1974); Horst Bergsten and Moran Bergsten, *American Multinationals and American Interests* (Washington, D.C., 1978); Lester R. Brown, *World Without Borders* (New York, 1972); Abdul A. Said and Luiz R. Simmons (eds.), *The New Sovereigns* (Englewood Cliffs, N.J., 1975); Lewis D. Solomon, *Multinational Corporations and the Emerging World Order* (Port Washington, N.Y., 1978); and Khrishna Kumar (ed.), *Transnational Enterprises: Their Impact on Third World Societies and Cultures* (Boulder, Colo., 1980).

one way in resolving domestic questions and a different way in dealing with external problems.

This is a serious defect of power-oriented approaches to American foreign relations. To be successful in adopting *Realpolitik* as the basis of their foreign policy, Americans would be required to change fundamentally many of their traditional ideals, values, and behavior norms. Accepting the pursuit of national power as a legitimate goal of diplomacy, *Realpolitik* is historically associated with aristocracy and autocratic government, control of foreign policy by an elite with little interest in public opinion, secret treaties, territorial expansionism and colonial rivalry, and other concepts alien to the American tradition. In recent years, public and congressional skepticism about the modern-day embodiment of *Realpolitik*—Henry Kissinger—reflects the American aversion to "power politics" divorced from the purposes for which national power is employed. It is noteworthy that no public leader in recent American experience has been able to interest the people or Congress in adopting "balance of power" as the central precept of the nation's diplomacy.[9]

A recent behavioral approach to the study of international politics and foreign policy is systems theory. For Americans, this perspective also suffers from serious shortcomings and inadequacies, preventing it from serving as a satisfactory paradigm for American foreign policy, for at least two fundamental reasons. First, systems theory makes the crucial assumption that an "international system" *actually exists*, which often appears totally contrary to the facts. Far from being an organized and structured system, contemporary international politics more often than not appears to be characterized primarily by anarchistic tendencies. Many scholars believe it is the *lack* of a system regulating the relationship among its major components that poses the principal threat to global peace and stability.[10] Pragmatists are inherently skep-

9. Ira S. Cohen, *Realpolitik: Theory and Practice* (Belmont, Calif., 1975). As applied to American foreign policy, realism is perhaps best represented in the voluminous writings of Hans J. Morgenthau. See particularly his *Politics Among Nations: The Struggle for Power and Peace* (4th ed.; New York, 1966) and subsequent editions; *In Defense of the National Interest* (New York, 1951); and "The Mainspring of American Foreign Policy," *American Political Science Review*, XLIV (1950), 833–54. See also Walter Lippmann, *U.S. Foreign Policy: Shield of the Republic* (Boston, 1943); T. V. Smith, "Power: Its Ubiquity and Legitimacy," *American Political Science Review*, XLV (1951), 693–702; and Hanson Baldwin, *Great Mistakes of the War* (New York, 1950).

10. Morton A. Kaplan, *System and Process in International Politics* (New York, 1962); Richard Rosecrance, *Action and Reaction in World Politics* (Boston, 1963); Oran Young, *Systems of Political Science* (Englewood Cliffs, N.J., 1968); Charles B. McClelland, *Theory and the International System* (New York, 1966); Klaus Knorr and Sidney Verba (eds.), *The International System* (Princeton, 1961); Roger D. Masters, "World Politics as a Primitive Political System," *World Politics*, XVI (July,

tical about the ability of systems theory or any other mechanistic conception of reality (whose model is Newtonian physics) to explain the political universe.

Second, systems theory has become so complex and abstract—including now both the concept of the international system and several regional sub-systems—that it is extremely difficult even for informed students of American foreign policy to understand its relevance for specific diplomatic problems, such as Soviet-American military competition, the Arab-Israeli conflict, or superpower rivalry within the Third World. It is virtually impossible to verify many basic propositions and tenets of systems theory empirically. (Systems theory is a notable example of the intellectual construct concerning which Charles Peirce would have asked: What real difference *in terms of its consequences* does it make whether we believe the theory or not?) To date, it is difficult to detect any evidence that systems theory has in any significant way affected the diplomatic conduct of the United States or the attitudes of the American people about foreign affairs.

A different defect is exhibited by game theory, useful as it sometimes is for illuminating challenges like disarmament and nuclear deterrence. Game theory is a highly rational approach to international politics. It emphasizes the extent to which the players engage in a rigidly logical analysis of the challenge confronting them, carefully evaluate all possible moves available, and ultimately decide upon a course of action that is viewed as most beneficial in the light of these rational calculations.

Yet every moderately well-informed student of American diplomacy is aware that on innumerable occasions, *nonrational factors* have momentously affected the course of foreign relations. Franklin D. Roosevelt's political charisma and his deteriorating health; President Truman's tendency to make major policy decisions intuitively; Secretary of State John Foster Dulles' strong religious convictions and personal aversion to communism; Lyndon Johnson's overweening ego and his belief that both his own and the nation's honor and diplomatic credibility were at stake in the Vietnam War; Reagan's deep distrust of the Soviet Union and his determination to make the United States "stand tall" on the global scene—these and other essentially nonrational forces sometimes crucially affect the diplomatic conduct of the United States.

1964), 595–619; and papers from the symposium on international systems, *International Studies Quarterly,* XIII (December, 1969).

Since 1789 American diplomatic experience has exhibited diverse and often contradictory strains, and it continues to do so in the contemporary period. One study of President George Washington's diplomacy, for example, has found that it shows clear evidence of "the tension between Idealism and Realism" which existed in American foreign policy in the earliest days of the republic. From the beginning, according to another interpretation, two basic and contrary themes—that America could successfully remain isolated from Europe's contentions and that it was intimately involved in events beyond its own borders—have been present in American diplomatic behavior. Still another scholar said that Thomas Jefferson, America's first secretary of state, was an idealist but could also be "as hard, as practical and as cynical . . . when the occasion arose, as any veteran diplomat of the Old World."[11]

Similarly, the Monroe Doctrine (1823) resulted from several major policy influences: a sense of idealism, power and strategic calculations, and not least the attempt by President James Monroe and his advisers to promote their party's political fortunes domestically. Richard Hofstadter concluded that after 1900 the foreign policy attitudes of many Americans combined an emphasis on idealism and antimaterialism with a "militancy" and a belief in the nation's unique mission in dealing with other countries. The diplomacy of the United States in Asia (specifically, toward Japan) constituted "a blend of evangelicalism, political calculation, benevolent paternalism, and crude self-interest."[12] An eclectic approach is, therefore, needed for any objective understanding of the events leading to the Japanese attack on Pearl Harbor.

Before World War II, the advocates of both isolationism and internationalism exhibited diverse policy motivations; neither approach was monolithic, and both proposed a variety of specific measures to achieve their goals. Meanwhile, the public opinion context of American diplomatic decision making was marked by pervasive "uncertainty" and by the "constant gyrations of public opinion" toward foreign policy issues. The Roosevelt administration's diplomatic moves reflect "a mixture of presidential initiative and

---

11. Ronald L. Hatzeneuhler, "The Early National Period, 1789–1815: The Need for Redefinition," in Haines and Walker (eds.), *American Foreign Relations,* 18; Felix Gilbert, *To the Farewell Address: Ideas of Early American Foreign Policy* (Princeton, 1961), 104; Nathan Schachner, *Thomas Jefferson: A Biography* (2 vols.; New York, 1951), I, 407.

12. Lester D. Langley, "American Foreign Policy in an Age of Nationalism," in Haines and Walker (eds.), *American Foreign Relations,* 42–43; Richard Hofstadter, *The Age of Reform* (New York, 1981), 270–80; Gerald K. Haines, "Roads to War: United States Foreign Policy, 1931–1941," in Haines and Walker (eds.), *American Foreign Relations,* 174–75.

caution."[13] For over a century and a half, America's isolationist record had been interrupted by interventionist episodes and diplomatic crusades to remake the world politically. It was not uncommon for some groups to exhibit both of these diplomatic attitudes simultaneously, or to advocate isolationist policies toward certain international issues and interventionist policies toward others.[14]

According to other interpretations, the American diplomatic record has been characterized by the presence of alternating cycles of isolationist and inward-looking periods, followed by eras of overt foreign interventionism in efforts to change the nature of foreign governments or the long-existing pattern of international political relationships.[15] America's crusade in behalf of universal democracy in World War I was followed by a powerful resurgence of isolationist sentiments, during which the popular motto was "Let Europe stew in its own juice." In the same pattern, by 1980 the mood of national disillusionment and self-doubt after the Vietnam War gave way to a widespread public demand that, under President Reagan, the United States "stand tall" abroad and regain its diplomatic credibility. Not untypically, since the Vietnam conflict Americans have remained highly suspicious of the concept of power even while they were in the process of using it to achieve desired diplomatic outcomes.

Similarly, peace has always ranked high on the list of historic American diplomatic goals. Time and again, Americans have been at the forefront of efforts within the international community to resolve global conflicts peacefully and to discover a substitute for violence as a method for settling interna-

13. Ernest C. Bolt, Jr., "Isolation, Expansion, and Peace: American Foreign Policy Between the Wars," in Haines and Walker (eds.), *American Foreign Relations,* 134–38.

14. The idea that before World War II American foreign policy exhibited both isolationist and interventionist impulses is explained more fully in Cecil V. Crabb, Jr., *Policy-Makers and Critics: Conflicting Theories of American Foreign Policy* (New York, 1976), 1–81. Specific examples of interventionist behavior by the American society are treated in Jan J. Lerski, *A Polish Chapter in Jacksonian America: The United States and the Polish Exiles of 1831* (Madison, 1958); Carl Wittke, *Refugees of Revolution: The German Forty-Eighters in America* (Philadelphia, 1952); Emil Lengyel, *Americans from Hungary* (Philadelphia, 1948); Thomas A. Bailey, *America Faces Russia: Russian-American Relations from Early Times to Our Day* (Ithaca, 1950); H. K. Beale, *Theodore Roosevelt and the Rise of America to World Power* (Baltimore, 1956); T. P. Wright, Jr., "United States Electoral Intervention in Cuba," *Inter-American Economic Affairs,* XIII (1959), 50–71; Gaddis Smith, *American Diplomacy During the Second World War, 1941–1945* (New York, 1965); William L. Langer, *The Diplomacy of Imperialism, 1890–1902* (New York, 1951); Ernest R. May, *American Imperialism: A Speculative Essay* (New York, 1968); and Thomas J. McCormick, *China Market: America's Quest for Informal Empire* (Chicago, 1967).

15. F. L. Klingberg, "The Historical Alternation of Moods in American Foreign Policy," *World Politics,* IV (January, 1952), 239–73; George F. Kennan, *American Diplomacy, 1900–1950* (New York, 1951); Justus D. Doenecke, *The Literature of Isolationism: A Guide to Non-Interventionist Scholarship, 1930–1972* (Colorado Springs, 1972).

tional disputes. Yet the United States acquired some of its territory by conquest; as in the months preceding America's formal entry into World War I, it has insisted that other countries respect such principles as freedom of the seas and neutral rights; and it has opposed territorial changes made as a result of aggression, as reflected in opposition to Japanese expansionism in Manchuria and China during the 1930s. After World War II, the United States consistently took the position that other independent nations have a right to defend themselves—and the United States is entitled to assist them in doing so—from external aggression and from foreign-instigated subversive movements. Again, American attitudes toward peace and war have clearly been characterized by an ambivalence that continues to be a feature of the nation's attitudes and activities in foreign affairs to the present day.

Innumerable studies of American public opinion since World War II have revealed the continued presence of paradoxical attitudes in the American mind about foreign affairs. Routinely, for example, Americans have concurrently indicated their desire for peace and their belief in the need to maintain a strong national defense; for a generation or more, Americans have exhibited considerable distrust of the Soviet Union, but they also want officials in Washington to conclude arms-reduction and other agreements with the USSR. Americans still subscribe to the principle of reciprocal trade unhindered by protective tariffs, but they want protection for domestic industries that are particularly vulnerable to foreign competition.

A pragmatic world view accepts the paradoxical quality of American foreign policy as a norm of diplomatic behavior, and it does not anticipate that this feature of American diplomacy will disappear in the near future. As was true of the leading proponents of pragmatism, a pragmatic world view is tolerant of such anomalies and implicitly believes that some outcomes are worse than a logically or ideologically inconsistent foreign policy. In the pragmatic view, several considerations—such as taking full account of the circumstances facing the United States at home and abroad, or recognizing the unique elements in specific problems facing America overseas, or calculating the resources the American society is willing to allocate to a particular diplomatic undertaking—normally rank ahead of logical and philosophical consistency as a requirement of successful diplomacy.

A pragmatic perspective on American foreign policy may not be the long-awaited "theory of theories" which many students of international politics anticipate and desire. A pragmatic world view unquestionably suffers from certain defects and limitations. Yet a pragmatically based explanation serves better than nearly all other available theories to make the international behavior of the United States intelligible. For the most part, the pragmatic perspective offered here fulfills the four major criteria which an acceptable theory of political behavior must satisfy: (1) it is capable of empirical verification by reference to the diplomatic experience of the United States over an extended period of time; (2) it is applicable to a broad range of more or less analogous political phenomena; (3) it permits greater predictability for the diplomatic conduct of the United States; and (4) it raises significant questions for future research. As applied to post–World War II American diplomacy, a pragmatic world view consists of the major elements outlined in the remainder of this chapter.

Experience as the Standard of Truth

Charles Peirce is often viewed as the father of American pragmatism, partly because he stated what might be called the first principle of pragmatic thought: that the truth of an idea cannot be distinguished from its validation in human experience. Time and again, Peirce called upon his philosophical opponents to demonstrate what difference it made for the realm of human experience whether their ideas were believed. When they could not, to the minds of Peirce and other pragmatists, the ideas were incapable of verification and had no practical application to human life. By experience, the pragmatic thinkers included all dimensions of human behavior and interaction: social, economic, and political affairs, as well as personal (or psychological) well-being, ethics, aesthetics, spiritual needs, and the individual sense of fulfillment and self-realization. In the pragmatic view, from natural science to ethics, a proposition becomes true to the degree that human experience is called upon to attest to its validity. In turn, throughout history new experiences have in time invalidated established truths and compelled humans to abandon or substantially modify them.

Many alternative standards for determining and validating truth are available to national policy makers. Conformity with the requirements of an *a priori* ideological system; the degree to which a given policy enhances (or detracts from) the power position of the United States; examples and precedents supplied by the practices of other nations; the extent to which a particular policy promotes (or hinders) the achievement of domestic political goals; a given policy's contribution to achieving and maintaining an internal consensus in behalf of American diplomatic activities; and the congruence of a particular policy or program with the demands of domestic pressure groups—this by no means exhaustive list is merely suggestive of available criteria.

From time to time, these criteria are employed by American officials and informed citizens for determining the meaning and utility of particular diplomatic undertakings. (In reality, the value of any given foreign policy venture will usually be determined by multiple criteria.) For example, in almost every realm of external policy, from relations with the Soviet Union, to interallied relations, to efforts to modernize the Third World, American officials are continuously mindful of the ideological criterion. The United States is the world's oldest functioning democracy. For two hundred years, Americans have remained deeply committed to democratic precepts; they wish to encourage and strengthen democracy abroad; and the ultimate political objective of pragmatic thought—creating and expanding what John Dewey called the "great community"—requires adoption of, and adherence to, fundamental principles and practices of democratic government.[16]

On other occasions, American officials are mindful of the impact of particular foreign policy decisions upon the power position of the United States and upon the global (or regional) balance of power. After World War II, for example, the Truman administration decided to preserve America's nuclear monopoly (which lasted until 1949) as a military counterweight to overwhelming Soviet superiority in ground forces. After Moscow acquired a nuclear arsenal, America was determined to maintain nuclear superiority—or at least sufficient nuclear strength to guarantee survival after a nuclear "first strike" and to give the United States a devastating "second strike" capability in the event of global war. John F. Kennedy was elected to the White House in 1960 in no small measure because of a public belief that the Eisenhower administration had permitted a missile gap to open in favor of the Soviet Union. After suffering a series of diplomatic reverses, in the closing months of his administration, President Jimmy Carter called for substantial increases in the national defense budget, a process carried even further by his successor, Reagan.[17]

Whether the idea is expressed as maintaining military equivalency or creating a military establishment "second to none," since the Korean War the

16. Frank Tannenbaum, *The American Tradition in Foreign Policy* (Norman, Okla., 1955); Dexter Perkins, *The American Approach to Foreign Policy* (rev. ed.; New York, 1968); and Lincoln P. Bloomfield, *In Search of American Foreign Policy: The Humane Use of Power* (New York, 1974).

17. Schlesinger, *A Thousand Days*, 301–302, 317–18. The fiscal year 1985 military budget of the United States reached the level of $292.9 billion. See the New York *Times*, September 21, 1984, dispatch by Jonathan Feurbringer.

American people and their leaders have repeatedly indicated their awareness that national power counts, sometimes decisively, in determining diplomatic results. Similarly, despite occasional alleged wrongdoing by the Central Intelligence Agency (CIA), Americans have made clear that they desire a large and efficient intelligence network; movements directed at disbanding the CIA have received very limited support on Capitol Hill and among the American people. In their typically paradoxical approach to foreign affairs, Americans concurrently favor efforts to negotiate Soviet-American differences and to resolve other global disputes peacefully, and to reduce the level of global armaments.[18]

A comparable analysis could be undertaken for the other criteria listed above. Yet the most frequently employed criterion—and the one most consistently favored by the American people—for determining the actual meaning and value of external policy is the pragmatic test of experience. Practically, the worth of any particuar diplomatic undertaking—or the overall impact and success of a given administration's diplomatic efforts—is normally measured *by its results or consequences,* intended and unintended. This was the case during the long era of American isolationism, and it remains true during the new age of American internationalism.

For some 150 years before World War II, the principle of isolationism governed the American nation's approach to foreign affairs. Yet the historic policy of isolationism was applied *pragmatically* to developments overseas. Isolationism, for example, did not apply to American foreign policy toward Asia; and toward Latin America, from around 1900 until the present day, the diplomacy of the United States has often been interventionist.[19]

To the American mind, a position of isolationism toward the Old World was logical and defensible for a long list of reasons. There was, for example, the geographical reality of America's physical separation from Europe by the "Atlantic moat." Americans also felt ideological estrangement from the European autocracies; they desired to avoid contaminating their new democratic system by overly close association with the Old World. Great Britain's example of "splendid isolation"—or unwillingness to engage in permanent alliances with other nations—served as a model for Americans. Isolationism also contributed to political stability for the new American democracy—a

18. Cecil V. Crabb, Jr., and Pat Holt, *Invitation to Struggle: Congress, the President and Foreign Policy* (2nd ed.; Washington, D.C., 1984), 161–87.

19. John A. Garraty, *Henry Cabot Lodge: A Biography* (New York, 1953), esp. 147–66, 255–58.

nation of immigrants—allowing the United States to avoid participation in political quarrels within and among the "old countries" of Europe.

With the passage of time, other factors such as religious influences, ethnicity, the geographical insularity of the isolationist heartland (the Midwest), domestic political factors, psychological forces, and the role of powerful individuals in diplomatic decision making strengthened the isolationist tradition. As Wayne S. Cole concluded, "Probably no single hypothesis explaining American isolationism is sufficient. The causes of isolation are varied and diverse."[20]

Yet for millions of Americans, experience weighed heavily in their attachment to the isolationist mentality. Even before they became independent, Americans had acquired firsthand awareness of the consequences to be expected from actively engaging in the power politics endemic in the Old World. While they were still under British dominion, Americans learned that an interventionist foreign policy drained nations financially, led to new and onerous taxes, enhanced the powers of autocratic governments (especially executive authority), and jeopardized domestic freedoms.[21] Great Britain's hated Stamp Tax imposed in 1764, for example, was a measure imposed by Parliament to help defray the cost of the recent war with France (the Seven Years' War, 1756–1763, or French and Indian War as it was known in North America). Another practice widely resented throughout the colonies—the quartering of British troops in American homes—was also an outgrowth of the necessity to station large numbers of British troops abroad. The disruption of American trade and commerce was another consequence of international conflicts which Americans often believed were remote from their interests and inimical to their well-being.

After independence, Americans were aware that their republic was weak and vulnerable. If it became allied with the stronger power in an international dispute, its influence in decision making was likely to be minimal. If, on the other hand, it became allied with a weaker power, which eventually lost an international conflict, America's newly gained independence might be se-

20. Wayne S. Cole, *Senator Gerald P. Nye and American Foreign Relations* (Minneapolis, 1962), 6; and Ray A. Billington, "The Origins of Middle Western Isolationism," *Political Science Quarterly,* LX (March, 1945), 44–64.
21. See Albert K. Weinberg, "The Historical Meaning of the American Doctrine of Isolation," *American Political Science Review,* XXXIV (1940), 539–47; Selig Adler, *The Isolationist Impulse: Its Twentieth-Century Reaction* (London, 1957); Ralph J. Smuckeler, "The Region of Isolationism," *American Political Science Review,* XLVII (1953), 386–97; and Cole, *Senator Gerald P. Nye and American Foreign Relations,* 1–13.

riously jeopardized. As George Washington and nearly every subsequent chief executive advised, therefore, the only sensible course for America was to avoid involvement in European political conflicts and to concern itself primarily with its own internal pursuits.[22]

Experience for the next 150 years repeatedly confirmed to the American mind the wisdom of the isolationist position. Democratic principles not only survived in America, but they were continually extended to new dimensions of national life. The American standard of living rose steadily, and the capitalistic economic system became a model of productivity and innovation. Countless thousands of immigrants entered the United States and were successfully assimilated into American life. Even the agony of the Civil War did not permanently disrupt the fabric of the American society or impair its progress in most realms of national experience. The boundaries of the United States were steadily enlarged, in most instances (the most notable exception was the Mexican War) by purchase and peaceful negotiations. Meanwhile, post-Napoleonic Europe remained gripped by deep social antagonisms and political upheavals, governed by entrenched autocracies, and immersed in diplomatic rivalries, colonial competitions, and arms races. By the early twentieth century, as war clouds gathered ominously on the European continent, Americans were virtually unanimous in their contention that the isolationist policy had been amply justified by experience. Woodrow Wilson's successful campaign slogan in the national election of 1916—"He kept us out of war"—proved extremely popular with the American people and was a key factor in his reelection.

For millions of Americans, the nation's participation in World War I was in time judged to have been a serious mistake, confirming the essential wisdom of the historic isolationist stance. Distinguished American writers created an influential school of "disillusionist" literature, which crucially affected American public thinking. On Capitol Hill, legislators devoted intensive efforts to proving that America had been duped into entering World War I by British propagandists, munitions makers, and other self-serving interests (a variation on the old theme that in foreign affairs, Americans were no match for the wily and treacherous diplomats of the Old World).[23]

22. The isolationist mentality is discussed in Cecil V. Crabb, Jr., *Policy-Makers and Critics: Conflicting Theories of American Foreign Policy* (2nd ed.; New York, 1986), 1–31. For John Dewey's views on the historic isolationist policy, see Jo Ann Boydston (ed.), *John Dewey: The Later Works, 1925–1953* (12 vols.; Carbondale, Ill., 1981), II, 167–72.

23. See U.S. Senate, *Hearings Before the Special Committee Investigating the Munitions Industry,* 73rd Cong., 2nd sess., pts. 1–39. An interpretive study is John E. Wiltz, *In Search of Peace: The Senate Munitions Inquiry, 1934–1936* (Baton Rouge, 1963).

For perhaps a majority of Americans, the observable results of World War I—widespread economic dislocations, social disorganization, the emergence of new totalitarian ideologies and systems of government—strongly reinforced the prevailing isolationist impulse. During most of his first two terms in office, not even Franklin D. Roosevelt—perhaps the most politically adroit leader in American history—was able to stem the isolationist tide successfully.[24]

By the end of the 1930s, the American people were conscious of the danger posed by Axis expansionism and gave at least tacit approval to Roosevelt's policy of "aid short of war" to Great Britain and other nations whose security was endangered. As Walter Lippmann said, "In foreign affairs, the country learned in the second World War that it was no longer among many great powers but that in fact it was the leading power upon which the whole Western world depended for its security and leadership." In assuming a position of diplomatic leadership, Americans would discover that "necessity will again be the mother of invention."[25]

According to the symbol of bipartisanship in postwar American foreign policy, Senator Arthur H. Vandenberg (R., Mich.), Pearl Harbor "ended isolationism for any realist" in the United States. Another vocal champion of the isolationist viewpoint, Senator Robert A. Taft (R., Ohio) said on one occasion that "only an idiot" would be an isolationist after 1941. In the popular phrase, Americans had learned their lesson painfully. A military disaster had showed that whatever the American people's wishes, the United States was not in fact isolated from global political events and could not remain so in the future. In the diplomatic phrase, the historic policy of isolationism had been "overtaken by events." However reluctantly, the vast majority of Americans, including most earlier proponents of isolationism, eventually adapted their thinking to that reality.[26]

The American nation's historic decision to abandon isolationism as its foreign policy position came about as the result of no national debate or public referendum over the theoretical merits of isolationism versus interna-

24. See Burton K. Wheeler, *Yankee from the West* (Garden City, N.Y., 1962), 31–33; and Cole, *Senator Gerald P. Nye and American Foreign Relations*, 9–10.

25. Walter Johnson, *The Battle Against Isolation* (Chicago, 1944); Lippmann's views are in Oscar Handlin (ed.), *American Principles and Issues: The National Purpose* (New York, 1981), 474.

26. Arthur H. Vandenberg, Jr. (ed.), *The Private Papers of Senator Vandenberg* (Boston, 1952), 1. During his administration, Harry S. Truman frequently alluded to the lessons and the mistakes of the past that had to be avoided in America's postwar diplomacy, especially in relations with the Soviet Union. See, for example, *Public Papers of the Presidents of the United States: Harry S. Truman, 1947* (Washington, D.C., 1963), 178, 193, 323–26, 486–87.

tionalism. It was the inevitable result of one of those dramatic lessons conveyed by experience—of which the American diplomatic tradition is replete—that was impressed indelibly upon the national consciousness and that profoundly affected public attitudes toward foreign affairs in the years ahead. After Pearl Harbor, Roosevelt never doubted that America's leadership role during World War II would extend into postwar planning and international decision making. His efforts to make wartime planning for the new United Nations a bipartisan undertaking stemmed in no small measure from awareness of a dual mistake made by the Wilson administration after World War I. One was the failure to consult the Republican opposition meaningfully in drafting the peace treaties and the Covenant of the League of Nations. The other was neglecting to assure an active role of American leadership after the war inside and outside the League of Nations to prevent a new international conflagration. The Roosevelt administration's determination to learn from Wilson's errors bore fruit on July 28, 1945, when the Senate approved the Charter of the United Nations by the overwhelming vote of 89 to 2.[27]

Even during and after World War II, as postwar experience time and again demonstrated, the American society's formal abandonment of the historic policy of isolationism was reluctant and unenthusiastic. A strong case can be made for the contention that emotionally and psychologically, if not by rational standards, isolationism remains the preferred diplomatic orientation of most Americans. The persistence of neoisolationist currents in the American mind testifies to the durability and appeal of the isolationist heritage.[28]

As in the past, in the new age of active international involvement by the United States, Americans continued to derive many of their diplomatic guidelines from experience. No dimension of national diplomacy perhaps illustrates this phenomenon better than postwar Soviet-American relations. Since the United States was isolationist down to World War II, and the Soviet Union was also preoccupied with internal problems until the late 1930s, each nation became significantly aware of the other's foreign policy goals and interests during and after World War II. Although the Allied cause—the "strange alliance"—remained sufficiently unified to assure an Axis defeat, even during the war Soviet-American relations were tense and characterized by major

27. Cordell Hull, *Memoirs* (2 vols.; New York, 1948), II, 1625–1743; and Vandenberg (ed.), *Private Papers of Senator Vandenberg*, 21–37, 90–126, 146–72. See also the discussion of bipartisanship in Cecil V. Crabb, Jr., *Bipartisan Foreign Policy: Myth or Reality?* (New York, 1957), 1–54.

28. See Vandenberg (ed.), *Private Papers of Senator Vandenberg*, 3–9. Postwar neoisolationist thought is analyzed more fully in Crabb, *Policy-Makers and Critics*, 214–99. An analysis of neoisolationist thought in light of the Vietnam War is Robert W. Tucker, *A New Isolationism: Threat or Promise?* (New York, 1972).

misunderstandings. Before his death, even Roosevelt had began to wonder whether Soviet-American cooperation would endure into the postwar era.[29]

More than most chief executives perhaps, President Harry S. Truman was conscious of the lessons of history, and his approach to diplomatic issues clearly reflected this awareness. A few weeks after entering the Oval Office, Truman became genuinely disturbed about the peace that would follow defeat of the Axis powers. Recalling the post–World War I era, Truman was afraid that the emerging postwar order might "carry within it the kind of self-defeating provisions that would enable another Hitler to rise to power." Several months later, in planning the American administration of defeated Japan, Truman "was determined that the Japanese occupation should not follow in the footsteps of our German occupation. I did not want the divided [Allied] control of separate zones. I did not want to give the Russians any opportunity to behave as they had in Germany and Austria." In asking the Senate to approve the United Nations Charter, Truman observed that "fascism did not die" with defeat of Germany and Italy. As in the past the enemies of freedom sought to divide and conquer the Allies; only continued unity among them, as during the war, could preserve peace and security.[30]

Soon after assuming the presidential office, the man from Missouri delivered one of the sharpest and most undiplomatic rebukes ever expressed to a Soviet official when he gave Soviet Foreign Minister V. M. Molotov a tongue lashing because of the Soviet Union's failure to observe the Yalta agreement and other accords respecting Eastern Europe. Urged by his advisers to demonstrate that "we were not afraid of the Russians" and to "be firm when we were right," Truman castigated Molotov because the Kremlin was not adhering to agreements reached with the United States. To Molotov's lament that he had "never been talked to like that in my life," the plain-spoken Truman replied: "Carry out your agreements and you won't get talked to like that."[31]

After his own frustrating experience in trying to gain agreement with Soviet officials on a number of key postwar issues, former Secretary of State James F. Byrnes concluded that a careful study of Russian history revealed a remarkable continuity in the Soviet state's diplomatic goals and tactics. "And the aims that Stalin and Molotov have pursued since the end of the war vary

29. For discussions of emerging Soviet-American tensions during and after World War II, see Robert Beitzell, *The Uneasy Alliance: America, Britain and Russia, 1941–1943* (New York, 1972); George C. Herring, Jr., *Aid to Russia, 1941–1946: Strategy, Diplomacy and the Origins of the Cold War* (New York, 1973); Thomas G. Paterson, *Soviet-American Confrontation: Postwar Reconstruction and the Origins of the Cold War* (Baltimore, 1973); and Diane S. Clemens, *Yalta* (New York, 1970).
30. Harry S. Truman, *Year of Decisions* (Garden City, N.Y., 1955), 308, 432, 292–93.
31. *Ibid.*, 75–82.

little from the demands they made of Adolf Hitler." Byrnes was convinced that, like Hitler, Stalin never intended to honor solemn international agreements made with the Allies during World War II. Experience had demonstrated convincingly that communist officials had "no scruples about violating laws and pledges to acquire the property they want for security."[32]

As much as any other single factor, the American perception of the role of experience in Soviet-American relations in time produced a profound change in American attitudes toward Moscow, inducing Washington to adopt a policy of "patience and firmness" in dealing with the Kremlin. This policy received its most forceful expression in the issuance of the Truman Doctrine early in 1947, when President Truman committed the United States to the policy of containment of Soviet expansionism.[33] Even before the end of World War II, American officials in Moscow such as Ambassador W. Averell Harriman and George F. Kennan had repeatedly warned Washington about postwar Soviet diplomatic aims in Europe and other regions. On the basis of his knowledge of Russian history and culture, Kennan frequently cautioned his superiors in Washington that after the war the USSR could be expected to pursue long-standing diplomatic ambitions, many of which were hallmarks of Russian diplomacy during the czarist period.

From firsthand experience and a careful study of Russian history, Kennan concluded that the Soviet Union was a "closed society" and would likely remain so; that gaining accurate information about most activities of the Soviet government would be extremely difficult; that written agreements (or what Kennan called "weak verbiage") would seldom deter the Kremlin from pursuing its diplomatic objectives; that idealistic or militant American foreign policy declarations unaccompanied by firm action would have little impact upon Soviet behavior; that Moscow could not be counted upon to observe treaties and other agreements that were not in its interests; and that Washington need not expect the USSR to serve as a "fit ally" in collaborative international endeavors. Instead, Americans could look forward to Soviet behavior based upon hatred and rejection of other countries, "abundant cruelties," "claims to infallibility," opportunism and unscrupulous methods, and "a love of power that so often and so obviously lurked behind the pre-

32. See the discussion of the Roosevelt administration's growing apprehensions about the future of Soviet-American relations in James F. Byrnes, *Speaking Frankly* (New York, 1947), 58–61, 282–97; Martin F. Herz, *Beginnings of the Cold War* (New York, 1966). Roosevelt's changing assessments of Moscow's postwar aims are discussed in W. Averell Harriman, *America and Russia in a Changing World: A Half Century of Personal Observation* (Garden City, N.Y., 1971), 37–39.

33. Truman's message to Congress on March 12, 1947, is in *Public Papers of Truman, 1947*, 176–80. His decision to aid Greece and Turkey early in 1947 is discussed in his *Years of Trial and Hope* (Garden City, N.Y., 1956), 93–110.

tense of high-minded ideological conviction." In any conflict involving other countries, Kennan believed, Moscow would endeavor to remain noninvolved, to enter at the end "if only in the capacity of a vulture." In brief, from an early date Kennan's assessments offered little ground for expecting cooperative Soviet-American relations in the future. Prophetically, Kennan anticipated that these relations in the years ahead would be marked by "a long series of misunderstandings, disappointments, and recriminations on both sides."[34]

Little evidence exists that Kennan's thinking significantly influenced the diplomacy of the Roosevelt administration. Yet by the closing months of World War II, Kennan and other competent observers of Soviet behavior played a key role in convincing the Truman administration that unilateral concessions and a conciliatory approach to the Soviet Union paid few dividends for the United States. Soviet behavior during and after World War II— in Central and Eastern Europe, the Mediterranean, Iran, Asia, and other settings—convinced the American people and their leaders that only a firm response by the United States could preserve peace and security in the postwar era.[35]

Out of this context, American officials formulated a fundamental principle—"deeds—not words"—that would regulate their relations with the Soviet Union with a high degree of consistency throughout the postwar era. As Truman's sharp remonstrance to Molotov forcefully illustrated, Washington believed that Soviet behavior provided the most reliable index of the Kremlin's diplomatic intentions.

Early in 1957, after witnessing what he and his diplomatic advisers became convinced was a concerted Soviet effort to penetrate the Middle East, President Dwight D. Eisenhower told the leaders of Congress, "The existing vacuum in the Middle East must be filled by the United States before it is filled by Russia." Congress accepted the president's evaluation by approving the Eisenhower Doctrine, designed to provide American economic and military aid to endangered countries in the region. Under this doctrine, American military forces intervened in Lebanon for several months, beginning in May, 1958.[36]

34. George F. Kennan, *Memoirs (1925–1950)* (New York, 1969), 53–59, 72–77, and *passim*; and "The Sources of Soviet Conduct," *Foreign Affairs*, XXV (July, 1947), 556–83. This article and other thoughts by Kennan on Soviet diplomatic behavior are reprinted in his *American Diplomacy.*
35. Kennan, "Sources of Soviet Conduct," 556–83.
36. Dwight D. Eisenhower, *Waging Peace* (Garden City, N.Y., 1965), 40–54, 178, 196–203. The Eisenhower Doctrine for the Middle East is analyzed more fully in Cecil V. Crabb, Jr., *The Doctrines of American Foreign Policy: Their Meaning, Role, and Future* (Baton Rouge, 1982), 153–93.

From their experiences during and after World War II in confronting an expansionist Soviet Union, Americans derived the concept of the power vacuum. In Washington's view, the evidence since the war indicated convincingly that Moscow was eager to exploit conditions of political conflict, economic weakness, or military vulnerability within the noncommunist world to promote its diplomatic goals. At some stage, every postwar American president has based his diplomatic moves upon the existence of a power vacuum in one or more regions abroad and upon the expectation that Moscow would endeavor to fill it.

During the late fall of 1984, President Ronald Reagan met with the experienced Soviet Foreign Minister Andrei Gromyko. It was not coincidence that this meeting took place following an intensive American military buildup, proposed by the Carter and Reagan administrations.[37] This development highlighted another diplomatic behavior guideline which Americans had derived from experience in recent Soviet-American relations: negotiating from strength. Even before World War II ended, Americans had witnessed the descent of the Iron Curtain on much of east-central Europe. The imposition of communist satellite regimes in this region had occurred for one primary reason: relying upon its military power, the Soviet Union had successfully communized these regions, and the other wartime Allies were powerless to prevent it. Similarly, many Americans concluded that the communist attack on South Korea in late June, 1950, had resulted from a perception by policy makers in the Soviet Union, Communist China, and North Korea that the United States was militarily weak, indifferent to South Korea's fate, and insensitive to its security interests in Asia and other regions.[38]

A related principle governed the diplomacy of the Johnson administration toward Latin America. After witnessing the communization of Cuba, followed by the Bay of Pigs episode and the Cuban missile crisis during the early 1960s, President Lyndon B. Johnson was determined to prevent the emergence of "another Cuba" in the Western Hemisphere—a goal that was reiterated several times by officials of the Reagan administration. His intervention in the Dominican Republic in 1965 was motivated in large measure by this goal. Similarly, the diplomacy of the Reagan administration was directed at preventing expanded Cuban and Soviet influence in Central Amer-

37. New York *Times*, September 29, 1984, dispatch by Steven R. Weisman; *ibid.*, October 1, 1984, dispatch by Bernard Gwertzman.
38. The causes of the Korean War are discussed in Matthew B. Ridgway, *The Korean War* (New York, 1967), 15–30; David Rees, *Korea: The Limited War* (Baltimore, 1970), x–xvi; and Dean Acheson, *Present at the Creation: My Years in the State Department* (New York, 1969), 358–65.

ica; both countries were regarded as sponsors of revolutionary movements throughout Latin America.[39]

The concept of détente (or what Moscow prefers to call "peaceful coexistence") between the superpowers also clearly illustrates the role of experience in shaping American foreign policy attitudes. As always, the viewpoints of Americans exhibited anomalies and contradictions. Relatively few Americans opposed the idea of a relaxation of cold war tensions. A peaceful resolution of international disputes has been a long-standing goal of the diplomacy of the United States. Yet Americans were convinced that the United States must "keep its guard up" in dealing with the Soviet Union; that "eternal vigilance is the price of liberty"; that the nation must maintain a military establishment "second to none"; and that negotiations with Moscow could be constructively undertaken only from a position of Western strength.[40]

A pivotal concept in the American understanding of détente was merely a contemporary variation on the old theme of "deeds—not words." This was *linkage*, or the idea that Moscow's professed interest in more cooperative relations with the United States had to be correlated with its actions abroad. If the Kremlin desired to improve relations with the United States, it could provide evidence of this intention by curbing its interventionist tendencies in Poland, Afghanistan, Southeast Asia, and Central America. Washington, in other words, was unwilling to accept a theory of détente which imposed restraints upon its own behavior while leaving Moscow free to sponsor "wars of national liberation" and other activities inimical to the peace and security of the noncommunist world. Once again, for Americans the meaning and value of détente were determined by reference to experience. In the absence of Soviet behavior consonant with the spirit of détente, Americans were inclined to view the concept as little more than a propaganda gambit or diplomatic tactic employed by the Kremlin to promote its own diplomatic ends.[41]

One final example of the key role of experience in shaping public and official American attitudes toward the Soviet Union may be cited. This was

39. The Johnson Doctrine for Latin America is discussed in Crabb, *Doctrines of American Foreign Policy,* 235–77; and Lyndon B. Johnson, *The Vantage Point: Perspectives of the Presidency, 1963–1969* (New York, 1971), 184–205. See the State Department publication "A National Response to the Crisis in Central America," *Current Policy,* No. 559, March 27, 1984, pp. 1–7.

40. President Kennedy's inaugural address, January 20, 1961, is discussed in Sorensen, *Kennedy,* 509–12.

41. Henry Kissinger, *Years of Upheaval* (Boston, 1982), 239–40, 746; see also Zbigniew Brzezinski, *Power and Principle: Memoirs of the National Security Adviser, 1977–1981* (New York, 1983), 147–50.

the dramatic transition in President Jimmy Carter's attitude toward Moscow during the late 1970s. Throughout most of his term in office, Carter had called for more cooperative Soviet-American relations; more than once, he indicated that rigidly anticommunist attitudes by Americans were a serious barrier to achieving that goal. Then, late in 1979, following the overt military intervention by Soviet troops in Afghanistan, Carter radically changed his assessment. Almost pathetically, he confessed that he had "learned more about communism" within a few days than he had known in his lifetime! In the months that followed, he issued the Carter Doctrine, forcefully warning the Soviet Union against threatening the security of the Persian Gulf area, and he recommended substantial increases in American defense spending.[42]

A Pluralistic Global Environment

Pluralism is a fundamental concept for understanding international politics, and especially American foreign policy, for a twofold reason. It accurately describes the *external environment* to which the diplomacy of the United States must be responsive, and it is no less applicable to the *internal environment* of American diplomatic decision making.

In its external dimension, the concept of pluralism relates directly to the American understanding of international politics. The successful American Revolution has frequently been cited as an example of a society that was determined to work out its own political destiny. In the Monroe Doctrine, the United States stated in effect that the Latin American nations had obtained (or were in the process of obtaining) their independence from colonial hegemony, and Washington would resist any new effort to impose a foreign regime upon them.[43]

In the twentieth century, the idea of pluralism was implicit in Woodrow Wilson's concept of self-determination during World War I. That this principle was applied almost exclusively to European nationalities did not mean either that Afro-Asian societies had abandoned their desire to become independent or that Americans had forgotten Wilson's concept. Presidents Roosevelt and Truman, for example, were outspoken opponents of colonialism. FDR linked the elimination of European colonialism to another pragmatic idea: the peaceful evolution of the post–World War II international system to

42. Brzezinski, *Power and Principle,* 426–69.
43. The text of President James Monroe's message to Congress on December 2, 1823, is in James D. Richardson (ed.), *A Compilation of the Messages and Papers of the Presidents, 1789–1897* (Washington, D.C., 1896), II, 207–20.

a new level of global cooperation and sense of community within the family of nations. General Charles de Gaulle, leader of the French government-in-exile during World War II and later president of France, became convinced that Great Britain and the United States were seeking to prevent Paris from reestablishing its colonial empire after World War II, and this was one factor influencing de Gaulle's suspicion of the "Anglo-Saxons" in the postwar era. Similarly, Winston Churchill, British prime minister, was convinced that a leading American diplomatic objective was to bring about the rapid dissolution of the British Empire. According to one well-informed student of the period, during World War II, Roosevelt and his advisers "worried less about the possibility of conflict with Russia than about the continued existence of western, particularly British, imperialism."[44]

After Roosevelt's death, the United States granted independence to the Philippines in 1946, and the Truman administration continued to insist that the European colonial powers relinquish their overseas dependencies. American influence was unquestionably a factor in India's acquisition of independence in 1947, in Indonesia's in 1949, and in Egypt's in 1954, when Great Britain agreed to evacuate the Suez Canal Zone. In the years ahead, the independence acquired by most societies in black Africa could be attributed in some measure to American diplomatic influence. Yet toward dependent societies in Africa and other regions, American foreign policy emphasized the importance of adequate preparation for self-government, of eventual independence for colonial possessions, and of the necessity for Afro-Asian societies demanding independence to demonstrate their capacity to exercise its responsibility.[45]

Altogether, 51 independent nations signed the United Nations Charter at San Francisco in 1945. By the mid-1980s, the organization had some 158 members. By this period, the United States maintained relations with more than 160 nations (not counting several, such as Iran, Cuba, and North Vietnam, with which Washington deliberately refrained from maintaining formal diplomatic relations). This transformation in the nature of the international

44. Robert E. Sherwood, *Roosevelt and Hopkins: An Intimate History* (New York, 1948), 511; and U.S. Senate, Foreign Relations Committee, *A Decade of American Foreign Policy: Basic Documents, 1941–1949,* 81st Cong., 1st sess., pp. 1–2. For American views on colonialism, see also Hull, *Memoirs,* II, 1235–38. Charles de Gaulle, *The Complete War Memoirs of Charles de Gaulle* (2 vols.; New York, 1959), II, 321–23. For Churchill's views, see Smith, *American Diplomacy During the Second World War,* 13, 81–98.

45. Acheson, *Present at the Creation,* 327; Vernon McKay, *Africa in World Politics* (New York, 1963), 288–361. For the views of Secretary of State Cordell Hull on independence for Afro-Asian societies, see *ibid.,* 319–20.

system within a relatively few years was remarkable, and it owed much to American diplomatic initiatives. American society, Truman observed in his memoirs, "fought her own war of liberation against colonialism, and we shall always regard with sympathy and understanding the desire of people everywhere to be free of colonial bondage."[46]

Admittedly, some American officials in the years ahead had difficulty accepting the implications of an increasingly pluralistic international order. A noteworthy case was provided by Secretary of State John Foster Dulles under the Eisenhower administration, who characterized a position of diplomatic neutralism (or nonalignment) as "immoral." Dulles' remark strongly implied that in the existing bipolar configuration of global power, all nations must choose to enter either the American or the Soviet diplomatic orbit. Yet Dulles' ideas did not fully reflect the viewpoints of President Eisenhower; after the former's resignation because of ill health in 1959, the Eisenhower administration's attitude toward nations espousing nonalignment underwent significant change.[47]

A diplomatic watchword of the Kennedy administration was "a world of diversity." More than any chief executive since World War II, John F. Kennedy identified with the concerns of the Third World and was widely admired throughout that zone. (Significantly, while he was a member of the Senate, Kennedy had achieved public prominence because of his active espousal of independence for nations on the African continent.) Convinced that Americans "cannot impose our will upon the other 94 percent of mankind," Kennedy favored what one of his advisers described as "a stable community of free and independent nations" as the best assurance of a peaceful and stable international system, and he believed that American foreign policy toward the Third World must have top priority in his administration's diplomatic activities.[48]

Against congressional critics, Kennedy and his advisers urged support for the principle of international diversity, and they advocated American foreign aid and other forms of assistance to several Afro-Asian nations whose policies were not always congruent with America's. These nations, Kennedy contended, "are entitled to national sovereignty and independence"; he did not insist that they always "agree with us" or choose to align themselves permanently with either superpower. He felt that for many newly independent

46. Truman, *Year of Decisions*, 275.
47. See Cecil V. Crabb, Jr., *The Elephants and the Grass: A Study of Non-Alignment* (New York, 1965), 168–98; and Eisenhower, *Waging Peace*, 103–106, 428–30.
48. Sorensen, *Kennedy*, 511, 529–30.

nations (as was true of the United States throughout much of its history) a foreign policy of nonalignment was inevitable. In 1963 Kennedy called for a "world made safe for diversity," and this idea became a dominant theme of his short-lived administration.[49]

By the early 1970s, the Nixon administration believed that the contemporary international system had become increasingly pluralistic. New nations "have found identity and self-confidence and are acting autonomously on the world state." Similarly, a once monolithic communist bloc "has fragmented into competing centers of doctrine and power." The earlier era of bipolarity had been superseded by "the fluidity of a new era of multilateral diplomacy." The international environment had become "increasingly heterogeneous and complex," meaning that "a shrinking globe and expanding interdependence" were hallmarks of international relations. A leading goal of American diplomacy, therefore, was "to realize the creative possibilities of a pluralistic world."[50]

In regard to Latin America, for example, Nixon asserted that it was the policy of the United States to maintain "contacts with governments spanning a wide political spectrum." Washington clearly preferred "free and democratic processes" among governments within the Western Hemisphere, and it did not disguise its hope that some governments "will evolve toward constitutional procedures." At the same time, the United States proposed to "deal with governments as they are"; America's relations with them would depend "on actions which affect us and the inter-American system." Nixon specifically singled out Cuba as an example of a government whose actions placed it outside the inter-American system "by its encouragement and support of revolution and its military ties to the Soviet Union." Moscow was attempting to use Cuba as a base to expand its hegemony throughout Latin America.[51]

The concept of pluralism was again uppermost in the diplomacy of the Carter and Reagan administrations toward Central America, and specifically toward the pro-Marxist government of Nicaragua. When the despotic, right-wing government of Anastasio Somoza was finally overthrown and replaced by a new government led by the Sandinista movement on July 17, 1979, for several months thereafter the Carter White House endeavored to preserve at

49. *Ibid.*, 537–39.
50. For the Nixon administration's view, see the White House publication *U.S. Foreign Policy for the 1970s: Building for Peace* (Washington, D.C., 1971), 155–65; and the White House publication *U.S. Foreign Policy for the 1970s: The Emerging Structure of Peace* (Washington, D.C., 1972), 16–26.
51. *U.S. Foreign Policy for the 1970's: Building for Peace*, 3–7, 53–55; *U.S. Foreign Policy for the 1970's: The Emerging Structure of Peace*, 3, 101–103.

least minimally cooperative relations with it, despite the new regime's Marxist coloration. This effort, however, met with considerable opposition in Congress, many of whose members believed that the Sandinista regime was
becoming a conduit by which Cuba (encouraged by the Soviet Union) was
seeking to export revolution to other Central American countries. Within
Nicaragua, the Sandinista regime was suppressing dissent and taking other
steps designed to impose a monolithic communist system upon the nation.

Predictably, the Republican administration of Ronald Reagan was even
more outspokenly opposed to Nicaragua's internal and external policies than
its Democratic predecessor. Increasingly, the Reagan White House adopted a
tough position toward the Sandinista regime. At a minimum, it demanded
the Nicaraguan government's abandonment of interventionist behavior
abroad and adherence to promised democratic reforms at home. In actuality,
many critics of Reagan's policies believed, by supporting the anticommunist
Contra movement based in Honduras, and other means, the Reagan White
House actually sought the overthrow of the Marxist regime in Nicaragua,
followed by the installation of a new government more favorably disposed
toward the United States and less dependent upon Cuba and the Soviet
Union. (Elsewhere, however, as in the "normalization" of relations with
China, the United States had accepted the idea of wide diversity among
Marxist-based governments.)[52]

The concept of pluralism is central to American foreign policy for three
fundamental reasons. First, on ideological grounds it is integral to the concept
of democracy, a principle with which American society has been identified for
over two centuries and which remains pivotal in its approach to external
issues. Second, American officials have emphasized the concept of pluralism
abroad because of their belief that Afro-Asian nationalist movements—resulting in the emergence of the Third World—had become increasingly
powerful and, by the end of World War II, irresistible. The defeat of the
European powers by Japan, for example, gave a potent impetus to nationalist
demands in Asia, and the wartime debilitation of Great Britain, France, and
the Netherlands meant that as a rule they were incapable of reimposing their
colonial empires upon unwilling subjects by force. From the *Realpolitik* perspective, Washington urged its European allies to face the reality that traditional colonial systems were doomed.

52. For President Reagan's view, see the New York *Times*, August 6, 1983, dispatch by
Hedrick Smith; *ibid.*, January 25, 1985, dispatch by Gerald M. Boyd; see also the statement by
Assistant Secretary of State Langhorne A. Motley on April 17, 1985, in "The New Opportunity for
Peace in Nicaragua," U.S. State Department, *Current Policy*, No. 687, April 17, 1985, p. 1.

Third, as cold war between the superpowers became the dominant fact of international political life, American officials advocated the concept of pluralism for another reason: the belief that societies that were politically independent (even from the United States) were determined to maintain their newly won freedom and to resist efforts by Moscow or other communist nations to impose a new alien political regime upon them. To the degree that this happened, as it has throughout the Third World since World War II, the phenomenon would contribute to the goals of America's containment strategy vis-à-vis the Soviet Union.

Five

Pragmatic American Diplomacy

Cognition, Challenge, and Response

_____

The "Crisis" Nature of American Diplomacy

A fundamental pragmatic tenet is that the process of human perception and cognition is triggered by the mind's awareness of the existence of a problem or challenge affecting human well-being. Among the almost infinite number of sensations, stimuli, perceptions, and the like impinging upon it from the environment, the mind sorts these out and concentrates upon those perceived as being most directly related to human survival and welfare. Anyone familiar with the diplomatic record of the United States is aware of the American tendency to engage in "crisis diplomacy" in response to a perceived threat to national security or some other acute problem in the external milieu.

That crisis diplomacy is a perennial trait of American diplomacy can hardly be doubted. The issuance of the Monroe Doctrine in 1823, for example, was Washington's response to two perceived crises: the possible reimposition of European colonial regimes upon the Latin American nations and the threatened expansion of czarist colonialism into the western territories from the Pacific Northwest. (In the case of the Monroe Doctrine and later instances in the nation's diplomatic record, Americans may well have misperceived the nature and gravity of the external crisis confronting them. Yet whether understood correctly or not, Americans *acted upon their perceptions,* and these became the basis of the nation's foreign policy attitudes and behavior.) At the end of the century, the Open Door policy toward China was issued in response to a perceived threat to the integrity of that country, which offi-

162

cials of the McKinley administration believed jeopardized China's future and American economic and other ties with it. The Open Door policy was expected to neutralize that threat and prevent its recurrence in the future.[1]

Attention has already been devoted to the impact of a crisis—the successful Japanese attack against Pearl Harbor on December 7, 1941—in accounting for the historic transition from isolationism to internationalism in American foreign policy. Postwar diplomatic experience exhibited the same pattern. From the Truman Doctrine in 1947 to the Carter Doctrine in 1980, every recent doctrine of American foreign relations (with the possible exception of the Nixon Doctrine) was issued in response to an existing crisis abroad. Without discussing these individually, we may briefly take note of three of them.[2]

The Truman Doctrine, committing the United States officially to the policy of containment of the Soviet Union, was the answer to what Washington viewed as a clear communist threat to Greece and Turkey. Containment was also applicable to countries such as South Korea and South Vietnam, which faced comparable threats in the years ahead.[3]

The second Johnson Doctrine for Latin America in 1965 in effect reiterated the principle contained in the Monroe Doctrine that the United States would oppose any attempt by a foreign power to establish itself in the Western Hemisphere. LBJ's doctrine was issued in response to what he and his advisers believed was a communist-instigated attempt to overthrow the govern-

1. The Monroe Doctrine is discussed more fully in Cecil V. Crabb, Jr., *The Doctrines of American Foreign Policy: Their Meaning, Role, and Future* (Baton Rouge, 1982), 9–56; Dexter Perkins, *A History of the Monroe Doctrine* (Boston, 1955); and James W. Gattenbein (comp. and ed.), *The Evolution of Our Latin American Policy: A Documentary Record* (New York, 1950). See the discussion of the Open Door policy in Crabb, *Doctrines of American Foreign Policy*, 56–107. More extended discussion is available in John K. Fairbank, *The United States and China* (New York, 1958); and Warren I. Cohen, *America's Response to China: An Interpretive History of Sino-American Relations* (New York, 1971).

2. The principal postwar doctrines of American diplomacy were the Truman Doctrine (1947), the Eisenhower Doctrine (1957), the Johnson Doctrine for Southeast Asia (1964), the Johnson Doctrine for Latin America (1965), the Nixon Doctrine (1969), and the Carter Doctrine (1980). The diplomacy of the Reagan administration after 1980 indicated clearly that President Reagan accepted most of these doctrines—especially the Johnson Doctrine designed to prevent the emergence of another Cuba in Latin America, and the Carter Doctrine pledging the United States to preserve the security of the Persian Gulf area. These doctrines are analyzed individually in Crabb, *Doctrines of American Foreign Policy.*

3. Washington's perception of the threats posed by Soviet conduct in Iran, Greece, Turkey, and other settings in the early postwar period is emphasized in Harry S. Truman, *Years of Trial and Hope* (Garden City, N.Y., 1955), 93–109; Arthur H. Vandenberg, Jr. (ed.), *The Private Papers of Senator Vandenberg* (Boston, 1952), 337–73; Joseph M. Jones, *The Fifteen Weeks* (New York, 1955); and Bruce R. Kuniholm, *The Origins of the Cold War in the Near East: Great Powers Conflict and Diplomacy in Iran, Turkey and Greece* (Princeton, 1980).

ment of the Dominican Republic, and it led to American military intervention to frustrate that objective.[4] Acceptance of this same principle underlay the Reagan administration's efforts during the 1980s to counter a communist-directed effort by Nicaragua (assisted by Cuba and the Soviet Union) to undermine the government of El Salvador.[5]

In 1980, in response to a series of threats over preceding months to American diplomatic interests and credibility, President Jimmy Carter issued the Carter Doctrine, pledging the United States to preserve the security of, and continued access to, the oil-rich Persian Gulf area. This objective also became a paramount diplomatic goal of the Reagan administration; it was forcefully reiterated by the Reagan White House after the attack on the USS *Stark* in the Persian Gulf in mid-1987.[6]

Numerous other examples might be cited to illustrate the point that American diplomacy has normally been crisis-oriented and directed at the solution of specific international and regional problems. The European Recovery Program (or Marshall Plan) during the late 1940s was formulated to meet Western Europe's increasingly critical social and economic needs in the postwar era. President Truman's Point Four program of aid to developing nations in 1950 was similarly designed to counteract such problems as widespread poverty, malnutrition, disease, and other disorders throughout the emerging Third World. The Cuban missile crisis of 1962 resulted from what officials of the Kennedy administration perceived as an ominous Soviet challenge to national and regional security. America's growing involvement in the Vietnam conflict resulted from a belief by successive administrations that communist expansion in Southeast Asia endangered the security of the region and perhaps of the world. Under the Reagan administration, the modernization and expansion of America's armed forces, the intervention by the

4. See the discussion of the Johnson Doctrine for Latin America in Crabb, *Doctrines of American Foreign Policy*, 235–77. More detailed treatments are Abraham F. Lowenthal, *The Dominican Intervention* (Cambridge, Mass., 1972); Tad Szulc, *Dominican Diary* (New York, 1965); Theodore Draper, *The Dominican Revolt: A Case Study in American Policy* (New York, 1968); and John B. Martin, *Overtaken by Events* (Garden City, N.Y., 1966).

5. See the statement by Assistant Secretary of State Thomas O. Enders, "Nicaragua: Threat to Peace in Central America," in the State Department series *Current Policy*, No. 476, April 12, 1983, pp. 1–5; the statement by Secretary of State George Shultz, "The Struggle for Democracy in Central America," *Current Policy*, No. 478, April 15, 1983, pp. 1–4; and Shultz, "U.S. Efforts to Achieve Peace in Central America," in the State Department series *Special Report*, No. 115, March 14, 1984, pp. 1–8.

6. The Carter Doctrine is examined more fully in Crabb, *Doctrines of American Foreign Policy*, 325–71. Firsthand accounts are available in Jimmy Carter, *Keeping Faith: Memoirs of a President* (New York, 1982), 465–66, 471–72, 586–92; Cyrus Vance, *Hard Choices* (New York, 1983), 384–98; and Zbigniew Brzezinski, *Power and Principle* (New York, 1983), 426–70.

marines in Lebanon, the successful intervention in Grenada, and the effort to prevent communist gains in Central America were all diplomatic undertakings induced by Washington's belief that a crisis or serious problem confronted the United States abroad.

In the absence of a crisis or serious problem overseas requiring a response by the United States, the usual tendency of the American society is *to exhibit apathy and lack of sustained concern about international questions*. By the late twentieth century, this observation would perhaps qualify as a truism, requiring no elaborate documentation. Since the earliest days of the republic, Americans have been predominantly absorbed with domestic issues. With rare exceptions, national political campaigns in the United States tend to revolve around "pocketbook issues"—the cost of living, the level of taxation, or the rate of inflation. Unless and until their attention is diverted by the eruption of a crisis abroad, Americans accord very low priority to diplomatic questions and are poorly informed about international developments. The news media, for example, devote minimal coverage to events abroad vis-à-vis internal problems and developments. For any given international issue, only a small minority of Americans—variously estimated as encompassing 15 to 25 percent of the people—comprise the "attentive public" that is interested in, and reasonably well informed about, foreign affairs.[7]

Once the average American becomes conscious of the existence of a crisis abroad, the reaction is likely to be as much intuitive and emotional as it is analytical and rational. In the popular mind, sloganizing—"Remember the Maine" or "No More Munichs" or "No More Vietnams"—not infrequently becomes a substitute for an informed and objective understanding of the diplomatic issues involved. By the mid-1980s, for example, skeptical as they were about growing American military involvement in Central America, members of the House and Senate were no less mindful of such politically damaging episodes as the "loss of China" to communism during the 1950s and public anxieties about the emergence of "another Cuba" in the Western Hemisphere.[8]

Crisis-oriented diplomacy has another significant implication for Americans. Since they are seldom interested in diplomatic issues in the absence of

7. See Alfred O. Hero, *Americans in World Affairs* (Boston, 1959), 6; and Bernard C. Cohen, *The Public's Impact on Foreign Policy* (Boston, 1973), 50–56, 62–63.
8. The tendency of Americans to engage in diplomatic "crusades" is a major theme of George F. Kennan's *American Diplomacy, 1900–1950* (New York, 1952). The same idea is emphasized in Walter Lippmann, *U.S. Foreign Policy: Shield of the Republic* (Boston, 1943), and *Isolation and Alliances: An American Speaks to the British* (Boston, 1952).

an overt crisis abroad, when a crisis exists the American people are nearly always prone to let the president deal with it, and the popular expectation is that the chief executive will do so effectively. It is significant that in the American democracy, relatively few citizens expect Congress, or other possible rivals to the president's preeminent position in the foreign policy process such as the secretary of state, to play this vital role. Despite post–Vietnam War apprehensions about the emergence of an "imperial presidency" and the impact of the Watergate episode on national experience, for example, Americans have not abandoned their preference (evident since the New Deal) for a strong presidency. President Carter's political demise stemmed in no small measure from a pervasive public conviction that his administration had failed to provide the dynamic and effective diplomatic leadership expected by the leader of a superpower. The presidency of Ronald Reagan witnessed a return to the normal pattern in the American foreign policy process: forceful direction of foreign relations by the White House, with Congress for the most part unable to deflect the president from his diplomatic course.

Since the emergence of the United States as a superpower after World War II, the American people have in effect conceded that they are largely apathetic and uninformed concerning foreign affairs. In brief, most Americans "know that they don't know" in the sphere of external policy. That being the case, citizens are normally content to leave the management of foreign relations to those who do—meaning, in practice, the president and his diplomatic advisers. From Franklin D. Roosevelt to Ronald Reagan, the American people have accorded the incumbent president wide latitude to respond to external crises and problems as he and his advisers think best under prevailing circumstances. Almost invariably, the public perception of an external crisis results in a tendency to rally around the White House and to accept the president's proposed course of action for responding to it (a tendency usually evident also among the people's representatives on Capitol Hill). Public anxieties about the emergence of the imperial presidency in recent years have not fundamentally altered the dominant position of the chief executive in the American foreign policy process.[9]

This fact means that in recent diplomatic experience, the president continues to serve as the dominant actor in the foreign policy process in the face of a twofold challenge: by those seeking to make the United States a "participatory democracy" and those advocating that Congress become an equal

9. The reasons why the chief executive remains the primary actor in the foreign policy process are explained more fully in Cecil V. Crabb, Jr., and Pat Holt, *Invitation to Struggle: Congress, the President, and Foreign Policy* (2nd ed.; Washington, D.C., 1984).

partner with the executive in the management of foreign relations. The goal of converting the American system into a participatory democracy by making it directly responsive to vocal (and sometimes violent) demonstrations and protests has been prominent among certain anti–Vietnam War groups, critics of American policy toward South Africa, and others. Studies have shown, however, that for most Americans not only do such tactics usually fail to achieve their objective, but the effect of highly emotional, extremist, and sometimes violent protests against American foreign policy in Southeast Asia, Africa, and other settings is often to strengthen public support and sympathy for the president. President Lyndon B. Johnson was determined that crucial diplomatic decisions by the United States would not be made "in the streets" by extremist groups, and other chief executives have adhered to the same principle.[10]

The other contender to a preeminent role by the president in foreign relations has been a diplomatically assertive Congress. The period since the Vietnam War has seen unprecedented activism by Congress in the foreign policy field. Many proponents of this movement were convinced that the Vietnam conflict proved the necessity for Congress to assert its constitutional prerogatives to the point of becoming an equal partner with the president in the conduct of foreign affairs.

Although there has unquestionably been a resurgence in legislative interest and influence in the diplomatic sphere since the Vietnam conflict, with some notable exceptions advocates of congressional assertiveness have failed to achieve their objective. At best, Congress remains a junior partner in the foreign policy process. Congress has been much more successful in preventing or limiting actions by the executive branch in external affairs than it has in formulating or administering the foreign policy of the United States. In most crucial respects, the locus of effective diplomatic decision making remains in the White House. Congress' evident *desire* for a more decisive role in foreign affairs has greatly exceeded its demonstrated *capacity* to play such a role effectively.[11]

The preeminent position of the president in the American foreign policy

10. Seymour M. Lipset, "The President, the Polls, and Vietnam," in Robert J. Lifton (ed.), *America and the Asian Revolutions* (New Brunswick, N.J., 1973), 101–17.

11. Crabb and Holt, *Invitation to Struggle,* esp. 217–47. Other detailed treatments of the recent experience with congressional diplomatic assertiveness are Louis Fisher, *Politics of Shared Power: Congress and the Executive* (Washington, D.C., 1981); Thomas Franck and Edward Weisband, *Foreign Policy by Congress* (New York, 1979); Edward P. Haley, *Congress and the Fall of South Vietnam and Cambodia* (East Brunswick, N.J., 1982); Pat M. Holt, *The War Powers Resolution: The Role of Congress in U.S. Armed Intervention* (Washington, D.C., 1978); and Alan Platt and Lawrence Weiler, *Congress and Arms Control* (Boulder, Colo., 1978).

process does not, of course, mean that the general public (or what is some-times called mass opinion) makes a totally inconsequential contribution. In any democracy, the domestic and foreign policies of the incumbent govern-ment must process legitimacy or be acceptable to a majority of the people. The diplomacy of the Johnson administration toward Southeast Asia, for exam-ple, ultimately lost legitimacy in the minds of the American people. President Reagan came close to losing a public mandate in behalf of his diplomacy in Lebanon and Central America. In these and other instances, the American people must overtly discern (or, at a minimum, unconsciously sense) a rela-tionship between the diplomatic behavior of their government and the pro-motion of objectives shared by the American society.

In such cases, mass public opinion clearly prescribes the boundaries within which any chief executive must operate within the foreign policy process. Some Americans (always a relatively small minority) believed that the Johnson administration's diplomacy in Southeast Asia was objectionable on moral-ethical grounds. Several years later, the Reagan administration confronted public disaffection centering upon "covert action" by intelligence agencies and other methods used to achieve Washington's foreign policy goals in Iran, Central America, and other settings. In recent years, the anti-nuclear war movement has similarly invoked the moral and ethical precepts that have long been identified with the American way of life and ought to apply to the external, no less than the domestic, policies of the United States government. Several years earlier, former Secretary of State Dean Acheson observed that largely because of such moral-ethical constraints upon its dip-lomatic behavior, it was not possible for the United States to undertake a diplomatic offensive against the Soviet Union such as the Kremlin engaged in routinely; in this sense, American policy toward Moscow had to remain essentially defensive.[12]

Yet for a majority of Americans, the Johnson administration's diplomacy in Southeast Asia ultimately lost legitimacy because it failed a fundamental pragmatic test: based on accumulating evidence, the results of America's growing involvement in the Vietnam War were not commensurate with the national effort involved. In brief, Americans in time concluded that the John-son administration's policies in Vietnam were not working, and they could not be made to succeed without exceeding the price most Americans were prepared to pay to achieve the goal. Only a small minority of citizens accepted

12. Dean Acheson, *This Vast External Realm* (New York, 1973), 35.

the contention that America's participation in the Vietnam War was immoral, or that the United States undertook this commitment for some ulterior purpose, or that President Johnson and his advisers had imposed the Vietnam commitment upon an unwilling public and Congress. By the late 1960s, the people objected to continuing the conflict in Southeast Asia primarily because the evidence indicated that the nation's goals apparently could not be achieved within the limits of acceptable costs.[13]

The American people took basically the same attitude toward the Reagan administration's intervention in Lebanon. For many Americans, the difference between Presidents Johnson and Reagan was that the latter had the good sense to realize the failure of his Lebanese venture and to liquidate it before a dramatic diplomatic failure precipitated a national trauma. Confronted with an intractable problem in Lebanon, Reagan "cut his losses" and withdrew American forces. To many citizens, as Reagan's overwhelming re-election to the White House in 1984 indicated, the exhibition of such common sense was a hallmark of effective national leadership.[14]

One additional aspect of America's response to crises or problems abroad is illustrated by an event during the national election of 1964 in which incumbent President Lyndon B. Johnson overwhelmingly defeated the Republican challenger, Senator Barry Goldwater of Arizona. During the campaign, Goldwater, who was noted for his right-wing approach to national issues, asserted that "extremism in the defense of liberty is no vice."[15] Many political observers became convinced that Goldwater's comment significantly contributed to his defeat.

As is illustrated also by the judicial concept of the "reasonable man" or reasonable person, pragmatism values moderation, flexibility, restraint, and reliance upon common sense in the solution of human problems. In most instances, this has been no less a hallmark of post–World War II American diplomacy. The Truman Doctrine, for example, was a limited and restrained response by American officials to the challenge of Soviet interventionism: it avoided the extremes of both acquiescence by the United States in Soviet

13. As one student of American diplomacy expressed it, Vietnam was "America's longest conflict," entailing direct military expenditures of over $100 billion, 44,000 Americans killed in combat, and Vietnamese civilian casualties numbering over 1 million people.

14. See Ralph B. Levering, *The Public and American Foreign Policy, 1918–1978* (New York, 1978); and the discussion of public attitudes toward foreign affairs in Ben J. Wattenberg, *The Real America: A Surprising Examination of the State of the Union* (Garden City, N.Y., 1974), 203–13.

15. Senator Goldwater repeated his statement in an address to the Republican National Convention on August 22, 1984. See the New York *Times*, August 23, 1984, dispatch by Martin Tolchin.

hegemony and actual or threatened "preventive war" as America's answer to it.[16]

Despite militant right-wing rhetoric about liberating Eastern Europe from the communist grip, in reality the Eisenhower administration carefully avoided overt interventionism (especially military interventionism) in this sensitive zone. It gave little more than verbal support to the Hungarian revolt against Soviet rule in 1956. Similarly, Secretary of State John Foster Dulles' new strategy of "massive retaliation" against Soviet expansionism was widely viewed as a provocative and extremist position by Washington in dealing with Moscow. Yet events soon made clear that in reality, massive retaliation was largely anticommunist rhetoric. In practice, Eisenhower, Dulles, and other officials of the Republican administration were nearly always restrained in their approach to the Soviet Union and international issues likely to precipitate nuclear war; they recognized that certain external threats could not be met by reliance upon nuclear weapons.[17]

Even during the Cuban missile crisis of 1962—the most dangerous Soviet-American encounter in the postwar period—it became evident that both Washington and Moscow were conscious of the potential risks of a nuclear conflagration. On several occasions, the Kennedy administration took steps to avoid provoking the Soviet Union and was careful to offer Moscow a way out of the impasse without sacrificing its vital diplomatic interests.[18] During 1979–1980, President Jimmy Carter's attempt to gain the release of American hostages held captive in Iran was similarly nonprovocative and restrained.[19]

By the mid-1980s, the Reagan administration was no less required to

16. See, for example, Frederick Barghoorn's assessment of the Truman Doctrine in Robert A. Divine (ed.), *American Foreign Policy Since 1945* (Chicago, 1969), 88–89; Adam B. Ulam, *The Rivals: America and Russia Since World War II* (New York, 1971), 125; and Ronald Steel, *Pax Americana* (New York, 1970), 22–23.

17. See President Eisenhower's statement on October 25, 1956, regarding the Soviet intervention in Hungary, in Dwight D. Eisenhower, *Waging Peace* (Garden City, N.Y., 1965), 65–70; Richard Goold-Adams, *John Foster Dulles: A Reappraisal* (New York, 1962), 107–109; and the assessment of Secretary Dulles' views by Hans J. Morgenthau, in Norman A. Graebner (ed.), *An Uncertain Tradition: American Secretaries of State in the Twentieth Century* (New York, 1961), 294–96. Both critics agree that inaction was the hallmark of the Eisenhower administration's diplomacy.

18. See the Introduction by Robert McNamara to Robert F. Kennedy, *Thirteen Days: A Memoir of the Cuban Missile Crisis* (New York, 1968), 14–15. Former British Prime Minister Harold Macmillan commended President Kennedy's "combination of flexibility and determination" in responding to the Soviet challenge in the Caribbean. His diplomacy exhibited both a readiness "to act, and to allow his adversary the opportunity to retreat." Unlike some leaders in modern history, Kennedy successfully achieved "both Peace and Honour" (*ibid.*, 19–20).

19. See Hamilton Jordan, *Crisis: The Last Year of the Carter Presidency* (New York, 1982); and Carter, *Keeping Faith*, 433–597.

demonstrate moderation and flexibility in dealing with a variety of international issues, from arms control to American involvement in Central America. President Reagan's political advisers were aware that his image as a right-wing ideologue and outspoken opponent of communism alienated many citizens, who preferred prudence and restraint in dealing with critical external problems. During the presidential election of 1984, Republicans made a concerted effort to depict the president as a diplomatic leader whose approach was marked by willingness to seek new agreements with the Soviet Union on issues such as arms limitation, to renew the quest for peace in the Middle East, to seek moderate solutions in Central America, and otherwise to engage in diplomatic activities acceptable to mainstream opinion in the United States.[20]

Habituation and the American Diplomatic Tradition

Habituation as a central tenet of pragmatic thought was examined in Chapter 2. This concept can be related directly to American diplomacy as it was applied to the foreign relations of the United States before and after World War II. We shall do so selectively, by focusing upon several ideas and behavior traits that have long been identified with the American approach to foreign relations.

One of these is the notion that the political principles of the New World are distinctive vis-à-vis those of other nations. It follows that, just as America's "democratic experiment" profoundly affected the theory and practice of modern governments, the active participation of the United States in foreign affairs should make a difference in the conduct of international politics. The isolationist era was punctuated by interventionist interludes directed at what Americans believed was enhancing the prospects of global peace and security, promoting democracy abroad, and otherwise contributing to human well-being.[21]

20. See, for example, the discussion of President Ronald Reagan's forthcoming meeting with Soviet Foreign Minister Andrei Gromyko in the New York *Times*, September 29, 1984, dispatch by Steven R. Weisman; and of efforts by the pragmatically inclined Secretary of State George Shultz to influence Reagan's diplomatic moves, in *U.S. News and World Report*, XCVII (October 8, 1984), 13.
21. For specific examples of American interventionism during the isolationist era, see Cecil V. Crabb, Jr., *Policy-Makers and Critics: Conflicting Theories of American Foreign Policy* (New York, 1976), 34–81; Raymond H. Buell, *The Washington Conference* (New York, 1922); Harriet E. Davis, *Pioneers of World Order: An American Appraisal of the League of Nations* (New York, 1944); Merle E. Curti, *Bryan and World Peace* (Northampton, Mass., 1931); Harley Notter, *The Origins of the Foreign Policy of Woodrow Wilson* (Baltimore, 1937); Thomas A. Bailey, *Woodrow Wilson and the Lost Peace* (New York, 1944); Roland N. Stomberg, *Collective Security and American Foreign Policy from the League of Nations to NATO* (New York, 1963); and Merze Tate, *The United States and Armaments* (Cambridge, Mass., 1948).

The Monroe Doctrine presupposed the existence of a Western Hemispheric community. Although Washington was unwilling to act on that idea for many years after 1823, it did play an energetic role during the 1930s and 1940s in giving the idea tangible expression in the form of the Organization of American States (OAS). In later years (sometimes in the face of considerable opposition south of the border), the United States attempted to make the OAS a more effective regional body with power to deal with hemispheric political crises.[22]

John Foster Dulles was convinced that in Western Europe in the post–World War II period the Allies must not rebuild the same "demonstrated firetrap" on the European continent that had produced two global conflagrations within less than a generation. Accordingly, American leadership was conspicuous in encouraging and supporting the emergence of new regional institutions in Europe, culminating in the creation of the European Community. The emergence of regional organizations in Asia in more recent years also owes much to American encouragement.[23]

American-sponsored innovations have been noteworthy also in the sphere of international organization and the codification and extension of international law to new areas of global concern. Leadership by the United States was crucial in the formulation and establishment of both the League of Nations and the United Nations. Efforts to outlaw war during the 1920s, culminating in the Kellogg-Briand Pact (or Pact of Paris) in 1928, were spearheaded by American officials, citizens, and organizations.[24]

President Theodore Roosevelt was primarily responsible for the convening of the Second Hague Conference on disarmament in 1907; during the Wilson administration, Secretary of State William Jennings Bryan called for

22. See Arthur P. Whitaker, *The Western Hemisphere Idea: Its Rise and Decline* (Ithaca, N.Y., 1965); Inis L. Claude, "The OAS, the UN, and the United States," *International Conciliation*, No. 547 (March, 1964), 1–67; John C. Dreier, *The Organization of American States and the Hemisphere Crisis* (New York, 1962); and John Gantenbein, *The Evolution of Our Latin American Policy* (New York, 1950).

23. Dulles' views are quoted in Department of State, *American Foreign Policy, 1950–1955*, Publication 6446, General Foreign Policy Series, 117 (2 vols.; Washington, D.C., 1957), I, 1442. American initiatives in behalf of European unification are emphasized in F. C. S. Northrop, *European Union and United States Foreign Policy* (New York, 1954); Richard Mayne, *The Recovery of Europe: From Devastation to Unity* (New York, 1970); Walter Z. Laqueur, *The Rebirth of Europe* (New York, 1970); U. W. Kitzinger, *The Politics and Economics of European Integration: Britain, Europe and the United States* (New York, 1964); Robert Kleiman, *Atlantic Crisis: American Diplomacy Confronts a Resurgent Europe* (New York, 1964); and Gordon K. Douglass (ed.), *The New Interdependence: The European Community and the United States* (Lexington, Mass., 1979).

24. See, for example, Merle Curti, *Peace or War: The American Struggle, 1636–1936* (Boston, 1959); L. Ethan Ellis, *Republican Foreign Policy, 1921–1933* (New Brunswick, N.J., 1968); and Frank Merli and Theodore A. Wilson (eds.), *Makers of American Diplomacy* (New York, 1974).

"cooling off" treaties designed to limit the violent resolution of international controversies; and during the 1920s, the United States led the way, as in the Washington Naval Armaments Conference (1921), in efforts to reduce the level of global armaments. Then in the 1930s, the Roosevelt administration repeatedly sought to persuade the great powers to resolve their differences by negotiations rather than by armed conflict.

Post–World War II American diplomacy has exhibited a continuation of this same spirit of creativity and innovation. During and after the war, the United States played a decisive role in formulating the United Nations and gaining international support for this second experiment in global organization. Again in 1950, American diplomatic leadership was largely responsible for the passage of the Uniting for Peace Resolution, which saved the UN from impotency by permitting the General Assembly to deal with an issue when the Security Council was deadlocked. Despite the prevailing crisis of confidence in the United States toward the United Nations in recent years, America continues to provide a substantial share of the UN's operating budget.[25]

In a different dimension of American diplomacy—Allied policy toward defeated Germany and Japan after World War II—the United States sought to bring about fundamental changes within these societies, assuring that they would no longer disturb the peace and security of the world. Owing in no small measure to American influence, the democratization of West Germany and Japan appears now to have been successful; neither nation has exhibited any tendency to pursue its goals in the postwar era through military force. Indeed, by the 1980s many Americans complained that these nations— especially Japan—were *not* assuming international responsibilities commensurate with their power. In this sense, continued evolution in the international role of both nations was anticipated as Japan, for example, exerted greater diplomatic responsibility for preserving the security of Asia.

Another imaginative and highly effective diplomatic undertaking after World War II was the European Recovery Program (or Marshall Plan), whose goal was the reconstruction of war-torn Europe. This program not only made possible Western Europe's phenomenal economic recovery, but, because of the Marshall Plan's emphasis on treating Europe's problems *regionally,* it gave

25. American efforts in establishment of the United Nations are fully described in Cordell Hull, *The Memoirs of Cordell Hull* (2 vols.; New York, 1948), II, 1625–1743; and Vandenberg (ed.), *Private Papers of Senator Vandenberg,* 172–220. Informative studies of the American role in the United Nations in the postwar period are Lincoln P. Bloomfield, *The United Nations and U.S. Foreign Policy* (rev. ed.; Boston, 1967); and Richard N. Gardner, *In Pursuit of World Order* (New York, 1964); William B. Bader, *The United States and the Spread of Nuclear Weapons* (New York, 1968); and Wolfram F. Hanreider (ed.), *Arms Control and Security: Current History* (Boulder, Colo., 1979).

powerful impetus to the emergence of regional organizations such as the European Community in the years ahead.[26]

President Truman's Point Four program of aid to the developing nations (the fourth major proposal in his inaugural address in 1949) was viewed by the president and his advisers as a bold new program designed to promote modernization throughout the Third World. Once again drawing upon the lessons of experience (Truman emphasized that American society had been developed by the infusion of foreign investment capital in its economic enterprises), the president believed that his new program would contribute to political stability within the Third World, produce a relationship that would be of mutual benefit for both developed and developing nations, and enhance the prospects for global peace. Truman conceived the program as a venture that would enable Third World societies to help themselves in their efforts to achieve modernization. The Point Four program stemmed no less from his conviction that the alternative to it was "to allow vast areas to drift toward poverty, despair, fear, and other miseries of mankind which breed unending wars." The program was also justified as "a practical expression of our attitude toward the countries threatened by Communist domination" and as an extension of America's policy of "preventing the expansion of Communism in the free world."[27] To anticipate a subject we shall deal with in the next chapter, the Point Four program provides an outstanding illustration of the fact that multiple influences—idealism and humanitarianism, economic considerations, strategic calculations, the containment strategy, national self-interest, lessons derived from experience and common sense, and other motivations—combined to shape the American foreign aid program toward the Third World and have been responsible for its continuation since 1949.[28]

The American approach to foreign relations has had a profound impact on the theory and practice of modern diplomacy. More than any other single individual, Woodrow Wilson was responsible for the tendency toward public or "democratic" diplomacy in the modern period. Franklin D. Roosevelt re-

26. The European Recovery Program is discussed more fully in Truman, *Years of Trial and Hope*, 109–31, 230–50; Dean Acheson, *Present at the Creation: My Years in the State Department* (New York, 1969), 226–36; and Vandenberg (ed.), *Private Papers of Senator Vandenberg*, 373–99. Useful commentaries are H. A. Schmitt, *The Path to European Union: From the Marshall Plan to the Common Market* (Baton Rouge, 1962); and William A. Brown and Redvers Opie, *American Foreign Assistance* (Washington, D.C., 1953).

27. Truman, *Years of Trial and Hope*, 230–33.

28. See the discussion of the rationale of American foreign aid in Lloyd D. Black, *The Strategy of Foreign Aid* (Princeton, 1968), 3–22; Edward S. Mason, *Foreign Aid and Foreign Policy* (New York, 1964), 26–52; and John D. Montgomery, *Foreign Aid in International Politics* (Englewood Cliffs, N.J., 1967).

lied heavily upon heads-of-state meetings—later called summit conferences—to resolve outstanding international issues. Summitry has subsequently become an established diplomatic mechanism; both in American
society and abroad, it is now widely expected that the American president
will take the lead in scheduling summit meetings periodically to discuss and
resolve international issues. During the presidential campaign of 1984, for
example, Ronald Reagan was widely criticized because he had *not* engaged in
a summit meeting with Moscow. During the early 1970s, the White House
national security adviser, later secretary of state, Henry Kissinger, resorted to
"shuttle diplomacy" in an intensive effort to resolve the Arab-Israeli conflict
in the Middle East. Several years later, the successful negotiation of the Camp
David peace accords between Israel and Egypt could be attributed in large
measure to Jimmy Carter's personal and intensive involvement in the
process.[29]

The common denominator to many of these diplomatic efforts was an
idea, widely expressed during the national political campaign of 1984, that
the influence of the United States should be cast in the direction of producing
"movement" and renewed efforts in the attempt to resolve serious international issues. In its approach to the Soviet Union, to the Arab-Israeli conflict,
to problems of political instability in Central America, and in other areas, the
Reagan administration confronted a public expectation that it would be creative, flexible, and moderate in pursuing its diplomatic objectives. Its attempt
to review moribund arms limitation discussions with the Kremlin, to renew
the search for peace in the Middle East, and to keep its diplomatic and military
commitments in Central America limited were clearly responsive to these
public expectations, which, in turn, expressed ideas long associated with the
pragmatic approach to problem solving.

Former Secretary of State Dean Rusk once observed that the inscription
which Dante had placed above the entrance to the Inferno should be inscribed
over the main entrance of the State Department: "ABANDON HOPE ALL YE WHO
ENTER HERE." Rusk's comment calls attention to another important element in
the American approach to foreign relations derived from habitual viewpoints: a traditional distrust of diplomacy and those involved in it. Since the

29. For a discussion of summitry, see Thomas A. Bailey, *The Art of Diplomacy: The American Experience* (New York, 1968); Robert B. Harmon, *The Art and Practice of Diplomacy* (Metuchen, N.J., 1971); Elmer Plischke, *Conduct of American Diplomacy* (3rd ed.; Princeton, 1967); and Kenneth W. Thompson, *American Diplomacy and Emergent Patterns* (New York, 1962). "Shuttle diplomacy" is discussed in Henry Kissinger, *White House Years* (Boston, 1979), and *Years of Upheaval* (Boston, 1982); see also Richard Valeriani, *Travels with Henry* (New York, 1980). See Carter, *Keeping Faith*, 267–431.

earliest days of the republic, Americans have exhibited misgivings about the diplomatic process and its results—a factor supporting their preference for an isolationist foreign policy.[30]

Almost without exception, since World War II every secretary of state has found his assignment frustrating, enervating, and often inherently impossible, in large part because of the lack of public and congressional understanding of the State Department's mission. One of the many unique features of President Franklin D. Roosevelt's approach to foreign affairs was his repeated bypassing of Secretary of State Cordell Hull. Other presidents since FDR (such as John F. Kennedy) have exhibited a lack of confidence in the State Department and have, in various ways, managed foreign relations directly or entrusted its control to other executive officials. Alternatively throughout the postwar era, the State Department has been severely criticized (as during the 1950s) for having lost China to communism and generally being under communist influence, or (as during the late 1960s) for being part of the foreign policy establishment that led the nation into the Vietnam War and engaged in other interventionist moves abroad. A pervasive complaint has been that the department lacks creativity, that it has been slow to adapt to postwar challenges, and that it epitomizes a tradition-bound and lethargic bureaucracy which is more devoted to its own customary procedures than to producing imaginative responses for a rapidly changing global environment.

Even today, in the size of its operating budget and number of personnel, the Department of State ranks near the bottom among the principal departments of the federal government. For example, by the late 1980s, the cost of one new Trident submarine exceeded the State Department's annual operating budget! Many key ambassadorships are still political appointments, in part because Congress is reluctant to appropriate sufficient funds to operate the larger embassies in London, Paris, Bonn, and other major capitals. This means that the American ambassador must have an independent income to subsidize embassy expenses out of his own pocket. Moreover, Congress has shown little or no discernible enthusiasm for the establishment of a diplomatic academy (comparable to the three military academies) for the training of American diplomatic officials. A former State Department official has deplored the tendency in American society to believe that experience in busi-

30. Historic American skepticism about diplomacy is a major theme of Smith Simpson, *Anatomy of the State Department* (Boston, 1967); and see several of the selections in Norman A. Graebner (ed.), *Ideas and Diplomacy: Readings in the Intellectual Tradition of American Foreign Policy* (New York, 1964), 1–334; and Elmer Plischke (ed.), *Modern Diplomacy: The Art and the Artisans* (Washington, D.C., 1979).

ness, politics, or other professions qualifies an individual for a diplomatic assignment—a traditional American idea that can easily "lure prestigious amateurs into disastrous miscalculations in the foreign environment."[31] Despite such admonitions, most Americans continue to regard professional diplomacy with skepticism, if not outright suspicion.

From the colonial period, Americans believed that diplomacy was closely associated with monarchy, aristocracy, political intrigue and machinations (often "behind the backs of the people"), conflict, and war—in short, with the political behavior of the Old World. In the American view, the intrigues and ambitions of Old World diplomats were in large measure responsible for such destructive encounters as the First World War. Ethnocentric conceptions of their national interests by diplomats and governments throughout the world contributed to the failure of the peace and, within less than two decades, to the eruption of the Second World War. During that even more destructive global conflict, traditional American skepticism about diplomacy was reinforced by the results of several wartime conferences, especially the Yalta Conference early in 1945, where, many Americans concluded, Roosevelt was diplomatically outmaneuvered by Soviet Premier Stalin to the detriment of peace and security in the postwar era. (It is, of course, another paradox of American diplomacy that citizens disdained diplomacy even while they called for a new summit meeting between Washington and Moscow.)

Referring to the Monroe Doctrine—historically perhaps with the Truman Doctrine America's most influential foreign policy declaration—an authoritative State Department publication said, "No other power of the world has any relationship to, or voice in, implementing the principles" contained in it. Monroe's proclamation was "our doctrine, to be invoked and sustained, held in abeyance, or abandoned as our high international policy or vital national interests shall seem to us, and to us alone, to demand."[32] This was a particularly forceful and candid expression of one of the oldest principles of American foreign policy, which continues to guide national diplomacy today, as during the isolationist era—the concept of American *unilateralism*.[33] In 1823 the Monroe administration chose to issue the Monroe Doctrine alone, rather than jointly with Great Britain (as London had suggested). Again at the

31. Charles Yost, *The Conduct and Misconduct of Foreign Affairs* (New York, 1972), 147–48.
32. See J. Reuben Clark, *Memorandum on the Monroe Doctrine*, December 17, 1928, 71st Cong., 2nd sess., 1930, Document 114, p. xxiii.
33. The unilateral nature of these diplomatic doctrines is emphasized in the discussion of them individually in Crabb, *Doctrines of American Foreign Policy, passim.*

end of the century, the Open Door policy in China was a diplomatic principle issued unilaterally by the United States. During the 1930s, the Roosevelt administration stated on several occasions that it was prepared to support the policies of the League of Nations in dealing with Axis expansionism, but the United States would act alone in doing so, not formally in collaboration with other nations.

Beginning with the Truman Doctrine in 1947, every postwar diplomatic doctrine of the United States has been a unilateral policy proclamation. Although it is true that Truman brought the defense of South Korea under United Nations auspices, in reality the military campaign in the country largely remained a United States–South Korea undertaking, with American officials usually making the key decisions.

Similarly, the defense of South Vietnam against communist expansionism under the Johnson and Nixon administrations was almost exclusively a commitment assumed by the United States and South Vietnam alone. The Reagan administration's military buildup in the Persian Gulf area, its military interventions in (and later withdrawals from) Lebanon, and its efforts to contain communist expansionism in the Caribbean and Central America were also examples of unilateral diplomatic undertakings by Washington. In many of these cases, the Western allies not only did not collaborate in them, but in several instances the United States encountered overt criticism from its allies in these diplomatic ventures. America's historic tendency toward diplomatic unilateralism has unquestionably served also as a major cause of disarray within the NATO alliance. Even when Washington has consulted the European allies in advance of important diplomatic undertakings (as during the Cuban missile crisis of 1962), such consultation usually consisted of informing the allies of impending actions, rather than seeking to devise an agreed-upon NATO strategy in which all the members of the alliance had participated.[34]

That unilateralism has been a pronounced quality of American diplomacy historically—and that it remains one in the contemporary period—is undeniable. For example, in 1987 the Reagan administration once again unilaterally affirmed America's determination to defend the security of the Persian Gulf region. Yet this tradition has also existed concurrently with a

34. See, for example, the discussion of the Kennedy administration's consultation with French President Charles de Gaulle during the Cuban missile crisis of 1962, in Theodore Sorensen, *Kennedy* (New York, 1965), 676, 705–706. Yet as some American officials have also complained, it has often been difficult to get the European allies to agree upon *any* common strategy or course of action. See Brzezinski, *Power and Principle*, 301–302.

contrary impulse in American foreign relations: time and again, the United States has led the way in *multilateral and cooperative approaches* to the solution of global problems. Woodrow Wilson's influence, for example, was crucial in the establishment of the League of Nations after World War I, and Franklin D. Roosevelt played a decisive role in gaining acceptance (sometimes in the face of an evident lack of enthusiasm by other governments) for the United Nations. During the 1930s, Washington played an energetic role in establishing the Organization of American States, and after the war, it repeatedly sought (often with no very conspicuous success) to expand and strengthen the powers of that organization. American influence in the postwar era was again crucial in encouraging the emergence of regional institutions, culminating in the creation of the European Community, on the European continent, and it has sought to promote a comparable tendency toward regionalism in Asia and other areas. American diplomatic and financial support has similarly been indispensable for the successful operations of such multilateral agencies as the World Bank, the International Monetary Fund, the General Agreement on Tariffs and Trade (GATT), and other organizations.

In this and other dimensions of foreign affairs, Americans have not hesitated to embrace dissimilar and sometimes antithetical principles and attitudes as they believed circumstances dictated in responding to global problems. The interplay between the two themes of American unilateralism and multilateralism, it may safely be predicted, will be a central theme of external policy for many years in the future.

Six

The Pluralistic Decision-Making Process

According to a former State Department official, the administration of President John F. Kennedy was successful in part because JFK understood clearly "the untidiness, the inconsistencies and internal contradictions" inherent in the American foreign policy process. In other words, Kennedy understood that, in pragmatic terms, the internal foreign policy setting is highly pluralistic, containing subjective and objective, random and predictable, and familiar and inexplicable forces that combine (sometimes in strange ways) to determine the behavior of the United States in foreign relations. The real sources of the external policies followed by the United States, former Secretary of State Dean Acheson once observed, are "undiscoverable." If Acheson's comment seems exaggerated, it does underscore the inevitable presence of the unforeseen, the contingent, and the mysterious in what is sometimes depicted as a highly rational and orderly process of decision making.[1]

It is often extremely difficult to determine precisely how and when a particular president decides upon a course of action in foreign affairs. Much of the discussion by President Truman's advisers of his decision to resist communist aggression against South Korea appeared to be a *pro forma* attempt to provide a rationale for a decision the president had already reached. Yet on other issues related to the Korean War—such as whether the United States should employ nuclear weapons against communist forces—Truman sus-

1. See Roger Hilsman, *The Politics of Policy Making in Defense and Foreign Affairs* (New York, 1971), 15; and the same author's analysis of President Kennedy's diplomatic leadership in his *To Move a Nation: The Politics of Foreign Policy in the Administration of John F. Kennedy* (Garden City, N.Y., 1967), 581. For Dean Acheson's views, see his *Grapes from Thorns* (New York, 1972), 110–11.

pended judgment and continually reexamined the question as circumstances changed.[2]

In a favorite phrase of economists, "all things being equal," the foreign policy of the United States results from the interaction among nine principal forces determining the nation's diplomatic behavior. (No effort is made here to assign any overall value or weight to these forces.)

Traditional and Historical Influences

For the United States, as for all nations, certain historically derived influences affect its diplomatic behavior. These include the American society's long attachment to an isolationist foreign policy. Neoisolationist currents can be identified in popular attitudes toward foreign relations in the contemporary era. The American people's historic belief in their unique mission to uplift and improve the lot of mankind also remains part of the American approach to foreign relations. Moreover, the old habit of American diplomatic unilateralism continues to be a conspicuous trait of the nation's diplomacy and contributes to the disarray usually present within the Western alliance. The thought of leading pragmatic philosophers emphasizes that such habitual influences upon diplomatic behavior are likely to change very slowly and only as new and more beneficial habits evolve to replace them.

Ideological Policy Influences

Ideological influences are nearly always present and sometimes play a decisive role in the foreign policy of the United States. The historic isolationist policy; the Monroe Doctrine; America's championship of the Open Door policy in China; President Wilson's "democratization" of the diplomatic process; the Roosevelt administration's opposition to Axis expansionism and FDR's advocacy of idealistic principles like the Four Freedoms; American leadership in planning and gaining international support for the United Nations; the Truman administration's conviction that communist expansionism endangered both American security and international peace and well-being; the Kennedy administration's conception of nation-building throughout the Third World; President Jimmy Carter's commitment to the cause of human

2. See David S. McClellan, *Dean Acheson: The State Department Years* (New York, 1976), 273–76; John W. Spanier, *The Truman-MacArthur Controversy and the Korean War* (Cambridge, Mass., 1959), 15–40; and Donald R. McCoy, *The Presidency of Harry S. Truman* (Lawrence, Kan., 1984), 229.

rights abroad and his active role in achieving peace agreements between Israel and Egypt; the Reagan administration's diplomacy in Central America—different as they are, these landmark developments in American diplomacy illustrate the impact of ideological considerations on the foreign relations of the United States.[3]

The ideological component of American diplomacy is genuine and authentic. For nearly all nations today—but especially for American society—ideology serves as something more than what French President Charles de Gaulle once called "the fig leaf of national ambition."[4]

Yet developments in the postwar American diplomatic record have made clear that this realistic assessment of the role of ideology in international relations frequently exhibits a curious lack of realism. Ideals, as pragmatic thought has always insisted, are an integral part of human experience. In the pragmatic conception, human action is oriented toward problem solving in a manner that best promotes human well-being. In turn, the concept of human well-being inescapably implies man's ability to *differentiate among possible solutions* depending on their effect on, or consequences for, the human condition. In brief, a pragmatic world view is postulated upon the twofold belief that an improvement or amelioration of the human condition is possible and that intelligent action can contribute to that result. The human mind, in other words, can conceive of beneficial change in the condition of society, and human intelligence can formulate the steps necessary to achieve that goal.

A long list of goals of postwar American diplomacy—support for the United Nations, encouragement of regional organizations abroad, Washington's opposition to colonialism and extensive assistance to emerging Third World nations, efforts to limit international armaments, ongoing efforts to resolve the intractable Arab-Israeli conflict, attempts to promote the cause of human rights abroad, international efforts to reduce impediments to world trade, more recent programs to solve global environmental problems—have been significantly influenced by traditional American ideological values and preferences. In some cases, the American conception of the good life has supplied the primary motivation for such diplomatic undertakings. This con-

3. The impact of ideals on American diplomacy is discussed in Arthur A. Ekrich, Jr., *Ideas, Ideals and American Diplomacy* (New York, 1966); Norman A. Graebner (ed.), *Ideas and Diplomacy: Readings in the Intellectual Tradition of American Foreign Policy* (New York, 1964); and Frank Tannenbaum, *The American Tradition in Foreign Policy* (Norman, Okla., 1955).

4. See, for example, de Gaulle's statement: "The banner of ideology in reality covers only [national] ambitions. And I believe that it has been thus since the world was born." Even America's liberal ideology, in de Gaulle's view, was a thinly disguised mask to hide its hegemonial impulses. See Roy C. Macridis (ed.), *De Gaulle: Implacable Ally* (New York, 1966), 6–7.

cept derives in some measure from the Christian precept that not only should man have life, but he should have life *abundantly*. Or, in the language of pragmatic philosophy, humans are able both to envision and to engage in activities designed to promote their growth, development, and evolution. Although survival is, of course, the minimum condition for the realization of all human goals, pragmatism does not view survival as a sufficient goal of human society. Indeed, in the pragmatic conception, it is doubtful that human society can long survive in the absence of continuing adaptation and growth in response to a pluralistic and dynamic environment.

The pragmatic assessment of the role of ideology in American foreign policy, therefore, emphasizes the following aspects of the relationship: (1) ideals have always been an integral feature of the American way of life, and they continue to be a prominent element in it in the contemporary era; (2) Americans have traditionally justified the exercise of political power by reference to certain ideal standards or criteria, that is, the degree to which the programs and actions of government promote human well-being; (3) as the public reaction to America's involvement in the Vietnam War and to the Reagan administration's diplomacy in Central America have indicated convincingly, the exercise of power by the United States abroad must be related to some ostensible, worthwhile *human purpose* that is understood (or at least intuitively sensed) by the American people; (4) applications of American power overseas which are not so understood—which do not possess legitimacy in the eyes of the American people—are not likely to succeed or to prove enduring; and (5) in judging the extent to which ideologically based diplomatic objectives have been successful or unsuccessful, American society customarily relies upon the pragmatic standard of assessing its consequences for human well-being at home and abroad.[5]

Power: Its Use and Legitimacy

As advocates of *Realpolitik* have properly insisted, both before and after World War II, from time to time American diplomacy has been guided by power

5. See P. A. Reynolds, *An Introduction to International Relations* (Cambridge, Mass., 1971), 46–47. Before his death, former Secretary of State John Foster Dulles chose the following passage to be inscribed at the Dulles Library at Princeton University: "This nation of ours is not merely a self-serving society but was founded with a mission to help build a world where liberty and justice would prevail." These and other definitions of American national interest, emphasizing the idealistic content of the concept, are included in Cecil V. Crabb, Jr., *Policy-Makers and Critics: Conflicting Theories of American Foreign Policy* (New York, 1976), 166–85; and see Stephen R. Graubard, *Kissinger: Portrait of a Mind* (New York, 1974), 271–97.

calculations. Paradoxically, this tendency has sometimes been exhibited by the nation's most avowedly idealistic presidents. Jefferson's acquisition of the Louisiana Territory was motivated both by his conviction that this step would strengthen and extend democracy on the American continent and by his understanding of the strategic value of the Mississippi Valley and the port of New Orleans for the security of the new American republic. The chief executive who most clearly symbolized American idealism—Woodrow Wilson— actually carried out more military interventions in Latin America than any other occupant of the White House, and in his determination to "teach Latin Americans to elect good men," Wilson came close to precipitating a new war with Mexico.[6]

The same President Franklin D. Roosevelt who epitomized the idealism of the Allied cause during World War II was also a masterful political manipulator, who understood the use of power in achieving his objectives. FDR believed that key wartime and postwar decisions ought to be made largely by the "Big Five" (the Soviet Union, Great Britain, France, China, and the United States). In practice, as often as not, it was the "Big Two" (the Soviet Union and the United States) that decided crucial military and diplomatic questions.

After World War II, President John F. Kennedy became a symbol of American idealism. Yet the Kennedy administration launched the ill-fated Bay of Pigs invasion of Cuba, engaged in an ominous confrontation with the Soviet Union in the Cuban missile crisis, pledged the United States to defend Berlin from communist annexation, and reiterated the determination of the United States to prevent the communization of Southeast Asia. By the late 1970s, another embodiment of American idealism—Jimmy Carter—relied on military intervention in an unsuccessful effort to rescue American hostages in Iran; delivered an ultimatum, in the Carter Doctrine, to the Kremlin not to jeopardize Western access to the oil-rich Persian Gulf area; and, before he left office, proposed a substantial expansion and modernization of the American military establishment.

Very few diplomatic undertakings by the United States after World War II have been totally devoid of power considerations. Take the European Recovery Program (or Marshall Plan), inaugurated by the Truman administration in the late 1940s to promote Western Europe's economic, social, and political

6. Howard F. Cline, *The United States and Mexico* (rev. ed.; Cambridge, Mass., 1963), 139–62; David F. Healy, *Gunboat Diplomacy in the Wilson Era* (Madison, 1976); and Dana G. Munroe, *Intervention and Dollar Diplomacy* (Princeton, 1964).

rehabilitation in the postwar era. This program unquestionably stemmed in some measure from America's perception of Europe's acute needs, from traditional American humanitarianism, and from awareness that the United States had escaped the physical devastation suffered by the other Allies during the war.

The Marshall Plan, however, was no less a decisive instrument in implementing the Truman administration's containment strategy. During the late 1940s, Truman and his advisers believed that Western Europe was rapidly becoming a "power vacuum" that invited overt Soviet aggression or indirect efforts by Moscow (with help from European Communist parties) to gain political power within France, Italy, and other Western nations. A dominant American goal, therefore, was to undermine the appeal of Marxism for Europeans by providing an effective alternative to the adoption of revolutionary and other extremist political programs. As subsequent experience in Western Europe demonstrated, this American objective was largely achieved; the region recovered its economic vitality and political stability. In 1949 the creation of the North Atlantic Treaty Organization was another step that strengthened the ability of the West to resist communist encroachments.[7]

Power calculations have no less influenced the provision of American foreign assistance to Third World nations since the inauguration of Truman's Point Four program, initially proposed early in 1949 and adopted in 1950. In some measure, foreign aid served as a tangible expression of the American people's historic generosity in responding to societies in need; a humanitarian incentive has nearly always been a motive in the foreign assistance program since World War II. At the same time, American officials seldom denied that foreign aid was an indispensable step in counteracting communist influence throughout the Third World. Economic and technical assistance by the United States provided Third World nations with an alternative to exclusive reliance upon Moscow (or in some periods, Peiping) in meeting their internal needs. Moreover, many Americans envisioned foreign aid as a method of retaining some influence within the host country.[8]

Numerous other examples might be cited of this same phenomenon. During the presidential election of 1984, Ronald Reagan stated that he knew

7. See Harry S. Truman, *Years of Trial and Hope* (Garden City, N.Y., 1956), 109–31; Dean Acheson, *Present at the Creation: My Years in the State Department* (New York, 1969), 226–35; and Arthur H. Vandenberg, Jr. (ed.), *The Private Papers of Senator Vandenberg* (Boston, 1952), 374.

8. The Point Four program was the fourth proposal contained in Truman's inaugural address on January 20, 1949. To Truman, the "proper development" of the Third World was a crucial key to maintaining global peace. See Truman, *Years of Trial and Hope*, 227–29; and *Public Papers of the Presidents of the United States: Harry S. Truman, 1949*, 286–91, 545–47, 555–57.

of no wars in modern history in which the United States had become involved because it was "too strong." The Reagan White House proposed, and Congress ultimately approved, the largest peacetime military budget in American history. The Reagan administration's "Star Wars" proposal for the creation of a new and extremely expensive system of satellites in outer space capable of intercepting Soviet offensive missiles was designed to give the United States a clear and decisive advantage in this aspect of military technology.[9]

Yet in recognizing the power component that has frequently been present in postwar diplomatic decision making, it is essential to bear in mind that Machiavelli, Hobbes, Richelieu, Metternich, Bismarck, and other proponents of *Realpolitik* have never been widely admired by American society. Although it has been advocated from time to time by individuals and groups interested in American foreign relations, the concept of *Pax Americana* has never elicited widespread support within the United States. After World War II, the United States neither attempted to impose a *Pax Americana* upon a debilitated world, nor have the American people subsequently expressed any discernible desire that Washington do so now.

To the contrary, as Dean Acheson emphasized, Americans have an inordinate preoccupation with their standing in world public opinion and are easily given inferiority complexes because of their actions abroad. Americans, Acheson emphasized, are "setups for the caricatures of the Ugly American, of the stupid diplomat, of the contemptuous, grasping, wily foreigner taking our money at the other end of the rat hole down which we fatuously pour it." This caricature also includes frequent complaints about America's "obtuseness in getting into wars we should have stayed out of, and getting out of wars we should have stayed in and enlarged." By the late 1960s, many Americans were convinced that their own "arrogance of power" posed the most serious threat to international peace and stability. At one stage, President Jimmy Carter expressed his belief that the American people had an inordinate phobia about communism, which he believed constituted a major barrier to more peaceful and stable global relations.[10]

Throughout the postwar era, widely publicized "exposés" of wrongdoing, covert activities, and other questionable behavior by the Central Intel-

9. Estimates of American vis-à-vis Soviet military power, significant trends in national defense spending, the development of new weapons systems, and other significant issues are examined in the Defense Department's analysis (published annually), *U.S. Military Posture, 1984* (Washington, D.C., 1984).

10. Acheson, *Grapes from Thorns*, 167; Raymond A. Moore, "The Carter Presidency and Foreign Policy," in M. Glenn Abernathy *et al.* (eds.), *The Carter Years: The President and Policy Making* (New York, 1984), 54–84.

ligence Agency and other federal agencies abroad have been a staple of the American news media. In recent years, pervasive fears that the United States was in danger of becoming involved in "another Vietnam" have testified to the persistence of the American society's psychological aversion to reliance upon military power to achieve diplomatic objectives. As vocal congressional opposition to new weapons systems proposed by the Reagan administration indicated, Americans have not traditionally favored the mere accumulation or expansion of power for its own sake. In foreign affairs, they have tended to exercise power reluctantly—and often with an obviously uneasy conscience.

In effect, they have operated under the conception of power identified with William James, John Dewey, and other pragmatic thinkers. Americans have (often reluctantly and belatedly) acknowledged that power is a crucial element in determining global and regional political relationships. Since World War II, and especially since the Korean War, they have realized that the United States cannot be indifferent to the status of its own power or that of its adversaries in international relations. For many years, they have supported the stationing of large American military contingents in the NATO area, in South Korea, and in innumerable overseas bases. By the mid-1980s, Congress and the American people accepted the necessity for an extensive and costly modernization of the American military establishment to preserve approximate military equilibrium with the Soviet Union.[11]

Nevertheless, it is evident that Americans rely upon military and other forms of coercive power to achieve their diplomatic goals with an uneasy conscience. Even when a majority of the people acknowledge that there is no feasible alternative, Washington's overt reliance on armed force to achieve diplomatic ends makes the American people visibly nervous and uncomfortable, nearly always elicits vocal opposition among certain groups within the society, evokes considerable skepticism on Capitol Hill, and in time gives rise to a vocal school of thought which holds that it was not necessary. At a minimum, sooner or later, Americans demand that their leaders demonstrate the relationship between the use of power abroad and the achievement of *some worthwhile human purpose.* In the absence of such a demonstrable relationship, the nation's foreign policy decision makers are likely to find that their use of power to accomplish diplomatic objectives is rapidly losing legitimacy with the American people and therefore cannot be sustained. Ameri-

11. A detailed description of the composition of American forces may be found in the New York *Times,* October 26, 1983, dispatch by Drew Middleton. The total size of all American armed forces exceeded 2.3 million troops.

cans, in other words, continue to rely on a pragmatic standard in evaluating the use of power in the diplomatic field: What are the *results* of doing so, and how do these contribute to some beneficial human purpose?

The Lessons of Experience

The lessons of diplomatic experience nearly always influence the process of arriving at diplomatic decisions in the United States. Without repeating my earlier analysis of that subject, it is enough to reiterate here that certain landmark experiences—the remembrance of the military disaster at Pearl Harbor; the unsuccessful efforts by the Roosevelt and Truman administrations to arrive at equitable and durable agreements with the Soviet Union during and after World War II; the traumas of the Korean and Vietnam wars; diplomatic setbacks because of American weakness during the Carter administration; and, more recently, the Reagan administration's successful intervention in Grenada—have potently affected official and public attitudes toward foreign relations. Diplomatic maxims such as "You can't trust the Russians," or the idea that Washington's efforts to arrive at arms control agreements with Moscow must involve "negotiating from strength," reflect the lessons that the American people and their leaders believe can legitimately be drawn from diplomatic experience.

Significantly, many informed students of American foreign relations would point out, Washington's diplomatic activity has often been guided initially by motivations such as idealism. A high idealistic content, for example, was unquestionably characteristic of the Roosevelt administration's approach to the Soviet Union during World War II. President Roosevelt had a vision or highly idealized conception of the postwar international order and of Soviet-American relations in the postwar era, and it seems clear that he believed that Stalin's government shared these goals. FDR's growing uneasiness about Moscow's postwar intentions—a skepticism that pervaded Washington under the Truman administration—derived mainly from the change in his perspective produced by wartime experience in negotiating with Soviet officials and in observing Moscow's behavior in Eastern Europe, the Middle East, and other settings during the war. The United States, millions of Americans ultimately concluded, had given the Kremlin a fair chance to demonstrate its good faith by its conduct. Only after the Soviet hierarchy failed that test were Americans willing to abandon Roosevelt's conciliatory approach to the Kremlin and to support the Truman administration's containment strategy. For a majority of Americans, experience had demonstrated convincingly that a foreign policy based primarily on idealistic expectations simply did not work in dealing with the Soviet Union.[12]

Similarly, Americans employed the criterion of experience by the end of the 1960s in judging the "policeman of the world" mentality which culminated in the nation's traumatic involvement in the Vietnam War. As the containment strategy was incrementally extended to one country and region after another during the 1950s and 1960s—and as the international commitments of the United States appeared to multiply without limit—the American people concluded that the nation was overextended in foreign affairs. President Kennedy had clearly anticipated this diplomatic overcommitment, although he did little during his brief tenure as president to change the situation.[13]

The Vietnam War convinced a majority of Americans that the United States was overcommitted diplomatically and that considerable retrenchment was required in the nation's overseas obligations. The Nixon administration attempted to translate that pervasive conviction into a new set of diplomatic guidelines for the United States, called the Nixon Doctrine.[14] In whatever degree his new doctrine was discredited by Richard M. Nixon's subsequent resignation from the presidency, a number of the principles associated with it did guide the behavior of the United States abroad in the post–Vietnam War era. Once again, American diplomatic conduct was profoundly affected by what the people and their leaders believed were applicable lessons of experience.

Perceptions and Misperceptions of the Challenge

Perceptions of the nature and implications of the challenge facing the United States abroad comprise another important component of the process of diplomatic decision making. Inevitably in a democracy, such perceptions often differ widely; and assessments of external developments are not infrequently characterized by the presence of serious misperceptions as well, in the viewpoints both of citizens and of officials directly involved in the foreign policy

12. See Robert E. Sherwood, *Roosevelt and Hopkins: An Intimate History* (New York, 1948), 875–934; W. Averell Harriman, *America and Russia in a Changing World: A Half Century of Personal Observation* (Garden City, N.Y., 1971), 36–39; and George F. Kennan, *Memoirs: 1925–1950* (New York, 1969), 213–30.

13. Kennedy is quoted in Theodore Sorensen, *Kennedy* (New York, 1965), 511.

14. The Nixon Doctrine is analyzed in Cecil V. Crabb, Jr., *The Doctrines of American Foreign Policy: Their Meaning, Role, and Future* (Baton Rouge, 1982), 278–325.

process. Almost any major diplomatic decision by the United States in recent history would illustrate the point. In limited space, however, let us take note merely of two fundamentally different examples.[15]

The first is Soviet-American arms competition, which by the late 1980s had reached unprecedented levels. For a generation or more, officials in the United States, along with well-informed students of international politics, held highly divergent views concerning the origins, nature, and consequences of this problem. One interpretation held that the contemporary military rivalry between the superpowers was merely a recent manifestation of an old historical phenomenon: the tendency of all powerful nations to expand their powr and to use it for diplomatic purposes. A different explanation is that the phenomenon is nothing more than an intensification of the cold war existing between the superpowers since the end of World War II (détente, in other words, had not basically altered the nature of the cold war). Other students of the problem believed that Soviet-American military rivalry provided a graphic illustration of the tendency of any arms race to get out of control and to result in increasingly intense suspicions, tensions, and perhaps conflict among the participants.

An alternative explantion was that the underlying cause of the military competition between the United States and the Soviet Union was quite simple: relying on its already large and expanding military arsenal, Moscow was planning to undertake some new diplomatic offensive, perhaps in the Third World. The Kremlin, in other words, would attempt to convert its military advantage into diplomatic leverage in pursuing its global objectives.

Soviet officials, along with some commentators in the West, had a totally different explanation. As exemplified by the diplomatic rhetoric of President Ronald Reagan, in this view the United States remains implacably hostile to the Soviet Union, does not acknowledge its status as a superpower, refuses to recognize its legitimate diplomatic interests, and is determined to impose a *Pax Americana* upon the world.

A still different explanation is that the spiraling military budgets of the superpowers provide a graphic example of the potent influence of the "military-industrial complex" on the decision-making process within both societies. Irrespective of their differences, both the United States and the

15. The impact of misperceptions in producing tensions and conflicts in international relations since World War II is the major theme of John G. Stoessinger, *Nations in Darkness: China, Russia, and America* (3rd ed.; New York, 1981). See also Peter G. Filene (ed.), *American Views of Soviet Russia* (Homewood, Ill., 1968); and Ralph K. White, *Nobody Wanted War* (Garden City, N.Y., 1980).

Soviet Union find it difficult to restrain those groups that demand ever higher defense expenditures! Another interpretation is that on both sides of the Iron Curtain, prevalent misperceptions and misunderstandings between the superpowers have led to continuing suspicions, animosities, and expanding military arsenals. According to this theory, Americans have repeatedly exaggerated the aggressive nature of Soviet postwar behavior, and Moscow has erroneously persisted in its belief that America was engaged in "capitalist encirclement" or other attempts to destroy the communist system within the USSR.[16]

Since World War II, these and other explanations of the Soviet-American arms competition have been offered and, in varying degrees, have influenced American foreign policy. Official and public assessments of the nature of the problem will be crucial in determining how the United States responds to it. Although it may safely be said that every incumbent administration since World War II has been convinced that the arms race was engendered primarily by Soviet actions and beliefs, the validity of alternative explanations— such as the idea that arms races generate their own momentum, or the conviction that American policy must take account of the Soviet society's historic preoccupation with its security[17]—has also at least implicitly been admitted. Once again, American foreign policy has normally been predicated upon the belief that the challenge confronting the United States has multiple and interrelated origins—a reality which American diplomacy must reflect.

A fundamentally different diplomatic challenge confronted the United States during the 1980s in Central America. What factors accounted for that region's extreme political instability and volatility? And how did political turbulence in Central America affect the diplomatic interests of the United States? Again, a wide range of answers has been offered.

The Reagan administration's position was that in Central America and other settings, communism posed the primary threat to the region's continued independence and well-being. Assisted by its willing "proxies"— Cuba and Nicaragua—the Kremlin was endeavoring to exploit conditions of poverty, underdevelopment, and political unrest to promote its own global and regional objectives. These included periodically "testing" America's diplomatic resolve in the Western Hemisphere.[18]

16. Comparative data on military spending by the United States, the Soviet Union, and other countries are available in *World Military Expenditures and Arms Transfers, 1972–1982* (Washington, D.C., 1984) and subsequent publications in this series.
17. Department of Defense, *U.S. Military Posture, 1984*, and other volumes in this series.
18. See the interview with CIA Director William Casey in *U.S. News and World Report*, XCII

Other Americans rejected this explanation and offered alternative interpretations. Some groups and individuals believed that political upheaval throughout Latin America was traceable chiefly to continuing efforts by the United States to dominate and exploit the region. A leading goal of Latin America's political revolutions, therefore, was to counteract hegemonial tendencies by the United States. From another perspective, revolutionary groups throughout Latin America sought to achieve modernization, including greater freedom from Washington's control and reduced economic dependency upon the United States.

Relatively few informed students of Latin American affairs adopted a unicausal explanation of the region's tendency toward political unrest and conflict. Most interpreters offered several reasons to explain the phenomenon, ranging from its Spanish-derived political legacy, to the traditional role of military elites in its political process, to the existence of extremely sharp social and ethnic antagonisms, to the presence of pervasive poverty and income maldistribution, to the implications of runaway population growth, to rivalries between the Soviet Union and the United States within the hemisphere.[19] The challenge to American diplomatic interests in Central America, in other words, was not a *single* problem but several interrelated ones that had to be met by a multifaceted American program, combining military assistance and advice to friendly countries and political movements, long-range economic assistance, efforts to induce Latin American nations to undertake long overdue internal reforms, reliance on the mediatory efforts of other nations, and concessions to disaffected groups who believed that thus far their demands have been ignored by indigenous governments.

Prevailing perceptions of the challenge confronting the United States abroad, of course, are often modified in light of new conditions and new interpretations of available facts. The danger of overt Soviet aggression

---

(March 8, 1982), 23–24; the analysis of anti-Sandinista activity by the United States government in *Newsweek*, CII (November 8, 1982), 42–49; the dispatch by Drew Middleton in the New York *Times*, March 9, 1983; excerpts from President Reagan's speech on Central America in the New York *Times*, July 10, 1983; and the speech by Secretary of State George Shultz, "Struggle for Democracy in Central America," in the State Department's series *Current Policy*, No. 478, April 15, 1983.

19. See, for example, the analysis of Central America's political instability and propensity for violence by the Kissinger Commission, *Report of the National Commission on Central America* (Washington, D.C., 1984). Alternative perspectives are offered in Willard L. Beaulac, *The Fractured Continent: Latin America in Close-Up* (Stanford, 1980); Cole Blaiser, *The Hovering Giant: U.S. Responses to Revolutionary Change in Latin America* (Pittsburgh, 1976); Howard J. Wiarda, *The Continuing Struggle for Democracy in Latin America* (Boulder, Colo., 1980); and Michael Erisman (ed.), *The Caribbean Challenge: U.S. Policy in a Volatile Region* (Boulder, Colo., 1984).

against the NATO area, for example, had clearly receded by the 1980s vis-à-vis Western estimates of that danger during the 1950s. Similarly, in contrast to the alarmist predictions often expressed by officials of the Eisenhower administration, by the 1970s most officials in Washington believed that (with a few exceptions) Moscow was actually making little headway in its effort to dominate key Third World nations. (By the latter period, the Soviet Union was perhaps experiencing even less success in controlling the Third World than the United States!)

In contrast to the Johnson administration, later administrations did *not* view expansionism by North Vietnam against its Southeast Asian neighbors as a direct security threat to the United States. In Asia also, after the Vietnam War many Americans became convinced that the danger of a resurgent Japan was minimal; the greater danger was a militarily weak Japan that failed to assume major responsibility for regional security in the face of growing Soviet strength in East Asia.

President Jimmy Carter freely acknowledged that his view of Soviet diplomatic objectives changed fundamentally after Moscow's military intervention in Afghanistan. After originally opposing the idea strongly, the Reagan administration at length concluded that the construction of a Soviet-built pipeline to supply natural gas to the NATO area did not endanger Western security. Implicitly at least, the Reagan administration also conceded that the problem of acute political instability in Lebanon could not be solved by direct American military intervention in the country (which in several aspects merely aggravated the existing crisis).

The Institutional Setting

The American foreign policy process operates in a unique and complex institutional setting. It is beyond the scope of this study to present a detailed analysis of the roles of the president, the White House staff, the State Department, other executive agencies, and Congress in the foreign policy process of the United States.[20] Several significant points about their contributions, however, seem directly related to our subject and require brief mention.

In understanding the formulation and administration of American foreign policy, it must continually be remembered, the hallowed American con-

20. Cecil V. Crabb, Jr., *American Foreign Policy in the Nuclear Age* (4th ed.; New York, 1983). See also Kenneth A. Oye *et al.* (eds.), *Eagle Defiant: United States Foreign Policy in the 1980s* (Boston, 1983); and Charles W. Kegley, Jr., and Eugene R. Wittkopf (eds.), *Perspectives on American Foreign Policy: Selected Readings* (New York, 1983).

cept of separation of powers does not apply in any meaningful sense. This point has been emphasized time and again by the Supreme Court in a succession of cases related to foreign policy issues. In contrast to the judicial activism witnessed in domestic affairs in recent years, the Supreme Court remains extremely reluctant to intrude itself into the conduct of foreign relations. In its view, this sphere involves "political questions" that inherently do not lend themselves to judicial solutions; their solution must be found by executive and legislative officials and by the people. In the rare instances when it does consider foreign policy issues, the Supreme Court nearly always rules in favor of executive control over the decision-making process.[21]

After more than two centuries' experience as an independent nation, for the United States the transcendent reality about the foreign policy process is that it is largely controlled by—and sometimes clearly dominated by—the president. The president serves as the nation's diplomat-in-chief, and his decisions affect the future and well-being not only of Americans but of millions of people outside the United States as well. More than ever, today the president is a world leader—in some respects, the most powerful head of state in history. It has proved almost impossible for rivals to the president's position in the executive or legislative branches, or contenders outside the government, to challenge his preeminent role of diplomatic leadership successfully. As the "Great Communicator," President Ronald Reagan provided an especially graphic example of the emergence of the chief executive as the unrivaled captain of the American ship of state. Relying on his constitutional powers—and what may be even more decisive on some occasions, his historical and informal powers—the president is in a position to make and implement crucial diplomatic decisions.[22] As a rule, the constraints on his leadership role are indirect and long-range checks, and resourceful presidents have proved to be skillful in circumventing many of them. Even former legislators have acknowledged that clear and decisive diplomatic leadership by the White House is essential for the success of American foreign policy.[23]

21. Leading Supreme Court decisions affirming the president's control of foreign relations are the *Prize Cases*, 67 U.S. (2 Black) 635 (1963), and *United States v. Curtiss-Wright Export Corp.*, 299 U.S. 304 (1936). Informative studies of the Supreme Court's foreign policy role are Louis Henkin, *Foreign Affairs and the Constitution* (Mineola, N.Y., 1972); and Anthony A. D'Amato and Robert M. O'Neil, *The Judiciary and Vietnam* (New York, 1972).

22. See Sidney Warren, *The President as World Leader* (New York, 1964); Cecil V. Crabb, Jr., and Pat Holt, *Invitation to Struggle: Congress, the President, and Foreign Policy* (2nd ed.; Washington, D.C., 1984).

23. See, for example, the views of former Senator J. William Fulbright in "The Legislator as Educator," *Foreign Affairs*, LVII (Spring, 1979), 723–27; and Senator John Tower, "Congress Versus the President: The Formulation and Implementation of American Foreign Policy," *Foreign Affairs*, LX (Winter, 1981–82), 229–47.

A related phenomenon has been the decline of the State Department, which has been particularly evident since World War II. Traditionally, of course, the State Department managed foreign affairs under the president's ultimate authority. The erosion of the State Department's historic position has been accompanied by (and in some respects caused by) the increasingly influential role of the White House national security adviser, graphically illustrated by Henry Kissinger's diplomatic activism during the early 1970s, when, by contrast, Secretary of State William Rogers' contribution to the foreign policy process was usually limited.[24]

Other bureaucratic rivals such as an assertive Defense Department have intruded into the State Department's historic domain. In fact, today almost every department and agency within the executive branch has some foreign policy responsibilities. The result has been a steady diffusion of power and responsibilities among an ever-growing circle of executive agencies. During some periods, and especially in the Reagan administration in the early 1980s, a condition of virtual anarchy existed within the executive branch in dealing with foreign policy issues. Time and again, informed commentators at home and abroad asked who was really in charge of American foreign policy and whether, in view of the internal disunity among executive officials on diplomatic questions, the Reagan administration really had a foreign policy. The high level of dissonance within the executive branch on diplomatic questions since the Vietnam War increases the likelihood that policy proposals and recommendations submitted to the president will be a product of compromise and bargaining among rival executive agencies.[25]

The problem is compounded by another tendency that has increasingly engaged the attention of students of American government: the growing burden of the presidential office so that today it is an almost impossible assignment for a single individual to perform adequately. Although the president does retain the power of ultimate decision making in foreign affairs, the chief executive is more than ordinarily dependent today upon his advisers and is less able than in earlier periods to devote his own energies and attention to specific foreign policy issues. The process of diplomatic decision mak-

---

24. See Cecil V. Crabb, Jr., and Kevin V. Mulcahy, *The President and Foreign Policy: FDR to Reagan* (Baton Rouge, 1986); and I. M. Destler, *Presidents, Bureaucrats and Foreign Policy: The Politics of Organizational Reform* (Princeton, 1972).

25. The problem of internal dissonance among executive officials involved in foreign affairs reached unprecedented levels during the Reagan administration. See the discussion of its approach to diplomatic decision making in Crabb and Mulcahy, *President and Foreign Policy*, chap. 8. Another recent study emphasizing this same disability in the American foreign policy process is I. M. Destler, Leslie Gelb, and Anthony Lake, *Our Own Worst Enemy: The Unmaking of American Foreign Policy* (New York, 1984).

ing has thus inevitably become diffuse: a growing number of major and minor actors and "kibbitzers" are involved in dealing with a given diplomatic question, and the goal of achieving unified positions within the executive branch becomes almost unattainable.[26]

Congress, of course, possesses several important constitutional and historical prerogatives in the foreign policy field. The Constitution provides that treaties must receive the advice and consent of two-thirds of the Senate; and the Senate also "confirms" (or approves) high-level appointments by the president (such as assistant secretaries of state and above, and ambassadors). Both houses of Congress must approve a declaration of war. Congress also determines the nature and size of the American military establishment, and it must appropriate the funds necessary to operate the foreign aid program, the State and Defense departments, the United States Information Agency (America's official propaganda arm), and other instruments of foreign policy. The regulation of foreign trade and commerce is another important legislative prerogative.[27]

Theoretically, Congress possesses ample constitutional authority to assert its influence in the diplomatic sphere. In practice, the remarkable fact, however, is how *seldom* its powers are actually used by Congress to determine the course of American diplomacy. Conceivably, at any time, Congress could rely upon the power of the purse to determine or change the course of American foreign relations in defiance of the president's wishes. Yet for a number of reasons, in practice this almost never happens, even in the post-Vietnam era of congressional assertiveness in foreign relations. Perhaps the most fundamental reason why it does not occur is awareness on Capitol Hill that there exists no discernible public support for Congress to replace the White House as the locus of diplomatic decision making. If apprehensions exist in the public mind about the emergence of an imperial presidency, most informed citizens are equally concerned about what might be called an immobilized Congress, which is so internally disunified and inefficient in its procedures that it is unable to deal with national problems effectively.[28]

26. See, for example, Harold M. Barger, *The Impossible Presidency: Illusions and Realities of Executive Power* (Glenview, Ill., 1984); Raymond Tatalovich, *Presidential Power in the United States* (Monterey, Calif., 1983); Hugh Heclo and Lester M. Soloman (eds.), *Illusion of Presidential Government* (Boulder, Colo., 1981); and Michael Nelson, *The Presidency and the Political System* (Washington, D.C., 1984).

27. The powers of Congress in foreign affairs are explained more fully in Crabb, *American Foreign Policy in the Nuclear Age,* 188–208; Crabb and Holt, *Invitation to Struggle,* 75–96; and the case studies on executive-legislative relations which follow, *ibid.,* 99–213. See also Thomas Franck and Edward Weisband, *Foreign Policy by Congress* (New York, 1979); and Pat M. Holt, *The War Powers Resolution: The Role of Congress in U.S. Armed Intervention* (Washington, D.C., 1978).

28. See Crabb and Holt, *Invitation to Struggle,* 213–53.

In recent years, therefore, Congress' role in the foreign policy process has remained subordinate. Congress can and does sometimes impose limits on the president's diplomatic freedom of action, as when it prohibited President Gerald Ford in 1975 from intervening in Angola. Relying upon its investigative powers, Congress can uncover and publicize maladministration, waste, abuses of executive power, and other problems in the foreign policy field—as in the Iran-Contra investigation during President Reagan's second term. Congress can take corrective steps or compel the president to do so.[29] Speeches and news conferences by individual legislators, reports by legislative committees and subcommittees, and studies by the Library of Congress can also direct public attention to problems in the foreign policy sphere and often compel the president to remedy them.

Two other legislative contributions to the diplomatic process have been highlighted by recent experience. One of these may be described by saying that in the foreign policy field, Congress often serves as a yellow light— flashing "caution"—for the chief executive. As the Reagan administration discovered on several occasions in its diplomacy toward Lebanon and Central America, congressional reactions told the president that he was sometimes coming very close to crossing the bounds of public acceptability or legitimacy in his diplomatic activities. Repeated warnings by Congress unmistakably signaled "danger ahead" to the White House, and in both settings, the Reagan White House modified its policies to take account of such admonitions.[30] Sensitivity to such viewpoints on Capitol Hill may well have saved the Reagan administration from the kind of public repudiation of its diplomatic undertakings experienced by the Johnson administration in Southeast Asia.

By contrast, the other contribution made by Congress to the foreign policy process is in some opposition to its yellow light role. On numerous occasions since World War II, Congress has served as a policy amplifier, strengthening and reinforcing diplomatic signals sent by the White House to foreign governments. This is clearly one of the contributions made by the House and Senate in a bipartisan approach to foreign relations. In 1947, for example, when the Truman Doctrine with its containment policy was enunciated by the president and overwhelmingly supported by majorities in the House and Senate, other governments could hardly mistake America's intentions or seriousness of purpose. This unanimity presupposes that the president and his advisers have fully consulted with legislative spokesmen in

29. See Gerald R. Ford, *A Time to Heal* (New York, 1979), 345–46. A useful compendium highlighting major congressional investigations is Arthur M. Schlesinger, Jr., and Roger Burns (eds.), *Congress Investigates: A Documented History, 1792–1974* (5 vols.; New York, 1975).

30. Crabb and Holt, *Invitation to Struggle*, 161–87.

the process of policy formulation, which has not always been true. During the Vietnam War, for example, legislators continually complained about the Johnson administration's failure to consult with them in devising political and military strategy. Yet when adequate consultation does exist, and both branches subsequently join in a unified statement of American foreign policy, this is a forceful demonstration of national unity which greatly strengthens the president's hand in dealing with other governments.[31]

Finally, in accordance with pragmatic tenets, the institutional setting of the American foreign policy process is dynamic, adaptive, and responsive to new conditions at home and abroad. This process was not consciously designed by anyone: for the most part, it evolved by a process of adaptation, in response to a series of external challenges, and it has continuously been modified over the years to serve the interests of the American society. Most especially, perhaps, in its institutional setting, the process of diplomatic decision making is untidy, illogical, inefficient, and often difficult to comprehend. At times, its defects are glaring and occasionally serious. The process continues to enjoy at least tacit public support, however, for one paramount reason: somehow *it works* better, perhaps because it has fewer disadvantages, than alternative systems that have been proposed to replace it.

The Domestic Constituency Setting

The American foreign policy process also operates within what might be called a "domestic constituency setting," which may be envisioned as consisting of three major components: public (mass and elite) opinion, interest groups, and internal political forces. (In practice, of course, these categories sometimes overlap and interact.)

What is the role of mass public opinion in the American foreign policy process? Some attention has already been devoted to this question. The average American has little sustained interest in, or knowledge about, foreign affairs. Preoccupied with domestic concerns, the ordinary citizen is largely content to leave the management of foreign affairs to the president and his advisers unless and until an external crisis engages his attention. Even then, however, the tendency of most citizens is to accept the president's account of the facts and to accord him wide latitude in responding to the challenge confronting the United States abroad. Practically never are the president's critics in Congress or elsewhere able to compete successfully with him in

31. See, for example, the discussion of the Truman Doctrine, the Eisenhower Doctrine, the two Johnson doctrines, and the Carter Doctrine in Crabb, *Doctrines of American Foreign Policy.*

gaining and retaining public support as long as the results of White House diplomatic efforts are at least minimally successful. In foreign affairs, even more than in the domestic realm, the president leads and educates public opinion, perhaps even more than he is influenced by it. Given the inchoate, ambivalent, and fragmentary nature of mass public opinion in the United States, executive officials can nearly always contend with some justification that the course of action they are following has widespread public support.[32]

Inert and apathetic toward foreign affairs as it usually is, mass public opinion nevertheless plays a crucial role in diplomatic decision making. In the American and other democratic systems, the nation's foreign policy must possess legitimacy. National policy makers must, so to speak, stay within a diplomatic channel demarcated by two sets of buoys. One of these is the American people's perception of diplomatic activity that crosses the bounds of common sense and moral-ethical acceptability. The most conspicuous example of a foreign policy that got "off course" was the Johnson administration's diplomacy in Southeast Asia, which, in time, lost legitimacy and was repudiated by the American people. Several years later the Reagan administration was hard-pressed to demonstrate that its diplomacy in Lebanon and Central America could be justified by this same criterion.

President Jimmy Carter was made painfully aware, however, of the dangers of veering out of the diplomatic mainstream in the opposite direction. During the closing months of his administration, the American people left no doubt that they expected the president to protect the lives and safety of American citizens abroad, to be concerned about the honor and diplomatic credibility of the United States, and to be diligent and resourceful in safeguarding American strategic and diplomatic interests overseas. In a word, the American people expect the chief executive to act *decisively.*

As the Reagan administration's diplomatic misadventure in Lebanon and its military strike against Libya subsequently illustrated, when circumstances abroad require it, the American people tend to be more tolerant of a president who acts—even if sometimes unsuccessfully—than one who appears to be immobilized, confused, or uncertain how to protect the nation's interests in the face of foreign threats.[33]

The elite or "informed" segment of public opinion makes a different

32. This is a major finding of the study by Bernard C. Cohen, *The Public's Impact on Foreign Policy* (Boston, 1973), esp. 137–43. See also Robert C. Hilderbrand, *Power and the People: Executive Management of Public Opinion in Foreign Affairs, 1897–1921* (Chapel Hill, 1981), esp. 198–205.

33. President John F. Kennedy's performance rating with the American people climbed after the Bay of Pigs invasion of Cuba in April, 1961. See the charts in John E. Mueller, *War, Presidents and Public Opinion* (New York, 1973), 200–201.

contribution to the foreign policy process. Seldom including more than 15 to 20 percent of the adult population, this stratum serves as the "opinion makers" for the mass public, supplies new ideas and proposals for consideration by policy makers, plays the role of informed critics for existing policies, and calls attention to tendencies and emerging problems likely to confront the United States abroad in the years ahead. The Council on Foreign Relations, the Foreign Policy Association, the Carnegie Endowment for International Peace, the Hudson Institute, and a long list of other organizations endeavor to counteract the average citizen's low level of interest in and understanding of foreign policy questions. The State Department, for example, relies heavily on elite opinion both for support of its policies and for enlightened criticisms of them. As a school of philosophy that drew heavily on the ideas of Charles Darwin, pragmatism emphasizes the necessity for variations in human society, if it is to evolve successfully. Elite groups within public opinion go far toward supplying such creative variations in the American foreign policy process.[34]

Americans are known as a "nation of joiners." By the late twentieth century, there were untold thousands of organizations and associations in the United States with direct or secondary interests in foreign affairs. John Dewey's emphasis on the group basis of the political process is nowhere better illustrated than in the pattern of pressure group activities in the United States. By some criteria, both the magnitude and effectiveness of lobbying have increased significantly since the end of World War II.[35]

Serving as an important component of the foreign policy process, pressure group activity in American society exhibits several noteworthy features.

34. Estimates of the size of "elite opinion" on American foreign policy vary, depending in large part on how the concept is defined or the criteria used to identify it. It is estimated, for example, that even within elite opinion, only some 1 or 2 percent of the American people could accurately be described as "mobilizers" of public attitudes on diplomatic questions. This group consists of those people who are extremely interested in, well informed about, and prepared to take action to influence the diplomatic behavior of the United States. See Barry B. Hughes, *The Domestic Context of American Foreign Policy* (San Francisco, 1978), 21–25; and Susan Shepard, "Foreign Policy Think Tanks: A Critical Guide," *Book Forum,* V, No. 4 (1984), 462–97.

35. Useful general studies are Bernard Cohen, *The Influence of Non-Government Groups on Foreign Policy-Making* (Boston, 1959); Mark W. Cannon, *The Makers of Public Policy: American Power Groups and Their Ideologies* (New York, 1965); and William O. Chittick, *State Department, Press and Pressure Groups* (New York, 1970). Informative treatments of specific lobbies and American foreign policy include David Horowitz (ed.), *Corporations and the Cold War* (New York, 1969); Raymond A. Bauer et al., *American Business and Public Policy: The Politics of Foreign Trade* (Chicago, 1973); James Clotfelter, *The Military in American Politics* (New York, 1973); Roscoe Baker, *The American Legion and American Foreign Policy* (New York, 1954); Alfred O. Hero, Jr., *American Religious Groups View Foreign Policy* (Durham, N.C., 1973); Lawrence H. Fuchs (ed.), *American Ethnic Politics* (New York, 1968); Symposium, "Labor's International Role," *Foreign Policy,* XXVI (Spring, 1977), 204–46; and George W. Shepherd, Jr. (ed.), *Racial Influences on American Foreign Policy* (New York, 1970).

Normally, individual pressure groups confine their lobbying on foreign policy questions to a narrow range of issues directly affecting the welfare of their members. Zionist groups, for example, are primarily interested in how the policies of the United States benefit (or perhaps harm) Israel; labor unions are concerned about the impact of foreign competition on employment in the United States; groups advocating a nuclear freeze concentrate on the single issue of arms control.

Group opinion is usually marked by a high level of intensity of feeling, which is seldom exhibited by the mass public on foreign policy issues. As a rule, lobbies representing organizations and citizens who feel strongly about selected diplomatic questions (especially those that oppose prevailing policy) communicate their viewpoints to executive and legislative officials.

For many national policy issues, perhaps, a crude equilibrium exists in the arena of pressure group activity. In trade policy, for example, protectionist lobbies are often counterbalanced by other groups (farmers, for example) whose prosperity depends upon a high level of exports and who demand continued American access to foreign markets. Pressure groups calling for higher defense expenditures are opposed by those advocating a nuclear freeze or other arms control measures. Organizations favoring an expansion of the foreign aid program are counterbalanced by those seeking to reduce the federal budget.

On certain diplomatic questions, however, no such equilibrium in competition among pressure groups exists. Throughout much of the post–World War II period, the pro-Israeli lobby has had little effective opposition from the pro-Arab lobby within the United States (although that situation began to change after the 1973 boycott which oil-producing states in the Middle East imposed on exports to the West).[36] On the Cyprus question, the Greek-American lobby has been infinitely more influential than the pro-Turkish lobby, to the detriment of America's relations with Turkey in recent years. During and after World War II, the Polish-American lobby also lacked significant competition from other pressure groups in its efforts to assure that American foreign policy was favorable to the cause of Polish democracy and independence from Soviet hegemony.[37]

36. See the discussion of the organization and activities of the Zionist lobby in the United States in *The Middle East: U.S. Policy, Israel, Oil and the Arabs* (Washington, D.C., 1980), 89–95; and Zvi Ganin, *Truman, American Jewry, and Israel, 1945–1948* (New York, 1979). The influence of the Greek-American lobby on Congress is discussed in Ford, *A Time to Heal,* 137–38, 199; and Laurence Stern, "How We Failed in Cyprus," *Foreign Policy,* XIX (Summer, 1975), 34–79.
37. See Sherwood, *Roosevelt and Hopkins,* 888–91; and Cordell Hull, *The Memoirs of Cordell Hull* (2 vols.; New York, 1948), II, 1265–73, 1436–50.

Such cases, of course, are likely to lead to a serious imbalance in pressure group activity and to produce distorted conceptions of America's national interest among executive and legislative officals. For almost forty years, American diplomacy in the Middle East has, with relatively few exceptions, been markedly pro-Israel. On Cyprus, the American position has predominantly favored the Greek position. Yet in these and comparable cases, we should be wary of concluding that the Zionist lobby has dictated postwar American foreign policy toward the Middle East, or that the Greek-American lobby controls the decisions of the American government on the Cyprus issue.

In these and analogous cases, lobbying activities have often operated in a public opinion environment already strongly predisposed toward a pressure group's position. The Zionist lobby, for example, may have been extremely successful in achieving its objectives mainly because most Americans were already sympathetic to the Zionist cause in Palestine vis-à-vis the Arab position. The popular conception of the goal of propaganda—that it seeks primarily to change the preexisting opinion of the hearer—is incorrect; such propaganda efforts in fact seldom succeed. In most instances, the objective of propaganda is to induce the hearer (sometimes called the "target") to *believe or act in accordance with his preexisting inclinations.* This phenomenon is known as *reinforcement;* propaganda supplies an explicit or persuasive rationale for individuals and groups to do what they already have a tendency to do. The successful record of the Zionist lobby in the United States since World War II can be interpreted, therefore, as indicating that this pressure group was operating within an already friendly environment. By contrast, the Arab lobby for the most part has operated in a milieu that is unfavorable to its efforts.[38]

Traditionally, lobbying has usually been viewed as an activity directed chiefly at the legislative branches of the national and state governments. In recent years, however, an important twofold tendency has become evident in pressure group activity in the United States. As often as not, pressure group activities, particularly with regard to foreign policy issues, are now directed at the White House and other executive agencies. Experienced lobbyists are well aware that, in the last analysis, the president determines the foreign policy of the United States.

Moreover, on several occasions in recent years, executive officials and interest groups have collaborated in efforts to gain public and congressional

38. See the Introduction by Konrad Kellen, in Jacques Ellul, *Propaganda: The Formation of Men's Attitudes* (New York, 1973), v–vii.

support for a particular undertaking in foreign affairs. President John F. Kennedy, for example, enlisted interest groups to join with the White House in persuading the American people and Congress to approve a liberalization of American trade laws. During the late 1970s, the Carter administration similarly gained the support of several interest groups to generate needed public support for, and ultimate Senate approval of, its new treaties for the Panama Canal.[39]

Domestic political considerations are seldom absent from the making of foreign policy decisions. Although he serves as diplomat in chief, an incumbent president is also the leader of his political party. Normally, a first-term president is interested in reelection, and he nearly always also wants his party to control the House and Senate. In national elections, as a rule the record of the incumbent administration is the dominant issue of the campaign—and a president's diplomatic performance comprises an important part of that record.

On the basis of post–World War II experience, three tendencies may be identified in the relationship between diplomatic issues and political outcomes on the national level in the United States. First, in the normal case, foreign policy questions *per se* play a subordinate role in determining political results. The major exception is when the voters perceive the existence of a foreign policy crisis, such as a threat to national security (as during wartime), or they become convinced that the incumbent administration has failed to protect the diplomatic interests of the United States (as in the political repudiation of the Johnson and Carter administrations). Otherwise, diplomatic issues are usually eclipsed by the personalities of the candidates and by domestic concerns in national political campaigns.[40]

The second tendency is that post–World War II political experience indicates convincingly that the American people have an aversion to diplomatic extremism and a decided preference for moderate or middle-of-the-road solutions for foreign policy problems. In time, for example, Americans repudiated the radical right-wing movement known as McCarthyism during the 1950s, which was distinguished by an almost fanatical and indiscriminate

39. See, for example, the account of the Kennedy administration's collaboration with private organizations to lobby nationally in behalf of the Trade Expansion Act of 1962, in Arthur Schlesinger, Jr., *A Thousand Days: John F. Kennedy in the White House* (Boston, 1965), 846–48. The national lobbying and informational campaign launched by the Carter administration to gain public and legislative support for the new Panama Canal treaties is discussed in Crabb and Holt, *Invitation to Struggle*, 75–96.

40. See the essays in Ellis Sandoz and Cecil V. Crabb, Jr. (eds.), *A Tide of Discontent: The 1980 Elections and Their Meaning* (Washington, D.C., 1981).

anticommunism, comparable to the Red Scare that swept the United States after World War I.[41] Similarly, during the Vietnam War, extremist behavior by antiwar critics alienated perhaps a majority of the American people. In the Vietnam conflict—as in later American military involvements in other countries—most of the people were neither overtly "hawkish" nor "dovish"; public attitudes tended to adhere to a centrist position and to vary considerably, depending on conditions confronting the United States abroad.[42]

By the 1980s, President Ronald Reagan was repeatedly required to demonstrate to the American people that, despite his often inflammatory ideological rhetoric, his policies toward a wide range of international issues were in fact moderate, reasonable, and flexible. Reagan's willingness to modify his viewpoints in the light of changing circumstances in the Middle East and Central America provided evidence of the diplomatic adaptability Americans approve and expect in a chief executive.[43]

A third significant tendency has been the pragmatic criterion applied by the American people to the administration of national affairs generally, but especially to foreign relations. Lacking deep and sustained interest in the latter, the people are primarily concerned about whether an incumbent president is managing foreign affairs *successfully*. As long as that appears to be so, relatively few citizens are interested in how that result is accomplished. When it is not the case—as the Johnson and Carter administrations discovered—an incumbent administration is likely to face a severe loss of credibility and confidence with the American people.

The Foreign Constituency Setting

Still another important dimension of the foreign policy process is the foreign constituency setting. In some respects, this aspect of the policy environment has become increasingly influential; yet in too many analyses of decision

41. The movement known as McCarthyism and other right-wing extremist groups in recent American political experience are described in Benjamin R. Epstein and Arnold Forster, *The Radical Right* (New York, 1967); Clinton Rossiter, *Conservatism in America* (New York, 1962); John H. Redekop, *The American Far Right: A Case Study of Billy James Hargis and the Christian Crusade* (Grand Rapids, Mich., 1968); Daniel Bell (ed.), *The New American Right* (New York, 1955); and Morris H. Rubin (ed.), *The McCarthy Record* (New York, 1952).
42. At one stage, a Gallup Poll showed that for a majority of Americans, student protests were a matter of greater public concern than the war itself! See Milton J. Rosenberg, Sidney Verba, and Philip E. Converse, *Vietnam and the Silent Majority* (New York, 1970), 33–34 and *passim.*
43. See, for example, the analysis of the meeting between President Reagan and Soviet Foreign Minister Andrei Gromyko, in *Time,* CXXIV (October 8, 1984), 12–16; and the text of Reagan's address to the U.N. General Assembly, in the New York *Times,* October 24, 1984.

making by the United States, its role has been neglected. In the pragmatic conception, human actions are viewed as responses to perceived problems or challenges, and many of these arise out of the foreign constituency setting.

More specifically, a number of major diplomatic decisions by the United States since World War II emerged in response to the requests and evident needs of foreign countries. The governments of Greece and Turkey, for example, requested assistance during the late 1940s to counter communist threats to their independence. The nations of Western Europe urgently requested large-scale American aid in the early postwar era, which took the form of various emergency programs and ultimately gave rise to the European Recovery Program. After the adoption of President Truman's Point Four program in 1950, at one time or another nearly every Third World nation has requested American economic and technical assistance—and they continue to complain that American aid is inadequate. The Kennedy administration took the lead in formulating the Alliance for Progress in the early 1960s in response to Latin American complaints that Washington had too long neglected their developmental needs.[44]

The same point can be made about American military aid and involvement abroad. Since World War II, innumerable more or less urgent requests have been received in Washington for American arms-aid by countries facing internal or external threats. (In some instances, and a leading example has been the intermittent conflict between India and Pakistan, both belligerents subsequently employed American-supplied weapons in the conflict.) In these situations, American officials have often found themselves in a difficult dilemma: if they provided military aid, they were accused of supporting authoritarian governments against political opposition groups or other countries in an external conflict and of encouraging the arms race throughout the Third World; if they refused to provide the military aid requested, they were charged with being indifferent to the country's defense needs, of "playing favorites" among the recipients of American military assistance programs, and of compelling the country that was refused aid to rely upon the Soviet Union or other sources for its military needs.

Basically the same point can be made about several cases of American military interventionism abroad. In Korea, Vietnam, the Dominican Republic, Lebanon, and Grenada, one or more foreign governments has nearly always

44. *The Rockefeller Report on the Americas* (Chicago, 1969); and J. Warren Nystrom and Nathan A. Haverstock, *The Alliance for Progress* (Princeton, 1966), 20–38; American Assembly, *Mexico and the United States* (Englewood Cliffs, N.J., 1981), v.

requested the United States to undertake such intervention. No doubt in some cases, such invitations have been "arranged" or otherwise instigated by Washington. Yet in many instances, they have been genuine. As in the well-known love-hate dichotomy in United States–Latin American relations, incumbent governments may denounce United States interventionism in the abstract while encouraging it in behalf of particular causes to which Latin American political leaders are devoted. Nor is it unusual for officials of such governments to condemn American interventionism publicly while privately expressing their appreciation to Washington for undertaking it![45]

Even in the period of diplomatic retrenchment that followed the Vietnam War, the United States continues to be the most powerful member of several military alliance systems—the most important being NATO. Accordingly, "alliance maintenance" remains another leading concern affecting the American foreign policy process. After they have been established, alliance ties must be continuously nourished; preserving the cohesion of the alliance is a perennial goal. It follows that American officials must listen to the viewpoints of their alliance partners; consult them in major diplomatic undertakings; take their positions into account, especially on issues of direct concern to the alliance; and give the allies the overall impression that their diplomatic and security interests are important to the United States and have been considered in the formulation of alliance policies. In accordance with pragmatic tenets, *how* decisions are made within the alliance system may be even more crucial in preserving unity within it than the substance of the decisions reached. The requirements of alliance maintenance are, of course, antithetical to the tradition of American diplomatic unilateralism.[46]

A different dimension of the foreign constituency setting relates to the image of the United States overseas. Elusive and intangible as this concept is, America's image abroad is an integral component of its national power. Since the inception of the cold war—sometimes described as "a battle for the minds of men"—the United States and the Soviet Union have been engaged in a contest to win the goodwill and support of leaders and masses throughout the Afro-Asian world. Pragmatic thought emphasizes that perceptions play a

45. See Herbert K. Tillema, *Appeal to Force: American Military Intervention in the Era of Containment* (New York, 1973), 34; John B. Martin, *Adlai Stevenson and the World* (Garden City, N.Y., 1977), 845.

46. The disarray that has been a chronic problem within NATO is examined in Robert Kleiman, *The Atlantic Crisis: American Diplomacy Confronts a Resurgent Europe* (New York, 1964), 154; and Alfred Grosser, *The Western Alliance: European-American Relations Since 1945* (New York, 1982), 183–208.

crucial role in determining human actions. How the United States is perceived throughout the Third World, therefore, is a major concern of policy
makers in Washington. Or, to take a different example, Soviet Premier Nikita
Khrushchev's perception (it turned out to be a major misperception) of the
supposed weakness of the newly inaugurated Kennedy administration contributed to Moscow's decision to install Soviet offensive missiles in Cuba,
leading in turn to the most serious Soviet-American confrontation since
World War II. Several years earlier, the Kremlin had seriously misjudged
America's determination to defend Berlin from Soviet pressures.[47]

Implicit in the concept of the foreign constituency is the idea of American
diplomatic credibility. Admittedly, this idea is also subjective and intangible,
but it is no less crucial in determining diplomatic outcomes. Does the Soviet
Union believe that America's nuclear deterrent is credible—that is, that it will
survive a possible Soviet first strike and will be used to retaliate massively
against a possible aggressor? Can Moscow count on Washington (and vice
versa) to negotiate arms control agreements in good faith and to honor their
provisions? Are the NATO allies convinced that the United States will actually
defend Western Europe at the risk of nuclear war? Do the Latin American
nations believe that Washington is determined to prevent the emergence of
"another Cuba" within the Western Hemisphere? Can Israel rely on repeated
American guarantees of its security in the face of continuing Arab hostility?
For these and numerous other external issues, the preservation of American
diplomatic credibility is essential for success in the foreign policy field.

Irrational, Random, and Subjective Influences

The pluralistic nature of the foreign policy process in the United States means
that it is affected—sometimes momentously—by a wide variety of irrational,
subjective, random, and unpredictable forces that play a role in determining
the nation's diplomatic course. Among these, an influential one is the administrative style of a particular president, which nearly always contains unique
elements. Since we cannot examine all incumbent administrations in recent
experience, let us concentrate merely upon three noteworthy examples to
illustrate the general point. Meanwhile, however, it is worth noting that in
the view of former Secretary of State Dean Acheson, what he called the
"personal" relationship or rapport existing between an incumbent president

47. See Schlesinger, *Thousand Days*, 796–97; and Theodore Sorensen, *Kennedy* (New York, 1965), 676–77.

and his secretary of state will be a crucial factor in determining the administration's diplomatic accomplishments.[48]

In the modern history of the presidential office, Franklin D. Roosevelt stands out as a prime example of a chief executive who served as his own secretary of state. Except for a few policy areas (Latin America and international trade), Secretary of State Cordell Hull was largely an ornamental and ceremonial figure in the Roosevelt administration. Especially after the United States entered World War II, FDR took the reins of foreign policy increasingly into his own hands—or, it might be more accurate to say that he dispersed that responsibility among a host of formal and informal advisers who were accountable to the president alone. Not infrequently, Secretary Hull was left in the dark concerning FDR's diplomatic intentions—and on some crucial occasions, even his decisions. Roosevelt routinely bypassed the State Department, preferring instead to rely on a wide range of personal advisers and friends and to reach decisions directly with other heads of state, often in secret negotiations. Roosevelt's great personal charisma; his skill in political manipulation and persuasion; his superficial knowledge of many complex foreign policy issues; his personal prejudices and preconceptions toward the Soviet Union, the British Empire, Poland, and a host of issues with which he dealt; and toward the end of World War II, his rapidly declining health and mental prowess were salient features of FDR's approach to American foreign relations and affected their outcome profoundly.[49]

By contrast, Harry Truman's administrative style was no less unique, if fundamentally different. A little-known political figure before Roosevelt's death on April 12, 1945, Vice-President Truman suddenly found himself the nation's leader, and he was determined to be such in fact as well as in name. The "man from Missouri" left no doubt that he was ultimately in charge of American foreign policy, although he delegated day-to-day responsibility for its management to his secretary of state. In time, Truman and Secretary of State Dean Acheson developed a close and continuing rapport, producing one of the most effective partnerships in the annals of American diplomacy.

It was not, of course, an equal partnership. Acheson never forgot that the ultimate power of diplomatic decision making belonged to the president; he kept Truman frequently and fully informed on major diplomatic develop-

48. See Dean Acheson's views on the relationship between the president and the secretary of state in Ronald J. Stupak, *The Shaping of Foreign Policy: The Role of the Secretary of State as Seen by Dean Acheson* (New York, 1969), 21–33, 113.
49. See the case study of President Roosevelt's serving as "his own secretary of state," in Crabb and Mulcahy, *Presidents and Foreign Policy,* chap. 3.

ments and defended the administration's foreign policy record capably and vigorously. Truman gave Acheson wide latitude to manage the Department of State, defended him against critics at home and abroad, and nearly always followed his policy recommendations. The result was perhaps the most diplomatically creative era in recent American experience.[50]

A third example was the process of foreign policy decision making adopted by the Nixon administration from early 1969 until President Nixon's resignation on August 9, 1974. Distinguishing features of this pattern were a president who had a better than average background in foreign affairs, who was keenly interested in external problems, and who was determined to make certain fundamental changes in American foreign relations. At the same time, Nixon was distrustful of the State Department, which he believed was dominated by the "Eastern Establishment." His appointment of William Rogers, who had few discernible qualifications for the position, as secretary of state underscored Nixon's determination to make the White House the dominant actor in the foreign policy process. Nixon's national security advisor, Henry Kissinger, emerged as the *de facto* secretary of state and the administration's principal foreign policy spokesman. The Nixon-Kissinger team successfully created and operated a rival State Department in the White House, establishing a precedent that was to change fundamentally the system of American diplomatic decision making in the years ahead.[51]

Several former government officials and informed students of American foreign relations have cautioned against the tendency to attribute to the process of diplomatic decision making a higher degree of rationality and order than is justified by the evidence. In Lloyd Jensen's view, "decision makers themselves often are not certain exactly what motivates them to advocate a given action" in foreign affairs. Similarly, Roger Hilsman cautions against accepting the assumption uncritically that external policy making is a highly rationalistic process, "with each step leading logically and economically to the next," and with the roles and responsibilities of each participant precisely defined, thereby permitting clear-cut accountability for decisions reached. In practice, foreign policy decisions emerge as the result of "a congeries of separate or only vaguely related actions"; not infrequently, they involve "an uneasy, even internally inconsistent compromise among competing goals or

50. *Ibid.*, chap. 4; Stupak, *Shaping of Foreign Policy, passim;* and Gaddis Smith, *Dean Acheson,* in Robert H. Ferrell (ed.), *The American Secretaries of State and Their Diplomacy* (New York, 1972).

51. The Nixon-Kissinger model of foreign policy decision making is analyzed in Crabb and Mulcahy, *Presidents and Foreign Policy,* chap. 7. More detailed treatment is available in Henry Kissinger, *White House Years* (Boston, 1979), and *Years of Upheaval* (Boston, 1982).

an incompatible mixture of alternative means for achieving a single goal." Almost never, in Hilsman's assessment, does American foreign policy emerge as the result of some "grand design." Instead, it is the result of "a series of slight modifications of existing policy," of "small and usually tentative steps," of a process of "trial and error," and of diplomatic "zigs and zags," producing a foreign policy that moves forward "in a series of incremental steps."[52]

The foreign policy process in the United States illustrates poignantly the contention of pragmatic thinkers that a pluralistic universe contains unique, random, and unpredictable forces that sometimes affect its destiny momentously. An example of such a force has been emphasized by several commentators on the diplomacy of the Truman administration. At the end of World War II and during the early prewar era, frequently the necessity for speed in arriving at American diplomatic decisions was a major factor in determining the results. The necessity to formulate a diplomatic response within a relatively brief period of time—as in the Greek-Turkish Aid Program of 1947 or the Truman administration's action after North Korean forces attacked South Korea—was often a key factor in accounting for the policy finally adopted.[53]

Concluding Observations

When applied to the internal environment of the American foreign policy process, the pragmatic concept of a pluralistic universe has had several significant implications for the diplomacy of the United States. First, in almost all instances, the nation's foreign policy is *the product of several major and minor influences* that combine to produce a given result. To the pragmatic mind, all unicausal or monistic interpretations of American diplomatic conduct are suspect, if not erroneous, because they tend to oversimplify a highly complex reality.

Second, the principal forces operating upon the process of diplomatic decision making by the United States vary over time; they are in turn affected by the dynamic character of the universe and by the particular conditions confronting the United States at home and abroad. As the experience of the

52. See Lloyd Jensen, *Explaining Foreign Policy* (Englewood Cliffs, N.J., 1982), 4, 13–44; and Hilsman, *Politics of Policy Making,* 4–5. Another study of the American foreign policy process concludes that policy recommendations are nearly always a "mixture of objective facts, subjective values, and personal motivations"; almost invariably for officials involved in diplomatic decision making, "personality needs and policy recommendations are closely related" (Stupak, *Shaping of Foreign Policy,* 114).

53. See McCoy, *Presidency of Harry S. Truman,* 36–37.

Carter administration graphically illustrated, the changing nature of these forces can produce significant modifications in the diplomatic behavior of a single administration. Or, from a different perspective, they can give rise to different courses of action by the United States in dealing with a single problem (the existence of communism in various countries, the modernization of Third World societies, or the promotion of human rights in diverse settings abroad).

Third, operating within a highly pluralistic domestic milieu, the American foreign policy process represents a complex "field of forces." How these forces are ultimately resolved—or determine the nation's diplomatic course of action in a particular case—is primarily the responsibility of the president, with participation by his executive advisers, Congress, public opinion, and foreign governments and opinion. In a given case, such, for example, as the Reagan administration's decision to expand and modernize the nation's military arsenal, a number of potent influences no doubt entered into the decision. The fact that the Carter administration had earlier called for a significant increase in national defense spending; the ideological aversion of President Reagan and most of his supporters to communism and their belief that it was still the most dangerous threat to global peace and security; the president's conviction that during the 1970s the nation's diplomatic credibility had suffered a serious decline; Moscow's evident determination since the Vietnam War to gain superiority in certain categories of strategic missiles and other weapons; the Kremlin's continuing intervention in Poland, Afghanistan, Latin America, and other settings; intensive and skillful lobbying activities by industries, labor unions, and local communities within the United States interested in developing new weapons; and requests by the NATO allies and other governments that Washington strengthen the military position of the noncommunist world—these were the main forces influencing President Reagan's diplomacy. It is seldom possible for an observer—and perhaps no less difficult for the president himself—to determine the *precise influence* of any of these forces in accounting for the decision that is ultimately reached.

Fourth, pragmatism teaches that is the interaction between humans and their environment which is crucial in determining the future of human society. As we have seen, environmental forces operate upon human decision makers, but the latter also continually *influence and change the environment.* For example, in a democracy, the president and his advisers must be mindful of, and responsive to, public opinion. Yet one of the president's most important diplomatic roles is to educate public opinion, lead it, and persuade it to accept a course of action that the White House believes is diplomatically essential. The relationship between a chief executive and public opinion is thus a two-way street: especially during crises abroad, skillful presidents can go far toward creating a public opinion environment that is supportive of their diplomatic undertakings.

Fifth, after identifying the principal influences operating on the process of diplomatic decision making by the United States, the pragmatic concept of a pluralistic universe cautions that this process remains at all times subject to random, accidental, subjective, and often mysterious forces, which can sometimes be crucial in determining the nation's diplomatic behavior. To what extent, for example, did President Woodrow Wilson's pride prevent him from accepting amendments to the Treaty of Versailles desired by Republicans, thereby assuring that the United States would not join the League of Nations? During late 1944 and early 1945, what role did President Franklin D. Roosevelt's declining health play in the diplomatic agreements reached at the Yalta Conference and in other foreign policy decisions by the Roosevelt administration? During and after the war, to what degree could the "failure" of American diplomacy in China be attributed to pervasive official and public ignorance about China and Asia generally? Then, in the 1960s, how important was President Lyndon Johnson's personal ego involvement in his Vietnam policies in explaining America's defeat in Southeast Asia? Under the Reagan administration, what was the impact of the president's unique administrative style—his tendency to permit full, frank, and often public debate among his advisers—in creating the impression that his administration lacked a coherent and unified foreign policy?

As pragmatic thought insists, such examples call attention to the fact that the universe *always* contains unique, random, and mysterious forces influencing human behavior. William James especially believed that a tendency always exists to attribute more order to the universe—often to fit an *a priori* belief system—than the evidence justifies. No theory of American diplomatic behavior that ignores James's warning can accurately explain the behavior of the United States in foreign affairs.

Seven

Pragmatic Guidelines of American Diplomacy

On the basis of the preceding analysis of the pragmatic mode of thought as it relates to American diplomatic behavior, it is possible to formulate a number of guidelines governing the foreign policy of the United States. These express significant and recurrent behavior patterns in the American approach to external policy; they embody what might be called the *normal and customary diplomatic conduct* of the United States, to which, of course, there are sometimes noteworthy exceptions. Yet insofar as the diplomatic behavior of the United States is predictable and consistent, to a significant degree it lies in the extent to which pragmatically derived principles govern American attitudes and actions toward the outside world.

1. Pragmatically based viewpoints and actions contribute to the belief of Americans in the uniqueness of their approach to foreign relations.

Since the earliest days of the republic, Americans have been convinced of the uniqueness of their democratic experiment in both its internal and external aspects. From the late eighteenth century until World War II, America's distinctive approach toward Western Europe was called isolationism—a policy that appealed to the nation for many reasons, some of which related to certain factors and conditions distinctive to the New World. After World War II, the United States adopted a policy of internationalism. Again, however, American internationalism differed in fundamental respects from the policies pursued by other powerful nations throughout history. As we have seen, the

Chapter 7 has no documentation, since it is a summary or recapitulation of pragmatic principles identified and discussed in earlier chapters.

post–World War II diplomacy of the United States combined elements of idealism and humanitarianism, political realism and power calculations, opportunism, personal diplomacy, and (in public, and sometimes even official, attitudes), pervasive apathy and ignorance about the world beyond America's own borders.

In the Monroe Doctrine, President James Monroe affirmed the uniqueness of American political principles vis-à-vis those of the Old World. That motif has been present in American diplomatic behavior to the present day. Americans not only believe that their approach to foreign relations is different from that of other countries; considerable evidence exists to support the contention that American diplomatic behavior *is* different from that of other great powers throughout history. To cite merely one example, the concept of foreign aid was an American innovation that has been emulated by several other nations in the contemporary world. Since the late 1940s, the foreign aid program of the United States has reflected such policy influences as genuine American concern for war-devastated and needy societies, strategic calculations and efforts to "contain" communism, domestic political factors (calling for massive and continuing aid to Israel), bureaucratic rivalries and inertia, compromises within Congress and between executive and legislative policy makers, and intense lobbying efforts by foreign governments and their supporters within the United States.

It is not contended, of course, that the influence of pragmatic thought on American attitudes and actions alone accounts for the unique quality of the nation's foreign policy. Yet just as pragmatism was the American society's most distinctive contribution to the philosophical heritage, the pragmatically based mode of thought and behavior has served as a major influence in maintaining the distinctiveness of American diplomatic conduct.

2. The thrust of pragmatic thought is to support and reinforce a policy of active and continuous involvement by the American society in foreign affairs.

Emerging in the late nineteenth century, the philosophy of pragmatism flourished and reached its zenith of popularity for a half-century or so before World War II. Ironically, this was also the period when the isolationist impulse dominated the American mind toward international issues. As we have seen, even William James, John Dewey, and other pragmatists were sometimes at the forefront of those calling for noninvolvement by the United States in foreign conflicts.

Nevertheless, the overall impact of pragmatic thought has been to enhance the American society's sense of its deep and inescapable *involvement* in international affairs, to demand a more intelligent understanding of the external environment, and to encourage the belief—epitomized by the diplomacy of President Franklin D. Roosevelt—that the United States must exert vigorous diplomatic leadership to create a global environment more congenial for the realization of worthwhile human goals.

Pragmatic thinkers such as James and Dewey often joined with isolationists in deploring *military* intervention and other hegemonial tendencies by the United States and all other nations to achieve their goals. At the same time, the pragmatists recognized that human society must be protected from predatory, egocentric, and comparable forces threatening its existence. A basic premise of pragmatic thought is that humans possess the capacity *to influence and change the nature of the environment within which individual and group activities occur,* and this principle applies no less to the political environment than to other realms of human existence.

More specifically, Americans do not have to accept passively whatever befalls them as a result of political tendencies beyond their own borders. To cite an extreme example, they are not required to endure a new Pearl Harbor before they exhibit concern about, and involve themselves actively in, developments overseas. More than once, John Dewey used the example of the physician who seeks to cure (or alleviate the condition of) sick patients and who routinely treats patients experiencing medical emergencies. Yet most physicians would infinitely rather prevent epidemics than treat their victims; the goal of medicine is the eradication of disease, not merely dealing with its consequences, often in acute form.

Consequently, pragmatic thought strongly supports the idea that, as in many respects the most powerful nation in modern history, the American society must recognize the degree to which developments in the external environment directly affect its well-being and future; endeavor to study and comprehend that environment; bring creative intelligence to bear at all times upon the process of formulating responses to external challenges; continually reexamine these responses in the light of experience and of their consequences; and pursue the goal of making the international environment as conducive as possible for the realization of positive human values and growth.

3. Implicitly and explicitly, pragmatic thought emphasizes certain underlying values and goals for human society that are reflected in the American approach to foreign relations.

One of the reservations sometimes expressed about pragmatism as a formal philosophy is the accusation that it is not a systematic set of ideas about truth but merely an approach to truth. The charge is partially, although by no means totally, valid. As indicated in earlier chapters, the views of Charles Peirce, William James, John Dewey, and other pragmatists did not make up a cohesive and logically integrated body of philosophical insights. Instead, their ideas were fragmentary, scattered, disorganized, and sometimes inconsistent; pragmatic thinkers were the first to admit that they had given the world no formal or tightly reasoned "system" of thought; and in fact they were congenitally skeptical that such closed systems in fact contributed to enlightenment about the nature of the universe.

Yet criticisms that pragmatism was devoid of concern for values, or that it was uninterested in ultimate questions of human destiny, or that it lacked a moral and ethical dimension have always been misdirected. (It would be more accurate to say that it was sometimes difficult to determine the precise sources of William James's or John Dewey's moral and ethical values.) Sometimes called the "new humanism," pragmatism was avowedly concerned with individual and group well-being, with the development and growth of human society, and with contributing to *human evolution* in all aspects of existence. As expressed in the biblical phrase, the pragmatists wanted the members of human society "to have life and to have it more abundantly."

Yet the leading pragmatic thinkers fully understood that no universal agreement existed about the meaning of, or the elements comprising, "the good life." They were well aware that Americans or Russians or Chinese or Egyptians would—and did—interpret this concept very differently. Moreover, they knew that gaining a global consensus about the goals of human society would be a difficult, sometimes frustratingly slow, and not always successful quest. At the same time, as John Dewey repeatedly emphasized, the task was by no means foredoomed to failure. Irrespective of their cultural differences, people everywhere tended to value good health over disease; they believed that an educated population is better than pervasive illiteracy; they viewed adequate housing as more desirable than slums; and they agreed that a reasonably adequate family income is a significant improvement over pervasive poverty. In the post–World War II period, even ideological adversaries, like the United States and the Soviet Union, acknowledged that nuclear restraint was better than a global nuclear holocaust. And in some aspects of Soviet-American relations (such as cultural and scientific exchange, trade, and the reduction in the level of ideological polemics) limited progress at least had been made in arriving at acceptable norms of international behavior.

Values, therefore, play a prominent and integral role in pragmatic thought. If the pragmatic American mind is cognizant at all times of the obstacles confronting the realization of such values, and if pragmatism teaches that few value questions can be dealt with dogmatically and ethnocentrically, the ultimate goal of international political activity is clear. By relying on creative human intelligence, it is to bring about those conditions throughout the world which are most conducive to the maximum realization of human potential.

4. In the pragmatic world view, American foreign policy operates in a highly pluralistic external environment, consisting of a wide range of uniform and unique, recurrent and random, and predictable and unpredictable forces that combine variously to affect the well-being of American society.

The pragmatic concept of a pluralistic universe is applicable both to the external setting of American foreign relations and to the process of internal policy formulation. Externally, the environment of American foreign policy is highly diverse, and in some respects, it is becoming more so with every passing year. Therefore, the diplomacy of the United States must take full account of the essentially pluralistic nature of the external milieu, and the nation's responses to challenges and problems arising out of that environment must reflect its diversity.

Largely because of the pluralistic nature of the environment, pragmatic minds place a relatively low value on diplomatic consistency, if by that term is meant rigid, indiscriminate, and completely predictable American adherence to diplomatic concepts and principles regardless of the particular conditions confronting the United States overseas. To the often-repeated charge that the post–World War II foreign policy of the United States has lacked consistency, the pragmatist makes a twofold reply.

First, the pragmatist concedes that there is a substantial element of truth in the observation. Second, in the pragmatic world view, as often as not, perhaps the lack of consistency in American diplomatic behavior is a source of *strength and resiliency,* rather than of weakness, in the nation's foreign policy. In the pragmatic view, a far more serious defect would be failure to adapt and adjust the diplomatic conduct of the United States to differing conditions and rapidly changing circumstances in a dynamic global environment. It would be no less detrimental for the United States blindly to adopt and adhere to some *a priori* set of ideological or diplomatic guidelines which govern its activities abroad, without regard for the facts of particular cases or of the consequences of following these guidelines blindly. Consequently, the pragmatically oriented mind urges the American people and their leaders to avoid *all* rigid ideological codes and concepts—whether they be "making the world safe for democracy," unthinking devotion to the cause of anticommunism, commitment to rapid modernization and nation-building throughout the Third World, attempting to achieve racial equality on the African continent, or allowing fear of another Vietnam to govern the use of American military power abroad.

Informed citizens whose international perspective is shaped by pragmatic precepts would point out that some of America's most significant diplomatic reverses since World War II—such as the failure to achieve democracy in Eastern Europe, the communization of China, the defeat in Vietnam, and the failure of the Reagan administration's intervention in Lebanon—could be attributed in no small measure to diplomatic rigidity and reliance on ideological dogmas by the United States.

By contrast, in responding to the communist challenge since World War II, officials in Washington have in time differentiated among several species or varieties of communism, according to their implications for the United States. Informed Americans, for example, recognize at least some beneficial changes within the Soviet system since the death of Stalin in 1953. Within the international communist movement, "polycentric" tendencies have destroyed the unitary nature of communism and resulted in the emergence of various forms of national communism. If expansive Soviet communism is still viewed by Americans as the primary threat to global peace and security, other forms (such as the Marxist systems in Yugoslavia, Poland, Romania, and China) present a less serious and more varied challenge to the diplomatic and security interests of the United States. By the 1980s, some movement could be detected in achieving more normal Cuban-American relations, and it was likely that this process would continue (perhaps slowly) in the future.

Similarly, by around 1960 American policy makers were prepared to come to terms with the reality that the vast majority of nations within the Third World were devoted to a foreign policy of nonalignment between the superpowers. If their position meant that they were unwilling to become diplomatic and military allies of the United States, it no less signified that they were determined to preserve their independence from Moscow as well. On balance, officials in Washington eventually realized, this diplomatic stance was *an affirmation of freedom* by Third World nations that was, in most fundamental respects, compatible with American diplomatic objectives.

The pragmatic conception of a pluralistic political universe, of course, contrasts sharply with the communist version of a monolithic political order (a "communist bloc") governed by Moscow. By definition, a pluralistic global environment is marked by diversity, freedom of choice, and the emergence of new political ideologies and systems of government. As the teachings of representative pragmatic thinkers emphasized, the ability of citizens and their leaders to function successfully in such a universe could well be the key to their future development—and even to their survival.

5. As pragmatists conceive it, the key fact of human experience is the interaction between human society and the environment.

As a philosophical movement momentously influenced by the theories of Charles Darwin, pragmatism has always acknowledged the influence of the environment upon human thought and conduct. Yet pragmatism was in some measure a reaction against Social Darwinism and other "deterministic" philosophies holding that human destiny is predetermined by inexorable environmental forces over which individuals have no control. In the more recent period, it follows that a pragmatic world view is equally skeptical that political relationships are ultimately determined by impersonal geopolitical, economic, cultural, "systemic," or other forces largely imperious to the will of man.

Pragmatists believe that the environmental context of human decision making always exhibits anomalous, contradictory, and discontinuous qualities. Life and death, symmetry and asymmetry, growth and decay, rationality and irrationality, progress and retrogression, order and disorder—such dichotomies are invariably present within an ever-changing environment. This reality alone is, in the pragmatic view, a forceful argument against basing human behavior upon an overly logical and consistent ideology or code of conduct.

In the pragmatic conception, the international environment contains both *benign and hostile forces* affecting human well-being. The power of nations, for example, may be used either to devastate the planet and jeopardize the future of civilization or to raise living standards, eradicate and control diseases, overcome pervasive poverty, raise educational and cultural levels, and for other worthwhile purposes. (From the record of modern history, it is clear that nations use their power for both constructive and destructive ends concurrently.)

Accordingly, the diplomatic pragmatist believes that the national symbol of the United States—the American eagle holding a quiver of arrows in one talon and the olive branch of peace in the other—accurately depicts the challenge confronting the nation in foreign affairs. Americans must always seek the peaceful resolution of global disputes, but they must simultaneously be prepared to preserve national security against forces inimical to it.

The old American adage "Trust your neighbor, but keep your powder dry!" accurately describes the pragmatic mentality in responding to environmental forces. On one hand, pragmatism emphasizes that at every possible opportunity, enlightened citizens must support efforts to improve the environment, making it more benign and favorable for the achievement of human aspirations. On the other hand, pragmatists do not underestimate the difficulty of this challenge; they do not believe that the environment is likely to be transformed rapidly and dramatically, even by the most energetic human efforts; and they caution against a tendency to believe that forces inimical to human welfare will *ever* be totally eliminated from the milieu of human experience. Therefore, the pragmatic mind urges nations to "keep at it"; to try again in the quest for arms control, global peace, and an effective system of international law and organization; and to take the calculated risk that, despite past failures, ultimately a breakthrough will occur that permits the solution of age-old problems confronting the family of nations. The possibility of failure in this course of action always exists; but the pragmatic American mind believes that it is outweighed by the certainty of failure inherent in not acting at all.

6. The pragmatic view of cognition holds that an almost infinite number of sensations, images, and perceptions impinge upon the human mind; the mind sorts or arranges them, concentrating the attention of the human organism on those perceived as posing a direct problem or challenge for human well-being.

Whatever modern psychology might say about this pragmatic view of the cognitive process, it seems clear that it is a reasonably accurate depiction of the way Americans have customarily responded to problems arising from the external environment and often from the domestic environment as well. More often than not, the foreign policy of the United States has been an exercise in "crisis diplomacy." Since the earliest days of the republic, the attention of Americans has been focused on actual or imagined crises abroad to which the United States has been required to formulate a response. The Monroe Doctrine, for example, was issued in response to two such crises: threatened intervention by the European powers in Latin America, and the Monroe administration's fear of expansionism by czarist Russia into the American Northwest.

No extensive documentation is required to support the contention that

220

this same mentality has dominated the American approach to foreign relations since World War II. Three landmark developments in the early postwar era—the Truman Doctrine (1947), the European Recovery Program (1948), and the North Atlantic Treaty Organization (1949)—were formulated in large measure as America's response to perceived crises abroad. Similarly, the policy of "patience and firmness" toward the Soviet Union, which was given formal expression in the containment strategy, emerged as a result of mounting anxiety in Washington about the implications of continued Soviet expansionism and interventionism. During the early 1960s, the Kennedy administration formulated the Alliance for Progress out of the conviction (shared by the Eisenhower administration) that the United States had too long neglected the critical needs of its Latin American neighbors.

In more recent years, President Carter issued an ultimatum to the Kremlin in the form of the Carter Doctrine in 1980, warning Moscow not to endanger the security of the Persian Gulf area. The Carter Doctrine was America's response to the Soviet invasion of Afghanistan a few weeks earlier. The Reagan administration's intervention in Central America was officially justified as an effort to counter moves by Nicaragua, Cuba, and the Soviet Union to export subversion within the region and to gain new communist bases in the Western Hemisphere.

As innumerable studies of public opinion have shown, even in the postwar era of internationalism, normally the attention of the American people is focused on domestic issues. As a rule, public interest in, and understanding of, foreign policy questions is extremely limited, rudimentary, and sporadic. For the most part, the same can be said about the involvement of Congress in foreign affairs. With rare exceptions, its role also tends to be episodic, dictated by the immediacy of the issue with which it is concerned, and characterized by a relatively brief attention span in dealing with particular international questions.

This is perhaps but another way of saying that the United States lacks an overall and sustained diplomatic strategy to which its manifold activities in foreign affairs can be related. We shall return to that question at a later stage. Meanwhile, our interest here is confined to observing that (in contrast to certain intellectual critics of American diplomacy), the American people have never viewed this lack of an overall diplomatic strategy as a serious deficiency. No convincing evidence exists that the pragmatically oriented American mind really desires such a strategy or would be willing to adhere to it consistently in dealing with specific foreign policy issues.

Instead, Americans are disposed to deal with diplomatic problems *as they arise* and are perceived as being related directly to national well-being. The American approach to foreign affairs continues to be directed at the solution of *specific problems* and to meeting external challenges on an *ad hoc* basis, often only after these problems are posed in an acute form. For good or ill, this is a characteristic of American diplomacy that is likely to remain a distinctive feature of the nation's external behavior for many years to come.

7. In their approach to foreign policy questions, Americans rely heavily on the pragmatic standard of experience as a guide to diplomatic behavior.

Charles Peirce's celebrated question—What difference does it make for human experience whether one idea is accepted over another?—finds its diplomatic counterpart in the recurrent tendency of the American people and their leaders to invoke the lessons of diplomatic experience in dealing with international problems. Innumerable examples are available from the recent diplomatic record to illustrate the point, beginning with the diplomacy of the Roosevelt administration.

In planning for the new United Nations, FDR and his advisers were mindful at every turn of the lessons taught by the failure of the League of Nations and of the need to avoid them in the establishment and operation of the United Nations. Among these lessons, none was perhaps more influential than the partisan storm that raged over the League of Nations during and after the Wilson administration. From this experience, the Roosevelt White House derived the necessity to place planning for the UN and other postwar undertakings on a firm bipartisan basis. Similarly, during World War II FDR was convinced that military and political questions arising within the Western alliance should be sharply separated, with the resolution of the latter being deferred until the Axis defeat.

The lessons of experience potently affected the diplomacy of FDR's successor, Harry S. Truman. At the top of the list—the principle that has in some measure guided the diplomacy of every administration in Washington since World War II—was the lesson of Munich or what is sometimes called the "Munich syndrome" in American foreign policy. This lesson has several specific corollaries, such as the belief that "you can't do business" with Hitler (or Stalin); the idea that totalitarian regimes view treaties as mere "scraps of paper" to be violated with impunity; and the beliefs that the time to stop aggression is now, before it threatens global peace and security and that appeasement does not pay but merely leads to new and more ambitious demands by expansionist regimes abroad. From the Truman to the Reagan administrations, these axioms have guided the foreign policy of the United

States toward the Soviet Union and other nations in the postwar era, and they continue to influence American thinking and conduct in foreign affairs.

Experience in dealing with the Soviet Union during and after World War II conveyed other lessons to the American mind. After witnessing the failure of President Roosevelt's conciliatory approach to Stalin's government in restraining Soviet expansionism and demands, the Truman administration concluded that a policy of patience and firmness was required, and this idea ultimately received formal expression in the containment policy. Many Americans became convinced that the only response the Kremlin understands is resolute resistance by the United States to Soviet demands. Another diplomatic precept—"You can't trust the Russians"—became a conviction underlying Washington's repeated insistence on adequate inspection and verification as a vital component of any acceptable arms control agreement between the superpowers. In the American view, lessons derived from Moscow's failure to observe wartime agreements dealing with Eastern Europe also reinforced prevailing skepticism about the Kremlin's intentions.

Still another precept of postwar American diplomacy—a maxim that has been influential for over forty years in shaping Washington's policies toward Moscow—is the familiar principle of "deeds—not words." As much as any other single guideline of American diplomacy, this one perhaps forcefully illustrates the impact of the pragmatic emphasis on experience on the foreign policy of the United States. As a diplomatic variation on the old American adage that "actions speak louder than words," the "deeds—not words" dictum has been central to Washington's approach to the Soviet Union since the early postwar era. By the early 1970s, the principle received a variant expression in the concept of "linkage," viewed by American officials as fundamental for the existence and maintenance of détente between the superpowers.

The common denominator of principles like "deeds—not words" and linkage was, of course, the American conviction that Moscow's often-expressed desire for "peaceful coexistence" with the United States must result in Soviet actions that are consonant with the goal. Americans believed that if the Kremlin is genuinely devoted to peace and a relaxation of tensions in international relations, Moscow must demonstrate this commitment by acting peacefully in settings like Afghanistan; if it truly desires to relax global tensions, the Kremlin can begin by relaxing its still-dominant grip on Poland and other satellite nations behind the Iron Curtain.

From the Vietnam War experience, Americans derived still other diplomatic guidelines, as embodied in the popular slogan "No more Vietnams!" Whatever that idea meant precisely (and, as always, the exact meaning of certain diplomatic lessons was subject to varying interpretations), it is clear that the desire to avoid another Vietnam remains a potent force affecting American attitudes and actions.

In both domestic and foreign affairs, pragmatic Americans have never been unduly troubled by the existence of paradoxes characterizing their beliefs and actions. Even though they were apprehensive about another Vietnam, for example, many Americans derived another, and somewhat contrary, lesson from recent diplomatic experience. This was the belief that the United States must not allow "another Cuba" to disturb the peace and security of the Western Hemisphere. President Lyndon B. Johnson invoked the lesson of another Cuba when he intervened in the Dominican Republic in 1965. During the 1980s, the Reagan administration repeatedly cited the same lesson as justification for its interventionist policies in Central America. From the statements and actions of legislators, it was evident that many members of the House and Senate—and in some cases, officials within the executive branch as well—were seeking a formula that would avoid both another Vietnam and another Cuba concurrently in American foreign policy toward Latin America. In effect, they believed that both lessons were instructive and provided valuable diplomatic guidelines for the United States.

8. The pragmatic world view believes that the universe is dynamic and in a constant state of change; by relying on his intelligence, however, man is able to influence the nature, direction, and pace of such change.

Historically, change, experimentation, and innovation have become synonymous with the American way of life. The very concept of the New World; the American society's ingrained belief in "the promise of the future"; one of the most perennial slogans of American political life— "It's time for a change"—these are merely selected examples illustrating the idea that Americans have routinely accepted the necessity for change in all dimensions of their national life.

As our earlier discussion indicated, this belief is fully compatible with the main tenets of pragmatic thought, and it has strongly colored the American approach to foreign relations. Before World War II, American officials and groups were at the forefront in calling for new efforts to limit global armaments; in reliance on negotiations, "cooling-off treaties," and other peaceful methods for resolving international disputes; in the attempt to outlaw war as an instrument of national policy; in the creation of new international organizations such as the League of Nations and the United Nations; and in efforts to devise new regional mechanisms (such as the Organization of American states).

One of the most far-reaching examples of insistent American support for change was the opposition expressed by officials of the Roosevelt and Truman administrations to Western colonialism. America's anticolonialist position was a potent force in the decision by Great Britain, France, the Netherlands, and other nations to relinquish their dependencies after World War II, resulting in the emergence of some one hundred new nations (the Third World) in the postwar era.

During and after the war, American diplomatic initiative was highly influential in the rehabilitation of Germany and Japan and in producing apparently stable democratic systems in these nations. Both cases serve as striking examples of America's twofold belief in the necessity for change and the possibility of undertaking it successfully.

A more recent example is provided by the diplomatic experience of the Kennedy administration, although the idea was implicit in Truman's Point Four program of aid to developing nations. This was the concept of "modernization" of less developed societies throughout the Third World. A variant of this concept (applied by President Kennedy and his advisers specifically to Southeast Asia) was "nation-building." The underlying premise of both concepts was the same: the United States must supply leadership and tangible assistance to Third World societies that are endeavoring to develop and modernize internally.

Implicit in the concept of modernization were a number of corollary ideas: that on the basis of its own domestic experience, the American society was committed to the process of change and could contribute many useful lessons to other countries in achieving it; that less developed societies must embark on a sustained and energetic process of change or risk almost certain retrogression; that the cold war between the United States and the Soviet Union (at least in its Third World manifestations) entailed competition between two fundamentally different models of socioeconomic and political change; and that unless the United States became identified with the process of national development abroad, Soviet communism would come to be viewed as the agent of change and Moscow would win the cold war by default.

On the basis of evidence from post–World War II experience, the accusation that the United States has been opposed to change abroad—that it advocates the *status quo* in other societies—is in general incorrect. American diplomatic influence has been in no small measure responsible for the emergence of an increasingly multipolar international system and for encouraging far-reaching changes in contemporary societies from Japan to Brazil.

Yet in accordance with pragmatic tenets, and despite their own so-called revolutionary heritage, in almost all cases, Americans have supported the principle of *evolutionary, gradual, and orderly change* vis-à-vis either attempts to maintain the *status quo* or to undertake radical and revolutionary transformations of other societies. As a mode of thought influenced by Darwin's findings, pragmatism has always acknowledged the possibility of retrogression, no less than progress, in human affairs. The pragmatic world view does *not*, therefore, necessarily equate all change with progress or improvement of the human condition. The pragmatic concept of habituation teaches that humans are likely to replace familiar and customary modes of behavior very slowly and often reluctantly; as a rule, they will adopt new modes of behavior only after experience has demonstrated that these are an improvement over established patterns.

Moreover, pragmatists believe that, beginning with the French Revolution late in the eighteenth century and extending through such recent examples as the Communist Revolution in Russia and Castro's Marxist regime in Cuba, the evidence provides little reassurance that revolutionary efforts to transform society actually result in *beneficial* changes for the people concerned. More often than not, as John Dewey emphasized time and again about the communist regime in the USSR, revolutionary movements have degenerated into varying degrees of tyranny, exploitation, and privilege by the group that won the revolutionary struggle; these movements become transformed into "personality cults" or systems of hero worship of the society's new leaders, and in the end, they result in little discernible improvement in the condition of the people. In many cases, also, such revolutionary movements have engendered violent antirevolutionary opposition, and the result has been a prolonged pattern of political conflict and upheaval.

The pragmatic emphasis on evolutionary change, therefore, normally places the United States in opposition to two contrary movements at home and abroad: those individuals and groups seeking to perpetuate the *status quo* and those calling for revolutionary changes within human society, frequently on the basis of some utopian or *a priori* ideological blueprint. In the vast majority of cases, informed Americans believe that both approaches are erroneous. In opposition to them, the United States nearly always advocates gradual change and incremental (although sometimes sweeping) reform, with experience serving as a guide to the utility of specific innovations.

9. The pragmatic world view holds that power is necessary for the achievement of most worthwhile human purposes; but it believes that the exercise of power derives legitimacy from the consequences resulting from its use.

As we have seen, pragmatic thought rejected most age-old dichotomies such as those between mind and matter, the material and nonmaterial universe, and matter and energy. Einstein's famous equation ($E = mc^2$) tells us that *matter is equivalent to energy.* Without power in some form—the brain-power needed for creative intellectual endeavor, economic and financial resources, the ongoing accumulation of knowledge, organizational skill, and determination, and in some instances, military force—the goals of human society remain elusive.

For these reasons, the pragmatic world view rejects all romantic or utopian and other approaches to international relations that in effect deny the existence of national power or minimize its often decisive role in determining political outcomes. On the basis of the evidence of human experience, pragmatists believe that such theories of political behavior are ill-informed, erroneous, and sometimes dangerous for the well-being of the United States and of human society generally. Pragmatists are aware that the root of the term *disillusionment*—and twentieth-century American diplomacy has witnessed several periods of widespread public disillusionment toward foreign policy issues—is *illusion.* As during the Wilsonian era, widespread official and public illusions about the role of power in international affairs contributed significantly to America's reversion to isolationism after World War I and to the period of pervasive national disillusionment about the results of that conflict during the 1920s and 1930s. Many years later, the "Vietnam War syndrome" of massive doubt, guilt, and frustration that shaped American foreign policy during the 1970s stemmed to no inconsiderable degree from pervasive misunderstandings in the public mind about the nature and role of American power abroad.

Yet the pragmatic world view also has serious objections to the *Realpolitik* conception of power. Pragmatists do *not* believe that a legitimate goal of American foreign policy is the pursuit of power or the mere acquisition of power for its own sake. Time and again, William James and John Dewey cautioned their fellow citizens against a "strong" foreign policy, or one whose dominant objective appeared to be primarily the enhancement of American power and influence abroad. James, for example, rejected the idea that the United States had a divinely appointed "mission" to civilize, uplift, or otherwise "save" foreign societies; and even while he denounced Nazism and communism, Dewey was scarcely less concerned about the implications of the growth of American military power. In more contemporary terms, the leading pragmatic thinkers cautioned against the tendency to believe that the United States has a mandate to serve as the policeman of the world.

Despite such admonitions, however, the pragmatists fully recognized the existence of national power and its key role in achieving human objectives. In their view, power was a fact of human experience; it could not be wished out of existence. From a moral-ethical perspective, power *per se* was neutral: its legitimacy or acceptability *derived from its use* by the members of human society. To cite a familiar example, the dawn of the nuclear age (which Dewey lived to witness) unquestionably presented new hazards and risks in the conduct of international relations, placing the future of civilization itself in jeopardy; but nuclear power has also made possible beneficial advances in medicine and in our understanding of the nature of the physical universe.

In the pragmatic world view, power must always be viewed *instrumentally.* Its use must be governed by the familiar pragmatic test: What consequences may reasonably be expected from its use, and on balance, do these promote, or do they impair, human well-being and development?

In turn, this test may be thought of as involving several specific questions: (1) What is the nature of the challenge confronting America abroad at any given time? (2) What are national objectives in responding to this problem? (3) What kinds of power are available to national policy makers for use in meeting the external challenge, and which are best adapted to responding to this specific problem? (4) What are the consequences to be anticipated from relying on different kinds (or combinations) of power in responding to the issue? (5) What forms of power can best be expected to produce the most positive consequences, with the fewest adverse results, for human well-being?

The pragmatic assessment of the problem of national power, it will be observed, is marked by an absence of dogma in applying it diplomatically. In the terminology of the Vietnam War, pragmatists are neither "hawkish" nor "dovish" on the subject of military and other forms of national power; their attitude might best be described as "owlish." In time, for example, most pragmatic thinkers condemned America's involvement in the Vietnam conflict primarily because national power, or the *instrument* of policy, was not adapted to, or did not contribute to achieving, the proclaimed goals of interventionism in Southeast Asia. Several years later, the Reagan administration's intervention in Lebanon miscarried for basically the same reason: experience in time indicated convincingly that Washington's reliance on armed force was not in fact promoting the objective of American peacekeeping in Lebanon.

In other cases, of course, America's reliance on military and other forms of power can and often does produce beneficial results. John Dewey could think of no feasible alternative to America's resistance to Axis aggression during World War II. The American contribution to the defense of the NATO area, Washington's determination to preserve the independence of South Korea, and the more recent American determination to preserve Western access to the Persian Gulf area are cases in which the nation's reliance on military power clearly has had more positive than negative results.

Sooner or later, the American people ask about the application of military and other forms of power abroad, "How are we doing?" or "Is the policy actually working?" Such inquiries usually mean that, in a crude and often unconscious way, Americans are relying on the familiar pragmatic test to determine the legitimacy of national policy. They are judging diplomatic effectiveness by the degree to which the means of policy are, or are not, adapted to, and conformable with, its avowed objectives.

10. The pragmatic concept of a pluralistic universe has clear application to the foreign policy process in the United States and enables us to understand a number of its significant features.

In the language of contemporary political science, democracy and pluralism have largely become synonymous. A democracy is, by definition, pluralistic, while nondemocratic systems are characterized by an absence of pluralism. As merely one example, in the mid-1980s the Reagan administration called upon the Marxist-controlled government of Nicaragua to implement reforms that would make the system more pluralistic, open, and democratic. The Sandinista regime was required to meet this condition before it could expect an improvement in relations with the United States.

As explained in detail in Chapter 6, the internal milieu or setting of American foreign policy is highly pluralistic. An almost infinite number of variables and forces play major or minor roles in the formulation and administration of foreign policy. In some periods—and conspicuous examples were supplied by the experience of the Carter administration and by the first Reagan administration—the decision-making process is marked by a high level of dissonance, static, and disunity among officials involved in it, to such a

229

degree that confusion exists at home and abroad concerning the goals and rationale of American diplomacy. In the post–Vietnam War era, the lack of a public consensus—or sometimes, even a consensus among executive officials—concerning diplomatic objectives has been especially striking; and this lack has had important consequences for American diplomatic behavior.

Our earlier discussion identified in considerable detail the main and recurring influences affecting the foreign policy process of the United States. These include traditional and habitual attitudes and behavior patterns; ideological concepts central to the American democratic system; power and strategic calculations; the lessons taught (or believed to derive) from diplomatic experience; perceptions (along with misperceptions) of the nature of the challenges and problems confronting the United States abroad; the dominant role of the president, and the contribution of other executive officials and agencies, in diplomatic decision making; the participation of Congress in formulating and implementing foreign policy decisions; the impact of public opinion (mass opinion, elite opinion, and interest groups) on American diplomatic behavior; the foreign constituency setting or the influence of foreign governments, political movements, and public opinion abroad on American foreign relations; and the ever-present existence of random, fortuitous, and irrational factors (such as the personalities of key officials, their administrative styles, the physical and emotional health of the president and other key actors, and bureaucratic rivalries and infighting) that sometimes crucially affect diplomatic outcomes.

To adapt a term from physics, the American foreign policy process comprises a highly complex "field of forces." The resolution of these forces into something called a "foreign policy" is ultimately the responsibility of the president, often with (but in many cases without) the participation of Congress. The precise nature and strength of these forces is likely to vary, not only from one administration to another but even during the same administration. In many cases, one force (or set of forces)—such, for example, as those favoring a more active and interventionist role by the United States abroad—will typically be counterbalanced by a contrary force (or set of forces) urging diplomatic retrenchment or a neoisolationist policy. In still other cases—and the leading example since World War II perhaps has been massive American support of Israel—this pattern of power and countervailing power may be largely lacking in the American foreign policy process.

The increasingly pluralistic nature of the American foreign policy process has led to an interesting and highly significant result: the steady enhancement of presidential power in the decision-making process. The emergence of what is sometimes called the "imperial presidency" is a key reality of post–World War II diplomatic experience. Yet the most noteworthy fact about it—since in nearly all modern governments, the management of foreign relations tends to be an executive function—is the degree to which this reality has been accepted and in some respects encouraged by American public opinion.

Exhibiting little sustained interest in, or understanding of, foreign affairs, the American people are usually content to let the president serve as the nation's diplomat-in-chief; during periods of crisis abroad, the people expect the president to take charge and to exemplify the leadership required to meet it successfully. In the vast majority of instances, a resourceful president is able to rally public opinion to his side. By contrast, even after the Vietnam conflict and Watergate, little discernible public sentiment exists in favor of the management of foreign relations by Congress. From the record in recent years, Congress has experienced mounting difficulty in managing itself or in producing unified legislative policies in both domestic and foreign affairs.

In more philosophical terms, the foreign policy process in the United States exemplifies a point that was prominent in the thought of William James. Paradoxical as it might appear, James saw no inherent conflict between the concepts of democracy and of elitism. The American foreign policy process contains elements of both. As the pragmatists taught, elites are necessary in any society; they provide the variations needed to make possible the process of human evolution. Implicitly, in their approach to foreign policy issues, the American people acknowledge and accept that reality. In effect, most citizens possess neither the incentive nor the background needed to understand the intricacies of foreign policy questions and are usually content to let the president and his advisers deal with them.

At the same time, ultimately the people decide whether their leaders have governed well or poorly in domestic and foreign affairs. In reaching that verdict, the people nearly always rely on the pragmatic test of experience, or the record of the incumbent administration, which they view, on balance, as promoting or impairing the welfare of the American society.

One final point, illustrated by the diplomatic experience of the Reagan administration, merits brief attention. Despite President Reagan's unimpressive foreign policy record—including the undisguised failure of his policy in Lebanon and pervasive public anxiety about his diplomatic moves in Central America—in 1984 an electoral landslide returned Reagan to the White House. As is customarily true in the United States, this outcome turned mainly upon the American people's assessment of *domestic policy* and their response to bread-and-butter issues. Throughout his tenure in the White House, the voters were extraordinarily charitable in judging Reagan's diplomatic performance.

Better understanding of the pragmatic tradition in the American ethos sheds at least some light upon this intriguing phenomenon. According to pragmatic tenets, action is nearly always better than inaction. Even when the effort fails (as in Lebanon), trying to resolve a problem abroad is preferable to not trying or to presidential immobilism, which voters came to associate with the earlier Carter administration. Based on the experience of the Reagan administration, Americans are less concerned about presidents who act—even those who sometimes act "imperially"—than they are about the consequences of confused, indecisive, and ineffectual presidential leadership.

Yet all principles, including pragmatic tenets, have their limits. If Ronald Reagan tried vainly to bring peace to strife-torn Lebanon, in contrast to Lyndon B. Johnson during the Vietnam War, Reagan also knew when to stop. In effect, after the failure of his diplomacy became evident even to the White House, Reagan did what Johnson was urged to do in Southeast Asia: he "declared a victory and came home." Americans were not overly critical of the Reagan administration for attempting to bring peace to the Middle East, but they commended Reagan's good judgment in "cutting his losses" and ultimately withdrawing American forces from a vulnerable and apparently hopeless position. Reagan's actions meant that at some more propitious time in the future, the United States could try again to bring peace to the troubled Middle East.

11. In the pragmatic perspective, the American foreign policy process entails a reasonably well-defined sequence of stages, culminating in the adoption of a policy and the evaluation of its results.

The principal stages in the foreign policy process of the United States, it must be admitted, are easier to delineate theoretically than they are to isolate in practice, since one stage often tends to overlap, or to merge imperceptibly into another. An understanding of the pragmatic tradition, however, makes this process more intelligible.

Initially, national leaders, and in time the American people, become aware of the existence of a problem or challenge in the external environment directly related to their interests and well-being. Frequently this awareness is perceived by the American mind as a crisis abroad. The communist threat to Western Europe in the early postwar era, or Soviet efforts to penetrate and dominate the Third World, or ongoing instability in the Middle East, or continuing political upheaval and communist interventionism in Central America, or some new threat to the security of the Persian Gulf area—these are examples of such crises, which have demanded diplomatic response by the United States.

Then there follows a stage in which the specific implications of the external problem for the United States are identified, assessed, and communicated to Congress and to the American people. What, for example, was America's stake in preventing communist gains on the European continent in the early postwar period? How was the well-being of the American society affected by the continued deterioration of war-devastated Europe during the late 1940s? To what extent are the diplomatic interests of the United States involved in a continuation of the ongoing Arab-Israeli conflict? In these and other cases, American officials have in time concluded that developments abroad *did* affect the welfare of the United States directly and significantly.

In other cases, of course, the president and his advisers may conclude that the diplomatic and security interests of the nation are *not* involved in developments overseas. Throughout most of the post–World War II period, for example, the United States has followed a policy of "low profile" toward sub-Saharan Africa. After the Vietnam War, Washington concluded that developments in Southeast Asia did not involve American well-being directly. Although it may not always be clearly articulated, national officials must operate upon some sense of *priority* in their response to events and tendencies abroad.

Once they determine that America's interests are involved in developments overseas, policy makers must decide upon the most appropriate response to the external challenge. This stage involves the consideration of possible alternatives and their anticipated consequences. As explained more fully in Chapter 4, however, in time the president and his advisers become aware that all possible responses by the United States possess advantages and disadvantages. Almost never will the nation's diplomatic course of action be clear-cut, in the sense of being devoid of adverse results and pitfalls. The determination of the national interest normally involves the weighing of the pros and cons of available policy alternatives. In the majority of cases a decision will normally be made in favor of the policy that is expected to have somewhat more positive than negative consequences. Not infrequently, the policy ultimately chosen will represent the "least of the evils" or the *least damaging* course of action available to the White House. The policy will inevitably encounter criticism, especially from groups whose approach to foreign relations is strongly colored by ideal (in some cases, utopian) conceptions of international politics.

The next stage involves policy implementation, or the formulation of appropriate means for achieving the desired goal. In this stage, the influence of Congress on the American foreign policy process is especially important, and sometimes decisive.

The final stage is concerned with policy review and evaluation—a process that is normally conducted concurrently on both official and unofficial levels. The policy's results are observed and reported to Washington continuously by the American diplomatic corps overseas, by officials of a growing list of other federal agencies, and by foreign governments and political commentators. In addition, one or more congressional committees investigate the results of the American economic and military aid program, the operations of the Voice of America, the activities of intelligence agencies, national trade policy, and countless other undertakings in the foreign policy field. Sometimes the president will appoint a committee (or "task force") of distinguished citizens to review existing policy toward a particular issue or region.

Unofficially, the foreign policy of the United States is subject to continuing scrutiny and assessment by the news media, by political commentators, by organizations and pressure groups, by "think tanks" and study groups, and by informed citizens. On the basis of postwar experience, one assertion that can safely be made about the foreign policy of the United States is that it never lacks critics at home and abroad!

In light of the multilevel and continuing review process, three courses of action are available to the president and his diplomatic aides with regard to a specific policy. They may decide to *continue it substantially unchanged* in the belief that it still serves the interests of the United States. Or they may *significantly modify existing policy* on the grounds that fundamental changes are indicated. Or they may *abandon the policy altogether* in the conviction that on balance its defects outweigh its advantages.

12. In a highly pluralistic policy-making context, the diplomatic goals of the United States are often diverse, multiple, and sometimes contradictory; in many cases, little overt sense of priority or hierarchy can be discerned among them.

Throughout the postwar period, considerable controversy has surrounded America's diplomatic objectives with regard to particular international issues. For almost any major diplomatic undertaking by the United States—the Greek-Turkish Aid Program in 1947, the Marshall Plan a year later, the foreign economic and military aid program, the nation's involvement in the Vietnam War, or the Reagan administration's diplomacy in Central America—wide differences of opinion have existed about what the United States was actually seeking to accomplish and whether, in fact, Washington was accomplishing it.

A noteworthy example is provided by the containment policy. Some forty years after its adoption by the Truman administration, there were almost as many theories purporting to explain the real goals of containment as there were commentators on American foreign affairs. These interpretations embraced a wide spectrum of opinion—from the belief that the objective of containment was (as President Truman initially defined it) to counter new expansionist and interventionist tendencies by the Kremlin; to the notion that containment was primarily an expression of the deep-seated and emotional anticommunist sentiments of the American people and their leaders; to the conviction that by adopting containment, the United States was engaged in the age-old diplomatic strategy of trying to preserve the balance of power; to the idea that the containment policy represented an ill-concealed effort by President Truman and his advisers to impose a *Pax Americana* upon the world. Several other explanations (such as the idea that containment stemmed from a fundamental misperception by the American people and their leaders of the nature and gravity of the Soviet threat) are available to explain the rationale of the containment strategy.

The Korean War experience provides another example of the same phenomenon. Initially, the purpose of American intervention was to "repel aggression" by communist forces against South Korea. As the war progressed, however—and especially after Allied forces in Korea gained the military initiative—new goals became uppermost in Washington. Teaching aggressors a "lesson" that would deter adventurism in the future, unifying the entire Korean peninsula under a democratic government (an objective of the United States since World War II), and preserving the diplomatic credibility of the United States and its allies in the Korean conflict in time tended to overshadow the more limited goal of repelling aggression. Then, even later, after Communist China's entry into the conflict, when the military tide shifted against the Allied forces, these new goals were largely abandoned. Finally, a cease-fire agreement was achieved, which more or less restored the 38th Parallel as the border between North and South Korea. Under these circumstances, it is small wonder that millions of Americans became confused about whether the United States had "won" or "lost" the Korean War. In more general terms, the outcome of the Korean conflict left a continuing legacy of doubt in the American mind about whether the nation's participation in *any limited war* was worthwhile. These doubts were, of course, greatly compounded by the unsatisfactory results of the Vietnam War several years later.

Basically the same problem beset the Reagan administration's diplomatic activities in Central America. Once again, pervasive doubts were expressed at home and abroad about what the White House was seeking to accomplish and whether in fact it was achieving these objectives. Was the primary purpose the familiar goal of containing communism in Latin America? Was it to prevent Moscow and Havana from gaining new military bases in the region, thereby threatening the balance of power within the Western Hemisphere? Was it to protect the continued independence of El Salvador in the face of communist-led efforts to subvert it? Was it to assure the future of democracy in El Salvador, Nicaragua, and perhaps Guatemala, Panama, and other neighboring countries as well? Was it, as President Reagan and his advisers frequently asserted, designed chiefly to prevent the emergence of "another Cuba" south of the border? Or was its dominant purpose to provide a forceful demonstration of American diplomatic credibility in the face of the continuing communist challenge?

These and comparable examples that might be cited permit several generalizations about the foreign policy goals of the United States. More often than not, the United States *pursues several diplomatic goals concurrently.* The order of priority among these goals is often unclear; and the order tends to change in response to new circumstances at home and abroad. Moreover, there is likely to be a lag or discrepancy between the goals currently being pursued by executive officials and those believed by Congress and the American people to be the nation's principal diplomatic objectives. As a result, for almost every major foreign policy venture by the United States since World War II, a wide diversity of opinion exists even among informed commentators concerning whether the nation has, or has not, accomplished its objectives abroad. For the ordinary citizen, the result may well be even greater mystification, bewilderment, and apathy toward foreign policy issues.

13. In the pragmatic world view, the choice of means and the concept of the ends-means continuum are viewed as crucial in determining diplomatic outcomes.

Theoretically, a distinction can be and often is made between America's goals abroad and the means needed to achieve them. In the pragmatic conception, goals are ideas, thoughts, and images, and means are what the United States actually *does, or its actions,* in relationships with other countries. The pragmatist is convinced that in diplomacy, as in everyday life, actions usually speak louder than words. In conformity with Charles Peirce's philosophical principle, the meaning of an idea is best conveyed by the extent to which it produces observable consequences in the realm of human experience.

In several key respects, this pragmatic precept has governed the postwar diplomacy of the United States. For example, it was the discrepancy between Moscow's verbal goals and wartime pledges, on one hand, and its behavior in Eastern Europe and other settings, on the other, that to the American mind was decisive in producing the cold war. Ever since the late 1940s, Americans have viewed Soviet *actions* as providing the most authoritative indication of the meaning and implications of communist ideology. As we have seen, in time this conception led successive administrations in Washington to insist upon "deeds—not words" by the Soviet Union as the precondition for a significant improvement in relations between the superpowers.

By the 1970s, the familiar deeds—not words principle was given a variant expression in the concept of "linkage," which was central in the American conception of détente. According to this concept, the professed Soviet desire for "peaceful coexistence" with the United States had to be given tangible expression in Soviet actions—in Eastern Europe, in the Middle East, in Latin America, and in other settings—which were compatible with Moscow's policy declarations. In the absence of such a correlation, pragmatically oriented Americans continued to conclude that Soviet deeds afforded the most reliable test of the Kremlin's actual diplomatic intentions.

The pragmatic concept of the ends-means continuum applies also, of course, to the foreign policy of the United States. Time and again, officials in Washington have discovered that *how the United States deals with other governments, public opinion, and groups abroad* is often more crucial than its professed foreign policy goals in determining diplomatic results. The foreign aid program, for example, may have (and nearly always does have) humanitarian, idealistic, and other worthwhile objectives. Yet as experience has repeatedly shown, how the program is actually administered—the means used to achieve the goal and their observable consequences—in various Third World settings are more often than not decisive in determining whether the foreign assistance program is a success or a failure.

In a different dimension of American diplomacy—relations between the United States and its NATO allies—the same pragmatic precept applies. For example, successive administrations in Washington have called for effective "partnership" among the members of NATO, and the cohesion of the Western alliance has been a high-priority issue in Washington for over a generation. Yet the European members of NATO judge America's devotion to the goal of partnership primarily by how the United States *actually treats its Western allies.* Does Washington consult the other members of NATO before it embarks upon new diplomatic initiatives? Does it give the European allies the feeling that their viewpoints are important and that they really matter to Washington in the formulation and implementation of American foreign policy?

American postwar diplomatic experience also illustrates a corollary idea about the relationship between the goals and means of diplomacy. A tendency nearly always exists for the means of foreign policy *to eclipse and to become the ends* of the nation's diplomatic activity. Although the comment may well have been partisan, the point is conveyed by an observation made several years ago by former Secretary of State Dean Acheson about the diplomacy of the Eisenhower administration. In Acheson's view, when the administration lacked clear diplomatic direction, officials in Washington "started moving around" (a reference to the fact that Secretary of State John Foster Dulles devoted much of his time to traveling abroad). Dean Acheson has not been the only commentator who has identified a tendency for activity, motion, movement, and "doing it" by officials in Washington to be mistaken for solid diplomatic accomplishment.

This frame of mind is clearly illustrated by the popularity which summit conferences continue to enjoy among the American people. Americans are nearly always sympathetic to the idea of a new heads-of-state meeting. In Charles Dickens' phrase, they look forward to a new summit meeting with "great expectations." When it is held, the meeting becomes a dramatic media event or extravaganza. Yet an objective assessment of the results of summit conferences, from World War II to the present time, provides little tangible evidence that they have contributed significantly to the long-term resolution of outstanding international issues. As illustrated by President Roosevelt's wartime exercises in summit diplomacy, it is at least as likely that such meetings will leave misunderstanding, unsolved problems, and public disillusionment in their wake.

Informed commentators have also often identified the phenomenon of the ends-means continuum as a central element in the ongoing arms race

throughout modern history. For the United States, as for most other countries, the expansion and modernization of military arsenals *per se* often appears to be the dominant goal. How creating an ever-larger stockpile of increasingly destructive weapons will contribute to national security—or how
the process will enable the United States to accomplish its diplomatic purposes more successfully—are questions frequently left unexplained. Yet to
the minds of foreigners, America's avowed devotion to peace is often eclipsed
by its determination to amass new instruments of war.

14. In its diplomatic implications, pragmatic thought exhibits a genuine
ambivalence about long-range planning versus meeting external challenges
as they arise on an *ad hoc* basis.

A perennial complaint about American foreign policy since World War II
is that the nation lacks a long-range diplomatic strategy, to which its approach
to the Soviet Union, its policies in the Middle East, its relations with Latin
America, and the other separate components of its foreign relations can be
meaningfully related. That is, commentators inside and outside the United
States have complained about its essentially *ad hoc* and "incremental" character. To cite merely one example, the point has been made many times that
incrementalism—or the piecemeal assumption of expanding diplomatic
commitments over time—was a key factor responsible for the nation's growing involvement in the Vietnam War.

Pragmatic thought, it must be recognized frankly, is highly ambivalent
on the subject of planning in governmental policy. Pragmatism emphasizes
the idea that, in John Dewey's well-known phrase, man "learns by doing";
pragmatists believe that experience serves as the laboratory in which competing ideas in human affairs can be tested, adopted as truth, or discarded. A
logical corollary of this idea, of course, is the expectation that human society
will apply truths gained from experience to *emerging and future problems;* in
other words, they will *plan* their responses to such problems so as to max-
imize human well-being.

This is one side of pragmatic thought which is clearly applicable to
American foreign relations. In too many cases since World War II—as in the
momentous changes occurring in the Soviet Union after the death of Stalin in
1953, or in the emerging split between Moscow and Peking (which American
officials recognized much too late), or in the collapse of the Iranian monarchy
in the late 1970s—the president and his diplomatic advisers appeared to be
taken by surprise and were unprepared for the major implications of such
developments. In these and other instances, the foreign policy of the United

States appeared to consist of hastily devised improvisations in response to perceived crises abroad.

Yet another side of pragmatic thought cautions against an undue preoccupation with planning by government in its foreign and domestic policies. Our earlier discussion has emphasized, for example, that a pragmatic world view conceives of the universe as being highly pluralistic: the environment always contains novel, contingent, and unpredictable forces. Sometimes these are crucial in determining political outcomes. Humans are required, therefore, to respond to problems whose nature, occurrence, and implications can seldom be fully and accurately anticipated. (As the modern history of economics has repeatedly illustrated, when forecasting becomes the dominant goal, and is sometimes viewed as an exact science, national policy makers are as much in a quandary as ever. The problem then becomes *whose* or *which prediction* of the future course of the economy is to be believed and made the basis of governmental policies?)

The ambivalence in pragmatic thought was especially pronounced in the views of John Dewey. The logical thrust of Dewey's ideas was that, on the basis of lessons gained from experience, man must plan in an attempt to identify and respond intelligently to emerging tendencies and problems. Otherwise, the insights gained from experience would have little value in the solution of human problems.

Yet Dewey was also an outspoken critic of the planning and ideological rigidity epitomized by the collectivist movements of modern history, specifically, fascism and communism. As Dewey assessed it, the evils and defects inherent in such planned societies outweighed their supposed benefits. Nor was Dewey enamoured of the almost frenzied planning that accompanied the New Deal in the United States. In his view, among its other defects, this planning inevitably expanded the size and influence of government bureaucracies and increased the power of the presidency in the American system. Therefore, Dewey drew a sharp distinction between a "planning" and a "planned" society; he favored the former but rejected the latter.

Recent American experience with diplomatic planning has exhibited the ambivalence in pragmatic thought identified here. Early in the postwar period, the Truman administration recognized the need for more systematic planning in the foreign policy field. The Policy Planning Staff (later renamed the Policy Planning Council) was established within the State Department to meet that need. (It is noteworthy that this innovation was undertaken when General George C. Marshall was secretary of state; the parallel with the "strategic planning" routinely engaged in by military staffs in the United States and other countries is evident.) This new administrative unit was initially headed by one of the nation's most experienced Foreign Service officers, the acknowledged Kremlinologist George F. Kennan; Kennan's staff consisted of some of the ablest officials within the State Department.

Yet from its inception, the Policy Planning Staff never operated as intended. By the 1980s, complaints were still widely expressed that the United States lacked a clear long-range strategy that controlled and unified its separate diplomatic activities. Even under the Truman administration, the tendency was for Kennan and his staff to be assigned other and more urgent responsibilities within the State Department. Moreover, high-ranking policy makers often exhibited little interest in diplomatic plans that were unrelated to day-to-day problems. The result was that with the passage of time, the planning function within the State Department largely atrophied.

In the years that followed, the American people and their leaders were repeatedly surprised by the Soviet acquisition of nuclear weapons, by the Anglo-French-Israeli invasion of Egypt in 1956, by Moscow's efforts to install offensive missiles in Cuba, by the determination and resourcefulness of communist-led rebel forces in Vietnam, by the energy crisis during the 1970s, by the reliance upon terroristic methods by anti-American groups throughout the world, and by the emergence of Moslem fundamentalism as a potent political force. As often as not, the United States has responded to such challenges on the basis of policy improvisations and *ad hoc* measures which reflected inadequate preparation for the event and little or no prior thought concerning how the United States could most effectively respond to it.

Two principles from pragmatic thought offer at least a partial explanation of why diplomatic planning by the United States has been only minimally successful. One is the pragmatic conception of the pluralistic universe: pragmatic minds are dubious about attempts to reduce human behavior in a pluralistic environment to a predictable set of guidelines or an exact science. The maxim that is instilled into every good military commander—"expect the unexpected" from the enemy—underscores this pragmatic admonition.

The other principle is the distinction which John Dewey drew between a planning and a planned society. It is a necessary inference from pragmatic thought that human beings should engage in intelligent planning, or attempts to anticipate and respond to emerging tendencies in all dimensions of their lives. Otherwise, human existence resembles certain forms of lower animal life which merely react to external stimuli. The pragmatic belief that man is capable of changing the environment also clearly implies the necessity for human forethought and planning. Yet, as Dewey recognized—and as Soviet experience has confirmed—the danger with planning is that it can result in a planned society, with all of its ideological rigidity, its political orthodoxy, its lack of spontaneity and creativity, and its inability to adapt itself to unexpected and novel challenges at home and abroad. To revert once more to a military analogy: every general wants his staff to plan for different kinds of possible military conflict, but he also wants to be left free to modify these plans drastically or to abandon them completely in the light of actual conditions and contingencies encountered on the battlefield.

As in other aspects of pragmatic thought, on the subject of diplomatic planning the pragmatic world view leaves thoughtful students of American foreign policy in a dilemma to which they must continually adapt. In this realm, as in many others, the pragmatist underscores the necessity for intelligent judgment, common sense, and balance in responding to the challenges confronting American society in a pluralistic, uncertain, and often volatile global environment.

Eight

Pragmatic Foreign Policy

Balancing the Diplomatic Books

Is the pragmatic approach to foreign affairs by the American people and their leaders on balance a positive or negative contribution to successful diplomacy by the United States? What are the main pitfalls and defects of a pragmatic world view? By contrast, what beneficial results can be expected from pragmatically based attitudes and behavior in foreign affairs? These are the central questions to be addressed in the concluding chapter. Our analysis begins by identifying and evaluating several criticisms which have been made of the pragmatic mode of thought, starting with its weaknesses as a school of philosophy, and then examining its main shortcomings as an approach to American foreign relations.

The Perils of Pragmatism

A former undersecretary of state has quoted the observation of a friend to the effect that when American civilization has run its course, its epitaph will read: "The United States—a great world power that died of a surfeit of pragmatism."[1] During an earlier stage of history, the label *pragmatist* was often considered an epithet, and among many philosophers and students of human problems, it remains so today. Certainly in the popular mind the term often has unsavory connotations, perhaps suggesting a political leader who is viewed as merely an opportunist, or one whose political activities are

---

1. Quoted in George Ball, *The Discipline of Power: Essentials of a Modern World Structure* (Boston, 1968), 343.

243

ostensibly devoid of any principles except promoting his own self-interest, or possibly one who adapts his position easily and readily to prevailing public opinion.

On a higher intellectual level, ever since its emergence in the nineteenth century, among philosophers and many students of intellectual history pragmatism has repeatedly encountered the criticism that it is not a fully respectable mode of thought, that it is in the second rank (or lower) among the philosophical movements witnessed in modern history. Other commentators have questioned whether pragmatism deserves to be described as a "philosophy" at all; in this view, it ought more properly to be viewed merely as a highly unsystematic approach to the acquisition and validation of truth. William James, John Dewey, and their followers admitted freely that pragmatism did not constitute an integrated system of thought, in part because they viewed all such philosophical systems as incapable of explaining infinitely complex reality. In the pragmatic view, monistic philosophical systems were more often than not serious impediments to deeper understanding of the universe.[2]

Critics of pragmatic thought have also called attention to the significant differences that can often be discerned in the ideas of Charles Peirce, William James, John Dewey, and their philosophical descendants. The leading spokesmen for pragmatism did not always agree upon what their philosophy would be called (James, for example, often referred to it as *meliorism*, whereas Dewey frequently used the term *instrumentalism*). Nevertheless, *pragmatism* remains the most widely employed term to describe this mode of thought, and most textbooks on modern philosophy discuss pragmatism as an identifiable and influential intellectual movement. Most other modern philosophies (existentialism is an outstanding example) may be even more difficult to define precisely than pragmatism. Or to cite another example, by the late twentieth century, as a philosophical movement Marxism had become as fragmented and had given rise perhaps to even more subspecies of thought than pragmatism.

Moreover, some criticisms of pragmatic thought derive from an inadequate or erroneous understanding of pragmatism's major tenets. Sometimes pragmatism has been rejected or blamed for deficiencies that are in fact totally contrary to the teaching of the leading pragmatic thinkers. Two examples of this phenomenon will illustrate the point.

2. See Robert J. Mulvaney and Philip M. Zeltner (eds.), *Pragmatism: Its Sources and Prospects* (Columbia, S.C., 1981), vii. In William James's view, philosophy embraces science, poetry, religion, and logic; it is "man thinking" about all dimensions of human experience. See John K. Roth (ed.), *William James's The Moral Equivalent to War and Other Essays* (New York, 1971), 93–106.

One is exemplified by the views of the conservative commentator Russell Kirk, who is prone to blame many of the evils of modern society on the ideas of Peirce, James, Dewey, and their intellectual descendants. The rise of totalitarian ideologies and political systems, the outbreak of World War II, the emergence of the cold war, and the high level of political "alienation" in contemporary modern society can, in Kirk's view, be attributed directly to the influence of pragmatic thinking on modern (especially American) life.[3]

Without denying the facts of which this indictment complains, however, it may be seriously questioned whether it reflects a correct understanding of pragmatic principles, as explained in earlier chapters. Fully as much as political conservatives like Kirk, James and Dewey were outspoken in condemning monistic and collectivist modes of thought such as Marxism. Pragmatists have consistently advocated democracy as the system that is indispensable for the successful operation of the scientific method and for the highest possible level of human development. It is equally erroneous to attribute a belief in the inevitability of progress to pragmatic philosophy. To the contrary, time and again, the leading pragmatists cautioned *against* this fatuous view of human destiny, which was prevalent during the late nineteenth and early twentieth centuries. Against the philosophical determinists, pragmatic thinkers contended only that progress in human affairs was possible, but only as a result of concerted human efforts guided by intelligence. This view of progress, of course, necessarily implied the possibility of failure by human society to achieve many of its goals.

Another misplaced criticism of pragmatism is that made by those who deplore the emergence and consequences of the approach to social science known as "behavioralism."[4] Without attempting a detailed discussion of the rise of behaviorally oriented research into social, economic, and political questions, it is enough to observe that its devotees emphasize the "value-free" nature of their investigations and findings. Relying heavily on statistical methods and data, they seek to produce reliable theories of socioeconomic and political behavior that will permit a high degree of predictability in human relationships. For the most part, the behavioral approach to political relationships is concerned with the political process, rather than with evaluations of the goals of political life or of the actual consequences, pro and con, that result from political interactions.

3. Russell Kirk, *A Program for Conservatives* (Chicago, 1962), 10–12.
4. The behavioral orientation in political science is described in Albert Somit and Joseph Tanenhous, *The Development of Political Science* (Boston, 1967); Marian D. Irish (ed.), *Political Science: Advance of the Discipline* (Englewood Cliffs, N.J., 1968); and Heinz Eulau, *The Behavioral Persuasion in Politics* (New York, 1963).

It is, of course, true that at one stage in his distinguished career, John Dewey was a leading member of the "Chicago pragmatists," who are credited with playing a key role in the emergence of the behavioral orientation in social sciences. It is no less true that Dewey's thought devoted considerable attention to the group basis of politics, a concept that became central in behavioral analyses of political phenomena.[5]

Nevertheless, it is a serious error to believe that behavioralism is merely an extension of pragmatism to the study of politics and other human relationships. A detailed examination of pragmatic thought as contained in an earlier chapter would reveal a number of points of fundamental divergence between it and the behavioral approach to political relationships—so many, in fact, as to support the overall conclusion that pragmatism and behavioralism are in many respects antithetical modes of analysis. For example, the pragmatic philosopher categorically *rejects* the notion of value-free scientific inquiry. A basic postulate of pragmatic thought also is the idea that the relationship between the observer and the environment is the key fact in the discovery of truth. As the Heisenberg principle of quantum mechanics expresses it, this interaction is intrinsic and inescapable, and it inevitably affects the results of scientific inquiry.

Consequently, for the pragmatic mind the really salient questions become: *Which* or *whose* values ought to guide the quest for knowledge and the application of discovered truths to human affairs? Pragmatists have never doubted that all scientists, philosophers, and others engaged in the search for truth have values (such as faith that the scientific method will yield reliable results); and it is better that such values be acknowledged *explicitly* rather than being left implicit in the investigator's methodology and findings. Moreover, the pragmatist believes that the scientific enterprise itself (especially in its application to human problems) can operate successfully only within an environment in which humans accept and preserve certain values (such as freedom of thought and speech) that are indispensable for objective and continuing scientific investigation. Once these ideas are accepted, concern by scientists, philosophers, and other scholars about the ends and actual consequences of group political activity becomes logical and inescapable.

It is instructive to observe that a comparatively new emphasis in the discipline of political science—known as "policy evaluation"—is much closer to the pragmatic tradition than behavioralism. The concept of policy evaluation reflects the pragmatic conviction that ultimately the political process must be judged by *its results or consequences* for the members of society, and

5. See Darnell Rucker, *The Chicago Pragmatists* (Minneapolis, 1960).

this approach implicitly recognizes that some consequences are more beneficial than others.[6]

Among students of modern philosophy, pragmatism has been criticized on a number of other grounds. As one study describes it, pragmatism is defective because it is an "open" approach to truth, which is "ragged around the edges" and is deficient in "precise logical analysis." Moreover, pragmatic thought often tends to evade a number of central philosophical questions. An Indian commentator has condemned the ideas of William James as merely "utilitarianism gone mad."[7]

Pragmatism, the eminent philosopher Jacques Maritain concluded, is a vague and emotional approach to truth, largely lacking in intellectual content; it is a mode of thought that appeals to "simple souls." In John Warbicke's assessment, a major objection to pragmatic thought is that the philosophy presupposed, and served as the instrument for achieving, an ethical ideal that was never clearly identified or analyzed. According to Woodbridge Riley, pragmatism reduces the quest for knowledge merely to fulfilling man's "felt needs," especially those that give humans "an emotional thrill." In George Geiger's view, Dewey's thought is philosophically unsound because it tends to waver between merely expressing the prevailing ethos of American society and denying that human relationships serve any ultimate moral purpose.[8]

As Ernest Gellner assesses it, pragmatism is merely a surviving example, among several, of evolutionary modes of thought that emerged in the nineteenth century in the wake of Darwin's findings. Pragmatism has always failed to acknowledge the uniqueness of the environment out of which it emerged; and the pragmatists sought to elevate a number of prevalent American beliefs (such as the Protestant work ethic) into universal norms of human conduct. To the mind of another critic, pragmatism was merely an Americanized version of Marxism: both philosophies are leading examples of "immanentalism," or a view of life which holds that the future will be better than the past and present. Yet the leading pragmatic thinkers seldom examined this assumption fully or critically.[9]

---

6. The concept of policy evaluation is discussed in Robert L. Lineberry, *American Public Policy: What Government Does and What Difference It Makes* (New York, 1978); and Aaron Wildavsky, *Speaking Truth to Power: The Art and Craft of Policy Analysis* (Boston, 1979).

7. See the Preface to Mulvaney and Zeltner (eds.), *Pragmatism*, vii; and the view of V. Kant, in Ignas K. Skrupskelis, *William James: A Reference Guide* (Boston, 1977), 96.

8. Maritain is quoted *ibid.*, 85; Warbicke, quoted *ibid.*, 82; Riley, quoted *ibid.*, 79; Geiger, quoted in Albert W. Levi, *Philosophy and the Modern World* (Bloomington, 1959), 318.

9. Ernest Gellner, "Pragmatism and the Importance of Being Earnest," in Mulvaney and Zeltner (eds.), *Pragmatism*, 62–63; Michele F. Sciacca, *Philosophical Trends in the Contemporary World* (Notre Dame, 1964), 45–46.

From a different perspective, a Polish student of modern philosophy has said that pragmatism was little more than a guide for those who merely wanted "to get on" in life and who actually had little serious interest in philosophical questions. A related criticism of pragmatism is that, in William McGovern's words, it is a species of "irrationalism"—the kind which contributed to the emergence and popularity of fascism before World War II. Still another commentator believes that the pragmatic mode of thought reflected the deeply ingrained anti-intellectualism characteristic of American life, and it sought to provide a philosophical justification for America's disdain of abstract intellectual inquiry. In the same vein, a commentator on the thought of William James accused him of numerous "metaphysical infidelities." As reflected in his ideas throughout his career, at various times James was tempted by the "fleshpots of rationalism, monism, intellectualism, and socialism." As a result, James's thought is characterized by "meanderings, zigzags, and [philosophical] circles."[10]

Other critics have denounced pragmatism because its ethical goals were never articulated and examined clearly; because James and Dewey merely projected their own (largely implicit) *personal* values as objectives for human society; because the pragmatists largely ignored the role of economic forces in determining human relationships; because representative pragmatic thinkers held equivocal and diverse views about the existence of God and about the role of supranatural forces in shaping human destiny; and because pragmatists (especially Dewey) often gave widely differing answers to the question of what is ultimately "good" for man and how it can be recognized and best achieved.[11]

As an approach to truth, other commentators have emphasized, pragmatism suffers from a lack of a central core of accepted philosophical principles. As such, one study concluded, pragmatism is a "corridor theory" of knowledge: its devotees "have interpreted and applied the theory in many different ways." One student of modern philosophy believes that at least five main "currents" of pragmatic thought may be identified. The philosopher A. O. Lovejoy identified some thirteen separate varieties of thought which could be described as "pragmatic." W. V. Quine has contended that differences among advocates of pragmatism have sometimes been greater than

10. See the views of Leszek Kolakowski, in Skrupskelis, *William James*, 159; of McGovern, quoted in *ibid.*, 113; and of Beverly Lawn, quoted in *ibid.*, 176; Ralph Barton Perry, *The Thought and Character of William James* (New York, 1954), 356–57.

11. See the views of Albert Dicey, quoted in Perry, *Thought and Character of William James*, 357; and A. H. Somjee, *The Political Theory of John Dewey* (New York, 1968), 175–76.

those between the pragmatists and advocates of rival philosophies. As a result, Morton G. White has observed, pragmatism has never been able "to present a single face to the world" or to agree upon its essential tenets.[12]

Pitfalls in Pragmatic Diplomacy

An identification of the philosophical shortcomings of pragmatism leads to specific criticisms of a pragmatic approach to American diplomacy. To the minds of many observers, a pragmatic world view creates major and minor problems for the United States in its foreign relations.

First, there is the general criticism that pragmatically oriented thinkers tend to evade difficult questions about the behavior of the United States beyond its own borders; or, at a minimum, the pragmatic world view provides answers to these questions that frequently are unclear and unsatisfactory. For example, Geiger and others discern a circularity in pragmatic thought on the question of democracy and the need to protect it from antidemocratic forces. Dewey was never able to provide a logically consistent and totally satisfactory resolution of the dilemma confronting the American democracy by the Axis threat before and during World War II. Basically the same uncertainty existed in his thinking about the cold war between the United States and the Soviet Union after 1945.

Dewey recognized the dangers to democracy posed by the threats of fascist and communist expansionism. Yet he was equally troubled by the tendency toward militarism and steadily growing presidential power within the United States during and after World War II. To Dewey's mind, both external and internal developments jeopardized the future of democratic government, and both should be resisted. Yet Dewey never clearly indicated precisely how one risk could be avoided without incurring the other.

Dewey thus recognized possible hazards in both an exclusively isolationist and an interventionist course for the United States in foreign affairs. American diplomatic experience since the 1930s has demonstrated convinc-

12. Milton R. Konvitz and Gail Kennedy (eds.), *The American Pragmatists* (New York, 1960), 7; Sciacca, *Philosophical Trends in the Contemporary World*, 41. For more detailed analysis of the varieties of pragmatic thought, see Arthur O. Lovejoy, *The Thirteen Pragmatisms and Other Essays* (Baltimore, 1963); Bernard Brennan, *The Ethics of William James* (New York, 1961), 156–57; and Marcus P. Ford, *William James's Philosophy: A New Perspective* (Amherst, Mass., 1982), 116–17. W. V. Quine, "The Pragmatists's Place in Empiricism," in Mulvaney and Zeltner (eds.), *Pragmatism,* 23; and William James's views, quoted in Frederick Mayer, *A History of American Thought: An Introduction* (Dubuque, Iowa, 1951), 281; Morton G. White, *Social Thought in America* (New York, 1949), 88.

ingly that Dewey was essentially correct: carried to an extreme, either policy entails genuine, and sometimes serious, risks for the United States at home and abroad. The lack of a clear public consensus about the nation's foreign policy following the Vietnam War could be attributed to a widespread desire by the American people to avoid *both* "another Munich" and "another Vietnam." As Dewey's philosophical predicament implicitly recognized, in practice this may be the equivalent to trying to "square the circle" diplomatically.

Admittedly, a pragmatic world view does not deliver the American people and their leaders from such painful dilemmas. Yet two things may be said about the utility of a pragmatically grounded approach to American foreign relations. If it leaves certain paradoxical aspects of the nation's external policy unresolved, so do alternative approaches. (In the *Realpolitik* tradition, for example, the pivotal concept of national interest may define either how foreign policy is *formulated* or how it is ultimately *defended and justified* by policy makers.) And the pragmatic world view possesses the merit of intellectual honesty. In effect, it asserts that Americans must somehow learn to live in a logically untidy world and to tolerate dilemmas and paradoxes in foreign relations, no less than in other dimensions of human experience. In the end, humans must choose among courses of action, all of which have shortcomings and disadvantages; and they must make such choices on a case-by-case basis within a particular context of time and circumstances. If that is not an answer that will be accepted enthusiastically by many individuals, it is the principle by which most Americans regulate their everyday lives, which they can live with, and which they prefer to other possible resolutions of the problems facing them in the external environment.[13]

A second criticism of pragmatism as a guide to American diplomacy is closely related. A former student of John Dewey's, Randolph Bourne, ultimately broke with his mentor, in part because Dewey's approach to political questions was too "rational." In Bourne's view, Dewey greatly overestimated man's capacity and inclination to be guided mainly by intelligence in arriving at political decisions. According to Bourne and other critics, the pragmatists greatly underestimated the impact of emotional, subjective, egocentric, and other irrational forces in determining political outcomes. Dewey and his followers, for example, uncritically assumed that political leaders are normally devoted to achieving such goals as adjustment, accommodation, growth, compromise, and development in human society. Or, as

13. See Cyrus Vance, *Hard Choices: Critical Years in American Foreign Policy* (New York, 1983).

several of his critics frequently observed about the genteel William James, James naively supposed that others were as ethical, humanistic, and personally virtuous as he was in his approach to human problems.[14]

It is true that, with some notable exceptions (as in James's essay on the moral equivalent of war), pragmatic thinkers devoted relatively little attention to the problem of irrational behavior in modern political life. Pragmatic thought affords only limited insight for understanding political conduct that is motivated by ideological fanaticism, by religious dogmas, by appeals to martyrdom, and by certain forms of terrorism witnessed in the post–World War II era. For reasons that are not altogether clear, what can be called the "irrational quotient" in international relations has grown steadily since World War II, as symbolized by the increase in global terrorism and in movements like the Islamic resurgence in the Middle East and parts of Asia.[15]

How, for example, can the internecine strife in contemporary Lebanon be understood by reference to the ideas of the American pragmatists? (The failure of the Reagan administration's intervention in Lebanon can be attributed in part to the prevalent assumption in Washington that the parties to the Lebanese conflict actually desired a resolution of it on a compromise or reasonable basis.)[16] Or, how does the thought of William James and John Dewey enable us to comprehend, and to respond more effectively to, terroristic attacks against American and other foreign embassies abroad? As Bourne contended, Dewey's "method of intelligence" seems an excessively rational, and minimally useful, approach to such contemporary diplomatic challenges.

If pragmatic thought quite clearly does not provide many useful guidelines for responding to the challenge of irrational political behavior—and if it does perhaps overemphasize the role of intelligence or rationality in shaping political relationships—this approach to foreign policy has at least one outstanding virtue. Dewey's method of intelligence offers the only feasible approach for *discovering the answer* to the riddle of irrational political conduct. If an answer to the problem exists, what better method of ultimately discerning

14. See Charles F. Howlett, *Troubled Philosopher: John Dewey and the Struggle for World Peace* (Port Washington, N.Y., 1977), 36–37.
15. David W. Marcell, *Progress and Pragmatism: James, Dewey, Beard, and the American Idea of Progress* (Westport, Conn., 1974), 328–29; Robert A. Kupperman and Darrell M. Trent, *Terrorism: Threat, Reality, Response* (Stanford, 1981); and Claire Sterling, *The Terror Network* (New York, 1981).
16. See P. Edward Haley and Lewis W. Snider (eds.), *Lebanon in Crisis: Participants and Issues* (Syracuse, N.Y., 1979); and David Gilmour, *Lebanon: The Fractured Country* (New York, 1984).

it is available than reliance on intelligence, common sense, the lessons of experience, and other pragmatic concepts? As in other aspects of pragmatic thought, these, of course, offer no guarantee that the desired answers will be found. What can be guaranteed is that, without relying on such pragmatic principles, the answers will almost certainly remain elusive.

Third, pragmatic thought—and the omission is especially noteworthy in the thought of John Dewey—devoted relatively little attention to the problem of political institutions vis-à-vis political organizations, group interactions, and political processes. By his own admission, Dewey was minimally interested in the institutions of the American (or any other) government. In the last analysis, he believed that institutions merely reflected the society's mores, needs, and patterns of group dynamics.

Consequently, Dewey and other pragmatists were not inclined to define democracy by reference to a particular set of institutions or specific political processes. The pragmatists believed—and experience in the twentieth century has clearly shown—that nations do not become or remain democratic merely because they have a written constitution, periodic elections, or a government with clearly delineated executive, legislative, and judicial functions. As is the case with many Third World societies today, nations may meet such formal criteria and still have authoritarian or totalitarian systems.[17] Conversely, as Dewey's thought repeatedly emphasized, a functioning democracy is sustained by an underlying belief by its members that principles of justice, equality, fair play, and the creation of new opportunities for human development are transcendent political goals.

In the process of directing attention to the group basis of political life, pragmatic thought suggests, by implication at least, that the institutions and formal processes of government are relatively unimportant. Yet this position leaves a significant gap in our understanding of foreign policy decision making in the United States. The institutional setting of American foreign policy plays a significant role in determining the nation's international behavior. In the American setting, the emergence of the president as the nation's diplomat-in-chief, for example, owes much to certain constitutional provisions dealing with the powers and responsibilities of the chief executive in the

17. Novel and emerging forms of democracy in selected Third World societies are identified and analyzed in Paget Henry and Carl Stone (eds.), *The Newer Caribbean: Decolonization, Democracy, and Development* (Philadelphia, 1983); Dennis Austin, *Politics in Africa* (Hanover, N.H., 1978); William Tordoff, *Government and Politics in Africa* (Bloomington, 1985); and Howard Handelman and Thomas C. Sanders (eds.), *Military Governments and the Movement Toward Democracy in South America* (Bloomington, 1981).

foreign policy field. The president's dominant role in diplomatic decision making is also clearly affected by the fact that (with the vice president) he is the only official of the federal government who is elected nationally. In large part for that reason, the president is in a position to define and articulate the national interest better than rival claimants in Congress or elsewhere. Similarly, the election of members of the House of Representatives on a two-year basis (versus six years for senators) is a factor influencing its role in, and impact on, foreign affairs.[18]

Such examples underscore the reality that institutions and formal political processes do matter in determining diplomatic results. As the government of Israel has repeatedly discovered since its creation in 1949, it makes a difference—sometimes crucial—whether it must deal with the White House or with Congress (or even with different committees of Congress) in matters affecting Israel's well-being.[19]

Fourth, a recurrent criticism of pragmatism is that it represents a uniquely "American" mode of thought. With this ethnocentric bias, pragmatism is poorly designed either to enable Americans to understand the attitudes and behavior of peoples in other societies or to provide useful guidance for the creation of an emerging global community.

In Chapter 2, detailed attention was devoted to the fact that the pragmatic mode of thought uniquely expressed the American ethos and the customary patterns of American thought and behavior. The leading pragmatists, of course, drew freely from the preexisting philosophical tradition. Yet the resulting pragmatic synthesis was a distinctively American way of viewing man's place in the cosmos and in human relationships. Even today, no other mode of philosophical inquiry rivals pragmatism in its unique identification with American ways of thought and conduct.

For many commentators, the close identification between pragmatism and the American ethos gives rise to a number of problems and shortcomings, detracting from the utility of pragmatic thought in serving as an adequate guide for understanding human relationships. The admittedly optimistic quality of pragmatic thinking, and its lack of restraint in assessing the pos-

18. See Stephen P. Soper, *Congress, the President, and Foreign Policy* (Chicago, 1985); Stephen L. Spiegel, *The Other Arab-Israeli Conflict: Making America's Middle East Policy from Truman to Reagan* (Chicago, 1985); Montague Kern *et al., The Kennedy Crisis, the Presidency, and Foreign Policy* (Chapel Hill, 1983); and Cecil V. Crabb, Jr., and Pat Holt, *Invitation to Struggle: Congress, the President, and Foreign Policy* (2nd ed.; Washington, D.C., 1984).

19. See Crabb and Holt, *Invitation to Struggle,* 99–127; Congressional Quarterly, *The Middle East* (5th ed.; Washington, D.C., 1981), and later editions; and Paul Findley, *They Dare to Speak Out: People and Institutions Confront Israel's Lobby* (Westport, Conn., 1985).

sibilities for human evolution and development, stand in sharp contrast to most modern European philosophies. A German observer has said, in reference to the ideas of William James, that pragmatism is a highly provincial way of thinking. He has pointed out that James and other leading pragmatists devoted little or no attention to Germany's traditions and experiences, which were, of course, in many respects very different from America's. William James's thought, another critic has lamented, reflected his own distinctively American values, such as a deep-seated belief in democracy, a commitment to the humanistic traditions, and a faith in the "sovereignty of the mediocre man." In Gellner's view, although pragmatism purported to offer universal guidelines for human behavior, in reality its supporting evidence was drawn almost exclusively from *Western experience* in the formulation of its principles. Pragmatism, said another critic, reflected the "experiences of the American middle class," and it projected these as the norm for humanity at large. Accordingly, pragmatic thought is much "too Western" to appeal widely to non-Western societies. From a different perspective, Marxists have always rejected pragmatism as an approach to truth because it attempted to rationalize and defend existing bourgeois attitudes and behavior patterns in the United States.[20]

That pragmatism is historically and intrinsically associated with the American way of life cannot be seriously doubted. Incontestably also, the leading pragmatic thinkers did draw their examples and evidence to support their philosophical insights primarily from Western experience. Yet these facts should not be interpreted to mean that pragmatic thinking has little or no utility for individuals and groups outside the American, or more generally the Western, cultural tradition. Increasingly, for example, ideological "decay"— the declining role of ideology in making internal and external policies—has come to be identified as *a global phenomenon*. Throughout the contemporary world, societies that have never heard of Charles Peirce are nonetheless in effect relying on his standard in judging incumbent governments by their performance or by the consequences of their policies at home and abroad. This tendency has been especially pronounced within the Soviet Union,

20. The French commentator Henry Bremond, quoted in Skrupskelis, *William James*, 90; an anonymous German commentator, quoted in *ibid.*, 80; M. H. Hedges, quoted in *ibid.*, 78; Gellner, "Pragmatism and the Importance of Being Earnest," 53; Thelma Herman, quoted in Skrupskelis, *William James*, 125; J. David Hoeveler, *The New Humanism: A Critique of Modern America* (Charlottesville, 1977), 42; and the commentary on pragmatism by Lewis Mumford in Gail Kennedy (ed.), *Pragmatism and American Culture* (Boston, 1950), 37–49. See the detailed and highly critical Marxist critique of pragmatism in Harry K. Welles, *Pragmatism: Philosophy of Imperialism* (New York, 1954).

where the communist hierarchy has been increasingly challenged to demonstrate the value of the Marxist system by its tangible benefits for the members of Soviet society.[21]

Some exceptions—and a noteworthy example is the Islamic resurgence witnessed in recent years—to this global process of "de-ideologization" exist. Nevertheless, as a generalization it remains true that the role of rigid ideological codes in shaping the domestic and foreign policies of governments throughout the contemporary world has declined. In the Soviet Union, in several Marxist states of Eastern Europe, in China, in Cuba, in North Vietnam and North Korea, communist authorities have become increasingly pragmatic in their responses to internal and external challenges—to the point of raising a substantial question of whether the chief role of ideology is now primarily to rationalize or provide legitimacy for policies adopted mainly for nonideological reasons. China's new "responsibility system"—combining Confucianist, Chinese, Marxist, capitalist, and other elements—is a prominent example of this tendency.[22]

Comparable examples might be cited from the experience of several Third World nations in the recent period. From 1952 until 1970, for example, under President Gamal Abdel Nasser, Egypt was governed by a highly ideological regime. Under Nasser's leadership, in both foreign and domestic affairs, Egypt's problems became increasingly critical. After Nasser's death in 1970, President Anwar Sadat adopted a more pragmatic approach to problem solving, and his successor, Hosni Mubarek, has carried that process even further.[23]

The Egyptian experience has been duplicated widely throughout the Third World. In Algeria and Tunisia, in the Ivory Coast and Nigeria, in Burma and Indonesia, and in other developing societies political elites have in-

21. See Curtis Keeble's view that Soviet policy cannot be adequately understood by reference to ideology or any other unicausal explanation. Instead, it is a product of "a multitude of separate acts, often with no clear linkage to an underlying philosophical concept, often uncoordinated and not infrequently conflicting" (Keeble [ed.], *The Soviet State: The Domestic Roots of Soviet Foreign Policy* [Boulder, Colo., 1985], 1). See also Stephen F. Cohen, *Rethinking the Soviet Experience: Politics and History Since 1917* (New York, 1985); Richard Lowenthal, *World Communism: The Disintegration of a Secular Faith* (New York, 1966); David Childs (ed.), *The Changing Face of Western Communism* (New York, 1980); and Robert Wesson, *The Aging of Communism* (New York, 1980).

22. See Peter Zwick, *National Communism* (Boulder, Colo., 1983); Timothy J. Colton, *The Dilemma of Reform in the Soviet Union* (New York, 1984); David Ottaway and Marina Ottaway, *Afrocommunism* (New York, 1981); and Maurice Halperin, *The Taming of Fidel Castro* (Berkeley, 1981).

23. Raymond W. Barker, *Egypt's Uncertain Revolution Under Nasser and Sadat* (Cambridge, Mass., 1978); and Jimmy Carter, *The Blood of Abraham: Insights into the Middle East* (Boston, 1985), 153–77.

creasingly abandoned ideological rigidity in favor of a more adaptive, flexible, and philosophically syncretistic approach to their nations' problems. By the late 1980s, even such ideologically militant governments as Syria, Iraq, and Iran were reported to be exemplifying a more "pragmatic" outlook in their attempt to solve pressing national problems.[24]

As one student of modern philosophy has observed, in the second half of the twentieth century, societies throughout the world have everywhere "become more pragmatic." Insofar as America can successfully provide a model for other societies, it does not derive mainly from the unique nature of the Constitution or the distinctiveness of the American two-party system. Instead, it is more likely to stem from the example of the American society's adaptability, its ideological flexibility, its spirit of experimentation and innovation, and its reliance upon trial-and-error methods and other concepts central to the pragmatic tradition. With the exception of groups like the Islamic fundamentalists, societies throughout the world have become increasingly willing to accept the twofold pragmatic principle that *truth continually evolves* and *methods of ascertaining truth also change* in the light of human experience and understanding.

Fifth, as many commentators assess it, a critical defect of pragmatic thought was identified in a recent study of the Kennedy administration. By many criteria, President John F. Kennedy was a leader whose approach to problems at home and abroad epitomized the pragmatic mentality. Yet as one official who was a member of the Kennedy team complained, the White House appeared to lack "a genuine sense of conviction about what is right and what is wrong." Kennedy and his closest advisers did not appear to have "a basic moral reference point" to which their ideas and actions could be related.[25]

In more general terms, James W. Smith believes that pragmatism lacks a "cosmic sense." It either evades or fails to come to grips with ultimate issues or the overriding political questions with which contemporary man is deeply concerned. In his view, John Dewey's "practicalism" fails to provide satisfactory answers to transcendent human problems. By contrast, on the interna-

24. See, for example, the discussion of the evolution in Iraqi policy in Adeed I. Dawisha, "Iraq: The West's Opportunity," *Foreign Policy*, XLI (Winter, 1980–81), 134–53. Changes in the internal and external policies of other Middle Eastern nations are analyzed in Michael C. Hudson, *Arab Politics: The Search for Legitimacy* (New Haven, 1977); and R. D. McLaurin *et al.*, *Foreign Policy Making in the Middle East: Domestic Influences on Policy in Egypt, Iraq, and Syria* (New York, 1977).

25. See the views of Chester Bowles, in David Halberstam, *The Best and the Brightest* (New York, 1972), 88.

tional scene, the American society is challenged by movements such as communism and resurgent Islam that are "extraordinarily vocal in their expression of cosmic perspective." In the same vein, Levi viewed Dewey's pragmatism as deficient because it lacked a "dominant moral aim" in the light of which human society could be reconstructed. According to Geiger, the great unanswered question in John Dewey's thought was "instrumentalism" for what? What *ultimate* moral and ethical ends were to be served or promoted by pragmatism's distinctive method for discovering truth? For these reasons, in Lewis Mumford's assessment, pragmatic thought has always exhibited a tendency to waver between "bland compliance" with existing political values and practices and (on the basis of little evident justification) an expression of "blind optimism" about the future.[26]

These criticisms are clearly applicable to any evaluation of post–World War II American diplomatic behavior. As a people steeped in the pragmatic tradition, Americans have exhibited difficulty discovering a cause or transcendent idea that serves as a common theme of their diplomatic activities. In its postwar foreign relations, the United States has had difficulty competing with revolutionary communism and other millenarian causes. As events by the mid-1980s demonstrated, it is difficult, for example, to envision the leaders and masses of black Africa exhibiting political fervor in behalf of an American-sponsored program of gradual and evolutionary change, of "adjustment," and of slowly emerging self-realization—or what the Reagan administration called "constructive engagement." To the contrary, we know from the record of recent American relations with the white-ruled government of South Africa that a pragmatically based approach to African questions does *not* elicit enthusiasm, either among black Africans or their supporters in the United States. In this and other settings, a widespread complaint about the foreign policy of the United States is that Americans have abandoned or forgotten their own revolutionary heritage.[27]

As explained more fully in Chapter 1, however, considerable misunder-

26. James W. Smith, "Religion and Science in American Philosophy," in James W. Smith and A. Leland James (eds.), *The Shaping of American Religion* (Princeton, 1961), 441–42; Levi, *Philosophy and the Modern World,* 318; George R. Geiger, "Dewey's Social and Political Philosophy," in Paul A. Schilpp (ed.), *The Philosophy of John Dewey* (Evanston, 1939), 365–67; Mumford, quoted in Kennedy (ed.), *Pragmatism and American Culture,* 56.

27. Evaluations of recent American policy toward South Africa are available in Clyde Ferguson and William R. Cotter, "South Africa—What Is to Be Done?" *Foreign Affairs,* LVI (January, 1978), 253–75; J. Gus Liebenow, "American Policy in Africa: The Reagan Years," *Current History,* LXXXII (March, 1983), 97–101, 133; and Frank J. Parker, *South Africa: Lost Opportunities* (Lexington, Mass., 1983).

standing often exists inside and outside the United States about the American Revolution. It was a "revolution" primarily in the sense that it was a successful anticolonial struggle against British rule. Otherwise, it was almost totally devoid of revolutionary content, in contrast to the French Revolution or the Communist Revolution in Russia. Indeed, after gaining their independence, Americans usually avoided revolutionary methods of change in favor of gradual, orderly, and piecemeal innovations, the effect of which over a long period of time might well be described as "revolutionary." Thus it is sometimes said that for some two hundred years American society has engaged in "continuing revolution" by constantly adapting its social, economic, and political institutions to the requirements of modern life. Or, as judged by its results over a period of years, it can perhaps accurately be said that Franklin D. Roosevelt's New Deal amounted to a revolution in many dimensions of national experience and that the abandonment of the isolationist position similarly produced a revolution in American foreign policy.

Admittedly, impatient and disadvantaged masses, radical political groups inside and outside the United States, those exhibiting a high degree of political alienation, and other advocates of revolutionary change are unlikely to be attracted to the pragmatic world view. Pragmatists, for example, do not promise or expect the political millennium; as evolutionists, they are realistic enough to acknowledge, and to say, that significant improvements in the conduct of international relations are likely to come about very slowly, sometimes imperceptibly. They do not believe that a new Soviet-American summit conference will eliminate the cold war; nor are they overly sanguine about the prospects for rapid and successful modernization or nation-building throughout most of the Third World.

Yet despite its evident lack of emotional appeal, especially for revolutionary-oriented groups, the pragmatic world view emphasizes two ideas that are in accord with the lessons of postwar experience. One is that lasting and beneficial political change is almost always a matter of slow growth, development, and continuing adaptations over time. Pragmatists are convinced that groups and political movements that contend otherwise are more often than not deceiving the people and are, in fact, creating new and serious impediments to beneficial changes in human political relationships. The other is that—as countless leaders and political movements throughout the Third World have discovered, often on the basis of painful experience—revolutionary slogans and ideological incantations are seldom substitutes for John Dewey's method of intelligence in the solution of urgent national problems. In the postwar period, innumerable Third World governments have (however reluctantly) acknowledged that modernization is in fact an extremely slow and often painful process; that it does entail the gradual substitution of a new set of habits for society's traditional modes of thought and conduct; and that this evolutionary process of change is most likely to occur successfully to the degree that the people understand *on the basis of experience* that new modes of thought and action produce better results than old ways. If this pragmatic assessment lacks political appeal, it has the considerable merit of being in accord with political reality throughout most of the contemporary world.[28]

Sixth, a French critic has identified another defect of a pragmatic approach to political phenomena. The pragmatically oriented American mind, this commentator complained, frequently offers "moral sincerity" to Europeans in lieu of genuine understanding of political issues. Or, as J. David Hoeveler has expressed the idea, the thought of William James promoted "a pursuit of speed and power for their own sake," instead of wisdom, as the motivating force of public policy. To paraphrase a popular song associated with the flapper era of the 1920s, everyone was "doing it" without knowing what "it" was. The American writer Irving Babbitt said that as a result of embracing the pragmatic mode of thought, the ancient judgment of Aristophanes had come true in American society: "Whirl is king, having driven out Zeus."[29]

Applied to American foreign policy, such judgments have several significant implications. As the comment by Dean Acheson (recounted in Chapter 7) emphasized, in a number of instances since World War II, there has been a discernible tendency for activity, energy, movement, and (a favorite concept with the Kennedy administration) "vigor" to be equated by Americans with solid diplomatic accomplishment. During the 1970s, the same basic criticism was made of Henry Kissinger's shuttle diplomacy in the Middle East: Kissinger's almost frenzied commuting among Middle Eastern capitals epitomized American diplomatic activism, which was often devoid of tangible diplomatic accomplishments.[30] Critics wondered whether considerably more might not have been achieved by relying on what is sometimes called quiet diplomacy

---

28. See Michael Todaro, *Economic Development in the Third World* (3rd ed.; New York, 1985), 61–94.

29. See the views of an anonymous French critic in Skrupskelis, *William James*, 83; Hoeveler, *New Humanism*, 33; Babbitt, quoted in *ibid.*

30. For fuller discussion and evaluation of Henry Kissinger's "shuttle diplomacy" in the Middle East, see Jeffery Z. Rubin, *Dynamics of Third Party Intervention: Kissinger in the Middle East* (New York, 1981); and Richard Valeriani, *Travels with Henry* (New York, 1980).

or less overtly active, sometimes almost frenetic, methods of resolving international disputes.

A variant criticism of pragmatism is Hoeveler's view that it has contributed to a world "with the lid off"; in the end, it engenders pervasive "confusion" and a concern with speed, motion, and activity for its own sake. As illustrated by the post-Vietnam era in American foreign policy, pragmatic thinking engenders highly disparate conclusions about the "lessons of Vietnam" and other major issues central to American diplomacy. The challenge of clarifying and applying the lessons of Vietnam to future diplomatic experience involves a twofold problem: gaining a consensus upon what *are* the principal lessons of the Vietnam conflict and determining how these lessons *apply* precisely to future diplomatic problems.[31]

The post-Vietnam diplomatic experience of the United States has called attention to another troublesome dimension of pragmatic thought, especially as it is associated with the ideas of John Dewey. As we have seen, Dewey's political goal was the emergence of a stronger sense of community among all peoples—the prerequisite for such specific objectives as the elimination of war and conflict among nations, growing international cooperation, and the promotion of human well-being throughout the world. His model was the scientific community, whose activities are characterized by the continual quest for knowledge, the collection and dispassionate evaluation of data, the formulation and testing of new hypotheses, and the modification of existing scientific truths in the light of new evidence. As earlier chapters have emphasized also, a major tenet of pragmatic thought was the idea that scientists and all those engaged in the quest for knowledge had an intrinsic interest in the application of their findings to human affairs.

As American diplomatic experience after the Vietnam War has clearly illustrated, however, in practice this pragmatic idea encounters a number of formidable obstacles, so as to raise serious questions about its utility as a guide to American foreign policy. For example, there is the ironic development that the most avowedly "scientific" approach to problems concerning social scientists today—the behavioral orientation, whose devotees claim intellectual

---

31. Hoeveler, *New Humanism,* 33. The list of "the lessons of Vietnam" is almost endless and continues to grow! The following call attention to many of these lessons: McGeorge Bundy, "Vietnam and Presidential Powers," *Foreign Affairs,* LVIII (Winter, 1979–80), 397–407; Michael Charlton and Anthony Monrieff, *Many Reasons Why: The American Involvement in Vietnam* (New York, 1979); Stephen A. Garrett, *Ideas and Reality: An Analysis of the Debate Over Vietnam* (Washington, D.C., 1978); Leslie H. Gelb and Richard K. Betts, *The Irony of Vietnam: The System Worked* (Washington, D.C., 1979); Paul M. Kattenburg, *The Vietnam Trauma in American Foreign Policy* (New Brunswick, N.J., 1980); and Richard M. Nixon, *No More Vietnams* (New York, 1985).

descent from the pragmatic philosophical tradition—is minimally interested in the application of its findings to internal and external policy questions. Among contemporary political scientists, for instance, behaviorally oriented scholars have often been reluctant to call attention to the public policy implications of their findings or to present their ideas in ways that are intelligible to, and useful by, national policy makers. As a result, more often than not their studies have been of marginal utility in formulating American foreign policy toward Central America, or toward a new arms control agreement with Moscow, or toward the problem of ongoing violence and upheaval in the Middle East.

Among natural scientists, social scientists, and other investigators whose research is not behaviorally oriented, a different problem frequently exists, which was not adequately understood and analyzed by Dewey and other thinkers in the pragmatic tradition. In its application to social, economic, and political affairs, Dewey's pragmatic model of scientific investigation underestimated the degree to which *disunity can and does exist,* even among well-informed students of human relationships. As a celebrated example, the scientific community has been sharply divided since World War II over the question of whether the United States should have developed and used the atomic bomb in the war against Japan. (Some scientists are persuaded that the United States should never have perfected nuclear weapons; others are convinced that the atomic bomb should have been developed but not used against Japan; still others are certain that American officials were justified in both developing and employing nuclear weapons against the Japanese enemy and, by extension, in the future against the Soviet Union or any other aggressive nation.) Comparable differences of opinion existed among members of the scientific community about America's development of the hydrogen bomb in the postwar era.

Then by the late 1980s, scientific opinion was again sharply divided over the question of the Reagan administration's Strategic Defense Initiative (SDI), or Star Wars proposal, as it was widely described by the news media. This long-range research project envisioned the use of space satellites to destroy Soviet (or any other nation's) offensive missiles before they were able to strike targets in the United States. President Reagan and his advisers were convinced that SDI was essentially a defensive breakthrough, which might offer a feasible alternative to dependence upon "mutually assured destruction" (the existing MAD strategy) for the maintenance of peace between the superpowers. Scientific and other critics of SDI, however, contended that the scheme was not scientifically possible, that even if it were possible, it would be prohibitively expensive, and that its implementation would seriously destabilize Soviet-American relations (by possibly provoking Moscow to attack before the United States gained a decisive military advantage.) From its inception, SDI proved to be a highly controversial undertaking, with well-informed observers taking sharply divergent positions concerning it. For our purposes, the most relevant aspect of the controversy perhaps is the reality that scientific opinion in the United States is seldom unified on this and other public policy questions. In the case of Star Wars, such opinion was more than ordinarily divided—even over the scientific feasibility of the proposal, not to mention its main diplomatic and military implications.[32]

On the basis of such examples, it seems clear that pragmatic thought does ignore or underestimate the degree to which scientific observers disagree— sometimes about the more narrow question of whether a particular proposal is scientifically feasible, but even more often about the implications and consequences of new scientific and technological developments for human society. Indeed, as experience with the Star Wars proposal has demonstrated, such disunity may be even more overtly conspicuous among members of the scientific community than among ordinary citizens, whose knowledge of, and interest in, the question is extremely limited. William James, John Dewey, and other pragmatic thinkers were convinced that, however much they might deny it, philosophers, scientists, and all those engaged in the search for truth were inescapably concerned with "values." From the evidence of postwar American diplomatic experience, even the pragmatists, however, were insufficiently aware of the implications of that reality for scientific opinions with respect to political and other human problems!

As a set of guidelines for American foreign policy, pragmatism exhibits a seventh weakness, identified by Henry Kissinger. In his view, the pragmatic mentality of Americans assumes that "the context of events produces a solution" and that "every [global] problem will yield if attacked with sufficient energy." Pragmatic thinking tends to break down a problem into its separate components; in the process, the wholeness of the problem becomes obscured, and policy makers are tempted to concentrate on its more technical and subordinate aspects. In Kissinger's assessment, this pragmatic mind-set is

32. For evaluation of the Star Wars concept and other recent proposals in national defense policy, see Richard Stubbing, "The Defense Program: Buildup or Binge?" *Foreign Affairs*, LXIII (Spring, 1985), 848–73; John Tirman (ed.), *The Fallacy of Star Wars* (New York, 1984); Gregg Herken, *Counsels of War* (New York, 1985); and Colin S. Gray, *America's Military Space Program* (Cambridge, Mass., 1983).

especially characteristic of lawyers, who are often heavily represented in the American foreign policy process. Legally trained minds tend to focus upon concrete, immediate, and *ad hoc* questions, and they are minimally concerned with the overall or collective impact of *ad hoc* decision making over time. Americans, Leland D. Baldwin believes, operate upon the premise that "problems could be easily solved." Since, in one way or another, such problems were in time usually solved *within* the United States, Americans believed "they could be just as easily handled in other societies."[33]

In the early post–World War II period, the perceptive Scotsman D. W. Brogan identified "the illusion of American omnipotence" as a striking characteristic of the American world view. To Brogan's mind, Americans normally approach international issues on the premise that diplomatic problems have a solution acceptable to the United States and that with sufficient diligence and energy, the solution can be found and implemented. Americans, said President John F. Kennedy, would "pay any price" and "bear any burden" in defense of freedom; and it was under his leadership that the United States assumed the ever-growing burden of defending Southeast Asia from communism. Moreover, JFK was convinced that the United States could successfully engage in "nation-building" throughout the Third World.[34]

America's traditional "can do" mentality—the unexamined assumption that most international problems have an "American solution"—unquestionably contributed to the indiscriminate American interventionism exemplified by the Vietnam War and, several years later, to the Reagan administration's ill-fated intervention in Lebanon. General Charles de Gaulle once observed that in its diplomacy, the American society had "a taste for intervention." According to Ronald Steel, such pragmatically based thinking led Americans to engage in interventionist behavior "indiscriminately and without measure," with the result that the United States became involved abroad "in struggles we do not understand, in areas where we are unwanted, and in ambitions which are doomed to frustration." In the words of Senator J. William Fulbright, the nation's foreign policy reflected the "arrogance of power" or the belief that American involvement, insight, and energy could resolve problems that had defied solution by others. More often than not, the

33. Henry Kissinger, "Conditions of World Order," *Daedalus*, XCV (Spring, 1966), 503–29; Leland D. Baldwin, *The American Quest for the City of God* (Macon, Ga., 1981), 326–29.

34. See D. W. Brogan, "The Illusion of American Omnipotence," *Harper's Magazine*, CCV (December, 1952), 21–28. John F. Kennedy's first Inaugural Address, in Theodore Sorensen, *Kennedy* (New York, 1965), 245–246; and see the discussion of JFK's policies toward the Third World in Arthur Schlesinger, Jr., *A Thousand Days: John F. Kennedy in the White House* (Boston, 1965), 506–85.

result of such thinking was to create more problems for the United States overseas than it resolved.[35]

Undeniably, the mind-set of William James, John Dewey, and other pragmatists was usually optimistic about the capacity of members of society to solve the problems confronting them. If the pragmatic conception of a pluralistic universe acknowledged the existence of environmental forces inimical to human welfare, and if pragmatism sometimes clearly reflected a tragic sense of human life, it remains true that as a rule pragmatic thought was in harmony with American society's deep-seated belief in progress and confidence in man's ability "to build a better future." The pragmatic emphasis on problem solving unquestionably implies that solutions to human problems *exist,* and by relying on the scientific method (or what Dewey called the method of intelligence) they can be found and applied to the challenges confronting human society.

Yet in evaluating this dimension of pragmatic thought, several other tenets and implications of pragmatism must also be kept in mind. For example, it is a misreading of the views of the major pragmatic thinkers to believe that they advocated automatic or inevitable progress in political affairs or any other realm of human existence. Time and again, James and Dewey acknowledged that humans may fail to respond effectively to challenges affecting their well-being. James was by no means certain that human society would succeed in discovering a moral equivalent to war. Toward the end of his life, Dewey became considerably less sanguine than earlier about modern man's ability to eliminate international conflict and to build a global community.

Nor is it a justifiable criticism of pragmatism to blame it for the "illusion of American omnipotence" or the impulse toward indiscriminate interventionism abroad. On several occasions, James, Dewey, and other pragmatists warned American society against the adverse consequences that would almost certainly accompany a "large" or increasingly interventionist foreign policy. Even before 1900, James cautioned his countrymen against trying to civilize the world or remake it in the image of the American democracy; James and Dewey were among the earliest critics of the policeman of the world mentality that eventually led to the nation's involvement in the Vietnam War.

Moreover, the pragmatic concept of global community implies collab-

35. De Gaulle and Steel are quoted in Robert A. Isaak, *American Democracy and World Power* (New York, 1977), 120; J. William Fulbright, *The Arrogance of Power* (New York, 1966).

orative efforts by the nations of the world to solve common problems. Pragmatic thought strongly argues against the diplomatic "do it yourselfism," or unilateral approach to global problem solving, that was an element in the Vietnam War tragedy and several other American diplomatic reverses since World War II.

Our discussion in earlier chapters has also emphasized the pragmatic concept of habituation, the belief that beneficial changes in human affairs are likely to come very slowly, as the members of society gradually exchange a new set of habits for old ones. Consequently, the pragmatic world view is antithetical to short-lived diplomatic "crusades" by the United States designed to eliminate communism, to modernize the Third World, to eradicate global poverty, and for comparable purposes. In the pragmatic view, a comprehensive and objective understanding of the problem—an element clearly lacking in the nation's intervention in Southeast Asia and in Lebanon—is the starting point of successful diplomacy. Pragmatic thinkers, like Dewey, repeatedly insisted that the means of foreign policy must be carefully chosen and must be consonant with the ultimate goal.

Pragmatic thought also supports another tendency, witnessed in American foreign policy since the Vietnam War: reexamination of recent diplomatic experience and modification of the nation's international commitments in light of it. In the pragmatic worldview, continuing *policy reevaluation on the basis of experience* is essential for diplomatic success and for the achievement of such goals as international peace, security, and an emerging sense of global community. A pragmatic approach to American diplomacy would strongly encourage the effort to learn from experience that has characterized the American foreign policy process in the post–Vietnam War period.

An eighth and final criticism of the pragmatic world view was highlighted by the members of the Russian delegation to the Soviet-American arms limitation talks in Geneva in 1985. According to one report, Soviet spokesmen were outspoken in complaining about the "zig-zags" in American foreign policy, especially when a new administration took office in Washington.[36] This is merely a contemporary example of one of the oldest and most enduring complaints about the diplomacy of the United States. During the 1950s, for example, a widely circulated Herblock cartoon depicted two mystified citizens discussing the Eisenhower administration's diplomacy. One citizen asked the other: "What is our 'firm and unswerving' Asian policy *today?*"

36. See the New York *Times*, May 30, 1985, dispatch by Seth Mydans.

A long list of examples might be cited to illustrate the inconsistencies, incongruities, and often abrupt changes of course that have marked American diplomatic experience since World War II. Under the Truman administration, for example, the containment policy was aimed at opposing communism in the Middle East, Asia, and other regions, yet the policy implicitly accepted its existence in Eastern Europe. Ever since the establishment of NATO in 1949, officials in Washington have deplored the lack of unity and common purpose in the Western alliance; at the same time, America's tendency to engage in unilateral decision making has often made such disunity inevitable. In the Middle East, Americans widely accepted the goal of self-determination for the Jewish people, which led to the creation of the state of Israel. Yet Americans have thus far been largely indifferent to the desire of the Palestinian people for their own homeland. The Carter administration was preoccupied with the problem of human rights violations by governments in Iran, the Philippines, South Korea, and other areas. It did not appear to be equally concerned about even more systematic and flagrant deprivation of liberty in the Soviet Union, Communist China, North Vietnam, and other Marxist-ruled states. On several occasions, President Ronald Reagan identified the Soviet Union as the "locus of evil" in the contemporary world. Yet Reagan lifted the existing grain embargo against trade with the USSR; he was extremely restrained in his reaction to possible Soviet violations of existing arms control agreements; and his administration entered into a new round of strategic arms control discussions with Soviet officials at Geneva. Meanwhile, even as the Reagan administration was endeavoring to ease tensions in Soviet-American relations, it showed no interest in a comparable resolution of outstanding differences with communist-ruled Nicaragua, Cuba, and North Vietnam.

These are merely a few examples illustrating the inconsistency of postwar American foreign policy. Writing in the mid-1970s, former Under Secretary of State George Ball complained that the foreign policy of the United States lacked an identifiable "frame of reference" to which its separate diplomatic moves could be meaningfully related. In Ball's view, White House adviser (and later, secretary of state) Henry Kissinger was the diplomatic "pragmatist" *par excellence.* Kissinger appeared to be interested in little more than "the managed play and counterplay of force," with no clear sense of direction to his diplomatic moves. Accordingly, Kissinger's "pragmatic diplomacy" had degenerated into "the manipulation of power without reference to any accepted body of rules or principles." A major defect of such diplomatic activity was that it was preoccupied with the short term and left no enduring diplomatic monuments.[37]

A few years later, a high-ranking Egyptian official expressed comparable judgments about the diplomacy of the Reagan administration. This official's assessment was that during the 1980s, American diplomatic moves in the Middle East and other regions were more often than not haphazard, disconnected, and unpredictable. In his view, the United States needs "a stable policy that is carefully planned and executed over a long period of time." For too many years, American diplomatic efforts had been marked by a lack of "a sense of direction" in dealing with global problems. Basically the same complaint was echoed earlier by a former American ambassador to Cairo, who said that during the 1950s the United States followed four different policies toward Egypt. The result was to foster the impression that "American diplomacy is unpredictable"; that it was not founded on "clear principles"; and that the United States lacked a consistent view of its own diplomatic interests. The record of American diplomacy toward Egypt convinced this spokesman that in the foreign policy field, Americans "react rather than act."[38]

Undeniably, pragmatism is a mode of thought that places a relatively low value on the logical consistency of human attitudes and behavior. The pragmatists implicitly accepted Ralph Waldo Emerson's assertion that "a foolish consistency is the hobgoblin of small minds." In the pragmatic conception of the process of cognition, mental activity is normally directed toward the solution of immediate problems, perceived by the mind as directly affecting human well-being. The pragmatists believed that these problems always existed *within a unique context of events and circumstances* and that effective solutions to them had to take full account of this reality. By contrast, closed ideological systems attempt to fit reality into a preexisting set of philosophical principles; in the process, they invariably oversimplify reality and ignore key (and often unique) conditions present within it. As applied to American foreign policy, such pragmatic tenets mean that the nation's diplomatic efforts must recognize the existence of highly diverse conditions overseas (along with related domestic forces affecting foreign affairs) and must tailor the American response to them.

37. George W. Ball, *Diplomacy for a Crowded World: An American Foreign Policy* (Boston, 1976), 307–309.

38. See the views of the Egyptian observer Osama el-Baz, in the New York *Times*, June 29, 1981. For a comparable complaint about the inconsistency of American foreign policy toward Japan, see Arafin Bey, "Japan's Defense Buildup," *International Journal of World Peace*, II (April–June, 1985), 30–33. Former American ambassador to Egypt John Badeau is quoted in Smith Simpson, *Anatomy of the State Department* (Boston, 1967), 122.

Take a specific problem in contemporary American diplomacy, such as the long-standing interest of the United States in promoting and strengthening democracy abroad. Few Americans would quarrel with the abstract assertion that, as the world's oldest democratic system, the United States should encourage the extension of democracy overseas. A long-range objective of American diplomacy remains the old Wilsonian objective of "making the world safe for democracy." Correctly or not, most Americans believe that a correlation exists between the growth of democracy abroad and the prospects for global peace and stability.

Yet as post—World War II diplomatic experience has repeatedly demonstrated, the American policy-making environment is highly pluralistic. Concurrently, Americans are committed to several other goals in foreign affairs, some of which may be in conflict with the promotion of democracy abroad. The American people also want their national leaders to preserve the security of the United States in the face of foreign threats; to create and maintain effective alliance systems so that the containment of communism and other goals involves a collaborative undertaking by several nations; particularly since the end of the Vietnam War, to avoid overcommitment abroad and to be more selective in assuming new overseas responsibilities; to respect the often strong sentiment in regions like Latin America against intervention by the United States in their internal affairs; and to formulate a clearer sense of diplomatic priorities, recognizing that some developments overseas directly involve America's diplomatic and strategic interests but others do not.

Faced with these manifold and often antithetical desires of the American people, officials in Washington have usually taken a pragmatic approach to the challenge of encouraging democracy abroad. Even under the Carter administration, which was more oriented toward international human rights questions than perhaps any other in the postwar era, considerable variation could be discerned in Washington's treatment of human rights issues in the Soviet Union, China, Iran, black Africa, and South Africa. In dealing with particular instances of human rights violations, American policy was governed by such diverse criteria as the strategic importance of the country to the United States; the nature of American ties with the country and the level of public and congressional interest in its political affairs; the assessment made by the president and his advisers of America's ability to influence the country's political development successfully; other overseas commitments and demands currently being made upon the power of the United States; and evaluations of the likely consequences to be expected from American efforts to change the country's political process fundamentally. For example, the pragmatic world view explicitly recognizes that in many cases (and American diplomacy toward the Iranian monarchy is a case in point), the *actual results* of overt American pressure on the incumbent government may be totally different from the intended results, and in some cases, the former may prove to be highly detrimental to the diplomatic interests of the United States.[39]

In brief, in company with the leading exponents of pragmatism, the diplomatic pragmatist is not unduly troubled by the existence of inconsistencies in American foreign policy, particularly over an extended period of time. If a choice must be made between judging each case on its merits and in the light of prevailing circumstances and blindly adhering to an ideologically rigid position in a dynamic external environment, the pragmatic mind seldom hesitates to choose the former course. In the pragmatic view, more damaging charges to bring against American diplomacy are that it is ineffectual, or that it is "out of touch with reality," or that it has not adapted to a highly diverse and often rapidly changing external environment. In the vast majority of cases perhaps, the more conspicuous failures in American diplomacy since World War II could be traced to these deficiencies rather than to the inconsistency of American attitudes and actions overseas.

Pragmatic Diplomacy: Profits and Payoffs

The distinguished American diplomatic historian Thomas A. Bailey once compiled a list of candidates for membership in the nation's diplomatic Hall of Fame. To his mind, towering above all other candidates for the honor was the "canny and urbane Jack-of-all-trades" Benjamin Franklin, the first minister to France. For Americans, Franklin exemplified a "practical," down-to-earth, and experimental approach to life—or the pragmatic spirit in the national ethos.[40]

The perceptive French student of American democracy Alexis de Tocque-

39. Highly varied assessments of recent American diplomatic efforts to promote human rights abroad are available in Sandra Vogelgesang, "What Price Principle?—U.S. Policy on Human Rights?" *Foreign Affairs*, LVI (July, 1978), 819–42; William Korey, "The Future of Soviet Jewry: Emigration or Assimilation?" *Foreign Affairs*, LVIII (Fall, 1979), 67–82; Robert C. Johansen, *The National Interest and the Human Interest: An Analysis of U.S. Foreign Policy* (Princeton, 1980); Donald P. Kommers and Gilburt D. Loescher (eds.), *Human Rights and American Foreign Policy* (Notre Dame, 1979); and Claude E. Welch, Jr., and Robert I. Meltzer, *Human Rights and Development in Africa* (Albany, N.Y., 1984).

40. Thomas A. Bailey, "Qualities of American Diplomats," in Elmer Plischke (ed.), *Modern Diplomacy: The Art and the Artisans* (Washington, D.C., 1979), 219–21.

ville once observed that the true genius of Americans lay in their ability to solve problems. A more recent student of the diplomatic process has said that skill in diplomacy is not acquired by abstract reasoning or any system of training but is "gained only after long experience."[41]

During an interview with Soviet Ambassador Anatoly Dobrynin on October 16, 1964, President Lyndon B. Johnson said that "his guard was up, but his hand was out." LBJ insisted that America's policy toward the Soviet Union was one of "peace and flexibility," and the president called on Moscow to reciprocate this approach in the interests of global peace and stability. Johnson's secretary of state, Dean Rusk, told his subordinates in the State Department that the foreign policy of the United States ultimately derived from "the kind of people we are . . . and from the shape of the world situation." A successful diplomat must be mindfull that "general principles" of American diplomatic behavior will "produce conflicting results in the factual situation with which he is confronted"; almost never will preexisting diplomatic positions "fit his problem because of crucial changes in circumstances." Every diplomatic decision involves "a galaxy of utterly complicated factors" that must be sorted out and handled "within a political system which moves by consent and in relation to an external environment which cannot be controlled."[42]

A leading student of recent Soviet-American relations has observed that in the United States (as in Great Britain), successful problem solving has resulted largely from the society's "pragmatic spirit." Pragmatic American minds realize that "most great problems are composed of a multitude of small ones"; they see little to be gained by raising "cosmic questions" or becoming endlessly bogged down in abstract debates over right and wrong. Indeed, the tendency of Americans is to avoid the search for the "philosopher's stone" that eliminates all doubts and uncertainties. Somehow, Americans learn to live with the paradoxes, dilemmas, and anomalies in which political decision making abounds. A White House adviser during the Reagan administration described himself as a "card-carrying pragmatist," who was interested primarily in "what works and what's feasible." Meanwhile, Reagan was described as "the picture of conciliation and caution" in his approach to foreign

41. Tocqueville is quoted in F. Clifton White and William J. Gill, *Why Reagan Won* (Chicago, 1981), 245–46; Hugh Gibson, in Plischke (ed.), *Modern Diplomacy*, 277.

42. The memorandum of Johnson's discussion with Ambassador Dobrynin on October 16, 1964, is in the Papers of Lyndon B. Johnson, National Security File (Aides File—McGeorge Bundy), Lyndon B. Johnson Memorial Library, Austin, Texas; Dean Rusk, "The Formulation of Foreign Policy," in *American Foreign Policy: Current Documents, 1961* (Washington, D.C., 1965), 22–28.

affairs. Above all, Reagan was interested in the *results* to be expected in choosing one course of action over another.[43]

In their diverse ways, each of these examples calls attention to the contribution of America's pragmatic tradition to the foreign policy of the United States. In Henry S. Commager's words, pragmatism became "almost the official philosophy of America"—and it largely remains so today. From the administrations of George Washington to Ronald Reagan, pragmatic modes of thought and behavior have profoundly influenced American diplomacy. On the basis of evidence provided by the outcome of the 1984 national election, the pragmatic impulses of the American people continue to shape their approach to internal and external policy questions; and no evidence exists that Americans are likely to abandon this historic propensity in the near future.[44]

The foreign policy of the United States has been momentously affected by pragmatically based attitudes and behavior patterns for several reasons. A major one is that pragmatic attitudes and actions have been characteristic of every major sphere of American life. Under these conditions, it would be strange if Americans did not apply these same pragmatic guidelines to the solution of diplomatic problems.

Yet the primary reason why Americans exhibit what we have called a "pragmatic world view," however, is that it possesses significant advantages over other approaches to external issues. To the American mind, pragmatically based diplomacy pays tangible dividends; it confers important benefits on the United States in foreign affairs; and, on balance, its advantages exceed its disadvantages. As emphasized earlier, a pragmatic world view unquestionably has shortcomings and defects. For informed Americans and their leaders, however, these are substantially outweighed by the attractions of a pragmatic approach to international problem solving. More specifically, what are the benefits to the United States of a pragmatic world view?

In the first place, a pragmatic orientation toward diplomatic questions is congenial to the American people because it "comes naturally" to them. It is compatible with their approach to the solution of domestic problems and is consonant with their customary behavior. It is the way most Ameri-

43. Adam B. Ulam, *The Rivals: America and Russia Since World War II* (New York, 1971), 281–82; Richard G. Darman's views are discussed in *Newsweek*, CIII (March 12, 1984), 37; *U.S. News and World Report*, XCIX (July 1, 1985), 23; and *ibid.* (July 22, 1985), 25. See also the views of Secretary of State George Shultz in the New York *Times*, November 25, 1982.

44. Henry S. Commager, *The American Mind: An Interpretation of American Thought and Character Since the 1880's* (New Haven, 1950), 97. See several of the essays in Ellis Sandoz and Cecil V. Crabb, Jr. (eds.), *Election '84: Victory Without a Mandate* (New York, 1985).

cans "meet life," often unconsciously and instinctively. Pragmatically based diplomacy, therefore, is a natural (and perhaps inevitable) application to the foreign policy field of long-established modes of thought and conduct that have been followed by Americans since colonial times.

By approaching international issues on a pragmatic basis, Americans are not required, in effect, to operate schizophrenically: it is not necessary for them to have one set of guidelines for solving internal problems and another (perhaps radically different) set for solving external problems. A pragmatic world view permits the American people and their leaders to "be themselves" or to rely on attitudinal and behavior guidelines that are familiar, natural, and whose application often requires little conscious planning and deliberation. Exhibiting a pragmatic world view is an almost automatic response of the American people to external problems. Indeed, given the minimal level of interest most Americans exhibit toward foreign affairs—a characteristic of general public opinion that continues to be a key reality of the foreign policy process—it seems questionable whether any other approach to foreign relations would actually work in the United States!

This is merely another way of acknowledging that, today as in the past, the United States continues to lack an overall theory of foreign relations that coherently integrates its diverse diplomatic activities. Historically (with the philosophical pragmatists), Americans have always been skeptical about monistic explanations and unicausal theories of reality. As in the New Deal, Americans have preferred to derive their ideological concepts from a wide range of sources and to blend these diverse ideas into their own unique ideological synthesis, which seems appropriate for prevailing conditions and existing problems. And they have preferred to test competing ideological claims by the pragmatic standard of *results,* in how well they enhance human well-being.

Neither the pre–World War II doctrine of isolationism nor the postwar concept of American internationalism constituted a unified and consistent theory of diplomacy. Isolationism was interrupted by numerous interventionist episodes and tendencies in American foreign policy. Similarly, since World War II (and most especially since the Vietnam War), the nation's internationalist policy has been characterized by *anti-interventionist* impulses and by strong neoisolationist currents in American public opinion. If, as the Carter administration discovered, the American people wanted to avoid another Vietnam abroad, in time they also insisted that the United States maintain its position and diplomatic credibility as a superpower. Or, as President Reagan and his advisers were clearly aware, in time the American people became deeply concerned about the relative deterioration of national military strength vis-à-vis the Soviet Union, and they were determined to regain a military position second to none in the world. Concurrently, however, as the Reagan White House was repeatedly reminded, the American people were no less apprehensive about the use of the nation's military arsenal abroad. Americans, however, showed no inclination to resolve or eliminate such paradoxes and inconsistencies by adopting a single, unified theory of foreign policy. In these and other dimensions of the nation's foreign relations, the American people routinely accepted such logical contradictions in their approach to external policy.[45]

In the second place, a pragmatic world view avoids (or endeavors to avoid) three pitfalls that are often associated with other possible approaches to American foreign policy. By insisting on the necessity for practicality and the need to place diplomatic activities in a specific context of time and circumstances, the pragmatic mentality serves to constrain the tendency toward utopianism that is always inherent in an idealistically motivated foreign policy. By definition, the idealist seeks to construct a political order existing only in the mind. By contrast, the pragmatist accepts Bismarck's well-known description of politics as "the art of the possible"; he believes that "half a [diplomatic] loaf is better than none"; he is always mindful that unintended consequences are likely to result from the commitment of American power abroad; and he understands that the means used to achieve foreign policy objectives may often be more crucial in determining the outcome than the goals themselves. The pragmatic mind is aware that when American diplomatic activity is motivated by pervasive idealistic illusions (as in many aspects of Wilsonian and New Deal diplomacy), the end result will likely be deep-seated disillusionment with the results achieved.[46]

But the pragmatic world view is no less conscious of certain serious shortcomings in an approach to foreign affairs based on *Realpolitik* principles. Our earlier treatment has emphasized that the pragmatic mind understands the dual nature of power in the political process. In international

45. See Norman R. Luttbeg (ed.), *Public Opinion and Public Policy: Models of Political Linkage* (Homewood, Ill., 1974); David W. Moore, "The Public Is Uncertain," *Foreign Policy,* XXXV (Summer, 1979), 68–74; and Daniel Yankelovich and John Doble, "The Public Mood," *Foreign Affairs,* LIII (Fall, 1984), 33–47.
46. Evidence of neoisolationist currents in recent American attitudes is presented in Ralph B. Levering, *The Public and American Foreign Policy, 1918–1978* (New York, 1978); and see the discussion of conservative and liberal neoisolationist thought in Cecil V. Crabb, Jr., *Policy-Makers and Critics: Conflicting Theories of American Foreign Policy* (2nd ed.; New York, 1986).

relations, the power of the United States and other nations may be used to devastate the planet and otherwise jeopardize human well-being, or it may be employed in a variety of useful ways for the benefit of human society. For the pragmatist, the standard is always *how power is used* in human relationships and the consequences of its use in particular cases. The salient question for national policy makers frequently is: In a specific context of events, *what kinds of power* will best promote the American society's goals? Yet pragmatists are no less mindful that, under certain circumstances, the *nonuse* of American power can lead to deleterious results, fully as much as its use.

In the pragmatic world view, other difficulties beset highly logical, elaborate, and often extremely abstract explanations of foreign policy such as game theory, systems theory, and decision-making theory. With rare exceptions (and the leading one, perhaps, is the application of game theory to such international problems as nuclear deterrence and arms control), such theories have had minimal appeal for the pragmatic American mind. Outside of academic circles, relatively few Americans understand such theories or are motivated to master their intricacies. Moreover, as even the devotees of these theories often concede, they can seldom be applied to specific diplomatic issues facing the United States. On the microanalytical level, their usefulness is severely limited. In addition, in recent years these theories have tended to proliferate, both in number and in complexity, at a rapid rate. Collectively, they encompass a constantly growing and highly diverse body of theoretical analyses.

Accordingly, for most Americans the standard of legitimacy for the nation's diplomatic efforts remains experience—or the same fundamental criterion relied upon by pragmatic thinkers for choosing among rival approaches to truth. For example, does the application of American power in an existing context of events at home and abroad make sense? Is it reasonable and defensible, in terms of the costs and probable consequences involved? Will it "create more problems than it solves" for the United States? Is it a step that Americans can "live with" in the months and years ahead? These pragmatically derived criteria are the ones Americans continue to apply to the conduct of foreign affairs, because they believe that such standards of judgment yield more satisfactory results than alternative criteria.

A former chairman of the Senate Foreign Relations Committee, Senator Frank Church (D.-Ida.), once observed:

The American people were not prepared by their national experience for the role of either ideological crusader or practitioner of the old-type 19th century Realpolitik. We came to believe that we could set a democratic example to the world by the way we governed our society, and we came to believe after each of the two world wars that it was worthwhile to try to build something new under the sun. There are, after all, no tried and true systems to fall back upon. The old Concert of Europe lay in ruins and the balance-of-power system had been utterly discredited. Under the circumstances, it seemed a reasonable, practical necessity to try to move forward in international relations from the rule of force to the rule of law. . . . That idea is still valid and it cannot be said that it has failed because it has never been tried.[47]

In Bruce Miroff's view, nearly all American presidents have "claimed the title 'pragmatic' for themselves." Routinely, an incumbent chief executive assures the American people that his administration is "not wedded to dogma" and that it will follow "a realistic and flexible course" in attempting to solve national problems. In the words of former President Richard M. Nixon, the American people expect their leaders to exhibit "pragmatism instead of dogmatism" in dealing with domestic and foreign issues. In the wake of their political defeat at the hands of Ronald Reagan in 1984, spokesmen for the Democratic party echoed basically the same idea. If they were to recover politically, said Governor Mario Cuomo of New York, Democrats had to "recapture the middle" of the political spectrum; they had to recognize that the voters were more interested in the results of public policy than in its ideological foundations or merits; and they had to avoid "extremist" positions on internal and external questions that alienated the average citizen. In brief, Cuomo contended, Democrats were compelled to become more closely identified with the American society's pragmatic tradition.[48]

In the third place, better than any alternative approach to international politics, a pragmatic world view equips the American mind to respond to the challenges posed by the existence of an increasingly pluralistic external uni-

47. See excerpts from Church's speeches in the New York *Times*, April 15, 1984.
48. Bruce Miroff, *Pragmatic Illusions: The Presidential Politics of John F. Kennedy* (New York, 1976), 283; interview with Nixon, in *Newsweek*, CIII (April 16, 1984), 34–35; interviews with several Democratic party leaders in *ibid.* (November 19, 1984), 60; and in the New York *Times*, November 17, 1984, dispatch by Fay S. Joyce.

verse. The pluralistic nature of the universe is a central tenet of pragmatic thought, and by the late twentieth century, it had become a dominant reality influencing American foreign policy. Pragmatists believe that, along with all other dimensions of human experience, the political environment is dynamic and ever-changing. A pluralistic environment contains both order and disorder, destructive and constructive, symmetrical and asymmetrical forces; invariably, it exhibits paradoxes, discontinuities, and contradictions. If humans are to survive and develop successfully in such a setting, the members of society must exhibit creative intelligence, adaptability, and common sense.

That the external political setting has become increasingly pluralistic since World War II is an assertion requiring no detailed proof. The postwar political milieu has been transformed by such momentous developments as the emergence of the United States and the Soviet Union as superpowers; the decline of Great Britain, Germany, France, and Japan as powerful global actors; the dawn of the nuclear age and the emergence of nuclear parity between the United States and the Soviet Union; the process of decolonization, followed by the emergence of some one hundred new members of the family of nations; the tendency toward polycentricity that has shattered the earlier unity of the Soviet-dominated communist bloc; and the growing unwillingness of America's allies to follow automatically diplomatic courses of action prescribed in Washington. By the late twentieth century, the pluralistic nature of the global political universe was perhaps its dominant characteristic.

A pragmatic orientation to American foreign policy both makes such changes more intelligible and equips Americans to respond to these tendencies more successfully. For example, the pragmatic mind is receptive to the idea—which is usually anathema to right-wing idealogues—that Soviet communism is susceptible to change and evolution in the light of experience. It believes that such changes have occurred in the USSR since 1917 and that other modifications can be expected in the Soviet system in the years ahead. At the same time, however, the pragmatic mentality is wary of the prospect that radical or dramatic changes can be anticipated in internal and external Soviet behavior, perhaps as the result of a new summit conference or because of a high level of scientific exchange or trade between the two superpowers.[49]

A pragmatically grounded assessment of Soviet-American relations, in

49. For evidence of reform within the Soviet system since 1917, see several of the essays in Curtis Keeble (ed.), *The Soviet State: The Domestic Roots of Soviet Foreign Policy* (Boulder, Colo., 1985), esp. 234–35; see also Richard Pipes, "Can the Soviet Union Reform?" *Foreign Affairs*, LXIII (Fall, 1984), 47–62.

other words, avoids two extremes that have sometimes characterized American attitudes toward the USSR. On one hand, it does not impute to communist ideology absolute doctrinal rigidity and imperviousness to change, which would render Soviet-American differences insoluble and perhaps guarantee the eruption of World War III. On the other hand, neither does the pragmatic world view expect sudden and drastic transformations in Soviet attitudes and behavior—least of all perhaps as a result of pressures from the United States or other external sources. The pragmatic world view is dubious that, with each successive change in Soviet leadership, the Kremlin's internal and external policies are automatically becoming more benign. (The pragmatists called attention to the biological reality that members of the animal species may retrogress as well as evolve). Yet the possibility of beneficial changes within the Soviet system exists, and American policy should be designed to encourage this evolution.

A pragmatic perspective on American foreign policy also believes that limited and modest progress in resolving some outstanding issues between the United States and the Soviet Union is possible. Furthermore, it holds that American officials must at all times assume the possibility of both rational and irrational behavior by the communist hierarchy in Moscow. The nation's leaders must presuppose that their Soviet counterparts are capable of perceiving existing realities (such as the nuclear balance of terror) and of responding rationally to them. Yet the pragmatic mind is no less cognizant that (as during the earlier Stalinist era), communist authorities sometimes engage in behavior dictated by aberrant psychological compulsions, personality traits, and other irrational and subjective forces. Prudence dictates, therefore, that the United States simultaneously be prepared for both rational and irrational Soviet conduct in foreign affairs. On that basis, the American people expect their leaders to keep trying to resolve the major sources of Soviet-American tensions, even while the United States maintains its military power in case such efforts fail or (as has occurred in the past) Moscow deliberately deceives Washington about its diplomatic intentions. In brief, the Truman administration's diplomatic principle of patience and firmness in dealing with Moscow continues to express American attitudes toward the Soviet challenge.

Another important sphere of recent American diplomacy that has been significantly influenced by the pluralistic nature of the universe is policy toward Eastern Europe. As much as any other single issue, disagreements between the United States and the Soviet Union over the future of this region—and, especially, over the political destiny of Poland—led to the disintegration of Allied unity after World War II. From the Roosevelt to the Reagan administrations, Americans have retained a keen interest in political developments in Eastern Europe.[50]

Following Yugoslavia's defection from the Soviet-dominated communist bloc in 1948, in time American officials acknowledged that polycentric tendencies were impairing the unity of international communism. Beginning with the Truman administration, Washington provided assistance to Yugoslavia—a vital step in enabling that country to preserve its position of independence in the face of continuing Soviet animosity. Yugoslavia ultimately emerged as a symbol of national communism and a spokesman for the nonaligned nations of the Third World. By the 1960s, American policy also recognized significant variations among the communist systems in Eastern Europe, between Poland and Romania, for example. The Johnson administration adopted a policy of "building bridges" to Eastern Europe in an effort to encourage the emergence of national communism behind the Iron Curtain.[51]

By the early 1980s, a report by the House Foreign Affairs Committee defined America's diplomatic goals toward Eastern Europe:

We intend to implement the policy of differentiation toward Eastern Europe in a manner which will encourage economic and political diversity in the region. We will proceed cautiously in calibrating our policy and our actions to grant more favorable treatment to those governments which either show relative independence from the USSR in the conduct of their foreign policy or which show relatively greater commitment to internal liberalization through the pursuit of political pluralism and economic decentralization. The U.S. Government will evaluate the actions and policies of each Eastern European nation on the basis of these criteria. Those nations which fail to show either internal relaxation or external independence will not be treated on a differentiated basis.[52]

Postwar American foreign policy toward Eastern Europe has been characterized by recognition that Soviet power throughout the region remains

50. See Piotr S. Wandycz, *The United States and Poland* (Cambridge, Mass., 1980); and the views of Secretary of State Edward Stettinius, quoted in Walter LaFeber, *America, Russia, and the Cold War, 1945–1984* (5th ed.; New York: 1985), 15.
51. Dean Acheson, *Present at the Creation: My Years in the State Department* (New York, 1969), 332–33; Alexander Dallin and Gail W. Lapidus, "Reagan and the Russians: United States Policy Toward the Soviet Union and Eastern Europe," in Kennedy A. Oye *et al.* (eds.), *Eagle Defiant: United States Foreign Policy in the 1980s* (Boston, 1983), 191–237.
52. U.S. Congress, House of Representatives, Committee on Foreign Affairs, *Developments in Europe, August, 1982* (Washington, D.C., 1982), 23.

pervasive and, in many respects, decisive; acceptance of the reality that historically and strategically, Eastern Europe *remains* a zone of extreme sensitivity for the Soviet Union, and this fact cautions against provocative American actions affecting the region; a conviction that the peoples of Eastern Europe are opposed to communism and to Soviet hegemony; a belief that the various Marxist systems of Eastern Europe differ in the prospects of their adopting democracy, their dependence on the USSR, and the nature of their ties with the West; and a realization that the United States possesses limited opportunities to "crack the Iron Curtain" or to encourage democratic tendencies within Eastern Europe, without at the same time provoking Moscow to impose even tighter control over its European satellites or precipitating new tensions in Soviet-American relations.[53]

Belief in a pluralistic universe, said William James, means that man must "live without assurances or guarantees"; humans must be content merely with "possibilities." Or, in the language of John Dewey, in accepting the idea of a pluralistic universe, man relinquishes the "quest for certainty" in the solution of human problems.[54] In many respects, America's policy of building bridges to Eastern Europe has disappointed both right-wing and left-wing critics. The former have been disaffected because the United States has not spearheaded a campaign to "liberate" the region from communist domination. Liberal critics have often been disconcerted because Washington has usually refrained from engaging in crusades designed to assure respect for human rights by governments behind the Iron Curtain.

Yet three things can be said in favor of postwar American policy toward Eastern Europe. One is that political conditions behind the Iron Curtain have not been made worse by overtly interventionist and emotionally dictated policies toward the region. Another has been that in several Eastern European societies, political conditions have improved moderately in the postwar era, and the possibility exists that communist authorities will allow at least limited political evolution in the future. Still another positive result of American policy—a precondition for evolution toward greater political freedom in all regions throughout the world—is that Soviet-American differences in Eastern Europe have not been permitted to escalate into World War III.

In the fourth place, a pragmatic mind-set in dealing with diplomatic problems contributes to *creativity and innovation* in the American approach to foreign affairs. For example, late in 1984 President Reagan called for "a better

53. See Alexander M. Haig, Jr., *Caveat: Realism, Reagan, and Foreign Policy* (New York, 1984), 238–61.
54. William James, *The Meaning of Truth* (Ann Arbor, 1970), 228–29; John Dewey, *The Quest for Certainty: A Study of the Relation of Knowledge and Action* (New York, 1929), 243–44.

working relationship" between the United States and the Soviet Union. The Reagan White House challenged Moscow to join Washington to "a new beginning" aimed at reducing the level of global armaments and resolving other outstanding differences between the two superpowers.[55]

In one way or another, nearly every American president in the twentieth century has called for a new beginning in efforts to resolve global problems. Theodore Roosevelt played a key role in concluding the Russo-Japanese War and in mediating a colonial dispute between Germany and France. Woodrow Wilson is identified with the concept of a "Brave New World" after World War I. More perhaps than any other single chief executive, Wilson was responsible for a long list of innovations, from the League of Nations to the democratization of diplomacy. Then, during the 1920s, Washington again led the way in efforts to reduce the level of global armaments, to outlaw war, and to settle international disputes by peaceful means.

The administration of Franklin D. Roosevelt was another innovative era in the nation's diplomatic record. FDR and his advisers produced one blueprint after another designed to create a more peaceful and stable international system after World War II. The reciprocal trade program, to which the United States has been committed for a half-century; the sweeping reform of the German and Japanese political systems under the Allied occupation following the Axis defeat; the second attempt to create an effective international organization, the United Nations; new multinational institutions such as the World Bank and the International Monetary Fund; efforts by the Roosevelt and Truman administrations to accelerate the process of decolonization in the postwar world; the Roosevelt administration's emphasis on the necessity for a bipartisan approach to postwar problems, in a largely successful effort to assure a high degree of national unity toward major diplomatic issues were among the leading examples of new and creative ideas in the diplomacy of the New Deal.

Other examples may be given of this same creative impulse in postwar American foreign policy. The Truman presidency was especially prone to this tendency. The Greek-Turkish Aid Program (1947), tangibly expressing the containment strategy; the European Recovery Program (Marshall Plan) the following year; NATO in 1949; the Point Four program of American aid to developing societies in 1949–1950, and the Uniting for Peace resolution, which saved the United Nations from total deadlock during the Korean

55. Reagan's speech is in the New York *Times*, September 25, 1984.

War were innovative landmarks of the Truman administration's diplomatic record.

President Eisenhower sponsored the Open Skies disarmament proposal in 1955, designed to give new impetus to the search for common ground between Washington and Moscow in arms control negotiations. President John F. Kennedy's administration witnessed an unprecedented interest in Washington in promoting the modernization of the Third World. The Kennedy White House sponsored the Alliance for Progress, whose goal was the rapid social, economic, and political development of Latin America. Moreover, by the early 1960s, officials in Washington had largely accepted the desire of most Third World societies to remain diplomatically nonaligned.

President Nixon took the lead in normalizing relations between the United States and the People's Republic of China, a process consummated by the Carter administration when the two nations reestablished formal diplomatic relations. Moreover, the Nixon Doctrine was an attempt to redirect American diplomacy in light of the Vietnam War experience. After prolonged negotiations, the Ford administration concluded the SALT I arms control agreement with the Soviet Union. Under the Carter administration, substantial progress was made in reaching a second agreement (SALT II), which was not ratified by the United States, primarily because of the Soviet invasion of Afghanistan.

With regard to the Soviet Union, for the most part, Washington has successfully avoided two diplomatic tendencies, either of which could have had highly deleterious consequences not only for the United States but for other countries as well. On one hand, the Roosevelt administration's disillusioning experiences with Moscow during the Stalinist era caused Americans to abandon the romantic expectation that goodwill gestures, expressions of friendship, and unilateral concessions by the United States would assure cooperative and constructive Soviet-American relations. On the other hand, as illustrated by the Kennedy administration's handling of the Cuban missile crisis in 1962, American officials have time and again been careful not to back the Soviet hierarchy into a corner, leaving it no alternative except to protect its diplomatic interests by force. Despite the high level of its anticommunist rhetoric, the Reagan administration was in nearly all cases extremely cautious in its diplomatic behavior toward the Soviet Union.

Our emphasis upon the more creative and innovative aspects of the recent American diplomatic record is not intended to imply of course that all these new ideas and proposals have been fully successful in achieving their objectives. A conspicuous example to the contrary, as most informed citizens are aware, is that since 1946 the United Nations has not fulfilled the high hopes of its founders. Similarly, in many cases American expectations associated with the foreign aid program have often been disappointed. Sometimes also, as with several aspects of Wilsonian diplomacy, Americans have been ahead of their time in proposing reforms and new initiatives for the international system. In still other cases (the Alliance for Progress is a prominent example), Americans have underestimated the obstacles in the path of achieving goals such as the rapid modernization of Latin American societies. Yet insofar as the conduct of international relations needed and benefited from a new beginning in the solution of age-old problems, as often as not the impetus has been supplied by the pragmatically oriented American society.

In the fifth place, a pragmatic perspective on international relations recognizes the essential untidiness and heterogeneity of both the American foreign policy process and the global environment toward which it is directed. This aspect of a pragmatic world view is illustrated by a recent study of American nuclear strategy. The nation's defense doctrine—sometimes called "countervailing strategy," or the ability to answer an enemy threat at any level of violence—has been described as plagued by "inconsistencies, incoherencies, and contradictions." Viewed from a strictly logical perspective, the policy "makes no sense" and should be discarded as an absurdity. Yet despite its logical defects, somehow the strategy has worked; it has preserved a relatively high degree of stability in Soviet-American relations since the early post–World War II era, and the threat of nuclear conflict between the superpowers has diminished in recent years.[56] As a result, less powerful nations can and do engage in conventional or nonnuclear conflicts with a high degree of assurance that the United States and the Soviet Union will not become directly involved in them.

Former Secretary of State Dean Acheson once observed that foreign policy is not "made" in the customary sense at the highest levels of government. Instead, foreign policy is usually "the sum total of many decisions"; experienced public officials know that the "springs of [foreign] policy bubble up; they do not trickle down." W. Averell Harriman recalled Edmund Burke's judgment, "Circumstances are infinite, are infinitely combined, are variable and transient." Therefore, in Burke's view, the statesman must always "be

---

56. See Robert Jervis, *Illogic of American Nuclear Strategy* (Ithaca, N.Y., 1984); and the review of Jervis' analysis by François Sauzey, *New York Times Book Review*, August 5, 1984.

guided by circumstances," and he must be wary of the advice of "true believers, doctrinaires and dogmatists" in resolving questions of public policy.[57]

Another experienced American diplomatic official, Roger Hilsman, has emphasized that decision making in foreign affairs always involves an attempt to harmonize or synthesize several more or less compatible goals and ideas. "It is not a question of whether this or that value should be pursued, but what *mixture* of values should be pursued." Hilsman has called attention to one of Kennedy's outstanding qualities as the nation's chief diplomat. Kennedy had very little confidence in anyone's "infallibility," including his own. By contrast, he exhibited a "large perspective," which took accout of "human weakness." As a result, he could simultaneously respond decisively to Moscow's effort to install offensive Soviet missiles in Cuba and seek new ways of lowering Soviet-American tensions. In brief, he understood the essential "untidiness, the inconsistencies and internal contradictions" of the foreign policy process.[58]

Former Under Secretary of State George Ball has said that foreign policy above all "is the art of the practical." In dealing with the Soviet Union since World War II, Ball believes that the United States has explicitly or implicitly accepted certain realities and practical constraints upon its diplomatic behavior. For example, Washington has largely accommodated itself to the existence of a Soviet sphere of influence in Eastern Europe. In waging the Korean War, the United States accepted the existence of North Korea and in time came to the realization that the Korean War could not be won decisively without risking a wider regional or global conflict.[59] By the late 1960s (owing in no small measure to George Ball's dissenting views), the Johnson administration finally concluded that the Vietnam War was unwinnable within the constraints imposed by public opinion, allied opinion, and overall costs. During the early 1980s, the Reagan administration came to basically the same conclusion about its efforts to achieve political unity and stability in strife-torn Lebanon.

Experience during the 1980s provided additional evidence of the growing untidiness and paradoxical nature of the American foreign policy process, particularly as it related to the role of public opinion in diplomatic decision

57. Dean Acheson, *Grapes from Thorns* (New York, 1972), 110–11; Introduction to W. Averell Harriman, *America and Russia in a Changing World: A Half-Century of Personal Observation* (Garden City, N.Y., 1971), x–xi.

58. Roger Hilsman, *To Move a Nation: The Politics of Foreign Policy in the Administration of John F. Kennedy* (Garden City, N.Y., 1967), 553, 581.

59. Ball, *Discipline of Power*, 301–302.

making. To a degree unprecedented since World War II perhaps, after the Vietnam conflict American public opinion exhibited ambiguities and anomalies toward foreign, and related domestic, policy questions. Although the polls showed that the American people were *nominally* identified 45 percent with the Democratic party and 25 percent with the Republican party, the political allegiances and ideological inclinations of the people were becoming progressively more fluid and difficult to categorize. One study found that the sentiments of a substantial number of Americans are somewhere between the positions of the two major political parties! Under Reagan's leadership, Republicans were described as having "become diplomatically isolationist and militarily internationalist. The Democrats . . . are becoming the opposite."[60]

"Our philosophic and religious development," William James once observed, "proceeds . . . by credulities, negations, and the negation of negations." A remarkable characteristic of the American mind, said Jacques Maritain, is that (in contrast to its European counterpart) the American mentality exhibits a certain "*modesty* before life and reality which is a great moral virtue and dynamic quality of considerable efficacy." The ordinary American does not believe he "has all the answers; he is able to say, 'I don't know.' "[61] And the American novelist F. Scott Fitzgerald once commented that an essential attribute of a mature and intelligent mind was its ability to entertain two contradictory ideas at the same time.

These observations have evident application to the conduct of American diplomacy. Since World War II, in nearly every dimension American foreign policy has exhibited paradoxical and contradictory qualities. The concept of "peace through strength" (a paraphrase of the old Roman dictum "If you want peace, prepare for war!"); the creation of an increasingly powerful American military establishment, designed in part to induce Moscow to *reduce* the level of global armaments; the maintenance of global peace by reliance on a "nuclear balance of terror"; the containment strategy—or the idea of American intervention abroad to counter Soviet intervention; the provision of large-scale and continuing American foreign aid to the developing nations to encourage them to become economically self-sufficient; repeated calls for partnership within the NATO alliance, while officials in Washington continue to engage in unilateral decision making; pleas from the

---

60. Richard Reeves, "The Ideological Election," *New York Times Magazine,* February 19, 1984, pp. 26–29, 80–91.
61. William James, "The Energies of Men," *Philosophical Review,* XVI (January, 1907), 1–20; Jacques Maritain, *Reflections on America* (New York, 1958), 96.

White House for bipartisan cooperation in foreign affairs, even as the president and his executive advisers continue to make crucial diplomatic decisions—these are among the more outstanding examples of paradoxical and illogical aspects of the American foreign policy process.

Pragmatically oriented minds readily acknowledge the existence of such paradoxes but are not unduly troubled by them. Pragmatists are aware that some of Western culture's most profound and widely accepted ethical and moral precepts are equally mind-boggling, enigmatic, and mystifying. The suffering inflicted on Job in the Old Testament and the concept of the "suffering servant"; such Christian principles as the teaching that "the meek shall inherit the earth" and that "the first shall be last, and the last first"; beliefs like "love conquers all" and "the pen is mightier than the sword"; legal precepts like "liberty under law"; political axioms like "that government is best which governs least" are merely a few examples of paradoxes existing in other realms of human experience that are familiar to Americans and are routinely accepted in their everyday lives.

Meanwhile, the pragmatically inclined American tries somehow to "get on" and to resolve urgent problems in domestic and foreign affairs on the basis of imperfect knowledge; to improve the human condition within the limits of finite capabilities; and to devote his energies mainly to the solution of concrete human problems, rather than endeavoring to construct a logically consistent world.

In the sixth place, a pragmatic world view equips the American mind to keep uppermost an idea that was dramatically conveyed by the Vietnam War experience and by more recent developments, such as the challenge posed by the growing incidence of international terrorism. This is greater public and official awareness of the *limits of American power.*

A pragmatic perspective on American diplomacy remembers General Andrew Jackson's order to his troops at the Battle of New Orleans, when he directed his men to "elevate them damn guns a little lower." Applying Jackson's principle to American foreign policy, it would not be amiss to say that many of the failures in the nation's diplomacy since World War II have had their origins in excessive popular and official *expectations* about what the United States was capable of accomplishing abroad. In instance after instance, the diplomatic efforts of the United States fell short of achieving goals that were partially or wholly unattainable, even by a superpower.

For all his personal magnetism and charisma, even President Franklin D. Roosevelt was unable to charm Stalin's government into abandoning many of its expansionist diplomatic goals and cooperating with the United States and other nations to maintain a peaceful postwar order. Most informed students of New Deal diplomacy are agreed that FDR's genuine quest for cooperative Soviet-American relations after World War II was probably doomed from the inception.

Both Roosevelt and Truman failed in their repeated attempts to assure the emergence of a democratically ruled and pro-Western China after World War II. Even if Chiang Kai-shek and his followers had won the Chinese civil war, American hopes were most likely doomed to disappointment. (The still authoritarian rule of Chiang's successors on Taiwan today testifies to the obstacles facing Western-style democracy in Chinese culture.) The United States "lost China" to communist rule on the mainland primarily because it never "had" China. The nation's political destiny would be—and was— determined primarily by forces, traditions, and behavior patterns indigenous to China itself and beyond the capacity of the United States, or any other foreign power, to influence decisively.[62]

The Kennedy and successive administrations in Washington have thus far failed to assure the survival of democracy, of stable political systems, and of corruption-free governments in Latin America. Admittedly, by the mid-1980s the prospects for the future of democracy south of the border appeared to be more favorable than during the 1960s (the restoration of civilian rule in Argentina, for example, was an encouraging development, as was Brazil's efforts to solve its internal problems by democratic means). Yet on balance, the high hopes associated with the Alliance for Progress during the Kennedy and Johnson administrations have not been realized.[63] Almost without exception, Latin American nations confront a long list of extremely serious and deeply entrenched problems, some of which will almost certainly become more acute with the passage of time. As illustrated by the recent experience of Mexico, corruption and maladministration continue to be pervasive throughout the region, with little prospect that long-promised reforms will be successfully implemented. Moreover, by the

62. America's lack of understanding of political developments in modern China is emphasized in the authoritative treatment by John K. Fairbank, *The United States and China* (New York, 1962). See also Warren I. Cohen, *America's Response to China* (New York, 1971); and Herbert Feis, *The China Tangle* (Princeton, 1953).

63. Recurring issues in United States–Latin American relations are identified and discussed in Martin C. Needler, *The United States and the Latin American Revolution* (Boston, 1972); Federico Gil, *Latin American–United States Relations* (New York, 1971); and Michael Oisken (ed.), *Trouble in Our Backyard: Central America and the United States in the Eighties* (New York, 1984).

mid-1980s—as illustrated by the vocal criticisms directed against the Reagan administration's diplomacy in Central America—relations between the United States and Latin America remained at a low ebb.

On a different front, efforts by successive American presidents to achieve an equitable and durable peace in the Middle East have proved unsuccessful. President Harry S. Truman and many of his advisers, for example, were confident that in time the Arab states would "accept" the state of Israel and arrive at a peace settlement with it. By the late 1970s, President Jimmy Carter similarly expected that the Camp David peace agreements between Israel and Egypt would provide impetus for an overall resolution of the Arab-Israeli conflict. Instead, throughout the years that followed, conflict between Israel and several Arab nations intensified, and by the late 1980s, Israel's overall position in the Middle East remained highly vulnerable.[64]

These examples call attention to the extent to which American diplomatic aspirations have often greatly exceeded the results achieved by the nation's diplomatic efforts. In these and other cases, it has sometimes been difficult for the American people and their leaders to understand the subtle but crucial distinction between possessing great power and *infinite power.* The emergence of the United States as a superpower since World War II does not mean that it has an unlimited ability to alter the global political environment at will, in accordance with American desires.

The nation's pragmatic philosophical tradition should serve to constrain such rampant illusions and diplomatic miscalculations. Despite certain widespread misconceptions, pragmatic thought does not encourage unlimited optimism about the human condition, about man's ability to transform the environment, and about the prospects of achieving such diplomatic goals as universal peace, security, democracy, and global understanding. In some measure, pragmatism was a philosophical reaction against fatuous Yankee optimism and the "rugged individualism" pervasive during the nineteenth century. For example, William James was outspoken in condemning what he called "naturalistic optimism," which to his mind was a form of philosophical "flattery and sponge cake." Even when they were characterized by the loftiest motives and most strenuous efforts, attempts to improve the human condi-

64. Relations between the United States and the Zionist movement, leading to the creation of the state of Israel in 1948, are examined in Spiegel, *The Other Arab-Israeli Conflict;* William B. Quandt, *Decade of Decision: American Policy Toward the Arab-Israeli Conflict, 1967–1976* (Berkeley, 1977); and Bernard Reich, *Quest for Peace: United States–Israeli Relations and the Arab-Conflict* (New Brunswick, N.J., 1977).

tion would not necessarily lead to what James called a "trimphant conclusion." As a rule, James cautioned, humans must anticipate that their efforts
will produce "limited success."[65]

John Dewey expressed basically the same idea (in uncharacteristically
theological terms), when he said that humans must always bear in mind that
they "are not the creators of heaven and earth"; only to a limited degree are
developments in the cosmos or on earth subject to the conscious will of man.
In Dewey's view, mankind does not have the capacity "to dominate the future. The power of man and mouse is infinitely constricted in comparison
with the power of events."[66]

Early in his political career, the nineteenth-century British political
leader William Gladstone was advised that he must quickly "learn to put up
with imperfect results." By contrast, the moral conveyed by literary master-
pieces such as *Faust* and *Paradise Lost* is that "grace derives from a sense of
one's limitations and that tragedy is the wage of losing that sense." Or, as an
experienced American diplomatic official observed, the foreign policy of the
United States is in large measure "a response to situations arising beyond the
national jurisdiction and therefore beyond our government's control." In a
literal sense, the effort to influence the behavior of other nations and political
movements abroad is *foreign* policy: it is action by the United States beyond
the compass of American law and frequently beyond the enlightened understanding of American citizens. At one point in his State Department career,
this official was confronted by a citizen who demanded that he predict the
course of American foreign policy several years ahead. His reply to the repeated inquiry was that "the main . . . predictable element" facing the
United States abroad "was *trouble,* which was bound to proliferate along our
course." Or in the words of a leading student of the diplomatic process,
relatively few individuals understand "how infrequent and adventitious is
the part played in great affairs by 'policy' or planned intentions"; in reality, it
is seldom that "the course of events [is actually] determined by deliberately
planned purpose." In a recent paraphrase of this idea, in the mid-1980s
Secretary of State George Shultz defined his diplomatic efforts to resolve the
Arab-Israeli conflict by saying that his limited goal was to "keep the level of
frustration down and the level of effort up."[67]

65. William James is quoted in Bruce W. Wilshire (ed.), *William James: The Essential Writings* (New York, 1971), xiii–xiv.
66. John Dewey, *Human Nature and Conduct: An Introduction to Social Psychology* (New York, 1930), 205–206.
67. The anecdote about Gladstone is recounted in Charles B. Marshall, *The Limits of Foreign*

Better understanding of America's pragmatic tradition should serve to constrain the disappointments, setbacks, and frustrations that nearly always accompany unlimited expectations associated with American diplomatic activities. Diplomacy based on pragmatic principles should enable the American ship of state to maintain a course of "steady as she goes" in often rough international waters. It would serve to prevent abrupt and perhaps dangerous changes of diplomatic course in one of two directions.

On one hand, the ideas of William James, John Dewey, and other pragmatic thinkers should go far toward inhibiting the national disillusionment and aversion to participation in global affairs that followed World War I and massively influenced American attitudes toward foreign relations in the wake of the Vietnam War. In these and other instances, the attitudes of Americans toward the outside world were marked by an abnormally high level of popular disenchantment about the results of American diplomatic efforts; by pervasive feelings of frustration, doubt, and guilt about the use of American power abroad; and by a resurgence of isolationist sentiments among the American people. The failure of America's effort to save Southeast Asia from communist domination was followed during the 1970s by widespread skepticism that the United States could accomplish *any* worthwhile purpose abroad, and some citizens became convinced that the arrogance of American power was the principal threat to global peace and security. From an ill-informed optimism about the nation's ability to transform the world (or a portion of it), American opinion had swung abruptly to a national mood of self-doubt, aversion to external problems, and serious neglect of the diplomatic interests of the United States.

A pragmatic world view no less serves to curb the opposite impulse in American diplomacy. This is diplomatic hubris or the tendency toward indiscriminate and poorly understood efforts to remake the world in the American image. Time and again—and the diplomacy of the Wilson and Roosevelt administrations provide numerous examples—the principle that "the Yanks are coming" has unquestionably governed the nation's foreign policy: Americans widely believed that their energetic and dedicated efforts would make possible the solution of global and regional problems that had thus far defied solutions by other nations. Thus President Franklin D. Roosevelt expected to solve the "Russian problem" by relying on his personal charisma, his position

---

Policy (New York, 1954), 27–28; the following quotation is from *ibid.*, 16, italics added. Sir Harold Nicholson, quoted *ibid.*, 11. Shultz's diplomatic activities in the Middle East are analyzed in the New York *Times*, May 17, 1985, dispatch by Bernard Gwertzman.

of global leadership, and his skill in political manipulation. President Truman believed that, despite failure by the British and others earlier, he could gain Arab acceptance of Zionist goals in Palestine. President John F. Kennedy and his advisers had few doubts that they could engage in successful nation-building throughout the Third World. President Richard M. Nixon and his chief foreign policy aide, Henry Kissinger, believed that they could create and maintain a "new structure for peace" in the post–Vietnam War era. The Reagan administration was equally confident that it could succeed, where earlier efforts had failed, in restoring peace and political stability to strife-torn Lebanon.

If more intelligent understanding of the American pragmatic tradition imparts steadiness, a greater degree of realism, good judgment, and common sense to the nation's diplomatic efforts, this fact will go far toward avoiding many of the setbacks and disappointments witnessed in the foreign relations of the United States since World War II.

In the seventh place, insight into the pragmatic tradition sheds light on another distinctive, and often mystifying, characteristic of the nation's diplomatic behavior. Beginning with the administration of Franklin D. Roosevelt, the foreign policy of the United States has usually existed on two levels. Normally, an incumbent administration has had a *declaratory or rhetorical policy* abroad, and it has also had an *operational policy* toward other countries. In many cases, these policies have been antithetical and contradictory. In turn, this quality of American diplomatic conduct has engendered confusion at home and abroad concerning the nation's true diplomatic intentions and raised questions about whether the United States in fact even *had* a foreign policy.

As much as any occupant of the Oval Office, Roosevelt can be viewed as the embodiment of American idealism, and considerable evidence can be cited from the record of the New Deal to support this contention. From the day he entered the White House in 1933, FDR made numerous idealistic pronouncements in the foreign policy field. During the 1930s, for example, Roosevelt time and again urged the nations of the world to resolve their differences by peaceful means, called upon them to observe international law, and offered his services in behalf of peaceful negotiations. With Winston Churchill, on August 14, 1941, FDR issued the Atlantic Charter, enunciating several high-minded principles that would guide the Allied war effort. At the Yalta Conference early in 1945, Roosevelt gained Soviet agreement to a Declaration on Liberated Europe, designed to assure the future of democracy in

Eastern Europe. Above all, perhaps, the Roosevelt administration was determined to create a new and successful international organization—the United Nations—that would assume primary responsibility for international peacekeeping in the postwar era.

Yet as has been true of nearly every other administration since the end of World War II, FDR's diplomacy also existed on another level—the plane of *pragmatic action.* This dimension of New Deal diplomacy consisted of a series of separate and often unrelated moves which the Roosevelt White House made *in response to specific circumstances and challenges confronting the United States abroad.* Collectively, these diplomatic activities constituted the operational policies of the Roosevelt administration, and as often as not, they were in marked contrast to its diplomatic pronouncements and rhetoric.

Noteworthy examples of FDR's operational policies include his efforts during the 1930s to subordinate foreign policy issues to the more compelling task of promoting the economic recovery of the United States; Roosevelt's approval of efforts (widely denounced in later years as appeasement of the Axis dictators) to resolve existing global disputes by negotiations; after 1941, his conception of himself as the leader of the Allied coalition and his readiness to make key military and political decisions with minimum consultation with spokesmen for other governments; his expectation that the Big Five (the Soviet Union, the United States, Great Britain, France, and China) would determine the nature of the postwar order (decisions often in fact made by Moscow and Washington alone); and FDR's penchant for secrecy, with neither Congress nor the American people cognizant of many of his far-reaching diplomatic decisions. With rare exceptions, the Roosevelt administration's operational policies were the ones that crucially affected the direction of American diplomacy and the course of world history during and after World War II.[68]

The same basic dualism could be discerned in the diplomatic behavior of the Eisenhower administration. Ideologically, of course, its foreign policy rhetoric contrasted sharply with that of the Roosevelt and Truman administrations. As exemplified by Secretary of State John Foster Dulles, during the 1950s the Eisenhower administration's rhetorical position was militantly anticommunist. Dulles conceived of the global conflict with communism in

68. The disparity between FDR's declaratory and his operational policies abroad is highlighted in James M. Burns, *Roosevelt: The Lion and the Fox* (New York, 1956). See also the fundamentally different interpretations of Roosevelt's diplomacy in Warren F. Kimball (ed.), *Franklin D. Roosevelt and the World Crisis, 1937–1945* (Lexington, Mass., 1973); and Gaddis Smith, *American Diplomacy During the Second World War, 1941–1945* (New York, 1966).

Manichean terms; other countries were either "for" or "against" the United States vis-à-vis the Soviet Union; and to his mind, the professed "neutralism" or nonalignment of most Afro-Asian nations was highly suspect. Dulles' announced approach to preventing new Soviet gains at the expense of the free world was his "brink of war" strategy, based on the premise that the United States was ready to use its superior nuclear arsenal at the first sign of communist expansionism. Under the Eisenhower administration the United States also greatly expanded its military alliance systems on the theory that communism presented mainly a military challenge to the free world.[69]

Yet several commentators believed that in reality the Eisenhower-Dulles team had two foreign policies—one declaratory and the other operational. If the former tended to be ideologically rigid, uncompromising, and sometimes even provocative, the latter was marked by caution, moderation, and flexibility and was, for the most part, consistent with the earlier diplomatic activities of the Truman administration. Right-wing ideological rhetoric to the contrary, the Eisenhower-Dulles team did not attempt to "liberate" Eastern Europe from communism during the Hungarian revolt in 1956. Nor, despite frequent Republican denunciations of it, did the Eisenhower White House repudiate the Yalta Agreement, which had served as the basis for American protests against Soviet intervention in Eastern Europe. With the Truman administration earlier, the Eisenhower administration did not escalate the Korean War, and it agreed to accept an armistice that in effect restored the territorial and political *status quo* in Korea. Eisenhower's intervention in Lebanon in 1957 was limited and short-lived. Eisenhower and Dulles were conscious of the Soviet Union's growing nuclear arsenal and of the dangers of unchecked arms rivalry between the superpowers for the future of civilization. Accordingly, the administration made several imaginative proposals designed to limit the arms race. In addition, by the late 1950s the Eisenhower White House was coming to terms with the idea that the vast majority of Afro-Asian nations desired to remain diplomatically nonaligned.[70]

The same dualism could be identified in the diplomacy of President John F. Kennedy. As a Democrat, JFK was in the Rooseveltian tradition;

69. See, for example, the discussion of Dulles' ideological rhetoric in Leonard Mosley, *Dulles: A Biography of Eleanor, Allen, and John Foster Dulles and Their Family Network* (New York, 1978), 306–308.

70. See the evaluations of the diplomacy of the Eisenhower administration in Fred A. Greenstein, *The Hidden-Hand Presidency: Eisenhower as a Leader* (New York, 1982); Herbert S. Parmet, *Eisenhower and the American Crusades* (New York, 1972); and Peter Lyon, *Eisenhower: Portrait of the Hero* (Boston, 1974).

more than any other postwar chief executive, perhaps, he became a symbol of American idealism and liberal political values. His popularity was high throughout the Third World (and particularly in black Africa). During his brief tenure in the White House, Kennedy time and again cautioned the world against the dangers of nuclear war and urged the superpowers to resolve their differences on the basis of a common interest in avoiding nuclear devastation. JFK also warned his fellow citizens against the "illusion of American omnipotence," and he specifically cautioned the nation against a tendency to believe that it could single-handedly save Southeast Asia from communism. As we have seen, Kennedy reversed Washington's long neglect of Latin America by sponsoring the Alliance for Progress, designed to promote development, modernization, and democracy within the Western Hemisphere.

Yet when viewed from an operational perspective, the diplomacy of the Kennedy administration can be assessed very differently. From this vantage point, JFK's diplomatic moves were highly pragmatic, heavily influenced by time and circumstances, and often in marked contrast to Kennedy's image as a symbol of American idealism. Shortly after he entered the Oval Office, for example, Kennedy approved the ill-fated Bay of Pigs invasion of Cuba—an overtly interventionist attempt to displace Castro's communist regime. The following year, Kennedy brought the world to the brink of nuclear war with the Soviet Union in the Cuban missile crisis—the most ominous Soviet-American confrontation since World War II. (Yet during this crisis the Kennedy White House was careful to give the Kremlin "a way out" to avoid the appearance of a one-sided Soviet diplomatic defeat.) On several occasions, President Kennedy reiterated America's determination to defend the Western position in Berlin from communist encroachments. Similarly (in tones reminiscent of the Eisenhower administration), the Kennedy White House affirmed America's determination to prevent the communization of Southeast Asia, and under Kennedy, the process of direct and growing American military involvement in the defense of South Vietnam was begun. Once again, by most criteria Kennedy's operational policies were the most decisive and enduring aspect of his diplomacy.[71]

Some two decades later, commentators at home and abroad identified the same dualism in the diplomacy of the Reagan administration. From a rhetorical perspective, by many criteria the Reagan White House was the

---

71. See Theodore Sorensen, *Kennedy* (New York, 1965); and Schlesinger, *Thousand Days*. A treatment of the Kennedy administration's diplomacy which questions JFK's idealism is Richard J. Walton, *Cold War and Counter-Revolution: The Foreign Policy of John F. Kennedy* (Baltimore, 1973).

most conspicuously ideological of any administration since World War II. After he entered the Oval Office in 1981, hardly a week passed in which Reagan and his advisers did not fire an ideological broadside at the Soviet Union as the "locus of evil" in the contemporary world, did not denounce "gangster governments" that encouraged or supported international terrorism, or did not otherwise vent their right-wing ideological indignation against diplomatic adversaries. From Western Europe to Japan, the Reagan administration raised the level of ideological confrontation throughout the world.[72]

Despite these right-wing ideological propensities, in practice the operational policies of the Reagan White House contrasted sharply with its militant ideological rhetoric. Particularly after George Shultz replaced Alexander Haig as secretary of state in 1982, Reagan's diplomatic behavior was consistently pragmatic. With occasional exceptions, the diplomacy of the Reagan White House was cautious, restrained, flexible, and in conformity with mainstream public opinion in the United States. For the most part, toward foreign policy issues Reagan and his advisers usually ignored their own ideological statements in favor of behavior that was reasonable, moderate, and responsive to the particular conditions confronting the United States abroad.

After repeatedly expressing his administration's adamant opposition to the idea, for example, the Reagan White House ultimately accepted the decision by the European allies to acquire natural gas from the Soviet Union. Nor did the Reagan administration's ideological hostility to communism prevent it from lifting the boycott on American grain sales to the Soviet Union or from encouraging an expansion in other commercial contacts between the superpowers. After it had become evident that his proclaimed goals could not be achieved in Lebanon, Reagan withdrew American forces from that country. Moreover, throughout the months that followed, more cooperative relations were cultivated with other ideological adversaries (such as Syria and Iraq); even toward the Islamic-based government of Iran, the Reagan White House was careful not to alienate the regime totally, to the point of causing it to become dependent on Moscow. And despite the administration's expressed opposition to the Sandinista government and other communist movements

72. The diplomatic rhetoric of Reagan and his Republican advisers is discussed in Hedrick Smith, "Reagan: What Kind of World Leader?" *New York Times Magazine*, November 16, 1980, pp. 161–77; Reeves, "Ideological Election," 26–29, 80–91; Laurence I. Barrett, *Gambling with History: Reagan in the White House* (Garden City, N.Y., 1983); Samuel Brittan, "A Very Painful World Adjustment," *Foreign Affairs*, LX (Special Issue, 1982), 541–69; and Seymour M. Finger, "Jeane Kirkpatrick at the United Nations," *Foreign Affairs*, LXII (Winter, 1983–84), 436–58; and Raymond Aron, "Ideology in Search of a Policy," *Foreign Affairs* (Special Issue, 1981), 503–35.

in the Western Hemisphere, Reagan's diplomacy in Central America was flexible, responsive to congressional and public apprehensions about involvement in another Vietnam, and modified from time to time to take account of changing conditions at home and abroad. In responding to the communist challenge in Latin America, the Reagan White House relied on a wide range of policy instruments—from economic and military aid, to propaganda and moral suasion, to various forms of overt and covert interventionism, to diplomatic cooperation with other governments—to achieve its objectives. Congress and the American people obviously desired to avoid another Vietnam in the hemisphere, and on the basis of Reagan's overwhelming reelection in 1984 his diplomacy in Central America appeared to have at least the tacit support of a majority of citizens. At any rate, Reagan's critics were severely challenged to produce alternatives to his diplomatic moves in Latin America that elicited a comparable degree of public approval.[73]

Better perhaps than most chief executives, Reagan understood the nation's pragmatic tradition and based his external policies on it. As even many leading Democrats conceded after the election of 1984, if they were to avoid another electoral defeat at Republican hands, Reagan's political opponents would be well advised to follow his example. As these examples indicate, an external policy existing on two levels—the rhetorical and the operational—appears to have become the *normal condition* of American diplomacy. Regardless of its ideological coloration or position on the political spectrum, every incumbent administration is likely to exhibit this diplomatic dualism.

Why does dualism exist as a seemingly permanent feature of the American foreign policy process? Although the question cannot be answered with complete assurance, certain tentative answers can be suggested. Periodically in its diplomacy every incumbent administration indulges in declaratory statements and rhetorical pronouncements. These serve various purposes, some of which have a remote relationship to the achievement of concrete foreign policy goals. They may be designed to enhance the president's image as a "man of peace"; to communicate his implacable opposition to alien political ideologies and political movements; to issue pointed warnings to other governments; and to state maximum or preliminary demands by the United States for the resolution of outstanding issues. In some cases, diplomatic oratory is no doubt designed mainly to serve domestic political pur-

73. See Brittan, "A Very Painful World Adjustment"; John E. Reilly, "American Opinion: Continuity, Not Reaganism," *Foreign Policy,* L (Spring, 1983), 86–105; Cecil V. Crabb, Jr., "'Standing Tall' as a Foreign Policy," in Sandoz and Crabb, *Election '84,* 179–204; and Henry Grunwald, "Foreign Policy Under Reagan II," *Foreign Affairs,* LXIII (Winter, 1984–85), 219–40.

poses such as promoting the cohesion of the president's political party, reassuring his more ideologically motivated followers, and undermining the position of his domestic political critics. In still other cases, ideological militancy in approaching foreign policy issues is obviously intended to appeal to certain pressure groups and constituencies at home and abroad which are identified with a particular diplomatic position. Sometimes also, the president and his diplomatic advisers may simply lose their tempers, vent their emotions, or otherwise express their frustrations about conditions in a disorderly, unpredictable, and often dangerous global environment that appears to be less amenable than ever to American control.

Yet from the Roosevelt to the Reagan administrations, the transcendent fact about the diplomacy of the United States is that, despite its particular rhetorical coloration, in practice it has usually been governed by the pragmatic principles identified in this book. *The operational foreign policy of the United States is essentially pragmatic.* On the basis of the evidence since World War II, this reality does not change significantly from one administration to another, and it is not affected fundamentally by the ideological orientation of the president and his principal foreign policy advisers. This constant in the foreign policy process is a reflection of the underlying pragmatic propensities of the American people in their approach to problem solving and to life generally.

Indeed, given the dynamic nature of the global political environment, it is not unreasonable to anticipate that many of the tenets of pragmatic thought will be even more applicable to American foreign relations in the future than in the past. It seems beyond dispute, for example, that the pragmatic concept of a pluralistic universe is increasingly useful in attempts to comprehend Soviet internal and external policies. One recent study of the Soviet Union has identified three contrary trends—called the reformist, the conservative, and the reactionary—that are operating concurrently within the Soviet system. Each of these tendencies presents a different challenge for, and demands diverse responses by, the United States.[74]

Or, as President Ronald Reagan expressed the idea in an address to European officials in 1985, Western leaders have "learned the lessons of history from the failures of their predecessors," among them being the realization that "aggression feeds on appeasement and that weakness itself can be provocative." Toward the Soviet Union, Reagan advocated an approach

---

74. See Stephen F. Cohen, "Soviet Domestic Politics and Foreign Policy," in *Common Sense in U.S.-Soviet Relations* (Washington, D.C., 1978), 11.

"based upon effective deterrence and the reduction of tensions." On that principle, Reagan asserted (in terms strikingly comparable to the language of William James or John Dewey), "I have directed the Secretary of State to engage with the Soviet Union on an extended agenda of problem-solving." Meanwhile, in the same period, a student of Polish-American relations called upon policy makers in Washington to utilize both "carrots and sticks" in an effort to achieve a twofold objective toward strife-torn Poland. The United States should seek "to encourage movement toward a more open and pluralistic society," and it should endeavor "to reduce Poland's dependence on the Soviet Union." Achieving these goals will require reliance on a multifaceted diplomatic strategy and a realization by Americans that success will almost certainly be limited and slow.[75]

Again, during the ongoing political crisis in Lebanon, in mid-1985 a New York *Times* editorial reflected the essentially pragmatic nature of American diplomacy. It identified the diplomatic alternatives available to the Reagan administration and found all of them unappealing. Americans, the editorial continued, must understand the policy dilemmas confronting national leaders, and they must exhibit patience toward the Reagan White House in its efforts to "make the best of a bad situation."[76]

In vernacular terms, "making the best of a bad situation" might describe with reasonable accuracy the American pragmatic world view. Even in the late twentieth century—almost a half-century after World War II—perhaps a majority of Americans has little enthusiasm for, or inherent interest in, foreign affairs. Psychologically and emotionally, most citizens still prefer isolationism over internationalism as the guiding principle of American diplomacy. More now than at the end of World War II, Americans are often repulsed and mystified by conditions in the external environment. Their participation in foreign affairs is, for the most part, reluctant, ill-informed, and episodic. Even less prospect exists today than in the past that the diplomatic behavior of the United States can be explained by reference to a single, unified, and consistent theory of American conduct in foreign affairs.

In responding to developments abroad, the attention of Americans will continue to be focused on concrete and immediate problems, especially those perceived as posing a crisis directly affecting the well-being of American society. Taken collectively, the American nation's responses to external

75. Reagan's address to the European Parliament is in the New York *Times*, May 9, 1985; see the views of F. Stephen Larrabee, *ibid.*, June 21, 1985.
76. "The Hostage Tangle," *ibid.*, June 18, 1985.

challenges will exhibit paradoxes, incongruities, and ironies—which will trouble the pragmatically inclined American people relatively little. As always, in both domestic and foreign affairs Americans expect national leaders to examine and respond to each case "on its merits," to adopt moderate and reasonable courses of action, and to modify national policies in the light of changing circumstances.

Above all, perhaps, Americans will continue to rely on the pragmatic standard of experience in judging the results of national efforts abroad. On the basis of the available evidence, is a given policy working? Are the results of the nation's diplomatic efforts commensurate with the time, funds, energy, and other resources required to achieve them? Do the observable consequences of American diplomacy accord with some worthwhile human purpose? Are the actions of national leaders abroad in conformity with mainstream opinion within American society?

These are the key questions which pragmatically minded Americans will almost certainly ask about the nation's foreign policy in the years ahead. And as was true of the philosophical pragmatists, Americans will do so in confidence that if the nation's diplomacy can satisfy these criteria, the probability exists that, by reliance on creative intelligence, mankind will somehow manage to make the international environment more benign and favorable for the realization of worthwhile American, and more broadly human, values.

Index

299

Index